Encounters with Emotions

Encounters with Emotions
Negotiating Cultural Differences since Early Modernity

Edited by
Benno Gammerl, Philipp Nielsen
and Margrit Pernau

berghahn
NEW YORK · OXFORD
www.berghahnbooks.com

First published in 2019 by
Berghahn Books
www.berghahnbooks.com

© 2019, 2025 Benno Gammerl, Philipp Nielsen and Margrit Pernau
First paperback edition published in 2025

All rights reserved. Except for the quotation of short passages
for the purposes of criticism and review, no part of this book
may be reproduced in any form or by any means, electronic or
mechanical, including photocopying, recording, or any information
storage and retrieval system now known or to be invented,
without written permission of the publisher.

Library of Congress Cataloging-in-Publication Data
Names: Gammerl, Benno, editor. | Nielsen, Philipp, editor. | Pernau, Margrit, editor.
Title: Encounters with emotions : negotiating cultural differences since early modernity / edited by Benno Gammerl, Philipp Nielsen and Margrit Pernau.
Description: New York : Berghahn Books, 2019. | Includes bibliographical references and index. |
Identifiers: LCCN 2019007908 (print) | LCCN 2019011477 (ebook) | ISBN 9781789202243 (ebook) | ISBN 9781789202236 (hardback : alk. paper)
Subjects: LCSH: Emotions--Social aspects--History. | Emotions--Political aspects--History. | Intercultural communication--History. | History, Modern.
Classification: LCC BF531 (ebook) | LCC BF531 .E545 2019 (print) | DDC 152.4--dc23
LC record available at https://lccn.loc.gov/2019007908

British Library Cataloguing in Publication Data
A catalogue record for this book is available from the British Library

EU GPSR Authorized Representative
LOGOS EUROPE, 9 rue Nicolas Poussin, 17000, LA ROCHELLE, France
Email: Contact@logoseurope.eu

ISBN 978-1-78920-223-6 hardback
ISBN 978-1-83695-077-6 paperback
ISBN 978-1-83695-215-2 epub
ISBN 978-1-78920-224-3 web pdf

https://doi.org/10.3167/9781789202236

Contents

List of Illustrations   vii

Introduction
Encountering Feelings – Feeling Encounters   1
Benno Gammerl, Philipp Nielsen and Margrit Pernau

Chapter 1
Missionaries: False Reverence, Irreverence and the Rethinking of Christian Mission in China and India   37
Stephen Cummins and Joel Lee

Chapter 2
Travellers: Transformative Journeys and Emotional Contacts   61
Edgar Cabanas, Razak Khan and Jani Marjanen

Chapter 3
Anthropologists: Feelings in the Field   85
Pascal Eitler and Joseph Ben Prestel

Chapter 4
Entrepreneurs: Encountering Trust in Business Relations   110
Agnes Arndt

Chapter 5
Diplomats: Kneeling and the Protocol of Humiliation   133
Ute Frevert

Chapter 6
Occupiers and Civilians: Facing the Enemy 160
Philipp Nielsen

Chapter 7
Prisoners: Experiencing the Criminal Other 184
Pavel Vasilyev and Gian Marco Vidor

Chapter 8
'Monsters': Emotional Incoherence and Familial Murder 207
Daphne Rozenblatt

Chapter 9
Performers: From 'Courtesans' to *Kathakali King Lear* 230
Kedar A. Kulkarni

Chapter 10
Lovers and Friends: Encounters of Hearts and Bodies 258
Margrit Pernau

Conclusion
After Encounters with Feelings: Outcomes and Further Issues 282
Benno Gammerl

Index of Subjects 297
Index of Names and Places 304

Illustrations

0.1	Detail of *Begum Samru's Household* (c. 1820), Delhi, India.	21
3.1	'Malinowski Watching Children at Play, Teyava Village, Kiriwina, May 1918'.	92
9.1	'Dancing Girls and Musicians'.	234
9.2	'Ruth St Denis with Native Hindus in Radha' (1906).	241
9.3	'Before Lear's Death'.	249
10.1	Thomas Hickey (Irish 1741–1824), *An Indian Lady, perhaps 'Jemdanee', Bibi of William Hickey* (1787), oil on canvas, 102 × 127 cm.	263
10.2	'Anita Delgado Posed at the Age of 22 Years with Indian Attire'.	266
10.3	Young Andrews, Tagore, Old Andrews.	273

Introduction
Encountering Feelings – Feeling Encounters

Benno Gammerl, Philipp Nielsen and Margrit Pernau

In January 2008, the Indian cricket team met the Australian team in Sydney for a test match. Feelings were running high on both sides when Harbhajan Singh, the Indian spinner, was heard calling the only non-white member of the Australian team, Andrew Symonds, a monkey. Singh was barred from play for three games for the racial taunt. Right from the beginning, however, doubts were raised as to whether he had really used the word monkey, or whether he had sworn at his opponent in Hindi, making a sexual innuendo about Symonds' mother – in its own cultural context no less offensive.[1]

This incident is a poignant example of how emotions move across cultural divides. The case triggered fierce debates about the potential for misunderstandings between languages. Many Indian commentators pointed to their country's leading role in the anti-apartheid movement in order to cast doubt on the accusations concerning Harbhajan's racism, claiming that it was highly unlikely that Harbhajan had used English rather than Hindi to abuse his opponent in a moment of stress. The case becomes even more complicated when viewed as the outcome of a series of previous encounters rather than as an isolated incident.[2]

During the Australian team's visit to India half a year earlier, Indian crowds at Baroda had taunted Symonds with monkey chants throughout the game. But for the Australian team, the victorious Indian team's extensive post-match celebrations really 'sparked passion inside of us', as Symonds put it in an interview. Describing their own celebrations in the

---

Notes for this chapter begin on page 23.

past as 'humble', the Indian players' multiday affair seemed excessive to Symonds. He continued: 'Something gets triggered inside of you, something is burning inside of you – it is your will for success or your animal instinct that wants to bring another team down'.[3] Harbhajan Singh, in turn, criticized the Australian team for being sore losers: 'They say they play the game in the right spirit, but they don't in reality. There is nothing gentlemanly about the way they play. . . . I was responding to a lot of vulgar words that were said to me'.[4]

Both teams were primed for the next round. Taking the tense atmosphere into account, they agreed to tone down their insults before the Sydney match. The Indian team had expressly promised to refrain from offending Symonds by calling him a monkey.[5] Yet this was not to be. Instead, the events that led to the international scandal and Harbhajan's suspension unfolded. The incident started with Harbhajan tapping bowler Brett Lee on the backside with his bat and saying 'hard luck'. Symonds said that he then 'had a bit of a crack at Harbhajan, telling him exactly what I thought of his antics'.[6] This 'telling' seems to have included the word 'fuck', whereupon Harbhajan furiously replied in kind – and uttered 'monkey' or 'maa ki . . .' (mother's . . .).[7]

This incident reveals a number of important things about emotional encounters. First, it draws attention to the fact that emotions are experienced through the body and that body language and gestures, like a slap on the backside, can also be used to convey and incite them. Additionally, it shows that the corporeal dimension of emotions inhibits neither their tactical use nor the intersubjective negotiation of their meaning. Finally, the example demonstrates how intercultural encounters are often laden with history. In this case, this history is not limited to that between two players and two teams but extends to a broader history of racist abuse, which in turn reaches back to the history of the construction of racial difference, a history that is far older than any of the players involved in the dispute. The Indian aristocrat Ranjitsinhji's cricket career in Victorian England is only one example of the role race politics have played in athletics: the first Indian to bat for the English team in 1896 and the supposedly racial or non-racial attributes of his body dominated his athletic life both at times of inclusion in and exclusion from English cricket and society.[8] This history, moreover, explains why an organization like the International Cricket Council sanctions racial abuse much more harshly in comparison to insults invoking the sexual behaviour of an adversary's mother.

Why Should Historical Research Focus on Emotional Encounters?

Sport is, of course, not the only field in which emotional encounters cross cultural boundaries – within societies as much as between them – on a regular basis. Encounters between people who have been socialized into different emotions have become almost commonplace at the beginning of the twenty-first century. People know, practise and value different emotions (or value emotions differently) and express them through a multiplicity of codes. Many experience cross-cultural encounters on a more or less regular basis, from tourists to refugees, from managers of multinational corporations or non-governmental organizations to migrant labourers, from residents of multi-ethnic metropolises to people who go abroad to seek knowledge or to find love. Encounters with culturally diverse forms of emotional expression in newspapers, television programmes and social media have become a part of everyday life.

Encounters with Emotions starts from contemporary emotional encounters and seeks to analyse them from a historical perspective, beginning with early modernity. By highlighting historical changes and transcultural dynamics, this approach promises to generate fresh and valuable insights for two fields of research that have up to now remained largely separated from each other: research on the history of emotions and research on cross-cultural encounters.

Encounters with Emotions first of all contributes to the study of the history of emotions by undertaking a much needed re-evaluation of the opposition between universalizing and particularizing understandings of them. Although overcoming this divide has been important for the field's agenda for a number of years now, it remains haunted by the distinction between nature and nurture to this day. Many neuroscientists and psychologists work with the assumption that all humans share the capacity to experience the same basic emotions, which are, so they claim, expressed through a universally valid set of facial micro-expressions. If this assumption is true, then communicating emotions across cultural divides should be relatively unproblematic. According to this theory, feelings experienced and expressed through the body are more transparent and easier to transmit than verbal utterances, which have to be translated. By contrast, many historians and anthropologists hold that within each particular cultural setting humans learn specific emotional behaviours and practices ultimately incommensurable with those of other cultures. Such practices are not limited to signs and symbols. They are also inscribed into, and expressed by, the body.[9] This theory implies the notion that a mutual understanding of feelings across cultural divides can only be achieved through processes at least as complicated and laborious as those involved in linguistic translation. In their analysis of individual case studies, the authors of this volume critically engage with these supposed dichotomies, maintaining that emotional encounters hold considerable potential for misunderstandings and failures of communication. Such misunderstandings can also spark further interaction. At the same time, body language and other forms of non-verbal communication are occasionally capable of bridging the gap and creating new meanings. Questioning both universalizing and particularizing assumptions, the authors are able to forge new approaches to the historicization of emotions.

Furthermore, the book contributes to the study of encounters, which has long been a staple of global history. Bringing emotions into the mix provides a concrete vantage point for analysing the local and bodily effects of, and reasons for, transformations of global power structures. Focusing on emotions offers a new perspective on the capacity of encounters to not only reproduce but also transform attitudes and behaviours, transformations that can trigger heretofore unforeseen developments. The focus on emotions in face-to-face encounters also enables the authors to scrutinize in greater detail how feelings impacted the very production and the shifting organization of cultural differences. It allows for investigating the interplay of language and visual codes with more bodily ways of learning. The integration of emotions into the study of global encounters is not intended to replace existing research on their cultural and cognitive dimensions but should rather complement it.[10]

Exploring the grounds between universalizing and particularizing understandings of emotion and between local and global dynamics of encounter is the main objective of this volume. The chapters will do so by examining a broad range of case studies. They thereby spin a number of interrelated threads, woven together in the conclusion by highlighting the specificities of emotional translation and by tracing major historical trajectories that have shaped emotional encounters since the seventeenth century.

Questions, Geographical Focus and Time Frame

Through discussing face-to-face encounters across cultural boundaries with the aim of rethinking the relationship between nature and nurture, *Encounters with Emotions* begins by addressing the culturally and historically specific preconceptions people bring to an encounter. Such preconceptions are informed by, among other factors, education, past experiences and assumptions about the other and his or her culture, all of which premediate each actor's behaviour and his or her interpretation of the encounter and its emotional content. At the same time, the authors stress the inherent openness of all encounters and their capacity to provoke unanticipated reactions, which in turn have the potential to challenge and ultimately overwrite earlier scripts. The authors claim that it is precisely this aspect of the encounter that can trigger historical change.

The case studies in the individual chapters thus address the following questions: firstly, which emotions – curiosity, disgust, fear or longing, among many others – have cross-cultural encounters caused in people with divergent emotional styles and behavioural habits? Secondly, what interpretive strategies have people employed in attempting to understand each other's emotions? Finally, what role have emotions played in facilitating or obstructing understanding and communication across cultural divides?

Looking at history over the longue durée while taking up a broad geographical scope enables the authors to consider a wealth of source material in which various actors describe their efforts to grapple with emotional differences. The area studied extends from Europe across the Arab world to Asia. While the book's scope does not encompass the entire world – a venture that might be more ambitious than wise – it draws attention to the close and complex interrelations that connect the geographical areas studied that have been in contact through trade, travel, conquest and migration since antiquity. This focus, however, is not an exclusive one: when our main actors wander into other regions, we follow them.

The period studied stretches from the seventeenth century to the present, thus combining early modern, colonial and more recent developments that have so far rarely been considered together. This broad time frame allows the book to trace changes in the dynamics of encounters and their emotional ramifications that often unfolded at a rather slow pace. With the foundation of the East India Company and the increase of missionary activities at the beginning of the seventeenth century, the level of interaction between Europe and Asia reached a new level of intensity. Within this time frame, particular emphasis is placed on the nineteenth and twentieth century. However, this does not deny earlier encounters, and the authors do not aim to privilege the eastward travels of European traders and envoys. Throughout the period under consideration, people travelled and migrated in both directions as well as between India, Persia and Central Asia, between the entire Islamicate world and the Hijaz. These flows were anything but negligible in terms of size and significance. The chapters map some of these movements, analysing the historical effects of the encounters they brought forth.

Emotions, Encounters and Cultures: Concepts and Key Terms

Striving for consistent definitions is one of the ways the social sciences attempt to avoid misunderstandings and ensure that the different authors of a book, as well as its readers, are reflecting on the same subject and grappling with the same problems. However, to suggest unified definitions is counterproductive once research begins to move across cultures, both temporally and spatially. If the ways actors conceptualize their experiences impact not only their interpretation of the world but also their actions and practices, then providing unequivocal definitions of core concepts at the outset unduly limits the analysis. Such definitions could at best provide equivalents for a small range of concepts used by certain actors or within certain cultures – usually those closer to the researcher in time and language – while remaining inadequate for other contexts. Overstepping the limits of a definition's validity and indiscriminately applying it to every culture thus harbours the danger of misleading researchers to liken things others hold to be dissimilar while separating things others may think are connected. Such one-sided definitions substantially minimize the explanatory value of historical analysis.

Changing concepts of what an 'emotion' is are a case in point. The word itself is a neologism that only came into use in English and French in the eighteenth century. It was an umbrella term that linked two concepts long viewed as distinct: affections and passions. The convergence of these two concepts was crucial for shifting the debates on emotions from theology and moral philosophy to psychology and medicine.[11] But concepts of emotions vary over time; and, as anthropological studies have shown, they also vary across space.[12] Studies on emotion concepts outside Europe are rare. Yet the existing research on South Asian understandings of emotions suggests that they differ from German or English perceptions, and South Asian concepts themselves also underwent considerable shifts from the eighteenth to the nineteenth century. Rather than attempt to come up with a universally valid definition of what an emotion is, or putting one region's conception in opposition to another, the authors of this volume hold that conceptions of what emotions are and how they work are determined by a multitude of factors. This approach highlights culturally contingent concepts of emotions that can be mapped onto the following questions: how and to what extent can emotions be controlled, either through effort of the will or through employing stronger counter-emotions? How are the boundaries between emotions and virtue and vice drawn? What role does the body play in emotional life? Is it placed in contradistinction to the mind? And how can it be affected by external agents like demons, other bodies, atmospheres or drugs? Are emotions considered to be rational or irrational phenomena, conventional or spontaneous? Are emotional dispositions viewed as products of education and cultivation, as inborn traits or as a mixture of the two?

However, beyond differences between regions and historical periods, conceptions of emotions also vary across – even within – present-day academic disciplines as the distinction between universalizing and particularizing approaches shows. In addition to this major divide, emotion research is further complicated by affect theoretical positions in the humanities that emphasize the bodily, immediate and involuntary force of affect, by appraisal theories in psychology that highlight the cognitive dimensions of feelings and by critical approaches in the neurosciences that challenge their discipline's assumptions about the hardwired nature of emotional responses. *Encounters with Emotions* does not subscribe to any single one of these positions, combining instead different aspects of them. For example, the authors draw on affect theory when they emphasize the fact that emotional dynamics exceed the limits of established structures of meaning, thus ascribing a certain openness to emotions; nevertheless they take recourse to cognitive and praxeological understandings of emotions when they describe them as culturally contingent and learned.

Encounters, too, the second key concept in the volume's title, may appear in many shapes and sizes. The authors' interest in debates on nature and nurture has motivated them to conduct research into a specific type of encounter that involves both minds and bodies: face-to-face encounters bring actors into the same physical space where they may share a common focus of attention and where they not only hear and see but also smell, touch and, in rare cases, even taste each other. Face-to-face encounters have figured prominently in certain strands of philosophy. The phenomenological tradition in particular has focused on the moment of encounter as constitutive for identity and ethics.[13] *Encounters with Emotions* extends these enquiries into intersubjectivity and subjectification by analysing the emotional dynamics that permeate them and addressing their broader social and cultural implications.

However, these assumptions about face-to-face encounters – shared space, co-presence and their multisensory dimension – are more ambiguous than they might appear initially. In the era of online video communication, face-to-face encounters can obviously take on a very different guise.[14] The notions of novelty, strangeness and familiarity that define the dynamics of encounters are themselves subject to historical change, as are the criteria that allow actors to consider an encounter as either a success or a failure. Equally, and even more decisively, face-to-face encounters rarely exist in a pure state. As the vignette in the introduction amply demonstrates, every face-to-face encounter is at least partially determined by the cultural knowledge of those involved. It follows that every such encounter draws on a history that precedes it and that every such encounter is permeated by the traces of collectively remembered experiences in which the actors themselves may have had no part. Thus, the focus on the immediacy of face-to-face encounters should not blind us to the fact that they always involve different levels of mediation, which adds depth to the interpretation.[15]

Although all encounters are informed by premediated concepts, their effects are by no means determined in advance. Every encounter holds the potential to bring those taking part in it into unforeseen situations, opening up space for experiences that transcend the limits of established categories.[16] Encounters can motivate a rearrangement of the frames of understanding that enable those involved to integrate the challenging experience into their worldview. Shifts in conceptual structures and learning processes are always bound up with the specific temporality of the encounter. While a certain degree of strangeness defines every encounter, it can give way to familiarity as the encounter turns into a more regular form of interaction. This familiarity can be based on trust, but it can also encompass experiences and expectations of violence. Encounters do not take place in a space beyond power relations. The authors of *Encounters with Emotions* do not understand encounter as an ethically or politically neutral counterconcept to conquest, but rather as a tool that brings along its own set of equally difficult ethical and political questions.[17]

The concepts of culture and difference play a decisive role in our research. Taking up face-to-face encounters allows us to enquire into the corporeal dimensions of emotions as potentially universal features. In the moment of an actual encounter, as the case studies presented here will show, the corporeality of emotions is not only capable of reproducing but also subverting established scripts. Moreover, integrating cultural differences and transcultural dynamics helps the authors to remind us of the fact that the shape an encounter can take is at least partially also conditioned by the culturally specific forms of socialization that inform the attitudes and opinions of the individual actors involved in it. As differences vary, the volume's authors are particularly interested in those differences that are not experienced on an everyday basis but occur once actors move out of their familiar surroundings and confront others who express and practise their emotions in unfamiliar ways. Their interest in cultural differences notwithstanding, the authors bear in mind that, depending on its usage, the concept of culture can be no less problematic than some of the more loaded concepts associated with it, such as civilization, ethnicity or race.

Thus, in order to avoid subscribing to any brand of essentialism, the authors of *Encounters with Emotions* view cultures as contested systems of shared meanings, ideas and practices. Every culture is constructed and changeable, lacking predetermined boundaries. The non-monolithic features of culture are further emphasized by paying attention to divergences not only between but also within cultures (intercultural and intracultural differences) as well as to the effects encounters generate in all parties involved (transcultural dynamics).[18] Furthermore, the authors specifically aim at investigating the historicity, the non-static and dynamic character of cultural identities and differences by highlighting their production within encounters and by scrutinizing the role emotions play in drawing ever new and divergent boundaries. Finally, the case studies also take care to note the historical intersections between divergent forms of differentiation; for example, along the lines of class, race and gender as well as the transformations they have undergone. The experiences people have with these intracultural differences and the strategies they develop to grapple with them intraculturally can have a significant impact on the ways intercultural encounters play out. In turn, intercultural encounters can impact the shape these differences take as well as the ways people approach them within each culture. Thus, analysing the intersectionality of cultural differences as well as the vicissitudes of their historical development lies at the heart of our research into the role of emotions in encounters.

Sources, Methods and Approaches for Researching Emotional Encounters

Encounters with Emotions draws on a large corpus of sources. While placing primary focus on ego-documents, the individual chapters also deal with material ranging from governmental records to advice books and novels. As mentioned earlier, the analysis of this source material will contribute to our understanding of the diverse ways people have attributed meaning to their engagement with emotional difference and their emotional coping with difference. In using these sources to grasp the nuanced emotional dynamics of face-to-face encounters, the authors are careful to remind us that the individual accounts detailed in the source material are informed by the particular positions – during the encounter itself and in the retrospective moment of writing about it – of those who composed them.

What, then, are the methodological approaches that can help us understand the ways people grapple with these differences in concrete historical situations? We have identified four main axes of inquiry: remediation, translation, mimesis and transmission. Placed on a scale, these approaches move from practices centred on knowledge to practices increasingly centred on the body.

Experiments that attempt to prove the universality of emotions are often conducted under circumstances that fail to take account of the test subjects' previous experiences. Some researchers claim that if people from a 'non-Western preliterate' culture in New Guinea and 'Westerners' who have never met each other before are able to correctly read each other's facial expressions, then this shows that the ways emotions are expressed and codified are universal. By implication, this assumption is used to support the claim that emotions are neither learned through previous encounters nor coloured by cultural expectations.[19] However, attention should be drawn to the fact that even 'first encounters' do not take place on a tabula rasa but are preceded by preconceived ideas about the other and by scripts that influence how the encounter might play out. This phenomenon has been termed premediation.[20] An example of premediation might be the significant role played by Tibetan and Chinese Buddhist representations of the devil as having round eyes and a big nose for these groups' first contacts with Europeans.[21] This shows the ambivalence of the concept: historical sources, whether textual or visual, can be read both as mediation of an experience (the encounter with the round-eyed Europeans) and also a premediation of further experience (seeing the similarity between devils and Europeans). Nevertheless, such scripts are not simply acted upon, and, while they certainly contribute to the content of emotions and the form of their expression, they do not wholly determine them. Encounters between two or more different scripts, encounters with an environment that does not conform to one's expectations and encounters between bodies lead to what has been called remediation. The content of these remediations can only be partially deduced from the scripts at play at the beginning of an encounter.[22] Changes in the scripts allow for different practices and for different ways of acting in the world. Although emotional expressions can have established meanings before the encounter, these can undergo change in the course of the interaction. Encounters thus open up space for those involved in negotiating the meanings of their emotions anew. Viewed from this perspective, it becomes clear that encounters force people to use their skills of adapting to, and learning about, unfamiliar emotional codes and practices. Such experiences contribute to an archive that can in turn support navigating the complexities of future encounters. Thus, returning to our interest in the nature/nurture debate, we might say that as a cultural phenomenon, emotions are expressed according to scripts, but as a natural phenomenon, their breadth and complexity escape the grasp of such scripts, so that they always remain capable of subverting and transforming them.

Translation enables the interlocutors to find or create equivalents in meaning between divergent expressions. The field of translation studies offers some helpful tools for analysing these processes. Over the last decades, the discipline has moved beyond its earlier focus on literary texts and philology and has entered into a fruitful dialogue with anthropology, which in turn has led to an increased focus on questions related to the historical context of acts of translation and the creative role of translators. Furthermore, the translation studies field has moved away from the assumption that there are either equivalents between languages (in which case it would be the task of the skilful translator to find them) or there are not (in which case translation is described as a story of loss and betrayal). Recent advances in translation studies have suggested that equivalents do not precede translation but are created through the very process of translation itself.[23] Applying the insights of translation studies to the study of encounters, which themselves always demand some sort of translation, it becomes clear that, like every translation, every encounter builds up an archive that informs further encounters. Rather than being carried in a closed box across a cultural and linguistic chasm, meanings and equivalents are constantly being negotiated. Thus, although emotional expressions have particular meanings before an encounter, a fact that our analyses will do justice to, the encounter itself has the potential to reconfigure them.

Nevertheless the negotiation of meanings does not take place in a vacuum. If the debates on Orientalism and the production of colonial knowledge have shown us anything, it is the power of epistemological shifts and reconfigurations. However, this does not imply that the colonized (or, more generally, the weaker actor) and their interpretation do not have an impact on the process of translation – negotiation is not power's other.[24] Nor does it mean that both sides have to completely agree on the meaning of equivalents for the encounter to proceed. While dictionaries (or ethnographies) can freeze meaning for a certain span of time, the translation process and its creation of equivalents remains an ongoing everyday activity. Society and culture are the sites where translation takes place; and they can themselves be regarded as products of ongoing translational activities.[25]

Bringing emotions into the debate allows us to show their similarity to linguistic codes while simultaneously demonstrating how they transcend the realm of language. Emotional expressions are undoubtedly endowed with meaning, which can but need not be the same across cultural divides. In this sense, they can be analysed like other signs that are translated between languages, signs whose meanings are not given but rather created and modified through encounters. However, things become more challenging when we consider the fact that emotional expressions have a surplus that cannot be reduced to the representation of an already existing, stable emotion. In this sense, emotional expressions, and even emotions themselves, can be interpreted as factors that play a crucial role in the creation of meaning and the process of translation in the encounter.[26]

Beyond translation, theories of mimesis offer another avenue for research on emotional encounters.[27] Theories on the mimetic imitation of bodily movements have been used to analyse the ways emotions were coordinated in early colonial encounters.[28] Although many theories of mimesis take care to account for the historical specificity of encounters and the cultural alterity that defines them, they ultimately rely on implicitly universalizing assumptions about the cross-cultural readability of emotions through sympathetically relating to the other's bodily gestures.[29] 'Yielding', a term used to denote an opening of the body towards the other, enables an emotional fusion between the participants of an encounter. The notion draws attention to the sensual aspects of attunement. Yielding highlights attunement's potential to produce new emotional expressions and to enable actors to experience new feelings. Current theories of embodied cognition in the neurosciences, which are explicitly based on a universalist understanding of emotions, have further advanced this model of mimesis.[30]

These anthropological and neuroscientific theories provide tools that can help us understand the role of the body in mimesis and its place in the construction of alterity and difference. However, mimesis also has a disruptive potential. It can create disturbing similarities between subjects that are supposed to remain distinct. Desires resulting from mimetic imitation can lead to envy and competition.[31] Furthermore, on the level of society, it has been suggested that intersubjective mimesis is constitutive for individuality itself ('interdividuality'). In light of the disruptive potential of mimetic behaviour and the emotions such disruptions can cause, mimesis is capable of bringing about change. Adaptation then does not necessarily imply that the capacities of two bodies must be brought into attunement with one another; rather, adaptation can also be brought about by a transformation of the power structures that codify and underlie the mimetic act.[32] For the authors of *Encounters with Emotions*, mimesis and mimicry thus allow us to think about bodily imitation as enabling a specific mode of cross-cultural understanding that need not necessarily result in harmonization but can also engender conflict and disagreement.[33]

If the bodily processes involved in mimesis are primarily intentional, the theory of transmission emphasizes the non-intentional dimension of emotional encounters and, more importantly, their emotional reverberation.[34] An offshoot of affect theory, it employs neurochemical theories of transmission with the aim of overcoming conceptions of contained selfhood as well as a supposed modern Western optocentrism.[35] Instead, the theory of transmission focuses on the permeability of bodies and on overcoming the dichotomy between subjects and their environments.[36] Changes in, and resonances between, the moods participants bring to an encounter are explained by the transmission of chemical properties between bodies.[37] *Encounters with Emotions* shares this concern with broadening the scope of the senses involved in encounters beyond the visual. At the same time, its authors acknowledge the impact that historically specific regimes of perception have on how bodies interact and resonate with each other. This allows the authors to conceive of feelings as being simultaneously non-intentional, non-representational, bodily and also culturally learned.[38]

Difference: Historicity and Intersectionality

Encounters with Emotions works with the basic assumption that emotions are neither self-identical entities that remain constant over time and space, nor are they always expressed in the same way. Nevertheless, differences can vary in degree and intensity. Moreover, the absence of precise equivalents does not prevent translation and communication, emotional or otherwise. All the same, the authors of this book view differences as products of the dynamics of the encounter. In addition, they operate within a broad spectrum of intersecting lines of differentiation. Thus the authors avoid making the problematic claim that there is a universally invariant nature of emotions and also avoid the opposite danger of exoticizing the other and considering particular cultural differences as absolutes.

People encounter differences – between emotional styles, cultural codes and shared histories, among other things – and learn to cope with them on a daily basis. For this reason, the individual chapters of this volume are not restricted to encounters on faraway shores but view intracultural and intercultural interactions as a continuum rather than as a dichotomy. Learning to understand the diverse ways others express their emotions and developing the ability to navigate unexpected emotional reactions are faculties that actors develop from a very early age, even if they never move out of their hometown or village. In this respect the categories of age, gender, class and race learned at home come to play a crucial role in colonial encounters.

Most children first encounter emotional difference in the family. Successfully navigating social interactions within the familial setting demands that children learn how to read different emotional codes and develop different emotional expressions depending on whom they are interacting with.[39] Gender and age, categories that should themselves be historicized, often define the ways in which these differences play out. Intrafamilial relations are structured by rules, codes and hierarchies that give rise to differences in the ways family members interact with one another; and these structures can vary across time and space – ranging from highly differentiated codes, which distinguish the emotional interaction with the father's elder brother from even that with his younger brother, to configurations that place individual variances among siblings at the core. Children's early experiences with the differences permeating intrafamilial interactions form the basis for their future emotional interactions, which increasingly encompass unfamiliar situations. Children not only learn how to encounter different emotional styles, they also learn how to learn, thus developing the ability to interpret unexpected situations, behaviour and expressions of emotion. In many cases, this interpretation proceeds through the translation of new differences into familiar ones.[40] This can be witnessed in the fact that cross-cultural encounters often employ metaphors of friendship and family in order to transform differences between strangers into familial relations, hierarchical or otherwise.

Finding effective ways to organize differences on a global scale in the age of colonial encounter and to make these differences both understandable and manageable was one of the central projects of the European Enlightenment. The idea of stages of development that all societies pass through – albeit at different times – offered one of the most important means for systematizing the observations of manifold diversity made by travellers, traders and early colonists. The idea basically holds that, like humans, all societies go through a life cycle: they are born, develop into childhood and adolescence, experience the strength and autonomy of adulthood and then slowly descend into old age. Childlike nations like the Irish or the Africans, so the theory went, thus co-existed with senescent nations that had gone through a long period of decline, like the Chinese or the Indians. The stage a particular nation or people had attained could be recognized not only by the social and economic structures that defined them but even more by the emotions that prevailed among them. For example, childlike nations were supposedly hot, boisterous and uncontrollable and thus in need of the guidance of adult nations with more refined emotions. Metaphors of family and age not only provided a frame for interpreting the emotions observed but also suggested and legitimized ways of responding to them. These responses were premediated through the earlier experience of the colonizers and their metropolitan readership, which in turn constituted premediation for encounters to come.[41]

The problem of basing colonial power and its interpretation of emotional encounters on a theory of stages of development was that these stages are transient: children grow up and parents lose their position of authority, becoming dependent on those they had governed only yesterday. Hence, the theory of historical stages of development could not provide sound footing for a long-term colonial project. Without being abandoned entirely, in the course of the nineteenth century the child metaphor was progressively replaced by gender metaphors that essentialized the difference between colonizers and colonized, giving it an element of permanence. Colonies were now viewed as being feminine, if not effeminate. The essentializing character of the gender metaphor supported the idea of a permanent polarization between the character of the colonizers and that of the colonized. These gender-based metaphors thus served to firmly place the colonies under the guardianship of their manly colonizers. What did not change, however, was the fact that colonial powers drew on familiar perceptions of emotions to interpret unfamiliar experiences.[42]

Over the course of the nineteenth century, the conceptualization of difference underwent a radical shift that intensified hierarchies within categories of race and gender. The ambiguity inherent to early modern concepts of 'race', which often viewed it in confluence with class, gender, religion and ethnicity, was succeeded by attempts to develop more precise definitions of racial identity.[43] These efforts were intimately intertwined with the rise of imperialism and the increasingly unequal distribution of agency and power on a global level. They coincided with the move towards a politics of racial segregation founded on coercion and subjugation and ran parallel to the gradual naturalization and biologization of race.[44]

Within the colonial setting, the kinship metaphors that were used in order to understand racial differences as stages of development faded in significance, while theories of sexual reproduction and genetic heredity gained ground. The concrete effects of this shift were important on many levels. For instance, 'mixed-race' children, especially those who had a European father from the middle or the upper classes, could be integrated into metropolitan societies relatively easily up until the early nineteenth century, when their supposedly tainted lineage led to them being largely excluded and discriminated against.[45] In line with this shift, strategies for understanding the other's emotions and the emotions bound up with cross-cultural encounters also underwent changes: strategies of adaptation and sympathy were succeeded by strategies of distancing, which were embodied in feelings of disgust and contempt. These strategies and feelings were no longer learned primarily within familial relations but within class relations.

As a result, the rigid distinctions and hierarchies that defined perceptions of class, race and gender mutually reinforced each other in separating certain bodies from others.[46] This became manifest in both the effeminization of non-European and the Orientalization and racialization of labouring bodies.[47] Growing fears of 'miscegenation' led to ever stricter surveillance over, and even prohibition of, intimate encounters, especially between European women and non-European men; they also motivated parallel attempts to prevent certain forms of close contact between elites and subalterns.[48] These widening gaps also had an emotional dimension, as stereotypes based on race, gender and class often relied on the ascription of specific emotional styles to subjugated groups.[49] Moreover, they triggered a dramatic shift in European evaluations of transcultural encounters, which could no longer be imagined as being peaceful, promising interactions or as harbingers of a future equality but could only be seen as dangerous, conflict-ridden and shot through with stark inequalities.[50] In this context, bodily desires for the forbidden other could subvert but also reinforce hierarchies.[51]

The historicity and intersectionality of differences not only contributed to shaping colonial relations but also relations among Europeans. In Europe, the homogeneity within and distinctions between different nations gained in importance over the course of the nineteenth century. Religious and denominational affiliations, for example, began to lose their capacity to cut across linguistic and political barriers and were instead used to bolster nationalist identities.[52] Along with religion, class and gender also played a significant role in reshaping understandings of national and racial identities and differences within Europe.[53]

These processes can be described as part of a process of universalizing the organization of differences.[54] Within the categories of gender, race, nationality, class and religion, rigid boundaries based on the logic of mutual incommensurability were increasingly enforced but in a more and more comparable manner. In some ways, this universalization of difference was countered by the universalism of sameness that was gaining ground during the nineteenth century, a universalism that advanced, among other ideas, the discourse of human rights.

Around the turn of the twentieth century, a new form of universalism of difference emerged that attempted to invert or dismiss hierarchies altogether. In their place, it propagated 'a radical attitude to difference' founded in 'a sensory experience and enjoyment of it'.[55] Aesthetic, spiritualist, pedagogical and other avant-garde movements criticized civilization, exoticized the other and praised cultural diversity and the 'cross-fertilizations' it enabled.[56] They also called for the protection of alterity against the forces of assimilation. These movements replaced the notion of progress and development with an emphasis on cultural relativity and an appreciation of '"primitive" . . . emotionalism'.[57] Emotionality itself came to be revered – at least by some – as a desirable quality of the other, whose example might enable overly rational Westerners to regain access to their feelings.

During the process of decolonization, attention was drawn to the detrimental psychological effects that colonial and other transcultural encounters had had on their 'non-European' participants.[58] Philosophers began advocating a new ethics of attentiveness towards the other, who was to reveal herself in face-to-face encounters – both intimate and distancing – 'not in a shock negating the I, but as the primordial phenomenon of gentleness'.[59] These developments ultimately paved the way for the multiculturalist and cosmopolitan discourses that started to gain prevalence in the 1960s. While some authors advocated a communitarian politics of recognition in place of earlier egalitarian models of universal individual rights,[60] others criticized forms of identification based on binaries, instead looking towards processes of hybridization or creolization as a way of fostering and valuing the productive and unforeseeable effects of cultural intermingling.[61] A further position aimed at establishing a new balance between universal human rights and cultural particularities.[62] Finally, other authors foreground transcultural encounters in 'the messy realm of everyday intermingling' as an embodied, affective and sensual form of cosmopolitanism or as a model for postcolonial hospitality.[63] This approach presumes the subjects' ability to draw emotional satisfaction from juggling with cultural differences. Taken together, all of these political and ethical theories provide specific models for grappling with difference through emotions.

These debates highlight an ongoing concern in contemporary societies with questions of cultural diversity. In this context, the dynamics of globalization engender frequent encounters, which can help to bridge differences through feelings of curiosity, trust and solidarity but which, at the same time, can reinforce boundaries through hate, disgust and shame.

Recent Historiography on Transcultural Encounters

Against the background of these debates, historical research on transcultural or cross-cultural encounters has also changed significantly since the 1980s and 1990s. Early contributions were primarily focused on researching large-scale contacts between civilizations, the economic and political conditions that enabled them and the conversions, conflicts and compromises that they brought with them.[64] Historical studies on transcultural or cross-cultural encounters have since moved beyond this approach, following three main avenues of research.

Firstly, the one-way street leading from Europe to the rest of the world has been replaced by the study of a network of manifold and multifariously connected routes. Instead of focusing exclusively on how Europeans moved to the colonial peripheries and spread their ideas and goods there, newer research has directed its attention to flows of people, things and thoughts towards Europe as well as to flows between non-Western regions.[65] One example might be studies of the trading networks that originated in the Hadhramaut in present-day Yemen in the sixteenth century, which connected places like Alexandria and Canton; these studies bring specific kinds of encounters into view that had escaped the attention of earlier historians.[66] At the same time, there has been growing interest in the study of settings before the establishment of a colonial state, when hierarchies were less clearly defined, agency was more broadly distributed and 'the dynamics of cross-cultural encounters were not always predictable'.[67] Yet, as many scholars have stressed, placing the study of these constellations on the research agenda should by no means serve to veil or relativize the violent and exploitative asymmetries of imperial formations. The aim of such studies should rather be to expose the historical contingency of colonial hierarchies in order to prevent the unintended reproduction of these structures in present-day discourse.[68] For the authors of *Encounters with Emotions*, this broadening of perspective has been particularly helpful, as it facilitates a more rigorous approach to the analysis of the historicity of encounters and the fact that they always unfold under specific political, social and economic conditions.

Secondly, the understanding of individual cultures as self-contained homogenous entities has given way to an emphasis on openness, connectedness and relationality. Thus, approaches that highlight hybridity and aim at 'eschewing all closed models of knowledge' have gained in prominence.[69] From this perspective, the Mediterranean, for example, does not constitute a cultural divide but rather a lively contact zone.[70] These reconsiderations have also engendered criticisms of the notion of the first encounter. Although this idea haunts research on cross-cultural encounters to this very day, many scholars emphasize that each encounter is informed by premediations that can have a decisive impact on the way encounters play out.[71]

Thirdly, cross-cultural analyses have long focused on representations of, and knowledge about, the other, as well as on narratives, memories and identities, thus largely remaining within the purview of discourse analysis and cultural history.[72] More recent research, however, tends to underscore the bodily and sensual dimensions of encounters. These fresh approaches offer some alternatives to the constructionist assumption that claims that it is impossible to know and understand the other and that one can therefore only access the ways in which one's own culture has produced the other and rendered them intelligible.[73] From this point of view, which largely follows Edward Said's Orientalist paradigm, attempts at translation are always distorting and, therefore, doomed to fail.[74]

Yet the question as to whether encounters hold the potential to foster contact across the divide between self and other – for those partaking in the encounter as well as for those studying it – has provoked other responses as well. Researchers have begun to move away from macro-structural frames of analysis, shifting their focus towards the everyday, towards 'the ways in which power and class and gender can be in a colour or a shape or a look'.[75] They often study the intersubjective constitution of subjectivities, drawing special attention to the body and the corporeal materiality of the encounter, accounting for its sensual and emotional dimensions.[76] However, this does not necessarily imply that there is a common bodily substrate that would enable universal transcultural human understanding. The debate about the extent to which one can comprehend the ways Hawaiians interacted with Captain James Cook and his crew – or whether one can comprehend these interactions at all – has clearly and succinctly laid bare the complexities of this issue.[77] Therefore, emphasizing the bodily and emotional dimensions of encounters does not necessarily require researchers to make assumptions regarding a shared physiological apparatus, but it does necessitate the development of methodological tools for crossing boundaries between and beyond languages.

* * *

The individual chapters cross these boundaries in manifold ways. Each chapter focuses on a specific group of actors – some of them less paradigmatic than others but all of them crucial for examining the multilayered complexity of transcultural encounters: topics range from missionaries, travellers and anthropologists across to entrepreneurs, diplomats and occupiers and on to prisoners, the mentally ill, performers and lovers. Taken together, these diverse perspectives shed light on crucial aspects of both intercultural and intracultural encounters. The book eschews a chronological or comparative structure, which would bind the authors to the problematic assumption that historical periods or specific regions can be treated as self-contained entities. Instead, the authors focus on actors, their movements and their encounters with others, thereby weaving together a longitudinal narrative with individual case studies that are paradigmatic for certain constellations. This approach enables them to home in on the complex interrelations between different regions and time periods. This actor-based approach, with its theoretical and methodological emphasis on emotions, practices and bodies, provides fertile ground for the authors' in-depth analyses of complex social and cultural interactions and the emotions that permeate them and that have played a crucial role in the creation and organization of globalized spaces. By conducting their research on these different actor groups and the emotional structure of their encounters in a historically sensitive way, the authors offer fresh insights into a phenomenon that is not only experienced by an increasing number of the world's population on a daily basis but that also allows us to rethink the dichotomous conception of emotions as being either a product of nurture or a given of nature, a dichotomy that structures academic and non-academic debates on feelings to this very day.

The focus on specific groups of actors provides methodological clarity and coherence to the individual chapters. Reality, however, is often much messier. Missionaries also facilitated diplomatic negotiations; diplomats and tourists fell in love; lovers could become insane or end up as prisoners. Traders provided anthropological knowledge, and anthropologists were recruited to the army for their local expertise. In order to trace these overlaps and connections, *Encounters with Emotions* contains numerous cross-references and threads, linking the chapters with one another.

The woman smoking the huqqah in the picture (Figure 0.1) embodies this plurality of roles.[78] Born as Farzana around 1750, she was raised in an establishment for dancing girls in northern India before being sold or gifted as a mistress to Walter Reinhardt, a soldier of fortune and mercenary from Austria, Luxembourg or Germany. Little is known about their emotional relationship, if they indeed had one at all. However, the events following Reinhardt's death in 1778 show that Farzana had by no means remained a submissive slave girl but had ambitiously used her position to establish a network of contacts and mutual obligations all over northern India. Relying on the personal loyalty of the army, over which she took command, she successfully placed herself at the head of the principality of Sardhana, some fifty miles northeast of Delhi, which had been given to Reinhardt by the Mughal emperor. She was recognized in her new role both by the Mughal court and the rising British colonial power. In the decades up until her death in 1836, she governed her territory with a firm hand and occasional cruelty, not only imprisoning her adversaries but in one instance even burying a slave girl alive and sitting on her grave until the victim's cries subsided. An astute diplomat, she moved between different cultural contexts without apparent difficulty. Known as Zeb un Nisa at the Mughal court, where the emperor called her his beloved

Figure 0.1 Detail of *Begum Samru's Household* (c. 1820), Delhi, India. © The Trustees of the Chester Beatty Library, Dublin (CBL In 74.7). Used with permission.

daughter, she was known as Begum Samru (after Reinhardt's nickname Sombre) in British circles. In her Mughal and British palaces she lavished hospitality on British travellers, not only introducing them to the Mughal court, increasingly an object of British curiosity, but also helping them to navigate the intricacies of imperial protocol. She converted to Catholicism in 1781, adding Princess Joanna to her names, built a church in Sardhana modelled on St Peter's Basilica in Rome and supported Christian missionaries. At the same time, she continued to celebrate Hindu and Muslim festivals at her cosmopolitan court, where Hindus and Muslims of all denominations intermingled with Catholics, Protestants and Jews from different regions of India and Persia, Armenia, England, Scotland, France, Germany, Poland and Portugal.[79] While she continued to dress like an Indian princess, she did not adhere to the rules of seclusion but interacted freely with the men, riding horses, drinking wine and smoking her water pipe. After her death, the principality of Sardhana was incorporated into British-Indian territory. David Dyce Sombre, her adopted son, had to leave India, was unable to find a place in Britain due to his cultural ambivalence, was declared insane and died at a young age.

In line with the overall argument of the book, the trajectory of Begum Samru's life exemplifies the fact that crossing multiple boundaries has only been possible in specific times and places. A life like Begum Samru's would have been unimaginable in the late nineteenth century. The encounter of feelings and the feeling of encounters have varied significantly over time, conditioned by the historical, political and cultural circumstances under which they took place. At the same time, cross-cultural encounters have always involved specific emotions and the bodily navigation of different emotional repertoires. This concurrence of the particular and the universal explains why actors and their feelings have never been fully transparent or completely opaque to one another. It is precisely this ambivalence that allows the authors of this volume to challenge the divide between nature and nurture that has long dominated research on the emotions.

Ultimately, this approach highlights the encounter's potential for bringing about unforeseeable outcomes and initiating processes of learning. Mediating between the theoretical frameworks of universal and particular approaches, *Encounters with Emotions* thus accounts for both the cultural dimensions of nature and the bodily dimensions of nurture by combining analyses of symbolic forms with analyses of historicized bodies.

Benno Gammerl is DAAD Lecturer in queer history at Goldsmiths, University of London and Associate Researcher at the Max Planck

Institute for Human Development's Center for the History of Emotions in Berlin. He published (with Jan S. Hutta and Monique Scheer) 'Feeling Differently: Approaches and their Politics', in *Emotion, Space and Society* (2017) and *Subjects, Citizens and Others: Administering Ethnic Heterogeneity in the British and Habsburg Empires, 1867–1918* (Berghahn, 2018).

Philipp Nielsen is Assistant Professor for Modern European History at Sarah Lawrence College and Associated Researcher at the Center for the History of Emotions at the Max Planck Institute for Human Development in Berlin. He received his PhD from Yale University in 2012. His publications include *Between Heimat and Hatred: Jews and the Right in Germany, 1871–1935* (forthcoming with Oxford University Press, 2019) and *Architecture, Democracy and Emotions: The Politics of Feeling after 1945* with Till Großmann (Routledge, 2018). His research interests include Jewish German history, German political and architectural history and the history of emotions.

Margrit Pernau is Senior Researcher at the Center for the History of Emotions at the Max Planck Institute for Human Development in Berlin. She has been Research Fellow at the Social Science Research Center Berlin, the Modern Orient Centre in Berlin, the Institute of Advanced Studies in Freiburg and the EHESS in Paris. Among her publications are *The Delhi College: Traditional Elites, the Colonial State and Education before 1857* (Oxford University Press, 2006), *Ashraf into Middle Classes: Muslims in 19th Century Delhi* (Oxford University Press, 2013) and *Civilizing Emotions: Concepts in Nineteenth Century Asia and Europe* (with Helge Jordheim et al., Oxford University Press, 2015). She has also written numerous articles on the history of emotions, modern Indian history and historical semantics.

Notes

1. Bose, 'Harbhajan Singh Row'. Many thanks to William Gould and Margrit's Facebook friends for finding this incident for us.
2. The history of cricket, its professionalization since the 1960s and the even older conflicts over race and masculinity are equally important. On the professionalization of cricket, see, for example, Sandiford, 'The Professionalization of Modern Cricket', 270–89; on race and masculinity in the sport, see Sen, 'Enduring Colonialism in Cricket: From Ranjitsinhji to the Cronje Affair', 237–49; McDevitt, 'Bodyline, Jardine and Masculinity', 70–84.
3. 'Symonds Sparked by Indian Celebrations', *ESPN Cricinfo*.
4. 'Harbhajan Attacks "Vulgar" Australia', *ESPN Cricinfo*.
5. Bose, 'Harbhajan Singh Row'.

6. 'Symonds Tells his Side of the Story', *ESPN Cricinfo*.
7. Hansen, 'Before the International Cricket Council Appointed Appeals Commissioner'.
8. See Satadru Sen's biography of Ranjitsinhji, *Migrant Races: Empire, Identity and K.S. Ranjitsinhji*.
9. Plamper, *The History of Emotions: An Introduction*, 75–146.
10. For a review of relevant literature, see the section 'Recent Historiography on Transcultural Encounters' below in this chapter. Hunt, *Writing History in the Global Era* and Iriye, *Global and Transnational History: The Past, Present, and Future* have recently argued for including emotional perspectives in global history.
11. Dixon, *From Passions to Emotions: The Creation of a Secular Psychological Category*; Frevert et al., *Emotional Lexicons: Continuity and Change in the Vocabulary of Feeling 1700–2000*; for a work on early modern emotions that also includes some thoughts on transcultural encounters, see Broomhall, *Early Modern Emotions: An Introduction*.
12. Lutz and Abu-Lughod, *Language and the Politics of Emotion*.
13. Levinas, *Totality and Infinity: An Essay on Exteriority*, 187–218.
14. Beneito-Montagut, 'Encounters on the Social Web: Everyday Life and Emotions Online', 537–53.
15. In a similar fashion, Erving Goffman stresses the physical co-presence of the participants in an encounter while simultaneously reminding us that encounters are always embedded in larger social structures; Goffman, *Encounters: Two Studies in the Sociology of Interaction*.
16. Affect-theory approaches highlight openness and unexpected potentials as well, often taking recourse to Spinoza's notion of encounter; Seigworth and Gregg, 'An Inventory of Shimmers', 3. From a Marxist perspective, Louis Althusser also emphasized the contingencies and aleatory dynamics of encounters; Althusser, *Philosophy of the Encounter: Later Writings, 1978–87*, xli and 193. For a similar conception, see also Schwartz, 'Introduction', 3.
17. Fabian, 'You Meet and You Talk: Anthropological Reflections on Encounters and Discourses', 25.
18. Fernando Ortiz introduced the notion of transculturation in 1940; Ortiz, *Cuban Counterpoint: Tobacco and Sugar*. For a different take on the phenomenon of cultural intermingling, see Stewart, 'Creolization, Hybridity, Syncretism, Mixture', 48–55.
19. Ekman, Sorenson and Friesen, 'Pan-Cultural Elements in Facial Displays of Emotion', 87, but for a counter-position based on further research in Papua New Guinea, see Crivelli et al., 'The Fear Gasping Face as a Threat Display in a Melanesian Society', 12403–7.
20. For an early example of this critique, see Hulme, *Colonial Encounters: Europe and the Native Caribbean, 1492–1797*; for premediation, see Ricoeur, 'Phenomenology and Hermeneutics', 85–102; Ricoeur, *The Course of Recognition*; Abulafia, *The Discovery of Mankind: Atlantic Encounters in the Age of Columbus*.
21. Linrothe, *Ruthless Compassion: Wrathful Deities in Early Indo-Tibetan Esoteric Buddhist Art*, 20–22, 134.
22. Balme, *Pacific Performances: Theatricality and Cross-Cultural Encounter in the South Seas*, 2–6; Douglas, *Science, Voyages, and Encounters in Oceania, 1511–1850*, 9, 18–19; Gruzinski, 'Découverte, conquête et communication dans l'Amérique ibérique: Avant les mots, au-delà des mots', 141–54; Jäger, 'Intermedialität—Intramedialität—Transkriptivität: Überlegungen zu einigen Prinzipien der kulturellen Semiosis', 301–23.
23. Pernau, 'Whither Conceptual History? From National to Entangled Histories', 1–11, with further references. For an early version of this argument, see Benjamin, 'The Task of the Translator: An Introduction to the Translation of Baudelaire's Tableaux Parisiens', 69–82.
24. Faiq, *Cultural Encounters in Translation from Arabic*.

25. Bachmann-Medick, *The Trans/National Study of Culture: A Translational Perspective*; Fuchs, 'Reaching Out; Or, Nobody Exists in One Context Only: Society as Translation', 21–40; Ho, *The Graves of Tarim: Genealogy and Mobility across the Indian Ocean*; Marjanen, 'Undermining Methodological Nationalism: Histoire crcisée of Concepts as Transnational History', 239–63; Renn, *Übersetzungsverhältnisse: Perspektiven einer pragmatistischen Gesellschaftstheorie*.
26. Reddy, *The Navigation of Feeling: A Framework for the History of Emotions*, 63–111; Pernau and Rajamani, 'Emotional Translations: Conceptual History beyond Language', 46–65.
27. Eitler, Olsen and Jensen, 'Introduction', 1–20.
28. Clendinnen, *Dancing with Strangers*, 11 and passim; Taussig, *Mimesis and Alterity*, 76, 78.
29. Taussig, *Mimesis and Alterity*.
30. Niedenthal et al., 'Embodiment in Attitudes, Social Perception, and Emotion', 193.
31. Girard, *Theatre of Envy: William Shakespeare*.
32. Dumouchel, 'Emotions and Mimesis', 76–81.
33. In order to describe how imitation produces and reproduces inequalities, Stephen Greenblatt developed the notion of *mimetic capital*; Greenblatt, *Marvelous Possessions: The Wonder of the New World*, 6.
34. See Brennan, *Transmission of Affect*. For a criticism of affect theory's bias against intentionality, see Leys, 'The Turn to Affect: A Critique', 443.
35. Brennan, *Transmission of Affect*, 17.
36. Brennan, *Transmission of Affect*, 7. On whether Brennan actually needs to use neurochemistry to make her argument, see 'Forum: Perspectives on Teresa Brennan's The Transmission of Affect', 103–17.
37. Brennan, *Transmission of Affect*, 9–10, 20. For a similar approach, see Garcia, '"Can You Feel It, Too?": Intimacy and Affect at Electronic Dance Music Events in Paris, Chicago, and Berlin'.
38. Gammerl, Hutta and Scheer, 'Feeling Differently: Approaches and Their Politics', 87–94.
39. Frevert et al., *Learning How to Feel: Children's Literature and Emotional Socialization, 1870–1970*.
40. Smith, *Intimate Strangers: Friendship, Exchange and Pacific Encounters*.
41. Pernau, 'Civility and Barbarism: Emotions as Criteria of Difference', 230–59. As far as the current state of research can tell us, this might indeed have been a particularity of the European tradition. While the Islamicate world and South Asia, for instance, made extensive use of family metaphors to make sense of encounters between strangers, this did not extend to the use of gender or age as ways of classifying different social groups.
42. Verheyen, 'Age(ing) with Feeling', 151–76.
43. Brown, 'Native Americans and Early Modern Concepts of Race', 79–100; Chatterjee and Hawes, 'Introduction', 28–30; Fisher, *Counterflows to Colonialism. Indian Travellers and Settlers in Britain 1600–1857*, 5.
44. Bank, 'Losing Faith in the Civilizing Mission: The Premature Decline of Humanitarian Liberalism at the Cape, 1840–60', 364–83.
45. Fisher, *Counterflows to Colonialism*, 183–84, 208; Saada, *Empire's Children: Race, Filiation, and Citizenship in the French Colonies*; Stoler, *Carnal Knowledge and Imperial Power: Race and the Intimate in Colonial Rule*.
46. McClintock, *Imperial Leather: Race, Gender and Sexuality in the Colonial Contest*, 257; Nagel, *Race, Ethnicity, and Sexuality: Intimate Intersections, Forbidden Frontiers*.
47. Fischer-Tiné, 'Reclaiming Savages in "Darkest England" and "Darkest India": The Salvation Army as Transnational Agent of the Civilizing Mission', 125–64.
48. Fisher, *Counterflows to Colonialism*, 9, 181; Hallam and Street, 'Introduction: Cultural Encounters—Representing "Otherness"', 3; Sinha, *Colonial Masculinity: The 'Manly*

Englishman' and the 'Effeminate Bengali' in the Late Nineteenth Century; Young, *Colonial Desire: Hybridity in Theory, Culture, and Race*, 8.
49. Borutta and Verheyen, *Männlichkeit und Emotion in der Moderne*; Pernau et al., *Civilizing Emotions: Concepts in Nineteenth-Century Asia and Europe*.
50. Douglas, *Science, Voyages, and Encounters*; Lüsebrink, 'Von der Faszination zur Wissenssystematisierung: Die koloniale Welt im Diskurs der europäischen Aufklärung', 17–18; Osterhammel, *Die Entzauberung Asiens: Europa und die asiatischen Reiche im 18. Jahrhundert*.
51. On the intricacies of cross-class, cross-gender and cross-race desires as they played out between the servant-lady Hannah Cullwick and her master-husband Arthur Munby in Victorian England, see McClintock, *Imperial Leather*, 132–80.
52. This process has been particularly well studied within the ethnically diverse regions of Central Eastern Europe; Himka, *Religion and Nationality in Western Ukraine: The Greek Catholic Church and the Ruthenian National Movement in Galicia, 1867–1900*; Judson, *Guardians of the Nation: Activists on the Language Frontiers of Imperial Austria*; Kaiserová, Nižňanský and Schulze Wessel, *Religion und Nation: Tschechen, Deutsche und Slowaken im 20. Jahrhundert*.
53. Gordon, 'Internal Colonialism and Gender', 427–51; McClintock, *Imperial Leather*, 353; Sluga, 'Identity, Gender, and the History of European Nations and Nationalisms', 87–111.
54. This seemingly contradictory simultaneity of universalization and difference has been analysed in an exemplary fashion by studies that view nationalism as an inter- or transnational phenomenon; Conrad, 'Globalization Effects: Mobility and Nation in Imperial Germany, 1880–1914', 43–66; Sluga, *Internationalism in the Age of Nationalism*. For an example from the history of religion, see Bayly, *The Birth of the Modern World 1780–1914: Global Connections and Comparisons*.
55. Blasco, 'Stranger to Us than the Birds in our Garden? Reflections on Hermeneutics, Intercultural Understanding and the Management of Difference', 31.
56. Booth, 'Making the Case for Cross-Cultural Exchange: Robert Byron's The Road to Oxiana', 167; Gandhi, *Affective Communities: Anticolonial Thought, Fin-de-Siècle Radicalism, and the Politics of Friendship*.
57. Young, *Colonial Desire*, 52. See also Gumperz, 'Contextualization and Ideology in Intercultural Communication', 35.
58. Gandhi, *Hind Swaraj, or, Indian Home Rule*; Fanon, *The Wretched of the Earth*; Nandy, *The Intimate Enemy: Loss and Recovery of Self under Colonialism*.
59. Levinas, *Totality and Infinity*, 150. See also Levinas, *Humanism of the Other*.
60. Taylor, 'The Politics of Recognition', 25–73.
61. Rushdie, *Imaginary Homelands: Essays and Criticism, 1981–1991*. See also Appadurai, *Modernity at Large: Cultural Dimensions of Globalization*; Bhaba, *The Location of Culture*; Glissant, *Introduction à une poétique du divers*; Gruzinski, *La pensée métisse: Cahiers de l'institut universitaire d'études du développement*; Knoblauch, 'Communication, Contexts and Culture: A Communicative Constructivist Approach to Intercultural Communication', 28; Stewart, 'Creolization', 48–55.
62. Benhabib, *Another Cosmopolitanism*; Benhabib, *The Claims of Culture: Equality and Diversity in the Global Era*.
63. Gilroy, *After Empire: Melancholia or Convivial Culture?*; Wise and Velayutham, 'Introduction: Multiculturalism and Everyday Life', 1–17.
64. Bentley, *Old World Encounters: Cross-Cultural Contacts and Exchanges in Pre-Modern Times*. See also Bitterli, *Cultures in Conflict: Encounters between European and Non-European Cultures, 1492–1800*; Bochner, *Cultures in Contact: Studies in Cross-Cultural Interaction*; Nelson, 'Civilizational Complexes and Intercivilizational Encounters', 79–105. For a more recent exploration of this approach, see Delanty, 'Cultural Diversity, Democracy and the Prospects of Cosmopolitanism: A Theory of Cultural Encounters', 633–56.

65. Thomas, *Islanders: The Pacific in the Age of Empire*, 3, 16f.; Bachmann-Medick, 'The Trans/National Study of Culture: A Translational Perspective', 14; Chatterjee and Hawes, *Europe Observed*; Fisher, *Counterflows to Colonialism*; Manjapra, *Age of Entanglement: German and Indian Intellectuals across Empire*; Shoemaker, *Native American Whalemen and the World: Indigenous Encounters and the Contingency of Race*; Subrahmanyam, *Explorations in Connected History: From the Tagus to the Ganges*; Vaughan, *Transatlantic Encounters: American Indians in Britain, 1500–1776*.
66. Freitag, *Indian Ocean Migrants and State Formation in Hadhramaut: Reforming the Homeland*; Ho, *Graves of Tarim*.
67. Chatterjee and Hawes, 'Introduction', 5. See also Konishi, Nugent and Shellam, *Indigenous Intermediaries: New Perspectives on Exploration Archives*.
68. Chatterjee and Hawes, 'Introduction', 23–24.
69. Davidann and Gilbert, *Cross-Cultural Encounters in Modern World History*, 3; Dening, *Beach Crossings: Voyaging across Times, Cultures and Self*, 13.
70. This approach goes back to the seminal work of Braudel; Braudel, *The Mediterranean and the Mediterranean World in the Age of Philipp II*. For recent works, see Horden and Purcell, *The Corrupting Sea: A Study of Mediterranean History*; King, *The Mediterranean Passage: Migration and New Cultural Encounters in Southern Europe*; Abulafia, *The Great Sea: A Human History of the Mediterranean*. On the concept of the contact zone, see Pratt, *Imperial Eyes: Travel Writing and Transculturation*.
71. Balme, *Pacific Performances*, 6; Daunton and Halpern, 'Introduction: British Identities, Indigenous Peoples, and the Empire', 5.
72. Hulme, *Colonial Encounters*; Hallam and Street, *Cultural Encounters — Representing 'Otherness'*; Lüsebrink, *Europa der Aufklärung und die außereuropäische koloniale Welt*; Mageo, *Cultural Memory: Reconfiguring History and Identity in the Postcolonial Pacific*; Pratt, *Imperial Eyes*.
73. Dallmayr, *Beyond Orientalism: Essays on Cross-Cultural Encounter*, xvii; Gustaffson and Blasco, 'Introduction–Intercultural Alternatives: Critical Perspectives on Intercultural Encounters in Theory and Practice', 16; Schwartz, 'Introduction', 1–2.
74. Asad, 'Muslims and European Identity: Can Europe Represent Islam?', 11–27; Faiq, *Cultural Encounters in Translation*; Said, *Orientalism*.
75. Dening, *Beach Crossings*, 18. See also Fabian, 'You Meet', 26; Rozbicki and Ndege, 'Introduction', 2.
76. Balme, *Pacific Performances*, 2; Gruzinski, 'Découverte', 145; Fabian, 'You Meet', 32–33; Hallam and Street, 'Introduction', 4; Jobs and Mackenthun, *Embodiments of Cultural Encounters*; Lobo, 'Affective Energies: Sensory Bodies on the Beach in Darwin, Australia', 104; Shellam, 'Mediating Encounters through Bodies and Talk', 85–102; Tamcke and Gladson, *Body, Emotion and Mind: 'Embodying' the Experiences in Indo-European Encounters*.
77. Obeyesekere, *The Apotheosis of Captain Cook: European Mythmaking in the Pacific*; Sahlins, *How 'Natives' Think: About Captain Cook, for Example*.
78. For her colourful biography, see Lall, *Begum Samru: Fading Portrait in a Gilded Frame*; for the biography of her adopted son, see Fisher, *The Inordinately Strange Life of Dyce Sombre: Victorian Anglo-Indian MP and 'Chancery Lunatic'*.
79. Fisher, *Inordinately Strange Life*, 33.

Bibliography

Abulafia, D. *The Discovery of Mankind: Atlantic Encounters in the Age of Columbus*. New Haven, CT: Yale University Press, 2008.

_____. *The Great Sea: A Human History of the Mediterranean*. London: Lane, 2011.

Althusser, L. *Philosophy of the Encounter: Later Writings, 1978–87*, ed. F. Matheron and O. Corpet, trans. G.M. Goshgarian. London: Verso, 2006 [Fre. orig. *Sur la philosophie*. Paris: Gallimard, 1994].

Appadurai, A. *Modernity at Large: Cultural Dimensions of Globalization*. Minneapolis: University of Minnesota Press, 1996.

Asad, T. 'Muslims and European Identity: Can Europe Represent Islam?', in E. Hallam and B.V. Street (eds), *Cultural Encounters – Representing 'Otherness'* (London: Routledge, 2000), 11–27.

Bachmann-Medick, D. 'The Trans/National Study of Culture: A Translational Perspective', in D. Bachmann-Medick (ed.), *The Trans/National Study of Culture* (Berlin: de Gruyter, 2014), 1–22.

Bachmann-Medick, D. (ed.). *The Trans/National Study of Culture: A Translational Perspective*. Berlin: de Gruyter, 2014.

Balme, C.B. *Pacific Performances: Theatricality and Cross-Cultural Encounter in the South Seas*. Houndsmills, U.K.: Palgrave Macmillan, 2007.

Bank, A. 'Losing Faith in the Civilizing Mission: The Premature Decline of Humanitarian Liberalism at the Cape, 1840–60', in M. Daunton and R. Halpern (eds), *Empire and Others: British Encounters with Indigenous Peoples, 1600–1850* (London: UCL Press, 1999), 364–83.

Bayly, C.A. *The Birth of the Modern World 1780–1914: Global Connections and Comparisons*. Malden, MA: Blackwell, 2003.

Beneito-Montagut, R. 'Encounters on the Social Web: Everyday Life and Emotions Online'. *Sociological Perspectives* 58(4) (2015), 537–53, doi: 10.1177/0731121415569284.

Benhabib, S. *The Claims of Culture: Equality and Diversity in the Global Era*. Princeton, NJ: Princeton University Press, 2002.

_____. *Another Cosmopolitanism*, ed. R. Post. Oxford: Oxford University Press, 2006.

Benjamin, W. 'The Task of the Translator: An Introduction to the Translation of Baudelaire's Tableaux Parisiens', in W. Benjamin, *Illuminations*, ed. H. Arendt, trans. H. Zorn (New York: Harcourt, Brace & World, 1968), 69–82 [Ger. orig. 'Die Aufgabe des Übersetzers' (1923)].

Bentley, J.H. *Old World Encounters: Cross-Cultural Contacts and Exchanges in Pre-Modern Times*. New York: Oxford University Press, 1993.

Bhaba, H.K. *The Location of Culture*. London: Routledge, 1994.

Bitterli, U. *Cultures in Conflict: Encounters between European and Non-European Cultures, 1492–1800*, trans. R. Robertson. Cambridge: Polity Press, 1989 [Ger. orig. *Alte Welt, Neue Welt*. Munich: Beck, 1986].

Blasco, M. 'Stranger to Us than the Birds in our Garden? Reflections on Hermeneutics, Intercultural Understanding and the Management of Difference', in M. Blasco and J. Gustafsson (eds), *Intercultural Alternatives: Critical Perspectives on Intercultural Encounters in Theory and Practice* (Copenhagen: Copenhagen Business School Press, 2004), 19–48.

Bochner, S. (ed.). *Cultures in Contact: Studies in Cross-Cultural Interaction*. Oxford: Pergamon Press, 1982.

Booth, H.J. 'Making the Case for Cross-Cultural Exchange: Robert Byron's The Road to Oxiana', in C. Burdett and D. Duncan (eds), *Cultural Encounters: European Travel Writing in the 1930s* (New York: Berghahn, 2002), 159–72.
Borutta, M., and N. Verheyen (eds). *Männlichkeit und Emotion in der Moderne*. Bielefeld: Transcript, 2010.
Bose, M. 'Harbhajan Singh Row Exposes Cultural Divide'. *The Telegraph*, 15 January 2008. Retrieved 12 September 2018 from http://www.telegraph.co.uk/sport/cricket/2288942/Harbhajan-Singh-row-exposes-cultural-divide.html.
Braudel, F. *The Mediterranean and the Mediterranean World in the Age of Philipp II*, 2 vols, trans. S. Reynolds. New York: Harper & Row, 1972 [Fre. orig. *La Méditerranée et le monde méditeranéen à l'epoque de Philippe II*. Paris: Colin, 1949].
Brennan, T. *The Transmission of Affect*. Ithaca, NY: Cornell University Press, 2004.
Broomhall, S. (ed.). *Early Modern Emotions: An Introduction*. London: Routledge, 2017.
Brown, K. 'Native Americans and Early Modern Concepts of Race', in M. Daunton and R. Halpern (eds), *Empire and Others: British Encounters with Indigenous Peoples, 1600–1850* (London: UCL Press, 1999), 79–100.
Chatterjee, K., and C. Hawes. 'Introduction', in K. Chatterjee and C. Hawes (eds), *Europe Observed: Multiple Gazes in Early Modern Encounters* (Lewisburg, PA: Bucknell University Press, 2008), 1–43.
Chatterjee, K., and C. Hawes (eds). *Europe Observed: Multiple Gazes in Early Modern Encounters*. Lewisburg, PA: Bucknell University Press, 2008.
Clendinnen, I. *Dancing with Strangers*. Melbourne: Text Publishing, 2003.
Conrad, S. 'Globalization Effects: Mobility and Nation in Imperial Germany, 1880–1914'. *Journal of Global History* 3(1) (2008), 43–66, doi: 10.1017/S174002280800243X.
Crivelli, C., J.A. Russell, S. Jarillo and J.-M. Fernández-Dols. 'The Fear Gasping Face as a Threat Display in a Melanesian Society'. *PNAS (Proceedings of the National Academy of Sciences)* 113(44) (2016), 12403–7, doi: 10.1073/pnas.1611622113.
Dallmayr, F. *Beyond Orientalism: Essays on Cross-Cultural Encounter*. Albany, NY: State University of New York, 1996.
Daunton, M., and R. Halpern. 'Introduction: British Identities, Indigenous Peoples, and the Empire', in M. Daunton and R. Halpern (eds), *Empire and Others: British Encounters with Indigenous Peoples, 1600–1850* (London: UCL Press, 1999), 1–18.
Davidann, J.T., and M.J. Gilbert. *Cross-Cultural Encounters in Modern World History*. Boston: Pearson, 2013.
Delanty, G. 'Cultural Diversity, Democracy and the Prospects of Cosmopolitanism: A Theory of Cultural Encounters'. *British Journal of Sociology* 62(4) (2011), 633–56, doi: 10.1111/j.1468-4446.2011.01384.x.
Dening, G. *Beach Crossings: Voyaging across Times, Cultures and Self*. Melbourne: Miegunyah Press, 2004.
Dixon, T. *From Passions to Emotions: The Creation of a Secular Psychological Category*. Cambridge: Cambridge University Press, 2005.

Douglas, B. *Science, Voyages, and Encounters in Oceania, 1511–1850*. Basingstoke, U.K.: Palgrave Macmillan, 2014.

Dumouchel, P. 'Emotions and Mimesis', in S.R. Garrels (ed.), *Mimesis and Science: Empirical Research on Imitation and the Mimetic Theory of Culture and Religion* (East Lansing: Michigan State University Press, 2011), 75–86.

Eitler, P., S. Olsen and U. Jensen. 'Introduction', in U. Frevert et al., *Learning How to Feel: Children's Literature and Emotional Socialization, 1870–1970* (New York: Oxford University Press, 2014), 1–20.

Ekman, P., R. Sorenson and W.V. Friesen. 'Pan-Cultural Elements in Facial Displays of Emotion'. *Science* 164(3875) (1969), 86–88.

Fabian, J. 'You Meet and You Talk: Anthropological Reflections on Encounters and Discourses', in S. Juterczenka and G. Mackenthun (eds), *The Fuzzy Logic of Encounter: New Perspectives on Cultural Contact* (Münster: Waxmann, 2009), 23–34.

Faiq, S. (ed.). *Cultural Encounters in Translation from Arabic*. Clevedon: Multilingual Matters, 2004.

Fanon, F. *The Wretched of the Earth*, trans. C. Farrington. New York: Grove Press, 1963 [Fr. orig. *Les damnés de la terre*. Paris: Maspero, 1961].

Fischer-Tiné, H. 'Reclaiming Savages in "Darkest England" and "Darkest India": The Salvation Army as Transnational Agent of the Civilizing Mission', in C.A. Watt and M. Mann (eds), *Civilizing Missions in Colonial and Postcolonial South Asia: From Improvement to Development* (London: Anthem Press, 2011), 125–64.

Fisher, M.H. *Counterflows to Colonialism: Indian Travellers and Settlers in Britain 1600–1857*. New Delhi: Permanent Black, 2004.

_____. *The Inordinately Strange Life of Dyce Sombre: Victorian Anglo-Indian MP and 'Chancery Lunatic'*. London: Hurst, 2010.

'Forum: Perspectives on Teresa Brennan's The Transmission of Affect'. *Women: A Cultural Review* 17(1) (2006), 103–17, doi: 10.1080/09574040600628724.

Freitag, U. *Indian Ocean Migrants and State Formation in Hadhramaut: Reforming the Homeland*. Leiden: Brill, 2003.

Frevert, U., et al. *Emotional Lexicons: Continuity and Change in the Vocabulary of Feeling 1700–2000*. Oxford: Oxford University Press, 2014 [Ger. orig. *Gefühlswissen: Eine lexikalische Spurensuche in der Moderne*. Frankfurt am Main: Campus, 2011].

Frevert, U., et al. *Learning How to Feel: Children's Literature and Emotional Socialization, 1870–1970*. New York: Oxford University Press, 2014.

Fuchs, M. 'Reaching Out; Or, Nobody Exists in One Context Only: Society as Translation'. *Translation Studies* 2(1) (2009), 21–40, doi: 10.1080/14781700802496191.

Gammerl, B., J.S. Hutta and M. Scheer. 'Feeling Differently: Approaches and Their Politics'. *Emotion, Space and Society* 25 (2017), 87–94, doi: 10.1016/j.emospa.2017.07.007.

Gandhi, L. *Affective Communities: Anticolonial Thought, Fin-de-Siècle Radicalism, and the Politics of Friendship*. Durham, NC: Duke University Press, 2006.

Gandhi, M.K. *Hind Swaraj, or, Indian Home Rule*. Madras: S. Garnesan & Co., 1921.

Garcia, L.-M. '"Can You Feel It, Too?": Intimacy and Affect at Electronic Dance Music Events in Paris, Chicago, and Berlin'. Ph.D. dissertation. Chicago: Department of Music, University of Chicago, 2011.
Gilroy, P. *After Empire: Melancholia or Convivial Culture?* Abingdon, U.K.: Routledge, 2004.
Girard, R. *Theatre of Envy: William Shakespeare.* New York: Oxford University Press, 1991.
Glissant, É. *Introduction à une poétique du divers.* Paris: Gallimard, 1996.
Goffman, E. *Encounters: Two Studies in the Sociology of Interaction.* Indianapolis, IN: Bobbs-Merrill, 1961.
Gordon, L. 'Internal Colonialism and Gender', in A.L. Stoler (ed.), *Haunted by Empire: Geographies of Intimacy in North American History* (Durham, NC: Duke University Press, 2006), 427–51.
Greenblatt, S. *Marvelous Possessions: The Wonder of the New World.* Chicago: University of Chicago Press, 1991.
Gruzinski, S. 'Découverte, conquête et communication dans l'Amérique ibérique: Avant les mots, au-delà des mots', in L. Turgeon, D. Delâge and R. Quellet (eds), *Transferts culturels et métissage Amérique/Europe, XVIe–XXe siècle* (Paris: L'Harmattan, 1996), 141–54.
_____. *La pensée métisse: Cahiers de l'institut universitaire d'études du développement.* Paris: Presses Universitaires de France, 1999.
Gumperz, J.J. 'Contextualization and Ideology in Intercultural Communication', in A. di Luzio, S. Günthner and F. Orletti (eds), *Culture in Communication: Analyses of Intercultural Situations* (Amsterdam: Benjamins, 2001), 35–53.
Gustaffson, J., and M. Blasco. 'Introduction–Intercultural Alternatives: Critical Perspectives on Intercultural Encounters in Theory and Practice', in M. Blasco and J. Gustaffson (eds), *Intercultural Alternatives: Critical Perspectives on Intercultural Encounters in Theory and Practice* (Copenhagen: Copenhagen Business School Press, 2004), 11–18.
Hallam, E., and B.V. Street. 'Introduction: Cultural Encounters – Representing "Otherness"', in E. Hallam and B.V. Street (eds), *Cultural Encounters – Representing 'Otherness'* (London: Routledge, 2000), 1–10.
Hallam, E., and B.V. Street (eds). *Cultural Encounters – Representing 'Otherness'.* London: Routledge, 2000.
Hansen, J. 'Before the International Cricket Council Appointed Appeals Commissioner'. *The Age,* 29 January 2008. Retrieved 7 October 2015 from http://www.theage.com.au/ed_docs/hansen.pdf.
'Harbhajan Attacks "Vulgar" Australia'. *ESPN Cricinfo,* 4 October 2007. Retrieved 12 September 2018 from http://www.espncricinfo.com/indvaus/content/story/313550.html.
Himka, J.-P. *Religion and Nationality in Western Ukraine: The Greek Catholic Church and the Ruthenian National Movement in Galicia, 1867–1900.* Montreal: McGill-Queen's University Press, 1999.
Ho, E. *The Graves of Tarim: Genealogy and Mobility across the Indian Ocean.* Berkeley: University of California Press, 2006.
Horden, P., and N. Purcell. *The Corrupting Sea: A Study of Mediterranean History.* Oxford: Blackwell, 2000.

Hulme, P. *Colonial Encounters: Europe and the Native Caribbean, 1492–1797*. London: Methuen, 1986.
Hunt, L. *Writing History in the Global Era*. New York: Norton, 2014.
Iriye, A. *Global and Transnational History: The Past, Present, and Future*. Basingstoke, U.K.: Palgrave Macmillan, 2013.
Jäger, L. 'Intermedialität – Intramedialität – Transkriptivität: Überlegungen zu einigen Prinzipien der kulturellen Semiosis', in A. Deppermann and A. Linke (eds), *Sprache intermedial: Stimme und Schrift, Bild und Ton* (Berlin: de Gruyter, 2010), 301–23.
Jobs, S., and G. Mackenthun (eds). *Embodiments of Cultural Encounters*. Münster: Waxmann, 2011.
Judson, P.M. *Guardians of the Nation: Activists on the Language Frontiers of Imperial Austria*. Cambridge, MA: Harvard University Press, 2006.
Kaiserová, K., E. Nižňanský and M. Schulze Wessel (eds). *Religion und Nation: Tschechen, Deutsche und Slowaken im 20. Jahrhundert*. Essen: Klartext, 2015.
King, R. (ed.). *The Mediterranean Passage: Migration and New Cultural Encounters in Southern Europe*. Liverpool: Liverpool University Press, 2001.
Knoblauch, H. 'Communication, Contexts and Culture: A Communicative Constructivist Approach to Intercultural Communication', in A. di Luzio, S. Günthner and F. Orletti (eds), *Culture in Communication: Analyses of Intercultural Situations* (Amsterdam: Benjamins, 2001), 3–33.
Konishi, S., M. Nugent and T. Shellam (eds). *Indigenous Intermediaries: New Perspectives on Exploration Archives*. Acton: Australian National University Press, 2015.
Lall, J.S. *Begum Samru: Fading Portrait in a Gilded Frame*. New Delhi: Roli Books, 1997.
Levinas, E. *Totality and Infinity: An Essay on Exteriority*, trans. A. Lingis. Pittsburgh, PA: Duquesne University Press, 1969 [Fre. orig. *Totalité et infini*. La Haye: Nijhoff, 1961].
Levinas, E. *Humanism of the Other*, trans. N. Poller. Urbana: University of Illinois Press, 2003 [Fre. orig. *Humanisme de l'autre homme*. Paris: Fata Morgana, 1972].
Leys, R. 'The Turn to Affect: A Critique', *Critical Inquiry* 37(3) (2011), 434–72, doi: 10.1086/659353.
Linrothe, R. *Ruthless Compassion: Wrathful Deities in Early Indo-Tibetan Esoteric Buddhist Art*. London: Serinidia Publications, 1999.
Lobo, M. 'Affective Energies: Sensory Bodies on the Beach in Darwin, Australia'. *Emotion, Space and Society* 12(1) (2014), 101–9, doi: 10.1016/j.emospa.2013.12.012.
Lüsebrink, H.-J. 'Von der Faszination zur Wissenssystematisierung: Die koloniale Welt im Diskurs der europäischen Aufklärung', in H.-J. Lüsebrink (ed.), *Das Europa der Aufklärung und die außereuropäische koloniale Welt* (Göttingen: Wallstein, 2006), 9–18.
Lüsebrink, H.-J. (ed.). *Das Europa der Aufklärung und die außereuropäische koloniale Welt*. Göttingen: Wallstein, 2006.
Lutz, C.A., and L. Abu-Lughod (eds). *Language and the Politics of Emotion*. Cambridge: Cambridge University Press, 1990.

Mageo, J.M. (ed.). *Cultural Memory: Reconfiguring History and Identity in the Postcolonial Pacific*. Honolulu: University of Hawai'i Press, 2001.

Manjapra, K. *Age of Entanglement: German and Indian Intellectuals across Empire*. Cambridge, MA: Harvard University Press, 2014.

Marjanen, J. 'Undermining Methodological Nationalism: Histoire croisée of Concepts as Transnational History', in M. Albert et al. (eds), *Transnational Political Spaces: Agents – Structures – Encounters* (Frankfurt am Main: Campus, 2009), 239–63.

McClintock, A. *Imperial Leather: Race, Gender and Sexuality in the Colonial Contest*. New York: Routledge, 1995.

McDevitt, P.F. 'Bodyline, Jardine and Masculinity', in A. Bateman and J. Hill (eds), *The Cambridge Companion to Cricket* (Cambridge: Cambridge University Press, 2011), 70–84.

Nagel, J. *Race, Ethnicity, and Sexuality: Intimate Intersections, Forbidden Frontiers*. New York: Oxford University Press, 2003.

Nandy, A. *The Intimate Enemy: Loss and Recovery of Self under Colonialism*. Delhi: Oxford University Press, 1983.

Nelson, B. 'Civilizational Complexes and Intercivilizational Encounters'. *Sociological Analysis* 34(2) (1973), 79–105, doi: 10.2307/3709717.

Niedenthal, P.M., et al. 'Embodiment in Attitudes, Social Perception, and Emotion'. *Personality and Social Psychology Review* 9(3) (2005), 184–211, doi: 10.1207/s15327957pspr0903_1.

Obeyesekere, G. *The Apotheosis of Captain Cook: European Mythmaking in the Pacific*. Princeton, NJ: Princeton University Press, 1992.

Ortiz, F. *Cuban Counterpoint: Tobacco and Sugar*, trans. H. de Onís. Durham, NC: Duke University Press, 1995 [Spa. orig. *Contrapunteo cubano del tabaco y el azúcar*. Havana: Jesús Montero, 1940].

Osterhammel, J. *Die Entzauberung Asiens: Europa und die asiatischen Reiche im 18. Jahrhundert*. Munich: Beck, 1998.

Pernau, M. 'Whither Conceptual History? From National to Entangled Histories', *Contributions to the History of Concepts* 7(1) (2012), 1–11, doi: 10.3167/choc.2012.070101.

———. 'Civility and Barbarism: Emotions as Criteria of Difference', in U. Frevert et al., *Emotional Lexicons: Continuity and Change in the Vocabulary of Feeling 1700–2000* (Oxford: Oxford University Press, 2014), 230–59.

Pernau, M., et al. *Civilizing Emotions: Concepts in Nineteenth-Century Asia and Europe*. New York: Oxford University Press, 2015.

Pernau, M., and I. Rajamani. 'Emotional Translations: Conceptual History beyond Language'. *History & Theory* 55(1) (2016) 46–65, doi: 10.1111/hith.10787.

Plamper, J. *The History of Emotions: An Introduction*. Oxford: Oxford University Press, 2015.

Pratt, M.L. *Imperial Eyes: Travel Writing and Transculturation*. London: Routledge, 1992.

Reddy, W.M. *The Navigation of Feeling: A Framework for the History of Emotions*. Cambridge: Cambridge University Press, 2001.

Renn, J. *Übersetzungsverhältnisse: Perspektiven einer pragmatistischen Gesellschaftstheorie*. Weilerswist: Velbrück Wissenschaft, 2006.

Ricoeur, P. 'Phenomenology and Hermeneutics'. *Noûs* 9(1) (1975), 85–102.
_____. *The Course of Recognition*. Cambridge, MA: Harvard University Press, 2005.
Rozbicki, M.J., and G.O. Ndege. 'Introduction', in M.J. Rozbicki and G.O. Ndege (eds), *Cross-Cultural History and the Domestication of Otherness* (New York: Palgrave Macmillan, 2012), 1–12.
Rushdie, S. *Imaginary Homelands: Essays and Criticism, 1981–1991*. London: Granta Books, 1992.
Saada, E. *Empire's Children: Race, Filiation, and Citizenship in the French Colonies*, trans. A. Goldhammer. Chicago: University of Chicago Press, 2012 [Fre. orig. *Les enfants de la colonie*. Paris: La Découverte, 2007].
Sahlins, M. *How 'Natives' Think: About Captain Cook, for Example*. Chicago: University of Chicago Press, 1995.
Said, E.W. *Orientalism*. New York: Pantheon Books, 1978.
Sandiford, K.A.P. 'The Professionalization of Modern Cricket'. *International Journal of the History of Sport* 2(3) (1985), 270–89, doi: 10.1080/02649378508713580.
Schwartz, S.B. 'Introduction', in S.B. Schwartz (ed.), *Implicit Understandings: Observing, Reporting, and Reflecting on the Encounters between Europeans and Other Peoples in the Early Modern Era* (Cambridge: Cambridge University Press, 1994), 1–19.
Seigworth, G.J., and M. Gregg. 'An Inventory of Shimmers', in M. Gregg and G.J. Seigworth (eds), *The Affect Theory Reader* (Durham, NC: Duke University Press, 2010), 1–25.
Sen, S. 'Enduring Colonialism in Cricket: From Ranjitsinhji to the Cronje Affair'. *Contemporary South Asia* 10(2) (2001), 237–49, doi: 10.1080/09584930120083837.
_____. *Migrant Races: Empire, Identity and K.S. Ranjitsinhji*. Manchester: Manchester University Press, 2004.
Shellam, T. 'Mediating Encounters through Bodies and Talk', in S. Konishi, M. Nugent and T. Shellam (eds), *Indigenous Intermediaries: New Perspectives on Exploration Archives* (Acton: Australian National University Press, 2015), 85–102.
Shoemaker, N. *Native American Whalemen and the World: Indigenous Encounters and the Contingency of Race*. Chapel Hill: University of North Carolina Press, 2015.
Sinha, M. *Colonial Masculinity: The 'Manly Englishman' and the 'Effeminate Bengali' in the Late Nineteenth Century*. Manchester: Manchester University Press, 1995.
Sluga, G. 'Identity, Gender, and the History of European Nations and Nationalisms'. *Nations and Nationalism* 4(1) (1998), 87–111, doi: 10.1111/j.1354-5078.1998.00087.x.
_____. *Internationalism in the Age of Nationalism*. Philadelphia: University of Pennsylvania Press, 2013.
Smith, V. *Intimate Strangers: Friendship, Exchange and Pacific Encounters*. Cambridge: Cambridge University Press, 2010.
Stewart, C. 'Creolization, Hybridity, Syncretism, Mixture'. *Portuguese Studies* 27(1) (2011), 48–55, doi: 10.5699/portstudies.27.1.0048.
Stoler, A.L. *Carnal Knowledge and Imperial Power: Race and the Intimate in Colonial Rule*. Berkeley: University of California Press, 2002.

Subrahmanyam, S. *Explorations in Connected History: From the Tagus to the Ganges*. New Delhi: Oxford University Press, 2005.

'Symonds Sparked by Indian Celebrations'. *ESPN Cricinfo*, 28 September 2007. Retrieved 12 September 2018 from http://www.espncricinfo.com/indvaus/content/story/312827.html.

'Symonds Tells his Side of the Story'. *ESPN Cricinfo*, 7 January 2008. Retrieved 12 September 2018 from http://www.espncricinfo.com/ausvind/content/story/329488.html.

Tamcke, M., and J. Gladson (eds). *Body, Emotion and Mind: 'Embodying' the Experiences in Indo-European Encounters*. Vienna: Lit-Verlag, 2013.

Taussig, M. *Mimesis and Alterity: A Particular History of the Senses*. New York: Routledge, 1993.

Taylor, C. 'The Politics of Recognition', in A. Gutmann (ed.), *Multiculturalism and 'The Politics of Recognition': An Essay by Charles Taylor* (Princeton, NJ: Princeton University Press, 1992), 25–73.

Thomas, N. *Islanders: The Pacific in the Age of Empire*. New Haven, CT: Yale University Press, 2010.

Vaughan, A.T. *Transatlantic Encounters: American Indians in Britain, 1500–1776*. Cambridge: Cambridge University Press, 2006.

Verheyen, N. 'Age(ing) with Feeling', in U. Frevert et al., *Emotional Lexicons: Continuity and Change in the Vocabulary of Feeling 1700–2000* (Oxford: Oxford University Press, 2014), 151–76.

Wise, A., and S. Velayutham. 'Introduction: Multiculturalism and Everyday Life', in A. Wise and S. Velayutham (eds), *Everyday Multiculturalism* (Houndsmills, U.K.: Palgrave Macmillan, 2009), 1–17.

Young, R.J.C. *Colonial Desire: Hybridity in Theory, Culture, and Race*. London: Routledge, 1995.

Chapter 1

Missionaries
False Reverence, Irreverence and the Rethinking of Christian Mission in China and India

Stephen Cummins and Joel Lee

In 1977, Daniel Everett, a Christian missionary, arrived in a remote region of Brazil in order to promote Christianity amongst the Pirahã, a tribe of Amazonians. As he recalls in his autobiographical account of Pirahã language and culture, his first impression was emotional. He wrote that the 'most striking thing . . . about seeing the Pirahãs for the first time was how happy everyone seemed'. For him this was evidenced by smiles that 'decorated' faces. He observed that '[n]ot one person looked sullen or withdrawn, as many do in cross-cultural encounters'.[1] Laughter and gentle touches meant he could not have imagined 'a warmer welcome'.[2] His pre-existing script of the difficult first encounter was contradicted. But the unexpected familiarity of happiness was soon matched by experiences of alienation. Everett writes that the missionary's 'body, mind, emotions, and especially his sense of self are all deeply strained'.[3] Some years into his mission, he recounted his testimony of Christian faith to an audience of Pirahãs, recounting how his stepmother had committed suicide, which led him to Jesus and away from drink and drugs:

> When I concluded, the Pirahãs burst into laughter. This was unexpected, to put it mildly. I was used to reactions like 'Praise God!' with my audience genuinely impressed by the great hardships I had been through and how God had pulled me out of them.
> 'Why are you laughing?' I asked.
> 'She killed herself? Ha ha ha. How stupid. Pirahãs don't kill themselves', they answered.[4]

Notes for this chapter begin on page 55.

Everett notes that this anecdote, which was meant to be emotionally appealing, had only 'highlight[ed] our differences'.[5] Daniel Everett's experiences amongst the Pirahã eventually led him to reject his faith.[6] Unexpected emotional reactions, whether welcome or unwelcome, shaped the narration of his mission. Despite Everett's loss of faith, his account remains marked by the missionary discourse of cross-cultural encounter that developed in the second half of the twentieth century.[7] Such modern missionary discourse has a notable preoccupation with the opportunities and challenges of emotions in the work of bridging cultures. The genre uses the vocabulary of popular psychology, anthropology and other social theories to define the 'cross-cultural'. By the end of the twentieth century, then, missions were self-consciously moments of 'cross-cultural' encounter in which preparation for difference was a vital part of training and in which bodily experiences and emotions were at the centre of the encounter. Emotions were bridges, but they were obstacles too. Yet this model did not emerge fully formed in the late twentieth century; the roots of such visions go much further back.

One of the paradigmatic figures in the emotional history of cross-cultural encounters must be the missionary. Traversing cultural distance, probing states of feeling on all sides of an encounter and documenting such reflections in laborious detail were not merely incidental pursuits for missionaries but vocational obligations. Missions are therefore fertile ground for both the history of cross-cultural encounters and the history of emotions. The unpredictable effects and inventive usages of imported religious belief have been central to some landmark studies of emotions.[8] More broadly, the effect of missionary encounters upon internal lives and social relations is a well-investigated field.[9] In recent years, scholars have opened new lines of enquiry by considering the particular intersection between missionary encounters and emotions.[10] Much of this writing concerns itself with the elusive category of conversion.[11] Missions have been argued to be channels for the circulation of emotional practices beyond the narrower category of didactic conversion.[12] Focusing on the perspective of the proselytized, some scholars have considered ways in which aspects of the Christian message appealed as a means to manage or transform emotional life, which in some contexts enabled the acquisition of social capital.[13] Missionary activity has also been linked to the emergence of certain forms of, or demands upon, 'interiority'.[14]

Christian missionaries of all varieties trafficked in messages about human sin – offences against God – that required forgiveness. In missionary discourse, it was the love of Christ that provided a way out of the wretchedness of sin. In addition to its metaphysical novelties, then, Christianity introduced particular emotional visions of the human condition. Different Christian denominations held different views over which emotional experiences should be cultivated and which emotional practices were to be taught. Any overly schematic divide between a highly emotionally expressive Catholicism and a restrained Protestantism is misleading. But there were significant distinctions. Amongst these there were, on the one hand, those who distrusted tears and cries as potentially false signs of piety and argued instead for the importance of reason and the intellect in conversion.[15] This intellectual apprehension of Christian doctrine was believed to anchor the drama of conversion and other moments of 'religious feeling' on solid ground. On the other hand, there were 'revivalist' missions characterized by the promotion of emotional expression in worship due to its status as evidence of grace moving through people.[16] Yet anxiety about the authenticity of emotion was present in all forms of missionary activity.

The diversity of ideas and practices concerned with emotion norms related to the broader heterogeneity of Christian missions. Missions differed in the social location of their personnel, the structure and ethos of their governing bodies, their relationship with local political structures in their 'fields' of operation and their orientation to particular populations within their host societies (whether elite, subaltern or otherwise distinct communities). The link between missions and empire – and the production of 'imperial emotions' – has been fruitfully studied.[17] Enmeshed in, and often benefitting from, imperial structures, many missionaries saw themselves as the vanguard of the European 'civilizing' mission with its emotional vocabulary of racialized paternalism.[18] Yet there were also missions that were dependent upon powerful non-European sovereigns and were allowed to operate only with the latter's consent. As Rupa Viswanath points out, a binary imperial sociology of missions – wherein there are only missionaries/colonizers and heathen/natives – distorts our understanding of what were often multipolar power relations.[19] The violent extirpation of 'traditional religion' in the early modern Americas – a paradigm of mission work sometimes assumed to have been the global norm – bore little relation to most missions in Asia; for example, the efforts of Protestant missionaries to negotiate between powerful local landlords and the colonial administration over the land or labour rights of Dalit Christians.[20]

One particularly helpful insight for connecting missions and emotions from the recent literature is that of the 'affective circuit'. As Claire McLisky persuasively argues, missionaries sought to incite religious emotions in their converts that would, both through face-to-face interaction in 'the field' and through discursive representation in missionary writing circulated 'at home', redound upon and indeed help constitute an expanding Christian 'affective community'.[21] These affective circuits were thus transnational networks through which emotion generated in missionary encounter reverberated beyond the immediate context. Affective circuits relied in part upon discursive techniques – evident in narrative genres like conversion or martyrdom stories – that related emotions produced in the missionary encounter to biblical and other Christian narratives. As Elizabeth Elbourne points out, these scripts privileged certain emotions such as love, pity and gratitude for representation in missionary writing while they concealed others such as frustration and anger that were arguably just as central to missionary experience.[22] Moreover, both in their adherence to and departure from the 'emotional script', missionaries tended to reproduce, in part, the affective vocabulary of the imperial projects in the context of which their missions operated rather than demonstrate a concern for the fine-grain of the local.

This chapter considers two historical moments in which the face-to-face encounter of missionaries and those they sought to convert compelled a rewriting of the emotional script of Christian mission. In these cases, the emotional habitus of the proselytized or the danger of the mistranslation of emotion across culture threatened to break a given affective circuit – to undermine, sabotage or bring an end to the mission. What resulted, however, was neither simply 'failure' or 'success' in missionary terms, nor merely an offstage release of frustration that left the onstage performance of Christian emotions intact. Rather, analysis of these two formative moments in the history of European missions in Asia – the papal missionary Matteo Ripa's mission to the court of the Kangxi Emperor in early eighteenth-century China and the Protestant 'mass movements' in colonial India in the late nineteenth century – illuminates how the emotions generated in the missionary encounter reshaped missionary practice.

Both cases occurred at important junctures in the global history of Christianity: Matteo Ripa's mission was entwined with the 'Chinese Rites' controversy that ultimately led to the expulsion of missionaries from Imperial China, a hardening of diplomatic relations between Rome and Beijing, the suspension of the Jesuit order and a rethinking of Catholic mission. A century and a half later, the 'mass movements' in which vast numbers of Dalits, or 'untouchables', converted to (predominantly) Protestant Christianity in Punjab, Travancore and the Madras Presidency at the height of colonialism produced the largest demographic shift to Christianity in the British Empire. Missionaries in China and India (unlike many of those who operated in the Americas or Oceania) largely acknowledged the societies in which they worked to be highly differentiated; while the category of 'heathen' operated in missionary accounts here no less than elsewhere, the pronounced class and caste distinctions within these societies forced missionaries to recognize more complex social fields. The institutional forms of social differentiation in which Ripa in China and the Protestant missionaries in India were necessarily embedded had important implications for their encounters with emotion.

Missions to China: Beijing or Babylon?

Evangelization, on its own terms, required the communication of concepts and appropriate feelings that were to accompany these concepts. For European missionaries, this project of boundary making and cultural policing was not only about emotions but was in itself a fraught emotional process: they faced fears of falling into heresy if they moved too far or, if they did not adapt enough, that their evangelizing would be ineffective. Yet perceived failure in navigating this problem did not simply lead to ineffective missionizing: it could also imperil their souls. The well-known scholarship that addresses the problems of the translation of Christian terms across cultures can be revitalized with attention to the way in which emotions were at stake in such issues.[23] For Christian missionaries, the difference between neutral cultural variation and heretical beliefs was not just an academic question but one that was felt and experienced as missionaries lived amongst the 'targets' of their missions.

This was at least a two-fold problem: on the one hand, it involved the question as to how far missionaries should endorse or partake in the practices of another society and, on the other, what parts of their own faith were malleable or disposable. These related issues formed a crucible for the creation of the cross-cultural category of the 'religious'.[24] The latter question about how far the Christian message could be altered (and the deeper question of what exactly composed Christianity) found its expression in debates over specific acts of translation and broader 'rites controversies'.[25] These debates have been productive topics for historical research.[26] But the history of emotions can aid understanding of these challenges of communication and translation. Abstract theological debate became lived experience when missionaries were present in ceremonies, the status of which could be, to them, ambiguous at best or idolatrous at worst. The emotional context of the face-to-face encounter changed the stakes of these problems.

This section considers the mission of Matteo Ripa, sent to Beijing as a missionary for the Roman Curia's missionary organization, the Sacra Congregatio de Propaganda Fide, as well as the broader context of Catholic missions to China.[27] Ripa's mission began during the initial stirrings of the Chinese Rites controversy. This was one of the most important debates over how to assess a non-European country's rituals and beliefs. The debate stretched from the late seventeenth century to the eighteenth century and questioned whether Confucianism and other Chinese ritual practices were religious or civil. If it was the former, they were heretical and inassimilable with Christian practice. If the latter was true, then they could be maintained and combined with Christian practice. This was a transnational controversy that involved the Jesuits, Dominicans, the Pope and the Kangxi Emperor (1654–1722, r. 1661–1722).[28] The Jesuits were the standard-bearers for the position that the rites should be considered civil, which led them into a bitter conflict with those who alleged that the rites had a religious content, most notably the Dominicans and, eventually, Propaganda Fide. What was at stake in the controversy was the exact nature of the respect shown to Confucius, the use of ancestral tablets and the translation of God (Deus) as *Shangti* or *Tian-zhu* (Lord of Heaven).[29] How did Ripa's perceptions of Chinese rites affect his embodied and emotional experience of partaking in Chinese ceremony?

In the late sixteenth century, the Jesuit Matteo Ricci had come to Beijing and cultivated friendships with the scholar elite.[30] After initial missteps, Ricci came to believe that in China integration within the scholarly system and the production of carefully researched books was the best path to evangelization. Ricci borrowed the vocabulary of Daoism and Buddhism to create his controversial translation of Christian terms in his texts *Tianzhu shiyi* (The true meaning of the Lord of Heaven). By the end of the seventeenth century, his name had become shorthand for a standpoint of accommodation to Chinese customs. At the start of the eighteenth century, the reciprocal expectations on both the European and the Chinese sides were that missionaries would follow 'the norms of Matteo Ricci'.[31] Ronnie Hsia's work emphasizes the self-doubt and melancholy that characterized his missionary experience, despite its achievements, as well as stressing the strong influence of Ming intellectual culture upon Ricci and the active critical engagement of Chinese elites with Ricci's works.[32]

The missionary Matteo Ripa was born in Eboli to a noble family. He began religious education under a member of the *Pii Operai* in Naples. Rather than join this order, he was recommended as a candidate for the Vatican's congregation for missionary work, the Propaganda Fide, which was recruiting priests to evangelize in China. In 1710, he embarked on a mission that would last until 1723. During his experiences, he kept a manuscript journal and oversaw the publication of a memoir during his lifetime.[33] When he returned from China, he brought with him four Chinese boys, sons of converts, with whom he founded a seminary in Naples for the training of Chinese-born missionaries.[34]

Ripa's encounter with Chinese culture and the court of the Kangxi Emperor was not a story of incomprehension but of complex negotiations among mandarins and European missionaries. Ripa arrived to a different dynasty than Ricci had known. The ruling Kangxi emperor of the Manchu dynasty had been raised with the presence of missionaries.[35] His rule was a period of tolerance for plural religious practices. Matteo Ripa's main employment while at the court of the Kangxi emperor was copper plate printmaking.[36] Ripa's career as an artist provided him unusual access to imperial palaces and gardens outside of Beijing. Like most missionaries in China in this period, Ripa's evangelization was a long-term project in which steps were taken cautiously and which did not rely on large-scale conversions. Instead, he made a handful of conversions and recruited the children of these neophytes. Missionaries at the Qing court were under the direct authority of the emperor and could be imprisoned and punished by him. They became fully involved in games of favour and political intrigues. Matteo Ripa repeated a scornful comment that the missionaries were like 'sold slaves'.[37] Missionaries had no unshakeable confidence in the security of their position, even after years of service, and they did not have the freedom to leave when they wished. Their whole existence in China rested on their ability or luck to navigate the politics of the nearby Qing court and those of faraway Rome.

Ripa's view was that the 'civility' of the Chinese was a major obstacle to conversion. He remembered many conversations with a certain mandarin who professed to be convinced by the messages of the Christian faith. Of this mandarin, Ripa wrote that with 'the excessive civility of a Chinese, he always affected to be convinced by my arguments; but the moment he joined his friends he turned my efforts into ridicule, laughing with them heartily'.[38] His journals describe many moments that suggest that he viewed trust with the Chinese as unstable, precisely because of their 'civility'. Chinese civility was interpreted as a barrier to understanding emotional responses to the Christian message. Ripa's encounter with Chinese culture was recorded in his numerous observations about the differences between Europeans and Chinese. Many of these focused on bodies, bodily practices and clothing. For Ripa and others, such customs of bodily care and difference were, in part, ways to think about economies of emotion on a societal scale. The binding of women's feet was linked by Ripa directly to male jealousy.[39] Ripa's journals are also replete with references to the 'obsequiousness' of the Chinese. He noted the prostrations and kneeling done between those of different hierarchies: sons to fathers, younger brothers to older brothers and wives to husbands. These issues of bowing, kneeling and standing in certain ways were not just of ethnographic interest but were central to his life in China. How Matteo Ripa was to hold his body was part of the involvement in rituals at the Qing court; missionaries had to hold their hands together, masked by robes, with their feet joined.

Ripa wrote of the embarrassment he felt during a visit to a Chinese mandarin when the mandarin's son returned. Ripa and the mandarin were seated but his son kneeled upon the floor for almost half an hour. When Ripa realized the man was the mandarin's son, he protested, saying that he should not be seated while his son knelt on the floor. A 'long contest' ensued: 'The father protested of not being able to stay seated while I was on my feet, I of not being able to sit when his son was on his knees, and the son of not being able to do anything but kneel in front of his father'. Ripa reported that he 'won' the contest, with the son being allowed to sit discreetly on a chest in the corner of the room.[40] Such tense moments of attempting to navigate appropriate reverence created embarrassment. It indicates that even with extensive knowledge of Chinese practices, difficulties remained that made moments of encounter into charged 'contests'. Embarrassment about the kneeling young man was accompanied by confusion over how best to show due reverence.[41] In this case, Ripa saw victory in asserting his objections.

Apart from these more everyday issues of etiquette, the risks, doubts and difficulties of assimilation were most pressing when concerned with ritual. Throughout his journal, Ripa notes his fears of accidentally falling into superstition and idolatry by offering inadvertent reverence during personal involvement in ritual. He relates that one of the first tasks he was asked to carry out was to copy a painting of Confucius, which he was warned against because Confucius was supposed to be a devil. Soon after arriving, he noted the practice of sacrificing animals 'to their false gods' and burning pieces of paper 'in the belief that they transform into true money in the next life'.[42] He claimed to never have held the view that these aspects of Chinese practice were civil rituals. Other missionaries had more forgiving attitudes. The Jesuits in particular sustained Ricci's views. The dilemma that faced Ripa was the problem of how to negotiate participation in the imperial court system without committing idolatry.

In 1704, Pope Clement XI condemned various Chinese rites with his bull *Ex illa die*, but the final confrontation stretched over many more years. Two years later, when the papal legation of de Tournon had displeased the Emperor with its critique of Chinese rites, the Kangxi Emperor ordered that, in order to stay in China, missionaries would have to agree to follow the 'customs of Matteo Ricci'. The next year, 1707, when de Tournon refused to approve the use of ancestral tablets, he was arrested and deported to Macau. In 1711, as the Chinese Rites controversy escalated and began to produce voluminous writings, Ripa found himself isolated from both other missionaries and imperial representatives, as he refused to take a clear stance; he neither censured Chinese rites publicly nor did he approve the Jesuit position. He later claimed that this had been the most difficult period of his life. He recorded that 'never did I find myself in greater anguish than in this case'. He was subject to 'scorn, insults and derision'.[43] What marked his memory of this event most was the laughter of the Jesuits. They mocked him for his unclear stance: he would neither affirm the Papal condemnation nor support Ricci's methods.

The controversy continued, and in 1717, in response to another proclamation, the Kangxi Emperor banned Christian preaching.[44] The controversy within the Catholic Church led to the removal of the Imperial toleration that had allowed the debate to even occur. This ban was not enforced fully until after the death of Kangxi. Awaiting a further papal legation, Kangxi sent a letter in 1720 to all missionaries, criticizing negative assessments of Chinese practices and arguing that they should present a united pro-Ricci front to the soon to arrive papal legate Mezzabarba.[45] In this letter, he defended the emotionality of Chinese funeral practice and filial piety, arguing 'that human beings are the soul of the myriad things, it is natural that within, they are sincerely moved *whilst externally they express their feelings*. Just as you religious people, if your parents should leave, will also *spontaneously* ... weep. If you did not do so, then you would not even be the equal of the animals'.[46] At stake were attempts to communicate Chinese emotional economies in the face of what Kangxi saw as ignorance due to a lack of learned study of Chinese practices.

Emotions surrounding death were one of the key parts of the encounter between European missionaries and the Chinese. The period of the Kangxi emperor saw Manchu elites confronting Han practices such as mourning.[47] Towards the end of the Ming period, emotions came to prominence in a range of cultural arenas.[48] Kangxi himself developed a 'consistent policy' on mourning.[49] A growing thought was that emotion, as Norman Kutcher has observed, 'was to be the starting point for rituals, rather than the result of their proper observance'.[50] Nicolas Standaert notes that the Kangxi Emperor believed that 'the correct intention concerns the right emotion, i.e., whether the ritual is a sincere expression of filial piety', whereas for missionaries 'the correct intention of a ritual is linked to the theologically correct meaning, i.e., whether the meaning leads to a superstitious act or not'.[51] Rituals were to be expressions of pre-existing emotions. For the missionaries, three aspects of funerals were most problematic: the inscription of ancestral tablets, the offering of food or wine and the burning of paper money. These were not simply intellectual issues. There was a visceral experience for those who believed they were idolatry. When did grief become reverence? When did signs of respect transgress into idolatry?

In 1722, after the Kangxi Emperor died, Matteo Ripa was confronted with these issues. In the extensive funeral rituals that ensued, the tightrope act of participating without revering became even more difficult. Apart from these spiritual costs, the mortal costs were higher still: in a time of political change, the missionaries could easily find themselves dangerously out of favour. Ripa claimed his participation in funeral rites filled him with concern. He wrote that upon entering the palace he found a 'vast number' of mandarins kneeling, dressed in mourning clothes and weeping together. He noted that 'from time to time, upon a signal from the master of the ceremonies, they all at once raised such a howl of lamentation as filled the sky; after which they performed their prostrations'. Next they were 'ordered to kneel also, but in a place apart from the mandarins', and then they adopted the practice of the mandarins: 'we wept with them, and made the same prostrations, not perceiving anything unlawful or unchristian in such marks of grief'. This was not a brief ritual participation: '[d]uring several days we repaired to the same spot, and repeated the same ceremonies'.[52]

The crisis for Ripa, as he told it, came after these highly emotional funeral rites were finished, and he sought clarification about their full nature. He asked a mandarin who had had a role in organizing the funeral 'in what manner it had been performed'. The mandarin's reply – which seems to indicate an awareness of the apprehension behind Ripa's question – was that while no paper money had been burnt while the body was in the palace, when it was moved out of the palace a large amount was burnt and 'the air around was for a time clouded with smoke'. Moreover, a libation of wine had been performed by the Emperor and 'at the same moment the master of the ceremonies gave a signal, at which the mandarins, and we missionaries with them, performed their prostrations'. Ripa wrote that upon 'hearing that we had, even unconsciously, taken part in this work of superstition, I was grieved and alarmed to a degree which it would be impossible for me to express; and in order to preclude the recurrence of such a misfortune, I resolved to quit that Babylon at any risk, and as soon as possible'.[53] Beijing had become Babylon for Ripa. He stayed some months more, but the final confrontation occurred when he was requested to make bells he knew would be used in what he considered idolatry. He writes that '[h]aving ... found myself in the critical alternative of either consenting to further the interests of idolatry or causing much prejudice to the mission, I determined upon returning to Naples' because of 'how little I could effect in China for the propagation of Christianity, and how repeatedly I was exposed to the danger either of participating in idolatrous practices or of perishing'.[54]

Ripa felt he had betrayed himself and placed his body in the service of rituals he believed to be unholy. There was, in this case, no stark absence of cultural knowledge. But the combination of certain interpretations of Chinese ritual practice with the demands of involvement in life at the Chinese court created situations in which Ripa believed his bodily actions betrayed his religious values and in which strong emotions were evoked. The rites controversy itself focused strongly on the nature of piety and reverence; to whom and how emotions were to be displayed. A 'culturalist' approach pioneered by Matteo Ricci and institutionalized under his name foundered upon the intransigence of Catholic authorities. The crucial issues of translation were, at heart, about which emotions were being shown to whom: true reverence was only to be shown to God. Later Protestant encounters with some of the same practices, especially the kowtow, were inflected by a growing racist disdain towards the Chinese. The kowtow and other markers of Chinese ritual would shift from being perilous to the soul to being humiliating.[55] No longer were they on a civilizational par to Europe. Instead, their obeisance was evidence of their feminized culture and their opposition to rational religion.[56]

Missions in India: Untouchability and Irreverence

The first nine decades of intensive Protestant missionary activity in colonial India – from the early 1790s to roughly 1880 – produced far more literature than it did converts.[57] Missionary writing, here as elsewhere, tended to replicate narrative tropes that sought to evoke particular sequential constellations of feeling in their readers: Elbourne's 'emotional scripts'.[58] The conversion narrative of Maulvi Imaduddin Lahiz, a Muslim scholar of a prominent genteel family whose baptism in Punjab in 1866 was considered a sensational victory for a mission desperate to demonstrate results, exemplifies this nicely. Translated and annotated by his baptizer, the British missionary Robert Clark, this 'autobiography' – in which Imaduddin's authorial voice cannot be distinguished from Clark's – describes Imaduddin's 'bigotry' and 'agitation' as a Muslim, his feeling 'alone, powerless, helpless, and needy' in his quest for a deeper truth and ultimately his 'comfort and joy' and 'great peace' upon his 'entrance into the grace of our Lord Jesus Christ'.[59] Moved by identification with the emotional itinerary of the native convert and the paternalist pride of his mentor, the reader is invited to admire 'the glowing brain and ardent heart of the Oriental Christian',[60] to feel membership in a transnational Christian community benignly inflected by racial difference and to contribute resources to the Church Missionary Society. Touching key themes of the emotional script of mission, this conversion story, like many others, functions 'to set up a series of affective circuits that would strengthen the faith of all involved'.[61]

The subsequent period in mission history – the 'mass movements' in which hundreds of thousands of 'untouchables' adopted Christianity in Punjab, Travancore and the Madras Presidency in the 1880s and 1890s – tested the limits of what the existing emotional script could accommodate, compelling missionaries to revise their ideas and narratives of appropriate religious emotion and indeed to rethink the very nature of their project. Until the late 1870s, the attention of Protestant missionaries in India had been, in the words of an American Presbyterian missionary,

> largely directed to people of good social position – the more intelligent and influential classes of the Muhammadan, Hindu, and Sikh population. These had been prominently before our minds in our study of the language, the preparation of our sermons, our public discussions, our educational efforts, and in our book and tract distribution. For the convincing and converting of such as these we had put forth our best efforts, and from their ranks chiefly we expected to receive our accessions.[62]

The conversion of Imaduddin and other educated individuals of elite Muslim and 'upper caste' Hindu families was the fruit of just such endeavours. Criticized by their sponsoring institutions for the small numbers of converts they produced, missionaries across a wide spectrum of denominations defended this approach, arguing that energy and time invested in proselytizing the elite would eventually yield an abundant 'harvest', since the general populace would follow their social superiors.

Thus, in the late nineteenth century when Dalits – in this period called 'untouchables', 'outcastes', 'aboriginals' and 'slave castes' among other, regional, names – began in increasing numbers to approach mission stations requesting baptism, they were often met with a tepid response. By all accounts, it was Dalits who initiated contact with the missionaries, sometimes taking mission stations 'by storm' rather than the other way around.[63] Missionaries in many places hesitated to baptize the newcomers.[64] They feared – with justification – that the influx of Dalits into their churches and Dalit students into mission schools would damage the mission's reputation among high status Hindus and Muslims, potentially killing prospects for this long-sought 'harvest'.[65] Missionaries were also apprehensive of a disruption of social relations within their fledgling native Christian communities. The degree of poverty and violent conditions of labour to which Dalits were subject – including outright slavery (*atimai*) in Madras Presidency and Travancore[66] – raised a host of pragmatic and political questions about the appropriate modes of missionary involvement in native society, questions that contributed to the missionaries' trepidation as the numbers of Dalit converts swelled.

Missionaries were also given pause by what they perceived to be a distinctively Dalit emotional habitus. Matilda Churchill, a Canadian Baptist who worked in the Northern Circars (northern Madras Presidency) from 1876 to her death in 1916, sketches the contours of this cluster of dispositions in one of her early letters to her sponsoring church, in which she describes evangelizing work among Dalit women.

> [T]hese are mainly Pariah settlements, the lowest class of natives about here. . . . They are often quarrelling among themselves, seeming not to listen, once in a while asking foolish questions to try to trouble us, and even scoffing, and our hearts are very sore and sad for them. When we tell of the love of God they will say 'Yes, He loves *you* and gives you everything you want, but He does not love us or He would not let us starve as we often do. We keeping crying "Davoordoo", [a name of god] but He does not give us *rice*, and we have to work so hard we have no time to worship as you do, we are so ignorant we cannot understand Him'.[67]

Churchill paints a collective portrait of Dalit women as insolent, irreverent, fractious and quick to argue with the missionary on materialist grounds. Admitting her own dismay at having to work with these women ('[t]hey are . . . not pleasant to labour with, nor are their children'),[68] Churchill tells her readers that the first boarder at her school, a Dalit girl, was caught stealing from the mission.

This portrayal is not exceptional but echoes themes in other missionary accounts from north and south India. A thinly fictionalized account of the adoption of 'an outcaste girl of Travancore' by a British mission station projects onto the eight-year-old protagonist, Aroogi, quarrelsomeness, a propensity for thieving and deceit, materialist preoccupations (she 'greedily devoured the food but seemed to have no desire to listen to a story') and a 'self-assurance' the missionaries find incongruous to her social standing.[69] As James Taneti demonstrates in his history of Bible women in colonial India, the Dalit women who took up this missionary occupation often earned reputations for a similar constellation of qualities and emotional proclivities. Exemplary is the case of one Annamma, 'the first Bible woman on the Akidu field', who Baptist missionaries depicted 'as an impetuous, worldly, and impenitent woman' who 'could meet any argument'. Her quality of being 'a better leader than a follower' at times ran afoul of her Canadian employers, notably when she negotiated for higher wages.[70]

In Punjab, it was above all the irreverence of Dalit women that stamped itself on the missionary archive. Some missionaries felt that Dalit women's untimely laughter threatened to disrupt the ritual life of the community and advocated against their participation in communion. As Hervey Griswold, an American Presbyterian missionary, put it: 'Lack of solemnity on the part of women at the communion has . . . been mentioned as a difficulty in the way of their being admitted [to the Lord's Supper]'. While Griswold argued in favour of the inclusion of Dalit women in communion, he admitted having witnessed their irreverent expressions of mirth 'at the time of baptism'.[71]

Not all of the elements of the distinctive emotional habitus sketched here were specifically gendered. Though to a lesser extent than Dalit women, Dalit men, too, appear in missionary accounts as disputatious, difficult for missionaries to control and inclined to impious and materialist 'scoffing' at religion in general. According to John Youngson, a Scottish Presbyterian missionary in Punjab at the turn of the twentieth century, the cynicism and impertinence of Dalit men (in this case Chuhras) was proverbial in his mission field. This was so much the case that a Muslim 'priest' advised him: 'Sir, it is quite useless to dream of making anything of these low caste people', and related an anecdote in which both Moses and God commiserate over the irremediable insolence of the Chuhras.[72]

In their writings, missionaries thus registered considerable disquiet regarding the emotional habitus they perceived in the Dalits, who in their numbers and persistence seemed poised to transform the Christian 'conquest' of India. From the internal perspective of missions, this should not have posed an enduring problem. The emotional scripts of missionary writing were well equipped to accommodate all manner of unfavourable conditions: problems like insolent or irreverent dispositions, discursively reframed as heathenish vice, provided fertile ground for an edifying tale of transformation and the acquisition of Christian virtue. Retaining its negative valence, the emotional habitus of the heathen would serve the narrative as a sign of the initially benighted state of the soul and then give way to a new constellation of feeling – in this case the reverent, gentle and obedient humility that the missionaries had been urging on Dalits all along – that would serve as an index of their salvation in Christ. The literature on the emotional history of missions, which emphasizes the conformity of missionary writing to such emotional scripts, would lead us to expect this kind of resolution to the predicament presented by the Dalit mass movements.[73] And indeed, some missionary sources accomplished this operation to varying degrees: 'impenitent' Annamma's biographer, for example, portrays the independent Bible woman as tearfully repentant when illness struck her in old age.[74]

To a considerable extent, though, the missionary record evidences the persistence of the 'problem' of the Dalit emotional habitus, a persistence that ruptured the emotional script and compelled missionaries to rethink their strategies. Consider again the reputation of Dalit women for (impiously) disputing with missionaries and particularly countering spiritual talk with material concerns. This did not, generally speaking, cease with a sustained programme of Christian instruction; women abandoned neither the argumentative style nor their prioritization of 'worldly' matters. In Madras Presidency, for example, a Dalit woman in tears told the Wesleyan Methodist missionary William Goudie: 'I cannot enter the Christian church. I cannot keep your law. You forbid lying and we cannot live without lying. We are in debt and we have constantly to promise [our creditors] to pay "to-morrow" when we know we cannot do it'.[75] What the woman described was a practice peculiar to the social conditions of caste servitude; for indebted Dalits to fail to perform the expected promise of repayment to their landlords meant potential eviction or other forms of violent reprisal. This woman's confrontation with Goudie – alongside similar encounters he recorded in which Dalit women stressed their hunger and lack of food[76] – led Goudie ultimately to reinterpret his role as a missionary by taking up legal advocacy in favour of basic land rights for Dalit ex-slaves and pressing the church to attend to these 'material' concerns as well. Rather than writing the Dalit woman into a typified script of heathenish deceitfulness yielding to Christian honesty, Goudie was pushed to revise the assumptions underlying such premediated narratives.

Sometimes it was through the opposite kind of recalcitrance – inhabiting the emotional script in too virtuosic a manner, beyond what missionaries encouraged – that Dalits compelled missionaries to rethink the implications of their labours in caste society. A runaway Dalit slave in Travancore, after conversion to Christianity, insisted on returning to his former master and confessing his sinful 'deceitfulness' in running away. The missionary who had baptized him tried to dissuade him, but the former slave went anyway; upon his return his former master had him tortured for several days and killed.[77] If conventions of missionary writing would have had the heathen ex-slave's adoption of an emotional habitus of repentant Christian meekness culminate in tears of joy meant to redound on the metropolitan reader, what actually transpired cast the anticipated narrative, and the missionary's role in it, in a rather different light: the missionary appeared as an accessory to slavery and murder. Encounters like these 'forc[ed] the missionary churches to engage with the questions of caste' in Travancore, notably by an institutional turn to the abolitionist cause.[78]

Another way in which Dalit emotions redirected the history of Christian missions involved Dalit evangelists. As we have seen, missionaries often initially perceived the emotional comportment of Dalit Bible women as conflicting with Christian models. Over time, though, the elements of this worrisome disposition, rather than disappearing, came to be revalued by missionaries as assets to the cause of promoting the gospel. As the mass movements developed, what first struck missionaries as insolence and quarrelsomeness began to register in missionary writing as assertiveness and a useful aptitude for righteous disputation. Dalit women came to be seen as desirable candidates for the post of Bible woman: more mobile than non-Dalit women (women of 'the Pariah class do not live in these Zenanas, they go out freely as we do'),[79] they also proved more 'brave and independent',[80] unafraid to argue religion with members of their local communities. The same goes for the impious scepticism that Youngson and others noted of Dalit men. When these men became Christian and the target of their disputatious scoffing was shifted from the Christian message to the beliefs of Hindu and Muslim 'heathen', this facet of their perceived emotional style began to attract missionary praise.[81]

There was one last way in which the Dalit emotional habitus, in its persistence, provoked missionaries to revise the emotional scripts so important to the transnational Christian community of affect. Dalit women's mirthful irreverence, while it initially distressed missionaries, eventually led some to entertain a culturalist framework for interpreting this aspect of emotional style. Griswold, in his argument for including Dalit women in communion despite their reputation for laughter, writes that:

> I have been present at a fair number of village communions when the sacred rite was administered for the first time, and have never yet noticed anything indecorous. . . . Nevertheless it is quite possible that now and then a woman may forget herself and smile. Think of the situation. Here is a woman who never in her life has eaten with her husband. But she is made to partake of the Lord's Supper in company with her husband. If she has a strong sense of humour, the whole situation may strike her as excruciatingly funny. I have seen this at the time of baptism.[82]

Here the question of heathenism, salvation and the state of the soul drop out of view; what remains is effectively a secular theory of cultural difference used to explain – indeed to excuse, to render innocuous – what emotional scripts since the time of Ripa could only interpret as a problem. Separated from a semiotic ideology that assigns every emotion religious significance, Dalit women's laughter ceases to alarm. But the operation of uprooting religious meaning from laughter, of recoding an act of 'irreverence' as something 'funny', transforms the ideology, and the scripts that it underwrites, in the process.

In ways like these, Dalit emotions incited missionaries to seriously consider the structural conditions of the society in which they laboured – Dalit subordination, gendered eating practices, caste slavery, 'untouchability' – and the ways in which such conditions could produce particular constellations of emotional dispositions. Such ruminations resulted neither in missionary 'failure' nor in the 'successful' fulfilment of preordained emotional scripts but in the structural transformation of missions. As a missionary in Punjab put it, as a result of the encounter with Dalits and their emotional dispositions:

> We have ... corrected some *fundamental* mistakes, and got down to the level on which [the Lord] himself labored. Instead of beginning at the top, with our large cities, principal stations and better classes of people, as we at first did, we have got down to the *Chuh'räs* and are beginning to build upwards.[83]

The passage alludes to institutional changes – redirecting of funds from urban to rural mission stations, allocation of resources to Dalit needs and advocacy with the colonial government to obtain land for settling Dalits as cultivators[84] – which mirrored transformations in Travancore and Madras such as the missionary turn to abolitionism and what Viswanath calls the 'Pariah-missionary alliance' for land reform.[85] The disputatious Dalit irreverence that dismayed many nineteenth-century missionaries provoked, through a series of encounters inassimilable to available emotional scripts, an overhaul of the missionary enterprise in India.

* * *

In 1868, Charles Henry Butcher, chaplain at the British Consulate in Shanghai, delivered an address titled 'The Trials and Consolations of Missionary Labour'. The address was published in several missionary journals. In it, Butcher discusses the difference between European missionaries and potential Chinese converts, stating: 'We are here to tell the truth, and to face things as they are; and therefore we must not, we *dare* not, conceal the fact that at first there is something like antipathy between the pioneer of the new faith and the callous, tradition girdled votary of the old one'. Butcher then advocates turning this antipathy anchored in difference into a stimulus for apparent critical self-reflection:

> When disappointments beset us, then let us examine our own hearts, and let us see if those disappointments are not caused by our having shown towards the natives some little lingering trace of this spirit of 'caste', the hardest thing in the world, as St Paul found, to shake ourselves quite free from the most fatal barrier to 'heart to heart' intercourse with those we come to seek and to save.[86]

To overcome this, Butcher recommends a conscious magnanimity that overcomes this apparently understandable condescension.

Butcher's assessment of missionary prejudice demonstrates the interconnection of the two major case studies of this chapter. Bad feelings between the missionary and his attempted converts should be noted and faced. This was not, of course, a meeting on equal ground. The call to be reflexive and to analyse one's own heart was part of the missionary's attempt to communicate across cultures. Yet Butcher's worldview was secure: the difference of which he speaks is not the space for the mortal peril that Matteo Ripa felt was at stake in the face-to-face encounter. Instead, as with Griswold, the emotions in the encounter with difference were to be dealt with in a less salvific and more sociological frame. The position of the missionary was less assailable by accidental involvement in idolatry. The varying assessments of non-Christian customs as religious, non-religious and as mere superstition or actually diabolic had deep impacts on the face-to-face nature of missionary encounter and upon the emotions that missionaries themselves felt and how they communicated their message. The fate of Catholic missionary projects to the Kangxi Emperor marked a blow to what might be considered a 'culturalist' approach to emotion in religion in the eighteenth century, an approach that had previously been influential in the Catholic missions of the early modern period. The mass movements in colonial India signalled one revival of a culturalist approach as certain emotions were once again released from bearing the burden of religious significance. In both cases, bodily gestures, comportment and expression played crucial roles in mediating emotion in the mission encounter.

Stephen Cummins is a researcher at the Center for the History of Emotions at the Max Planck Institute for Human Development in Berlin. He is a historian of early modern Europe, with a primary focus on early modern southern Italy. His major interests are the social, religious and legal histories of interpersonal relations and the changing role of emotions in rituals and practices of relationship. He is the co-editor, with Laura Kounine, of *Cultures of Conflict Resolution in Early Modern Europe* (Ashgate, 2016).

Joel Lee is Assistant Professor of Anthropology at Williams College in Massachusetts, in the United States. He has published articles on Dalit Muslim oral traditions, the sensory and environmental implications of caste and the politics of untouchability and religious majoritarianism in urban north India. He is co-author, with Jayshree Mangubhai and Aloysius Irudayam, of *Dalit Women Speak Out: Caste, Class and Gender Violence in India* (Zubaan, 2011).

Notes

1. Everett, *Don't Sleep*, 6.
2. Everett, *Don't Sleep*, 6.
3. Everett, *Don't Sleep*, 17.
4. Everett, *Don't Sleep*, 265.
5. Everett, *Don't Sleep*, 265.
6. Everett, *Don't Sleep*, 271.
7. See, for example, Harley, *Preparing to Serve: Training for Cross-Cultural Mission*; Reed, *Preparing Missionaries for Intercultural Communication: A Bi-Cultural Approach*.
8. Rosaldo, *Knowledge and Passion: Ilongot Notions of Self and Social Life*.
9. Comaroff and Comaroff, *Of Revelation and Revolution*. Much of this work has been focused on Africa. See also Nelson, *Christian Missionizing and Social Transformation: A History of Conflict and Change in Eastern Zaire*. See also Whiteman, *Melanesians and Missionaries: An Ethnohistorical Study of Social and Religious Change in the Southwest Pacific*.
10. Haggis and Allen, 'Imperial Emotions: Affective Communities of Mission in British Protestant Women's Missionary Publications, c1880–1920', 691–716; McLisky, 'Emotional Economies of Protestant Missions to Aboriginal People in Nineteenth-Century Australia', 82–98; McLisky, Midena and Vallgårda, *Emotions and Christian Missions: Historical Perspectives*.
11. Alberts, *Conflict and Conversion: Catholicism in Southeast Asia, 1500–1700*, 8–10.
12. Scheer, 'German "Shouting Methodists": Religious Emotion as a Transatlantic Cultural Practice', 45–72.
13. Mohan, *Modernity of Slavery: Struggles against Caste Inequality in Colonial Kerala*.
14. Keane, *Christian Moderns: Freedom and Fetish in the Mission Encounter*.
15. Warkentin, 'Begging as Resistance: Wealth and Christian Missionaries in Postcolonial Zaire', 146–49.
16. Maughan, *Mighty England Do Good: Culture, Faith, Empire, and World in the Foreign Missions of the Church of England*, 139–41 and details on the 'Great Awakening' in Lutz, *Opening China: Karl F.A. Gützlaff and Sino-Western Relations*, 15–17.
17. Etherington, *Missions and Empire*; Cox, *The British Missionary Enterprise since 1700*; Haggis and Allen, 'Imperial Emotions', 691–716.
18. Grimshaw, 'Faith, Missionary Life, and the Family', 271–72.
19. Viswanath, *The Pariah Problem: Caste, Religion, and the Social in Modern India*.
20. See Cervantes, *The Devil in the New World: The Impact of Diabolism in New Spain*; Županov, *Disputed Mission: Jesuit Experiments and Brahmanical Knowledge in Seventeenth-Century India*.
21. McLisky, 'Affective Circuits: Emotional Transfer and Christian Mission in Early Colonial Greenland and Australia', 151–76.
22. Elbourne, 'A Complicated Pity: Emotion, Missions and the Conversion Narrative', 123–50.
23. For translation, see L. Sanneh, *Translating the Message: The Missionary Impact on Culture*; Hsia, 'Translating Christianity: Counter-Reformation Europe and the Catholic Mission in China, 1580–1780', 87–108.
24. Keane, *Christian Moderns*.
25. Aranha, 'The Social and Physical Spaces of the Malabar Rites Controversy', 214–32.
26. See Županov, 'Prologue: Perils of Translation: Missionary Writing in/on South Asia (16th–18th c.)', 1–20.
27. On Ripa, see Fatica and D'Arelli, *La missione cattolica in Cina tra i secoli XVIII–XIX: Matteo Ripa e il Collegio dei cinesi*.

28. For these multiple actors, see Mungello, 'An Introduction to the Chinese Rites Controversy', 3–12; Spence, 'Claims and Counter-Claims: The Kangxi-Emperor and the Europeans (1661–1722)', 15–28.
29. Kim, *Strange Names of God: The Missionary Translation of the Divine Name and the Chinese Responses to Matteo Ricci's 'Shangti' in Late Ming China, 1583–1644.*
30. Hsia, *A Jesuit in the Forbidden City: Matteo Ricci 1553–1610.*
31. The Kangxi Emperor quoted in Ryden, 'Keep to the Method of Matteo Ricci: The Kangxi Emperor and Catholic Missionaries in China', 185–99.
32. Hsia, *Forbidden City*, 179.
33. See Ripa, *Storia della fondazione della congregazione e del collegio de' cinesi* and the partial English translation: Ripa, *Memoirs of Father Ripa: During Thirteen Years' Residence at the Court of Peking in the Service of the Emperor of China*. His journal has been published as Ripa, *Giornale (1705–1724).*
34. This *Collegio* would later become Naples' *Regio Istituto Orientale*, of which the institutional successor is today the University of Naples 'L'Orientale'.
35. Spence, *Emperor of China: Self-Portrait of K'ang-His.*
36. Lust, *Chinese Popular Prints*, 60–61.
37. Ripa, *Giornale*.
38. Ripa, *Memoirs*, 95.
39. Ripa, *Giornale*.
40. Ripa, *Giornale*.
41. For comments on prostrations and kneeling in late Imperial China, see Hevia, 'Sovereignty and Subject: Constituting Relations of Power in Qing Guest Ritual', 181–200.
42. Ripa, *Giornale*.
43. Ripa, *Giornale*.
44. Li, *China in Transition: 1517–1911*, 22.
45. See DiFiore, *La legazione mezzabarba in Cina (1720–21).*
46. Quoted in Ryden, 'Keep to the Method', 196–97 (emphasis in original).
47. Kutcher, *Mourning*.
48. Kutcher, *Mourning*, 47.
49. Kutcher, *Mourning*, 73.
50. Kutcher, *Mourning*, 50.
51. Standaert, *The Interweaving of Rituals: Funerals in the Cultural Exchange between China and Europe*, 181–82.
52. Ripa, *Memoirs*, 134.
53. Ripa, *Memoirs*, 134.
54. Ripa, *Memoirs*, 143, 144.
55. For this shift, see Chapter 5, Frevert, 'Diplomats' in this volume.
56. For this, see Reinders, *Borrowed Gods and Foreign Bodies: Christian Missionaries Imagine Chinese Religion*, 126–28.
57. The authors thank James Taneti, Rupa Viswanath and Sanal Mohan for directing us to several of the primary sources cited in this section.
58. Elbourne, 'Complicated Pity', 123–50.
59. Imad-Ud-Din, *A Mohammedan Brought to Christ: Being the Autobiography of the Rev. Imad-Ud-Din, D.D., of the Church Missionary Society's Mission at Amritsar, North India, and Honorary Chaplain to the Lord Bishop of Lahore*, 16, 19.
60. Clark, *Robert Clark of the Panjab: Pioneer and Missionary Statesman*, 297.
61. McLisky, 'Affective Circuits', 158.
62. Gordon, *Our India Mission: A Thirty Year's History of the India Mission of the United Presbyterian Church of North America, Together with Personal Reminiscences*, 428. On early missionary endeavour in Travancore, see Mohan, *Modernity of Slavery*, 51.

63. Gordon, *Our India Mission*; Taneti, *Caste, Gender, and Christianity in Colonial India: Telugu Women in Mission*; Viswanath, *Pariah Problem*; Webster, *The Dalit Christians: A History*.
64. Gordon, *Our India Mission*, 422–23; Griswold, *The Admission of Village Christians to the Lord's Supper*.
65. Gordon, *Our India Mission*, 174–76; Mohan, *Modernity of Slavery*, 62.
66. Mohan, *Modernity of Slavery*; Viswanath, *Pariah Problem*.
67. Churchill, *Letters from My Home in India: Being the Correspondence of Mrs. George Churchill (1871–1916)*, 73–74 (emphasis in original).
68. Churchill, *Letters*, 75.
69. W.B., *In a Tapioca Garden: The Story of an Outcaste Girl of Travancore*.
70. Craig et al., *Telugu Trophies: The Jubilee Story of Some of the Principal Telugu Converts in the Canadian Baptist Foreign Mission in India from 1874 to 1924*, 139; Taneti, *Caste, Gender, and Christianity*, 64–65.
71. Griswold, *Admission of Village Christians*.
72. Youngson, *Forty Years of the Panjab Mission of the Church of Scotland, 1855–1895*, 226–28, quotation 226.
73. Eyre, 'Converting Emotions: Domesticity and Self-Sacrifice in Female Missionary Writing', 179–201.
74. Craig et al., *Telugu Trophies*, 139.
75. Viswanath, *Pariah Problem*, 79.
76. Viswanath, *Pariah Problem*, 78.
77. Mohan, *Modernity of Slavery*, 99–100.
78. Mohan, *Modernity of Slavery*, 28 and passim.
79. Churchill, *Letters*, 97.
80. Craig et al., *Telugu Trophies*, 138.
81. Mohan, *Modernity of Slavery*, 89–90; Youngson, *Forty Years*, 228–31, 57–58.
82. Griswold, *Admission of Village Christians*, 14.
83. Gordon, *Our India Mission*, 432 (emphasis in original).
84. Gordon, *Our India Mission*, 428–32.
85. Mohan, *Modernity of Slavery*; Viswanath, *Pariah Problem*.
86. Butcher, 'The Trials and Consolations of Missionary Labour', 43, 44.

Bibliography

Alberts, T. *Conflict and Conversion: Catholicism in Southeast Asia, 1500–1700*. Oxford: Oxford University Press, 2013.

Aranha, P. 'The Social and Physical Spaces of the Malabar Rites Controversy', in G. Marcocci et al. (eds), *Space and Conversion in Global Perspective* (Leiden: Brill, 2014), 214–32.

Butcher, C.H. 'The Trials and Consolations of Missionary Labour'. *Chinese Recorder and Missionary Journal* 1(2) (June 1868), 43–46.

Cervantes, F. *The Devil in the New World: The Impact of Diabolism in New Spain*. New Haven, CT: Yale University Press, 1994.

Churchill, M.F. *Letters from My Home in India: Being the Correspondence of Mrs. George Churchill (1871–1916)*, ed. G.M. Rogers. New York: George H. Doran, 1916.

Clark, H.M. *Robert Clark of the Panjab: Pioneer and Missionary Statesman*. New York: F.H. Revell, 1907.

Comaroff, J., and J. Comaroff. *Of Revelation and Revolution*, 2 vols. Chicago: University of Chicago Press, 1991/1997.
Cox, J. *The British Missionary Enterprise since 1700*. New York: Routledge, 2008.
Craig, J., et al. (eds). *Telugu Trophies: The Jubilee Story of Some of the Principal Telugu Converts in the Canadian Baptist Foreign Mission in India from 1874 to 1924*. Toronto: Canadian Baptist Foreign Mission Board, 1925.
DiFiore, G. *La legazione mezzabarba in Cina (1720–21)*. Naples: Istituto Universitario Orientale, 1989.
Elbourne, E. 'A Complicated Pity: Emotion, Missions and the Conversion Narrative', in C. McLisky, D. Midena and K. Vallgårda, *Emotions and Christian Missions: Historical Perspectives* (Basingstoke, U.K.: Palgrave Macmillan, 2015), 123–50.
Etherington, N. (ed.). *Missions and Empire*. Oxford: Oxford University Press, 2005.
Everett, D. *Don't Sleep, There Are Snakes: Life and Language in the Amazonian Jungle*. London: Profile, 2009.
Eyre, A. 'Converting Emotions: Domesticity and Self-Sacrifice in Female Missionary Writing', in C. McLisky, D. Midena and K. Vallgårda, *Emotions and Christian Missions: Historical Perspectives* (Basingstoke, U.K.: Palgrave Macmillan, 2015), 179–201.
Fatica, M., and F. D'Arelli (eds). *La missione cattolica in Cina tra i secoli XVIII–XIX: Matteo Ripa e il Collegio dei cinesi*. Naples: Istituto Universitario Orientale di Napoli, 1999.
Gordon, A. *Our India Mission: A Thirty Year's History of the India Mission of the United Presbyterian Church of North America, Together with Personal Reminiscences*. Philadelphia, PA: A. Gordon, 1886.
Grimshaw, P. 'Faith, Missionary Life, and the Family', in P. Levine (ed.), *Gender and Empire* (Oxford: Oxford University Press, 2004), 260–80.
Griswold, H.D. *The Admission of Village Christians to the Lord's Supper*. Undated pamphlet [c. 1917].
Haggis, J., and M. Allen. 'Imperial Emotions: Affective Communities of Mission in British Protestant Women's Missionary Publications, c1880–1920'. *Journal of Social History* 41(3) (2008), 691–716, doi: 10.1353/jsh.2008.0047.
Harley, C.D. *Preparing to Serve: Training for Cross-Cultural Mission*. Pasadena, CA: Carey Library, 1995.
Hevia, J.L. 'Sovereignty and Subject: Constituting Relations of Power in Qing Guest Ritual', in A. Zito and T.E. Barlow (eds), *Body, Subject and Power in China* (Chicago: University of Chicago Press, 1994), 181–200.
Hsia, R.P. 'Translating Christianity: Counter-Reformation Europe and the Catholic Mission in China, 1580–1780', in K. Mills and A. Grafton (eds), *Conversion: Old Worlds and New* (Rochester, NY: University of Rochester Press, 2003), 87–108.
_____. *A Jesuit in the Forbidden City: Matteo Ricci 1553–1610*. Oxford: Oxford University Press, 2010.
Imad-Ud-Din. *A Mohammedan Brought to Christ: Being the Autobiography of the Rev. Imad-Ud-Din, D.D., of the Church Missionary Society's Mission at Amritsar, North India, and Honorary Chaplain to the Lord Bishop of Lahore*, trans. R. Clark, new edn. London: Church Missionary House, 1885.

Keane, W. *Christian Moderns: Freedom and Fetish in the Mission Encounter.* Berkeley: University of California Press, 2007.

Kim, S. *Strange Names of God: The Missionary Translation of the Divine Name and the Chinese Responses to Matteo Ricci's 'Shangti' in Late Ming China, 1583–1644.* New York: Lang, 2004.

Kutcher, N. *Mourning in Late Imperial China: Filial Piety and the State.* Cambridge: Cambridge University Press, 2006.

Li, D.J. *China in Transition: 1517–1911.* New York: Van Nortrand Reinhold, 1969.

Lust, J. *Chinese Popular Prints.* Leiden: Brill, 1996.

Lutz, J.G. *Opening China: Karl F.A. Gützlaff and Sino-Western Relations.* Cambridge: Eerdmans, 2008.

Maughan, S.S. *Mighty England Do Good: Culture, Faith, Empire, and World in the Foreign Missions of the Church of England.* Grand Rapids, MI: Eerdmans, 2014.

McLisky, C. 'The Emotional Economies of Protestant Missions to Aboriginal People in Nineteenth-Century Australia', in D. Lemmings and A. Brooks (eds), *Emotions and Social Change: Historical and Sociological Perspectives* (New York: Routledge, 2014), 82–98.

———. 'Affective Circuits: Emotional Transfer and Christian Mission in Early Colonial Greenland and Australia', in C. McLisky, D. Midena and K. Vallgårda, *Emotions and Christian Missions: Historical Perspectives* (Basingstoke, U.K.: Palgrave Macmillan, 2015), 151–76.

McLisky, C., D. Midena and K. Vallgårda (eds). *Emotions and Christian Missions: Historical Perspectives.* Basingstoke, U.K.: Palgrave Macmillan. 2015.

Mohan, P.S. *Modernity of Slavery: Struggles against Caste Inequality in Colonial Kerala.* New Delhi: Oxford University Press, 2015.

Mungello, D.E. 'An Introduction to the Chinese Rites Controversy', in D.E. Mungello (ed.), *The Chinese Rites Controversy: Its History and Meaning* (Nettetal: Steyler, 1994), 3–12.

Nelson, J.E. *Christian Missionizing and Social Transformation: A History of Conflict and Change in Eastern Zaire.* New York: Praeger, 1992.

Reed, L.E. *Preparing Missionaries for Intercultural Communication: A Bi-Cultural Approach.* Pasadena, CA: Carey Library, 1985.

Reinders, E. *Borrowed Gods and Foreign Bodies: Christian Missionaries Imagine Chinese Religion.* Berkeley: University of California Press, 2004.

Ripa, M. *Storia della fondazione della congregazione e del collegio de' cinesi*, 3 vols. Naples: Istituto Universitario Orientale, 1832.

———. *Memoirs of Father Ripa: During Thirteen Years' Residence at the Court of Peking in the Service of the Emperor of China*, selected and trans. F. Prandi. New York: John Wiley, 1849.

———. *Giornale (1705–1724)*, 2 vols, ed. M. Ripa. Naples: Istituto Universitario Orientale di Napoli, 1991/1996.

Rosaldo, M.Z. *Knowledge and Passion: Ilongot Notions of Self and Social Life.* Cambridge: Cambridge University Press, 1980.

Ryden, E. 'Keep to the Method of Matteo Ricci: The Kangxi Emperor and Catholic Missionaries in China', in C. Shelke and M. Demichele (eds), *Matteo Ricci in China: Inculturation through Friendship and Faith* (Rome: Gregorian and Biblical Press, 2010), 185–99.

Sanneh, L. *Translating the Message: The Missionary Impact on Culture*. Maryknoll, NY: Orbis Books, 2008.
Scheer, Monique. 'German "Shouting Methodists": Religious Emotion as a Transatlantic Cultural Practice', in C. McLisky, D. Midena and K. Vallgårda, *Emotions and Christian Missions: Historical Perspectives* (Basingstoke, U.K.: Palgrave Macmillan, 2015), 45–72.
Spence, J.D. 'Claims and Counter-Claims: The Kangxi-Emperor and the Europeans (1661–1722)', in D.E. Mungello (ed.), *The Chinese Rites Controversy: Its History and Meaning* (Nettetal: Steyler, 1994), 15–28.
_____. *Emperor of China: Self-Portrait of K'ang-His*. New York: Knopf, 2012.
Standaert, N. *The Interweaving of Rituals: Funerals in the Cultural Exchange between China and Europe*. Seattle: University of Washington Press, 2008.
Taneti, J.E. *Caste, Gender, and Christianity in Colonial India: Telugu Women in Mission*. New York: Palgrave Macmillan, 2013.
Viswanath, R. *The Pariah Problem: Caste, Religion, and the Social in Modern India*. New York: Columbia University Press, 2014.
W.B. *In a Tapioca Garden: The Story of an Outcaste Girl of Travancore*. London: Church Missionary Society, n.d. [1928].
Warkentin, R. 'Begging as Resistance: Wealth and Christian Missionaries in Postcolonial Zaire'. *Missiology: An International Review* 29(2) (2001), 143–63, doi: 10.1177/009182960102900203.
Webster, J.C.B. *The Dalit Christians: A History*. Delhi: Indian Society for Promoting Christian Knowledge, 1992.
Whiteman, D.L. *Melanesians and Missionaries: An Ethnohistorical Study of Social and Religious Change in the Southwest Pacific*. Pasadena, CA: Carey Library, 1983.
Youngson, J.F.W. *Forty Years of the Panjab Mission of the Church of Scotland, 1855–1895*. Edinburgh: R. & R. Clark, 1896.
Županov, I.G. *Disputed Mission: Jesuit Experiments and Brahmanical Knowledge in Seventeenth-Century India*. New Delhi: Oxford University Press, 2001.
_____. 'Prologue: Perils of Translation: Missionary Writing in/on South Asia (16th–18th c.)', in A. Amaladass and I.G. Županov (eds), *Intercultural Encounter and the Jesuit Mission in South Asia (16th to 18th Centuries)* (Bangalore: Asian Trading Corporation, 2014), 1–20.

Chapter 2

Travellers
Transformative Journeys and Emotional Contacts

Edgar Cabanas, Razak Khan and Jani Marjanen

Caminata Nocturna, a simulation of an illegal crossing of the United States–Mexico border, is one of the main tourist attractions of the theme park EcoAlberto. Since 2004, it has been offering tourists the chance to experience what it would be like to be an illegal migrant. Advertised as a rigorous and educational simulation aimed at discouraging migration and raising awareness about the physical and emotional perils of border-crossing (a reality for thousands of Mexicans every year), Caminata Nocturna stages an important part of Mexican history and identity[1] while simultaneously providing its visitors with an educational and shocking – albeit riskless – emotional experience. In Caminata Nocturna, tourists experience how a migrant feels by simulating the camaraderie, dependence, violence, humiliation and submission that often characterize migration; these experiences are then supposed to be accompanied by the corresponding emotions of shock, fear and suffering that migrants undergo in order to survive. Caminata Nocturna compels tourists to engage in a series of realistic tasks in which negotiating meaning and achieving mutual understanding with other unfamiliar participants and the persons staging the event is crucial for successfully navigating the simulated ordeal and achieving the sort of transformative experience offered by placing oneself in a threatening situation for a few hours.[2]

This example from contemporary tourism illustrates that while the phenomenology of the tourist experience comes in a wide variety of forms,[3] emotions and the desire for self-transformation have shaped and continue

---

Notes for this chapter begin on page 80.

to shape tourist experiences. Tourism advertising promises transformative experiences through encounters with the unexpected, the unknown and even the shocking. Contemporary tourists want to experience what they have never experienced before[4] and demand that their time be emotionally transformative.

The emphasis on self-transformation can be traced back to the elite travellers of the eighteenth century, who, unlike many explorers, missionaries, traders and anthropologists of their time, saw travelling as a self-edifying endeavour. However, the historical development from the traveller to the modern tourist has seen important changes both in the nature of face-to-face encounters between travellers and locals as well as in the ways people have conceived of the type of self-transformation that might be achieved through travel. In turn, the aims, duration, structure and availability of travel have set the foundations for various perceptions of self-transformation in different times. The advent of mass tourism and the democratization of travel have brought with it the proliferation of short-duration, structured, standardized face-to-face encounters with locals. Scholars have argued that tourists 'expect to be entertained and exposed to performances which ... are different from those of their familiar world',[5] and they are willing to accept the reproduction of the foreign culture as long as it is an 'authentic reproduction'. Experiences should be intense, shocking and exciting but only as long as they are safe and uncompromised.[6]

This chapter explores the role that emotions have played in the negotiation of power and meaning during face-to-face encounters between travellers and locals by examining cases characterized by different power dynamics and cultural sensibilities. The cases range from the Grand Tour in Europe (Gustaf Mauritz Armfelt) to Orientalist travel in the nineteenth century (Georg August Wallin), from the European travels of South Asian Muslim elites (Mirza Shaikh Itesamuddin, Mirza Abu Taleb and Syed Ahmed Khan) in the same century to the travel of early twentieth-century authors to Mexico (D.H. Lawrence) and the Caminata Nocturna simulation discussed earlier. The historical cases represent iconic genres in travel literature, from the period of the Grand Tour to the advent of mass tourism and (post)modern reactions to it in present-day travel. These genres have provided scripts for how people are supposed to experience admiration, awe, shock and disgust in encounters with the other.[7] They have since been emulated and challenged by later travellers. As a literally scripted encounter, the Caminata Nocturna differs from the other cases, but it also highlights something present in all of them because it poignantly puts on display the need many tourists feel to learn emotionally by experiencing something alien. Taken together, the cases illustrate a global practice of feeling difference characterized by different constellations of intercultural power dynamics. Intercultural asymmetries shape the image of who can afford to be disgusted or awed, but the cases also show that individuals still have emotional agency.

The chapter suggests that emotional transformations experienced through travel have often been determined by contingency and that they have often partially or wholly diverged from the travellers' initial expectations. Furthermore, the chapter shows that premediated emotions embedded in cultural prejudices, social location and power dynamics have affected the negotiation of power and meaning in encounters between travellers and locals. We argue that emotions are not just the outcome of cultural encounters but that they also shape the vocabulary of difference and similarities in their changing scripts. As discussed in the introduction, emotional sovereignty varies historically and is not necessarily predetermined but is rather negotiated during encounters. This chapter shows that the process is historically variable, and the cases selected here point to how emotions work both as resources that shape and are simultaneously transformed through such encounters. Political power is negotiated through the emotional power of possessing, performing and transforming emotions within a changing political and emotional economy.

The dominant scholarly opinion sees travel encounters – from early modern explorers to present day city-hopping youth and leisure tourists – as something that involves the pursuit of self-transformation.[8] It is also commonplace to understand travel encounters as circumspect, cold, intellectual explorations of otherness. However, this commonplace ignores the role that emotions play in people's attempt to understand otherness and power. More concretely, the role that wonder and curiosity might play in helping people bridge cultural gaps or co-adapt or the role that fear and disgust might play in intensifying cultural differences, leading to misunderstandings, has not been fully appreciated. At different times, travellers have explored and attempted to grasp the foreign as a way to problematize their own culture or self. They have done so not by maintaining intellectual distance but by emotionally engaging with the other. Such engagements have often resulted in emotionally ambivalent responses marked by a mixture of fascination, perplexity, disgust and, quite often, fear of the encountered other. Indeed, personal diaries and ego-documents describing travellers' own experiences with locals attest to the power of face-to-face encounters to transform travellers and test and contest their personal and cultural prejudices. Thus, the question is not so much whether travellers really achieved self-transformation during their sojourns but how these transformations were facilitated by emotional encounters and what kind of change the travellers themselves sought.

From Learning from the Past to Finding Yourself

Although travelling has a long history, it was only in the sixteenth century that guidebooks for collecting knowledge during journeys to foreign lands began appearing in Europe.[9] These guidebooks helped shape the tradition of travelling. Journeymen read them and planned their own trips in line with what others had done before them, basing their reports on previous accounts and thus subordinating expectations of the journey ahead to a particular script. Most accounts of the history of travel focus on eighteenth-century travellers when describing the Grand Tour that young men and women from privileged backgrounds made through Italy, France and other parts of Europe with the aim of educating themselves.[10]

The Grand Tour was not a unified form of travel, nor was it an exclusively British phenomenon. It was also adapted as a mode of princely education in other parts of Europe and in South Asia. The itinerary varied greatly depending on the origins and interests of the traveller. While Northern Europeans were interested in encounters with Europe's past through art and architecture in Italy and France to present themselves as cultured persons in domestic settings, South Asian tourists were more future-oriented in their travels, projecting themselves upon their return home as vehicles of progress. Most of those who undertook the Grand Tour also had other objectives, but the idea that travel could help an individual person polish their manners and personality was a central motive for all. In one of the most influential accounts of the Grand Tour, Goethe described a total transformation: 'Naples is a paradise; everyone lives in a state of intoxicated self-forgetfulness, myself included. I seem to be a completely different person whom I hardly recognize. Yesterday I thought to myself: Either you were mad before, or you are mad now'.[11] In most accounts, the transformation people sought was less fundamental and more instrumental. Improved manners and acquired knowledge were used to impress at home. But encounters with other people were not the only source of transformation. It could also be brought about through a fascination with foreign architecture, art, libraries or modern technological inventions, among other things. But in the end, the process of learning was most often facilitated either by premediated information about the artefacts or by local mediators who could point out the importance of particular sites and how to feel about them.

In a travel diary, Gustaf Mauritz Armfelt (1757–1814), a Swedish nobleman who accompanied the Swedish king Gustavus III on a ten-month tour in 1783–84, provides examples of how encounters with artefacts as well as other nobles were guided by established knowledge.[12] Gustavus III followed a rather typical Grand Tour itinerary: he travelled south from

Sweden through German-speaking Europe, continued to Italy, stayed in Rome for a longer period and continued by boat to Monaco and ultimately to Paris, the second main attraction of the trip.

The king travelled without revealing his identity and presented himself as a Swedish nobleman, the Count of Haga (sometimes Count of Gotland). This mode of incognito travel allowed for smoother movement and saved the king and potential hosts time and money they would have had to spend on arranging formal royal visits.[13] A travelling monarch demanded recognition, whereas a nobleman could enjoy the theatre, architecture and arts and educate himself in freedom.[14] Gustavus had with him a memorandum by Carl August Ehrensvärd that guided his interpretations and feelings about certain pieces of art: 'Your Majesty will among the ruins of antiquity gain a number of ideas that will not come to you in the North. And Your Majesty will reach clarity regarding a number of topics that have before been in the dark'.[15]

While keeping the king's true identity a secret rendered many practical arrangements easier, it also led to certain prefigured codes of honour and politeness to be renegotiated. Gustavus' role as a student seeking to learn new things clashed with his role as a king of a European state. For instance, Gustavus was constantly annoyed by local noblemen, who refused to leave him alone. In a Munich theatre, Armfelt was approached by a Count Daun, who sought to see the King of Sweden on the behalf of Prince Elector Karl Theodor of Bavaria. As the king hoped to remain anonymous, a complicated exchange took place between the disguised king, the Bavarian prince elector and their mediators. After much irritation and many apologies, they agreed to arrange an informal visit.[16]

The episode is telling of how diplomatic relations, power and honour codes were played out through emotional language. Anger, annoyance, embarrassment and joy were central in the process of setting up a meeting in a way that preserved the honour of both parties. Allowing him to retain his prerogative to grant or deny meetings seems to have been crucial for satisfying the travelling monarch.

The lack of interest in the royal party was equally problematic. In Augsburg, Armfelt was disappointed that the people there 'showed no curiosity, no boy ran there to stare, not a person seemed to let their projects be disturbed. . . . They could not be unknowing that this was the king of Sweden'.[17]

Travelling abroad seems to have served a liberating purpose for the group. Codes of conduct were important, but they could be relaxed while travelling, making it easier for the group to meet new people and learn from them. Overall, the noble tour enabled freer forms of engagement with foreigners, more open discussions about religion, politics and economy, new possibilities for love affairs, as well as a critical distance to domestic aesthetics and manners.[18] This freedom facilitated a self-transformation of the tourist that could later be capitalized on at home and thus lead to both emotional and material benefits. Gustaf Mauritz Armfelt is himself one example of this. He was sometimes described as the king's favourite, but initially the two did not like each other. However, Armfelt was able to prove his usefulness to the king and advanced quickly up the ranks after going on a European tour at the age of twenty-one, during which he learned Italian, improved his French and, above all, polished his 'provincial habits' to become an 'homme du monde'.[19]

Being familiar with Europe's past and using Antique motifs in the present was crucial for the Scandinavian tourist. But with the uptick in travel from the newly colonized territories to the capital of the new British Empire, London, inspiration in travel was no longer sought from the past. The logic of emulation came to be dominated by a more future-oriented perspective, as we shall see in the cases of Mirza Itesamuddin and Mirza Abu Taleb's travel accounts of London discussed later.

Self-transformation through travel is a persistent topos in travel literature, but the conditions of the transformation have evolved over time. In the eighteenth century, travellers were by and large a very exclusive group who represented the highest strata of society. Their travels served very diverse purposes, often all on the same trip.

Although ideas of national character and local manners were in circulation in eighteenth-century Europe – for instance, in a travelogue from 1780–82, Carl August Ehrensvärd obsessed over the differences between northern and southern nations[20] – networks necessary for organizing travel were not primarily founded on national loyalties but rather on aristocratic family ties. However, at the dawn of the nineteenth century, the emotional scripts that travellers could draw on to cope with otherness underwent shifts for a number of reasons: travel was perceived more and more in terms of encounters between national cultures, professional journeys were increasingly specialized and more people were able to travel. The emergence of a new culture of travel was no longer oriented towards the past but located within and defined by the national identities and emotions of the present.

Elite travellers were more concerned with seeking out experiences that would allow them to show how impressed – or unimpressed – they were with the foreign culture. Thus, they sought inspiration for learning, often without success. But as ideas of a less permeable self evolved and meetings with foreigners came to be increasingly conceived of as encounters between representatives of national cultures, new scripts for transforming oneself came into being. Travelling could be about more than just polishing oneself: it could be about finding your true self in something foreign. This is particularly apparent in European travellers' narratives on peoples who were perceived as untouched by modern culture and thus as representative of an authentic form of humanity. Such idealizations can be found in the travel diaries of Georg August Wallin (1811–52), a nineteenth-century Finnish Orientalist who travelled on the Arabian Peninsula and Sinai, in Egypt, Syro-Palestine and Persia between 1843 and 1849.[21] Wallin travelled as a scientist and studied spoken Arabic. But he is best known for immersing himself in local Bedouin culture and for being among the first twenty or so Westerners to visit Mecca in modern times.[22] He came from a Christian country but presented himself as a Muslim from Central Asia ('Abd al-Wāli). In his diaries, he describes with pleasure the locals' speculations about his origins, thus engaging in a playful performance of ethnicity.

A recurring theme in his diary and letters is the hypocrisy and luxury of Europe and the big cities as opposed to the simple but authentic life in the desert.[23] The desert functions as a harsh other that allows Wallin to escape modern life:

> I do not know what this love of mine for the desert can be – yet I already know it too well to expect anything of it but hunger and thirst and hot sun with no shade and at every moment the fear of being assailed and plundered by my friends the Bedouins.... And yet I know that in all the luxuriance of Persia and all the luxury of the English colony in Baghdad and the ample 'fleshpots' of Egypt I constantly yearned for the desert.[24]

Wallin's disdain for Europe was not a sentiment acquired during his immersion in Bedouin culture but was premediated. Even before the beginning of his journey he wrote to his teacher Sheikh Muhammad 'Ayyad al-Tantawi: 'Ever since I learned to know the strength of your language and the beauty in your literature, I have become weary of the frivolity of Europeans, been repulsed by the feebleness of their language, and despised the refinement of their knowledge'.[25]

Wallin not only wanted to leave his country in search of truth and authenticity. He was also actively working on his pronunciation, vocabulary, manners and facial expressions to better blend in during his travels in Egypt, Arabia and Persia. He spent longer periods among local friends and beneficiaries, which gave him the chance to mimic his hosts. This mimicking was based on ideas of companionship with educated men, while encounters with women and lower classes were seen as being less edifying.

While waiting for his travel grant to come through, Wallin frequently met with his teacher Sheikh al-Tantawi in St Petersburg, learning

Arabic, listening to stories about Egypt and strengthening his urge to travel:

> His good-natured, pure and almost childlike character, his ingenuity and sincerity are increasingly gaining my esteem and friendship; and now at last we are no longer on the narrow terms of teacher and disciple, but on terms that are completely amicable. ... [H]is endless tales of his beloved Egypt, its Storytellers, Singers and Dance Maidens and all its other delights have, if possible, aroused even further my inclination and desire to go there, and I really do not know how I shall be able to bear the news of the decision about my application, which must now come one of these days. If it is a 'nay' I fear that I shall sink into sorrow and vexation, and if it is a 'yea' I fear that my heart will leap from my breast.[26]

Wallin's relationship with his teacher was based on mimicking the expressions and pronunciation of al-Tantawi. While in Helsinki, Wallin described his desire to keep learning but complained that he could not make any progress without having someone to teach him spoken Arabic. For him, this meant that the relationship had to grow closer. Wallin described how al-Tantawi started talking more freely, even 'answering questions that would probably be touchy for a very strict Muslim'.[27]

Wallin's travels would not have been possible without Russia's imperial ambitions and the imperial practice of sending scientists to explore foreign territories. While the expansion of European empires allowed scientists to travel in service of the empire – whether directly or indirectly – it also enabled travel from the colonies to the new imperial centres.[28] The power relations that defined these journeys differed markedly from those that defined the Grand Tours of the eighteenth century. Consequently, the emotional scripts that travellers used to adapt changed too.

From Wonder to Civility

While the Grand Tour in Europe was at its high point, people began travelling from the newly colonized territories (especially from South Asia) to the capital of the new British Empire, London. However, unlike the European Grand Tour tradition, which was centred on learning about Europe's past, South Asian travellers were more interested in Europe's modernity and innovation.[29] The diaries of travellers Mirza Shaikh Itesamuddin and Mirza Abu Taleb are exemplary, marking the emergence of the modern travelogue in the Persian language. J.E. Alexander's 1827 English translation of Mirza Shaikh Itesamuddin's *Shigurf Nama-i-Velayet* (The wonders of Europe) changed the title to *Excellent Intelligence*

Concerning Europe: Being the Travels of Mirza Itesa Modeen.³⁰ The translation shifted the emphasis from 'wondrous experience' to 'useful knowledge'. Another English translation, this time from a Bengali version, claims to capture not only the literal meaning but also the 'emotional tone of Persian'.³¹ Mirza Abu Taleb Khan's *Masiri Talibi* (Travels of Taleb), which was written in Persian in 1803, had a similar fate. It was translated and published in English by Charles Stewart in 1810. However, Stewart removed the Persian poetry, which in his opinion 'disturbed' the narrative, but which actually conveyed the emotional experience of travel. As much as the texts benefited from the wider dissemination that came along with being translated, they were also profoundly changed if not completely lost in translation.

These travelogue writers were confident of their manners and behaviours as *Munshi* (learned scribes) when consorting with British gentlemen. Mirza Itesamuddin made known his noble Syed descent and gentlemanly status, as did Taleb, who discussed it repeatedly in his travel diaries. Their accounts of their travels are characterized by curiosity and a desire to make interesting observations that were crucial in establishing what Mohammad Tavakoli-Targhi calls 'Persianate Europology', which produced knowledge about Europe and the manners and habits of Europeans, especially their 'vices and virtues'.³² Wallin's criticism of Europe's emotional depravity in modern times should be regarded as an echo of the texts of 'Persianate Europology'. But these texts also expressed awe and admiration for modern European technology and architecture. Emotions were crucial in the critical engagement with, and evaluation of, European culture in South Asian travel literature.

Space, class and gender seem to have had a particular impact on shaping emotions and encounters in early travel literature written by South Asian visitors to Europe. The binary between colony and metropolis was not the only spatial distinction of significance for the encounters described in these travelogues. Significant, too, were the intermediary spaces of encounter during travel on ships and in ports. These encounters were often crucial in developing and transforming premediated knowledge about emotions and representations of the other, often sparking self-exploration and transformation. The encounter in the metropolis itself varied depending on the spatial context. Both Itesamuddin and Taleb's accounts described the spatially defined emotions and emotional styles of English society: in the street and other public places, they were 'unrestrained' and full of 'great curiosity', which stood in contrast to the 'restrained politeness' and 'friendliness' of clubs, high society, balls, operas, etc.³³ However, the emphasis on the curiosity of the masses and the politesse of the elite was reversed at masquerade and dance parties. As Daniel O'Quinn notes, masquerade balls were defined by the '"fanciful" construction of alterity', where people could experiment and play with emotional styles and behaviours. Such play could lead to confusion and misinterpretation. Paradoxically, however, such misunderstandings often led to greater emotional proximity and understanding.[34] The enhanced popularity of transcultural masquerades in the imperial metropolis should be understood in the context of the sexual and emotional economy of nineteenth-century England. They were characterized by mimicry, alterity and the tensions and pleasures associated with the cultural diversity of the British Empire in the age of colonialism.[35]

Physical appearance – and fashion in particular – was an important part of emotional encounters. Considering this aspect of the cultural dimensions of physical appearance might help us historicize and spatialize the contact between bodies in transcultural encounters.[36] For example, when Mirza Itesamuddin went to an elite dance party, even the respectable ladies and gentlemen 'thronged around' and examined his costume, which included a robe, a turban and a shawl. Based on their premediated knowledge, they concluded that he was a dancer or actor. Although he tried to explain that he was indeed not an actor, one gentleman thought he was just 'feeling shy' because of the presence of the ladies. According to the author's own account, however, this was far from the truth: he boasts that, while the ladies stared at his clothes, he also gazed at their 'astonishing loveliness'.[37] In the end, we might read this as a staged emotional encounter that was enabled by a specific space, namely the masquerade ball. Although it led to confusion, such misreading might be considered essential in making the stranger look familiar.

In other encounters in public spaces and streets, Itesamuddin writes that crowds followed him around and people gazed at him in wonder, while curious children and adolescents saw him as a 'black man' or feared him as a 'black devil'.[38] Appearance was thus very significant in the encounters between travellers from the new colonies and the English locals. It could spark curiosity or admiration or could lead to fear or even disgust against what was perceived to be an 'effeminate appearance' and manners. Itesamuddin himself seems to attribute considerable importance to his own appearance: because he wanted to be recognized as a gentleman, he strove to distinguish himself from the lascars familiar to the British and circumvent premediated knowledge about Indians in Britain.[39] In more general terms, one might say that culturally defined bodies and materiality were crucial factors in shaping the emotional encounter. This also raises important questions about how people engage with curiosity, as it is articulated through bodily emotional signs and responses like wide-eyed amazement, friendliness and hospitality. In addition, the account makes clear that curiosity can also lead to other emotions including fascination, fear and disgust.

Gender relations are a third aspect of these emotional encounters. Itesamuddin's account of the white woman's appearance is an example of the significance of gender. He was captivated by the beauty and splendour of white women, who he compares with the fairies (*houris*) of paradise. However, he attributes his emotions not to 'physicality' but to 'divine beauty'. He confesses that he is 'overwhelmed by the glory of Allah's creative power' and recites a distich. Poetry was the language of emotions and experience in an age of asymmetrical power relations.

> Out of dust he produces a living body
> And from seed makes a fair face[40]

Taleb articulated his emotions through his physical and moral charm, which he claims attracted women.[41] However, Taleb never engaged in romantic relationships with the women he admired and used his emotional restraint to assert his personal and moral superiority, thus drawing on Indo-Persian standards of personal character. His claim that he, unlike the Englishmen, was not emotionally swayed by the allure of ravishing beauty is also staged as a form of cultural agency and critique. Thus, we might claim that, instead of seeking self-transformation, Taleb asserted his emotional sovereignty in a time of political subordination. Taleb also expresses his sense of sovereignty and critique through poetry, most notably in the 'Poem in Praise of Miss Julia Burrell'. The poetic section on the 'Praise of Her Mole', mole being a metaphor for colonized India, underscores the connection between the emotional and political economy of colonialism, which was characterized by tensions within the empire and England's simultaneous allure for colonial subjects.

> The pupil of her eye is also its constant attendant.
> Although the European be ruler over a part of India;
> Yet behold an Indian who is sovereign of all Europe.
> What a mole! the essence of a hundred caskets of ottar makers[42]

The encounter at this historical moment does not reveal any emotional inferiority on the part of the colonized subject or guilt about the subject's attempts to civilize his colonized society. Indeed, the accounts of South Asian travellers maintain the idea that the colonized were spiritually superior to their colonizers, while conceding that Europeans had made material progress. Self-transformation was not simple mimicry but was defined by remediation, translations and emotional negotiations. This relative freedom within the cultural encounter and its interpretation itself underwent changes after Britain's violent suppression of the 1857 revolt.

Syed Ahmed Khan's travelogue was the first influential account of engagement with the colonial metropolis in the post-1857 political climate.[43] The land of the victorious Queen of England was no longer a remote place of curious wonders but had become the new centre of civility and culture for colonial subjects. Syed Ahmed Khan was a leading figure from the Indian elite, who started a movement for educational reform in Aligarh in northern India. His travel account has been regarded as a text of 'Anglo-Muslim rapprochement' based on a 'passion to build' a Muslim community with the help of the colonial masters.[44] He describes England as 'a world of hope and promise', especially due to its excellent education system. The travelogue is markedly different from previous accounts both in its observations and in the perspective it provides on English society and culture. The emphasis is on education with the aim of achieving progress. Khan writes that learning these new values required loyalty to the Raj,[45] and he believed that modern values had to be acquired and old feelings abandoned. These were the constant themes in letters that Khan wrote back to Aligarh, which were published in the *Aligarh Institute Gazette*. Important is the shift in language through translation: while earlier Persian travel accounts were translated into English, Urdu had now become the language of experience and expression of the travel account. These Urdu letters not only helped people in India acquire new information about England. They also helped them understand the new emotional knowledge conveyed by Syed Ahmed Khan's experiences, including his awe upon seeing the library in the 'city of books'.[46] He also offered encouragement and advice to students and other future travellers to England, writing that the trip was comparable to performing the Hajj.[47] Echoing Goethe's ideas, Syed Ahmed Khan particularly emphasized the emotional and self-transformative role of travel: 'And just as this travelling is necessary for the enhancement of wisdom, it is very useful for the refinement of morals: Travelling benefits a man's mind by widening his understanding and perception. His morality benefits from his developing softness towards and sympathy for "other" people'.[48]

Unlike travelogues that remained confined to the upper echelons of society, Syed Ahmed Khan interacted with people from both the nobility and the middle classes, particularly during his visits to academic societies and clubs. These were places where new knowledge and new values were learned, exchanged and disseminated. Particularly important was the Athenaeus club, where Khan met many distinguished Englishmen and marvelled at the scientific temperament of the people who studied there. He also admired the civility of educated Englishwomen. During his journey, he met famous social worker and educationist Mary Carpenter and praised her civility, cordiality and good intentions. However, Khan postponed the issue of education for Muslim women at Aligarh. Self-transformation remained an emotionally charged and historically contingent process marked by social anxiety about gender relations. He hoped that new appropriate values and emotions could be taught and cultivated in India; however, he also remained anxious about the social implications they might have.[49] Syed Ahmed Khan's travel experience was echoed by – but also criticized in – subsequent travel accounts, which shifted from wondrous narratives to a critical understanding couched in pedagogical language.

As Julie F. Codell argues, Indian travel accounts reversed the earlier European Grand Tour narratives defined by 'self-discovery', developing a new, alternative 'guest discourse' based on comparing the cultures of England and India.[50] While European accounts of the Grand Tour emotionally engaged with the Greek and Roman past for new imperial rulers, South Asian travellers experienced the modernity of European nations as a resource for cultivating new emotions that might be shared between the British and their imperial subjects. These colonial travel narratives of 'emotional encounters' should be placed within the larger history of counter-perspectives on the 'colonial encounter' in the imperial metropolis, which increased in frequency and became much more complicated in the twentieth century. Hence, self-transformative possibilities of travel also underwent a transformation in the age of mass tourism.

From Shocking to Staged Encounters

The political turmoil and years of war that followed Mexico's 1910 revolution – and the cultural boom that went along with it – attracted a number of North American and British writers, historians, journalists, political observers and students, who, with varying degrees of sympathy and ignorance, travelled to Mexico. They sought personal edification through shocking encounters, as well as alternative cultural settings through which they could examine and criticize the horrors of industrialization in their own countries.

Emotions not only shaped travel experience. They also shaped the production of knowledge about other cultures and subjectivities. As noted earlier, European accounts of the Arabic and Islamic world help set forth a tradition of Orientalism as described by Edward Said, and, for their part, South Asian travel experience and accounts were crucial in developing a Persianate Europology. Similarly, encounters with Mexicans would eventually shape (and be shaped by) what Elisabeth Mermann-Jozwiak, in analogy to Said, termed as Mexicanism: a set of romanticized, colonial prejudices held by Europeans and Americans towards Mexico, prejudices that entailed 'a search for the supposed innocence, simplicity, and authenticity before the Conquest'.[51] Although this idealization set the tone before any travellers had ever actually had any encounters with locals, few encounters of North American and British travellers with Mexicans were simple and clear-cut. On the contrary, these encounters often contested – or sometimes amplified – travellers' preconceptions by causing emotionally ambivalent reactions that combined fascination, astonishment, perplexity, disgust and, quite often, fear – not least because Mexico had one of the world's highest murder rates.

Alongside Katherine Anne Porter, Graham Greene, Malcom Lowry and Gertrude Diamant, to name just a few, D.H. Lawrence remains one of the most important and representative authors of British-American travel literature on Mexico in the first half of the twentieth century. Most of Lawrence's first-person descriptions of his face-to-face encounters with Mexicans during the 1920s are compiled in the volume *Mornings in Mexico and Other Essays*. However, they also find expression in popular novels like *The Plumed Serpent*.[52]

Like for the vast majority of other North American and British travellers and writers (and anthropologists), it was the life of Mexico's lower and indigenous classes that exerted the greatest influence on Lawrence's writings. There were three main reasons for this. First, agrarian society and indigenous culture were seen as the most informative and authentic representatives of the Mexican way of life. Second, lower and indigenous classes also confronted North American and British writers and travellers with the kind of cultural counterpoint, shocking encounters and alien experiences that many of them were seeking. And third, while access to the middle and upper classes was precluded for most foreigners, encounters with lower and indigenous classes in the countryside, the city streets, hotels, churches, markets etc. were not only easy to come by but also unavoidable.[53]

While elite clubs provided the spatial context of encounters between South Asian and British elites in London, the marketplace provided the setting for everyday encounters with the locals in Mexico and is well described in Lawrence's 'Market Day'. In this piece, Lawrence describes the Mexican market square as a crowded, noisy, smelly, shoddy place where buyers and merchants went '[t]o buy, to sell, to barter, to exchange. To exchange, above all things, human contact'.[54] According to Lawrence, commingling and interacting with others were the locals' main reasons for hanging out at the market, a place where '[o]nly that which is utterly intangible, matters.... That which can never be fastened upon, forever gone, forever coming, never to be detained: the spark of contact'.[55] Contact is also the main explanation why merchants 'like you to bargain', something that Lawrence, unaccustomed to haggling, found rather unpleasant:

> 'Señor! Señor! Look! Huaraches! Very fine, very finely made! Look, Señor!'
> The fat leather man jumps up and holds a pair of sandals at one's breast.... You take them in your hand, and look at them quizzically, while the fat wife of the huarache man reiterates, 'Very fine work. Very fine. Much work!'
> Leather men usually seem to have their wives with them.
> 'How much?'
> 'Twenty reales'.
> 'Twenty!' – in a voice of surprise and pained indignation.
> 'How much do you give?'
> You refuse to answer. Instead you put the huaraches to your nose. The huarache man looks at his wife, and they laugh aloud.
> 'They smell', you say.
> 'No, Señor, they don't smell!' – and the two go off into fits of laughter.
> 'Yes, they smell. It is not American leather'.
> 'Yes, Señor, it is American leather. They don't smell, Señor. No, they don't smell'. – He coaxes you till you wouldn't believe your own nose.
> 'Yes, they smell'.
> ...
> And you give another sniff, though it is painfully unnecessary. And in spite of your refusal to bid, the man and wife go into fits of laughter, to see you painfully sniffing.[56]

This example does not reveal misunderstanding as much as it does maladaptation, unease and awkwardness. It shows how emotions might amplify – and not only bridge or ease – cultural friction and differences by creating more distance between those involved in the face-to-face encounter. Lawrence's gestures, such as the quizzical look at the shoes, the complaint after smelling the leather or the 'voice of surprise and pained indignation', together with the merchant's laughs and coarse gestures of insistence, made it all but impossible for a process of adaptation – that is, mimesis or any other kind of corporeal, affective or cooperative coping – to take place. The interaction also heightened Lawrence's initial discomfort with the dynamics of the marketplace culture, which he initially perceived as 'a strange ... current of haste' where 'small men with lifted chests and quick, lifted knees, advancing with heavy energy in the midst of dust ... spy [on] you and whistle to you like ferocious birds'.[57] Thus, instead of closeness and adaptation, the absence of verbal communication and the failure to cope with emotional difference generated divides and intensified interpersonal frictions as well as power differences.

Lawrence's writings on his encounters with Mexicans are, indeed, filled with descriptions of the contrast between what we might call the different 'emotional styles'[58] of Britons and Mexicans. Lawrence depicts this contrast as a clash between the 'tension of the nerves' characteristic of the British and the 'exasperation of the temper' characteristic of the Mexicans.[59] He seems to have two reasons for drawing this contrast. On the one hand, in a vein similar to Georg Simmel, Lawrence underlines some of the perverse emotional consequences – such as apathy – caused by the routine, individualistic, mechanized, standardized life, characteristic of industrial societies.[60] As Simmel wrote, the metropolis, saturated with intense, individualized pleasures, 'stimulates the nerves to their utmost reactivity until they finally can no longer produce any reaction at all'.[61] On the other hand, Lawrence emphasizes the passion-driven character of the Mexicans, writing that whereas this passionate character often expressed itself in viciousness, violence and lack of self-control, it was also part of Mexicans' playfulness, lack of inhibition, intimacy and warmness. However, he wrote that it always felt overwhelming and often primitive, childish and careless in the eyes of an Englishman.[62]

On the whole, Lawrence's *Mornings in Mexico* was received with enthusiasm.[63] But some reviews, while praising Lawrence's genius and writing, criticized the 'snobbishness', 'contempt' and 'superiority' with which 'globe-trotting Englishmen' like Lawrence tended to 'gloat over the inferiority of the Mexicans'.[64] The point was that such power differences made it impossible for Lawrence to paint a neutral, respectful portrait of Mexicans and that he did not even feel the need to do so. Related to this criticism was the question of accuracy: how much did these writers' and travellers' descriptions of their encounters really reveal about Mexican character and culture?[65] In other words: what was lost in translation? And what role did emotions play in augmenting that loss? As George Woodcock pointed out, 'the curious exaggerations and distortions which appear in various accounts of Mexico in fact represent the imposition, over the true map, of the individual's personal fears and hopes'.[66] Furthermore, we might try to distinguish between those distortions that were caused by the inherent problems of translating emotions and meanings and those caused by the different aims that motivated writers and travellers, like curiosity and self-transformation, which stand in contrast to those that motivated anthropologists, like objectivity and knowledge. After all, travellers and writers were not anthropologists or ethnologists, as Lawrence himself remarked.[67] Nevertheless, despite many possible exaggerations, distortions and misunderstandings, the fact is that through their writings on their encounters in Mexico, North American and British travellers widely contributed to the construction and consolidation of both foreign and local cultural narratives on Mexican national character, thus setting a precedent for subsequent encounters.

North American and British literature on Mexico of the 1920s influenced the rise of the tourist guides in the 1930s. Among them, two bestsellers stand out: Anita Brenner's *Your Mexican Holiday* and Edith Mackie and Sheldon Dick's *Mexican Journey*.[68] However, these guides emerged in a different cultural and economic context, and their aims differed from Lawrence's. Concerned with the idea of accuracy and information rather than with interpretation and deep understanding, these guides tended to portray a less romanticized picture of Mexico. They were also informed by the growing derision of travelling, the increasing commodification of local cultures for consumption by outsiders and the expanded accessibility of travelling, which was now open to lower classes and women, groups that until then had mostly been excluded from 'serious travelling'.[69] These changes meant putting the notions of fun, health, leisure and relaxation at the centre of the travel experience.

Tourists still sought some kind of personal edification through the encounter with other cultures, but, contrary to travellers, tourists no longer sought out confrontations and casual experiences of learning through encounters with otherness.[70] In this regard, one of the most noticeable features of these guides is the almost complete lack of descriptions of any personal experience or face-to-face encounter with the locals. Unlike the travel literature of the 1920s, the guidebooks on Mexico do not contain any first-person commentary on Mexican character and culture, focusing instead on neutral third-person descriptions of costumes, language, landscapes and the people of Mexico. Of course, older traditions of travel writing did not disappear. Novels such as Jack Kerouac's 1954 *On the Road*, among others, are good examples of how the pleasures and fears of face-to-face encounters had not disappeared. They are also good examples of how the tradition of Mexicanism, characteristic of the North American and British literature of the 1920s, was, with some differences, still alive.[71] Nevertheless, the decade after the end of the Second World War saw a decline in the publication of travel literature and travel itself,[72] decline that ultimately gave way to the rise and expansion of a booming tourist industry in Mexico, which has been attracting thousands of North American and British visitors every year since.

Indeed, the North American and European interest in Mexico greatly intensified in the following decades. Mexican economy, both on a national and local level, became increasingly dependent on tourism, and places such as Cancún or the Mayan Riviera were developed in the 1980s and 1990s with the aim of producing pleasure, excitement and relaxation experiences for foreign tourists.[73]

The park EcoAlberto, opened by the Otomí community of El Alberto in the Valle del Mezquital, and the Caminata Nocturna experience in particular are good contemporary examples of the ways in which the Mexican tourism industry has deployed the commodification and advertisement of Mexican heritage in order to attract mass tourism. It is also indicative of the change in the type of encounters between foreign and local cultures already initiated in the 1930s, a shift that took place alongside the global transformation in the logic of travelling and that has intensified in the last decades. While the age of mass tourism in general promoted the search for self-transformation through leisure and relaxation, and not the interaction between cultures, the new experience industry again highlights the face-to-face encounter as a source of learning. At the same time, the 'experience-generation' has shifted the emphasis on travel encounters to something essentially harmless, fun and innovative.[74] Accordingly, the adventurous exploration of the foreign other characteristic of nineteenth- and early twentieth-century travellers was gradually succeeded by the riskless consumption of pre-packaged, theatrical experiences with other cultures, which is characteristic of late twentieth century tourism.

The vignette presented in the introduction highlights the contrast between historical and contemporary modalities of travelling aimed at self-transformation. At the same time, it underscores the growing importance of emotions for understanding late twentieth-century encounters between travellers and locals. Emotions not only play a key role in shaping the way in which meanings are negotiated in face-to-face encounters, as analysed throughout the chapter. They have also become a fundamental value in the production of authenticity and in the consumption of the transformative experience of travelling.[75]

* * *

This chapter has taken a longue durée, transregional approach to analysing the role that emotions play in bridging – or amplifying – cultural differences in travel encounters and the role they play in helping people cross emotional boundaries. The way in which travellers have historically dealt with the strange or the unknown reveals that these emotional practices are not static but are subject to historical transformations instigated by intercultural emotional encounters. In this process, practices and ideas related to self-transformation through travel have undergone significant changes. Eighteenth- and nineteenth-century European travel accounts gave precedence to the issues of civility and honour in negotiating curiosity, awe, disgust and pain. The reverse travel narratives from South Asia were also part of this history of travel and curiosity, which underwent changes during the colonial period, when travel became a pedagogical practice. Travel was part of a conception of pedagogy that not only aimed at transforming the self but at bringing about greater social reform in the colonies through the cultivation of new emotions. While this dimension persisted in later travel literature, the rise of the nineteenth-century notion that culture is rooted in nationality, and the breakthrough of mass tourism in the twentieth century, brought questions of authenticity to the fore. Travellers tried to reproduce authentic emotions by either seeking to interact with persons seen as proper representatives of their cultures – German monarchs, Egyptian sheikhs, high-class Englishmen, middle-class Muslim men, lower-class Mexican peasants – or, as in the vignette discussed at the beginning of this chapter, by staging an event in order to replicate real emotions that occur in actual life-threatening situations. Not only are emotional practices culturally constructed over time, but the ways in which the historical actors discussed in this chapter describe them are also further complicated by the fact that they are describing intercultural encounters. The dialogical nature of perceiving and describing emotions in encounters may be seen as an example of the ways in which historical enquiry is distanced from the actual emotions of past actors. At the same time, intercultural encounters have brought together diverse emotional practices, thus becoming a source of learning and emotional transformation for those involved.

Edgar Cabanas is Research Fellow at the Universidad Camilo José Cela (co-financed by the Community of Madrid, Spain [2017-T2/SOC-5414]) and Adjunct Researcher at the Center for the History of Emotions (Max Planck Institute for Human Development), in Berlin, where he had previously held a Postdoctoral Research position. He is the author of several scientific papers (in *Theory & Psychology* and *Culture & Psychology*) and book chapters (Oxford University Press and Suhrkamp), co-editor of Routledge's series on Therapeutic Culture and researcher in several research and development projects.

Razak Khan is Research Fellow in the Modern India in German Archives project in the History Research Group at the Centre for Modern Indian Studies (CeMIS) Göttingen University. He has edited a special issue of the *Journal of the Economic and Social History of the Orient* 58(5) (2015). He has also published blog posts and commentaries in the *Global Urban History Blog, TRAFO – Blog for Transregional Research and Economic and Political Weekly* and several book reviews. He is completing a book *Minority Pasts: Locality, Histories, and Identities in Rampur* for Oxford University Press.

Jani Marjanen is Postdoctoral Researcher at the University of Helsinki from where he gained his PhD in 2014. In 2014–15 he was a visiting scholar at the Center for the History of Emotions at the Max Planck Institute for Human Development, Berlin. He is the co-editor of *The Rise of Economic Societies in the Eighteenth Century: Patriotic Reform in Europe and North America* (with Koen Stapelbroek, Palgrave Macmillan, 2012) and the author of *Den ekonomiska patriotismens uppgång och fall: Finska hushållningssällskapet i europeisk, svensk och finsk kontext 1720–1840* (University of Helsinki, 2013). He is one of the editors of the journal *Contributions to the History of Concepts*.

Notes

1. Sarat, *Fire in the Canyon: Religion, Migration, and the Mexican Dream*.
2. Magelssen, 'Tourist Performance in the Twenty-First Century', 174–202.
3. Cohen, 'A Phenomenology of Tourist Experiences', 179–201.
4. Ogilvy, 'This Postmodern Business', 4–23.
5. Galani-Moutafi, 'The Self and the Other: Traveler, Ethnographer, Tourist', 211.
6. Bruner, 'Transformation of Self in Tourism', 238–50.
7. Rojek, *Ways of Escape*.
8. Rojek, *Ways of Escape*.
9. Stagl, *A History of Curiosity: The Theory of Travel 1550–1800*.
10. Black, *The British and the Grand Tour*; Black, *The British Abroad: The Grand Tour in the Eighteenth Century*; Chard, *Pleasure and Guilt on the Grand Tour: Travel Writing and Imaginative Geography, 1600–1830*. Scripts for encounters were provided also by fictitious or allegorical satires such as Jonathan Swift's *Gulliver's Travels*, but in general the travels for self-education were regarded as something separate.
11. Goethe, *Italian Journey (1786–1788)*, 198.
12. Armfelt, *Resan till Italien: Gustaf Mauritz Armfelts resedagbok 1783–1784*; Schück, *Gustaf III's Resa i Italien: Anteckningar af Gudm: Göran Adlerbeth*.
13. Conrads, 'Das Incognito: Standesreisen ohne Konventionen', 591–607.
14. See Chapter 5, Frevert, 'Diplomats' in this volume.
15. Ehrensvärd, *Matka Italiaan = Resa till Italien 1780, 1781, 1782*, 159. All Finnish and Swedish sources translated by Jani Marjanen unless otherwise noted.
16. Armfelt, *Resan till Italien*, 38–39; see also 28, 31–32, 33–34.
17. Armfelt, *Resan till Italien*, 35.
18. Black, *British and the Grand Tour*.
19. Bonsdorff, *Gustav Mauritz Armfelt: Levnadsskildring*, 28–55, quote 31.
20. Ehrensvärd, *Matka Italiaan*.
21. Wallin, *Travels in Arabia (1845 and 1848)*.
22. Öhrnberg, 'Vägen till Arabien: "Det förlofvade landet"', 46.
23. Öhrnberg, '"Långt skild från Europas flärd, fåfänga och öfverförfinade bildning": G.A. Wallin, Orienten och Europa', 494–507.
24. Translation by David McDuff quoted in Edgren-Henrichson, *Dolce far niente in Arabia: Georg August Wallin and his Travels in the 1840s*, 12 [Swe. orig. Wallin, *Skrifter*, vol. 2, 391].
25. Wallin, *Skrifter*, vol. 1, 232. The text provides the original letter in Arabic and in Swedish translation.

26. Translation by David McDuff quoted in Edgren-Henrichson, *Dolce far niente*, 40 [Swe. orig. Wallin, *Skrifter*, vol. 1, 227].
27. Wallin, *Skrifter*, 1: 232, 234, 238, quote 227.
28. Nabil Matar emphasizes the change that European imperialism meant for encounters between Arabs and Europeans; Matar, *Europe through Arab Eyes, 1573–1727*, 3–28.
29. Majchrowicz, 'Ideological Voyages: Nationalism, Colonialism and Identity in the Works of Qazi "Abdul Ghaffar"', 132–50.
30. I'tisam al Din, *Shigurf Namah i Velaët, or, Excellent Intelligence Concerning Europe; Being the Travels of Mirza Itesa Modeen, in Great Britain and France*; Jamana, *Mirza Shaikh Itesamuddin and His Travelogue: Shigurf Nama-i-Velayet (Wonders of Britain 1765–1769 AD)*; I'tesamuddin, *The Wonders of Vilayet: Being the Memoir, Originally in Persian, of a Visit to France and Britain by Mirza Sheikh Itesamuddin, an Eighteenth Century Indian Gentleman*.
31. Jamana, *Mirza Shaikh Itesamuddin*, xx.
32. Tavakoli-Targhi, *Refashioning Iran: Orientalism, Occidentalism and Historiography*, 207–24.
33. Gammerl, 'Emotional Styles – Concepts and Challenges', 161–75.
34. O'Quinn, 'Introduction', 20.
35. O'Quinn, 'Introduction'.
36. Ballantye and Burton, *Bodies in Contact: Rethinking Colonial Encounters in World History*.
37. Jamana, *Mirza Shaikh Itesamuddin*, 51.
38. Jamana, *Mirza Shaikh Itesamuddin*, 52.
39. Visram, *Ayah, Lascars and Princes: The Story of Indians in Britain 1700–1947*.
40. Jamana, *Mirza Shaikh Itesamuddin*, 51.
41. O'Quinn, 'Introduction', 30.
42. O'Quinn, 'Introduction', 30.
43. Ahmed Khan, *Voyage to Modernism*, 155.
44. Hasan and Zaidi, 'Introduction', 4, 1.
45. Hasan and Zaidi, 'Introduction', 7–10, 11–12.
46. Ahmed Khan, *Voyage to Modernism*, 155 (4 June 1869).
47. Ahmed Khan, *Voyage to Modernism*, 170 (10 September 1869).
48. Ahmed Khan in *Akhbar Scientific Society, Aligarh* (14 February 1868) in Abbas, *Print Culture: Sir Syed's Aligarh Institute Gazette 1866–1897*, 75.
49. Ahmed Khan, *Voyage to Modernism*, 177 (9 November 1869), 215–23 (27 May 1870), 224 (8 July 1870).
50. Codell, 'Reversing the Grand Tour: Guest Discourse in Indian Travel Narratives', 173–89.
51. Mermann-Jozwiak, 'Writing Mexico: Travel and Intercultural Encounter in Contemporary American Literature', 96.
52. Lawrence, *Mornings in Mexico and Other Essays*.
53. Gunn, *American and British Writers in Mexico, 1556–1973*.
54. Lawrence, 'Market Day', in Lawrence, *Mornings in Mexico*, 52.
55. Lawrence, 'Market Day', 55.
56. Lawrence, 'Market Day', 53–54.
57. Lawrence, 'Market Day', 51–53.
58. Gammerl, 'Emotional Styles'.
59. Gunn, *American and British Writers*, 129.
60. Roux, 'Emotions and Otherness in D.H. Lawrence's Mexican Fiction', 215–35.
61. Simmel, *On Individuality and Social Forms: Selected Writings*, 329.
62. Lawrence, 'The Mozo', in Lawrence, *Mornings in Mexico*, 37.
63. For example, Howe, 'Standard-Examiner Book Reviews', 4.
64. Currie, 'Mexico in the Eyes of D.H. Lawrence'.
65. Gunn, *American and British Writers*.

66. Woodcock, 'Mexico and the English Novelist', 23.
67. Lawrence, 'Indians and an Englishman', in Lawrence, *Mornings in Mexico*, 111–21.
68. Brenner, *Your Mexican Holiday: A Modern Guide*; Mackie and Dick, *Mexican Journey: An Intimate Guide to Mexico*.
69. Urry, *The Tourist Gaze: Leisure and Travel in Contemporary Societies*; MacCannell, *The Tourist: A New Theory of the Leisure Class*; Lefèbvre, *Everyday Life in the Modern World*; Clifford, *Routes: Travel and Translation in the Late Twentieth Century*.
70. Merrill, *Negotiating Paradise: U.S. Tourism and Empire in Twentieth-Century Latin America*.
71. Mermann-Jozwiak, 'Writing Mexico', 95–114.
72. Gunn, *American and British Writers*.
73. Merrill, *Negotiating Paradise*.
74. Rojek, *Ways of Escape*.
75. Gilmore and Pine II, *Authenticity: What Consumers Really Want*.

Bibliography

Abbas, A. *Print Culture: Sir Syed's Aligarh Institute Gazette 1866–1897*, trans. S. Asim Ali. New Delhi: Primus Books, 2015.

Ahmed Khan, S. *A Voyage to Modernism*, ed. and trans. M. Hasan and N. Zaidi. New Delhi: Primus Books, 2011 [Urd. orig. *Musafiran-i Landan*, 1961].

Armfelt, G.M. *Resan till Italien: Gustaf Mauritz Armfelts resedagbok 1783–1784*, ed. R. Knapas. Stockholm: Atlantis, 1997.

Ballantye, T., and A. Burton (eds). *Bodies in Contact: Rethinking Colonial Encounters in World History*. Durham, NC: Duke University Press, 2005.

Black, J. *The British and the Grand Tour*. London: Croom Helm, 1985.

_____. *The British Abroad: The Grand Tour in the Eighteenth Century*. New York: St Martin's Press, 1992.

Bonsdorff, C. von. *Gustav Mauritz Armfelt: Levnadsskildring*, vol. 1. Helsinki: Svenska Litteratursällskapet i Finland, 1930.

Brenner, A. *Your Mexican Holiday: A Modern Guide*. New York: G.P. Putnam's Sons, 1932.

Bruner, E.M. 'Transformation of Self in Tourism'. *Annals of Tourism Research* 18(2) (1991), 238–50, doi: 10.1016/0160-7383(91)90007-X.

Chard, C. *Pleasure and Guilt on the Grand Tour: Travel Writing and Imaginative Geography, 1600–1830*. Manchester: Manchester University Press, 1999.

Clifford, J. *Routes: Travel and Translation in the Late Twentieth Century*. Cambridge, MA: Harvard University Press, 1997.

Codell, J.F. 'Reversing the Grand Tour: Guest Discourse in Indian Travel Narratives'. *Huntington Library Quarterly* 70(1) (2007), 173–89, doi: 10.1525/hlq.2007.70.1.173.

Cohen, E. 'A Phenomenology of Tourist Experiences'. *Sociology* 13(2) (1979), 179–201, doi: 10.1177/003803857901300203.

Conrads, N. 'Das Incognito: Standesreisen ohne Konventionen', in R. Babel and W. Paravicini (eds), *Grand Tour: Adeliges Reisen und europäische Kultur vom 14. bis zum 18. Jahrhundert* (Ostfildern: Thorbecke, 2005), 591–607.

Currie, G. 'Mexico in the Eyes of D.H. Lawrence'. *Brooklyn Daily Eagle* 87(217) (7 August 1927), section Sunday Eagle Magazine, 15.

Edgren-Henrichson, N. (ed.). *Dolce far niente in Arabia: Georg August Wallin and his Travels in the 1840s*. Helsinki: Svenska Litteratursällskapet i Finland, 2014.

Ehrensvärd, C.A. *Matka Italiaan = Resa till Italien 1780, 1781, 1782*. Helsinki: Artemisia, 2002 [orig. Stockholm: 1786].

Galani-Moutafi, V. 'The Self and the Other: Traveler, Ethnographer, Tourist'. *Annals of Tourism Research* 27(1) (2000), 203–24, doi: 10.1016/S0160-7383(99)00066-3.

Gammerl, B. 'Emotional Styles – Concepts and Challenges'. *Rethinking History*, 16(2) (2012), 161–75, doi: 10.1080/13642529.2012.681189.

Gilmore, J.H., and B.J. Pine II. *Authenticity: What Consumers Really Want*. Boston: Harvard Business School Press, 2007.

Goethe, J.W. von. *Italian Journey (1786–1788)*, trans. W.H. Auden and E. Mayer. New York: Pantheon Books, 1962 [Ger. orig. *Italienische Reise*. Leipzig: Bibliographisches Institut, 1816].

Gunn, D.W. *American and British Writers in Mexico, 1556–1973*. Austin: University of Texas Press, 1974.

Hasan, M., and N. Zaidi, 'Introduction', in S. Ahmed Khan, *A Voyage to Modernism*, ed. and trans. M. Hasan and N. Zaidi (Delhi: Primus Books, 2011), 1–45.

Howe, M. 'Standard-Examiner Book Reviews'. *Ogden Standard-Examiner* 58(38) (21 August 1927), 4.

I'tesamuddin, M. *The Wonders of Vilayet: Being the Memoir, Originally in Persian, of a Visit to France and Britain by Mirza Sheikh Itesamuddin, an Eighteenth Century Indian Gentleman*, trans. K. Haq. Delhi: Chronicle Books, 2008.

I'tisam al Din, M. *Shigurf Namah i Velaët, or, Excellent Intelligence Concerning Europe; Being the Travels of Mirza Itesa Modeen, in Great Britain and France*, trans. J.E. Alexander. London: Parbury, Allen, 1827.

Jamana, S.N. *Mirza Shaikh Itesamuddin and His Travelogue: Shigurf Nama-i-Velayet (Wonders of Britain 1765–1769 AD)*. London: Shams N. Zaman, 2003.

Lawrence, D.H. 'Indians and an Englishman', in D.H. Lawrence, *Mornings in Mexico and Other Essays*, ed. V.C. Hyde (Cambridge: Cambridge University Press, 2009), 111–21.

_____. 'Market Day', in D.H. Lawrence, *Mornings in Mexico and Other Essays*, ed. V.C. Hyde (Cambridge: Cambridge University Press, 2009), 47–55.

_____. 'The Mozo', in D.H. Lawrence, *Mornings in Mexico and Other Essays*, ed. V.C. Hyde (Cambridge: Cambridge University Press, 2009), 35–45.

_____. *Mornings in Mexico and Other Essays*, ed. V.C. Hyde. Cambridge: Cambridge University Press, 2009.

Lefèbvre, H. *Everyday Life in the Modern World*. New Brunswick, NJ: Transaction Books, 1984.

MacCannell, D. *The Tourist: A New Theory of the Leisure Class*. New York: Schocken Books, 1976.

Mackie, E., and S. Dick, *Mexican Journey: An Intimate Guide to Mexico*. New York: Dodge Publishing Company, 1937.

Magelssen, S. 'Tourist Performance in the Twenty-First Century', in S. Magelssen and R. Justice-Malloy (eds), *Enacting History* (Tuscaloosa: University of Alabama Press, 2011), 174–202.

Majchrowicz, D. 'Ideological Voyages: Nationalism, Colonialism and Identity in the Works of Qazi "Abdul Ghaffar"', in R. Micallef and S. Sharma (eds), *On the Wonders of Land and Sea: Persianate Travel Writing* (Cambridge, MA: Harvard University Press, 2013), 132–50.

Matar, N. *Europe through Arab Eyes, 1578–1727*. New York: Columbia University Press, 2009.

Mermann-Jozwiak, E. 'Writing Mexico: Travel and Intercultural Encounter in Contemporary American Literature'. *Symploke* 17(1/2) (2009), 95–114, doi: 10.1353/sym.2009.0023.

Merrill, D. *Negotiating Paradise: U.S. Tourism and Empire in Twentieth-Century Latin America*. Chapel Hill: The University of North Carolina Press, 2009.

Ogilvy, J.A. 'This Postmodern Business'. *Marketing and Research Today* 18(1) (1990), 4–23.

Öhrnberg, K. '"Långt skild från Europas flärd, fåfänga och öfverförfinade bildning": G.A. Wallin, Orienten och Europa'. *Historisk Tidskrift för Finland* 76(4) (1991), 494–507.

_____. 'Vägen till Arabien: "Det förlofvade landet"', in G.A. Wallin, *Skrifter*, vol. 1: *Studieåren och resan till Alexandria*, ed. K. Öhrnberg and P. Berg (Helsinki: Svenska Litteratursällskapet i Finland, 2010), 15–73.

O'Quinn, D. 'Introduction', in M. Abu Talib, *The Travels of Mirza Abu Taleb Khan: In Asia, Africa, and Europe, During the Years 1799, 1800, 1801, 1802, and 1803*, ed. D. O'Quinn, trans. C. Stewart (Broadview Press, 1962), 9–48.

Rojek, C. *Ways of Escape: Modern Transformations in Leisure and Travel*. Basingstoke: Macmillan, 1993.

Roux, M. 'Emotions and Otherness in D.H. Lawrence's Mexican Fiction'. *Études Lawrenciennes* 43 (2012), 215–35.

Sarat, L. *Fire in the Canyon: Religion, Migration, and the Mexican Dream*. New York: New York University Press, 2013.

Schück, H. *Gustaf III's Resa i Italien: Anteckningar af Gudm: Göran Adlerbeth*. Stockholm: Bonnier, 1902.

Simmel, G. *On Individuality and Social Forms: Selected Writings*, ed. D.N. Levine. Chicago: University of Chicago Press, 1971.

Stagl, J. *A History of Curiosity: The Theory of Travel 1550–1800*. Chur: Harwood, 1995.

Tavakoli-Targhi, M. *Refashioning Iran: Orientalism, Occidentalism and Historiography*. Basingstoke, U.K.: Palgrave, 2001.

Urry, J. *The Tourist Gaze: Leisure and Travel in Contemporary Societies*. London: Sage, 1990.

Visram, R. *Ayah, Lascars and Princes: The Story of Indians in Britain 1700–1947*. New York: Routledge, 2015.

Wallin, G.A. *Travels in Arabia (1845 and 1848)* [repr. edn. Cambridge: Falcon-Oleander, 1979].

_____. *Skrifter*, vol. 1: *Studieåren och resan till Alexandria*, ed. K. Öhrnberg and P. Berg. Helsinki: Svenska Litteratursällskapet i Finland, 2010.

_____. *Skrifter*, vol. 2: *Det första året i Egypten 1843–1844*, ed. K. Öhrnberg and P. Berg. Helsinki: Svenska Litteratursällskapet i Finland, 2011.

Woodcock, G. 'Mexico and the English Novelist'. *Western Review* 21(1) (1956), 21–32.

Chapter 3

Anthropologists
Feelings in the Field

Pascal Eitler and Joseph Ben Prestel

In the 1970s, the American anthropologist Renato Rosaldo conducted fieldwork together with his wife Michelle Z. Rosaldo in the northern part of Luzon, an island in the Philippines. Living among the Ilongot, who inhabit this region, Rosaldo encountered an emotional practice that left him puzzled. From conversations and direct observation, he learned that some Ilongot men used headhunting as a way of coping with bereavement. The Ilongot told Rosaldo that it was 'rage, born of grief' that motivated them to kill other human beings. While the anthropologist found it difficult to elaborate on this practice in the 1970s, he took up the issue again in the 1980s, after the death of his wife. According to Rosaldo, his own experience of bereavement made him understand the practice of headhunting; he could now see how the kind of rage the Ilongot had described to him could result from grief. It was fourteen years after his first encounter with the particular emotional practice of 'headhunting' that he finally thought he had understood this aspect of local culture.[1]

* * *

The case of Renato Rosaldo is a prominent example of anthropologists discussing the role of emotions in their fieldwork. Between the late eighteenth and the late twentieth century, various scholars sought to understand the emotions of people living in what they perceived as other cultures. In this context, anthropologists developed influential frameworks for

---

Notes for this chapter begin on page 104.

investigating, describing and analysing internal and interactional feelings of different actors, milieus and societies. For several of these scholars, an everyday part of their fieldwork involved encountering the emotions of foreign people, whom they labelled at times as 'savage', 'primitive' or 'exotic'. Drawing on these encounters, anthropologists tried to understand the manifold possibilities, contexts and perhaps even necessary aspects of human relations to the world. From a historical perspective, anthropologists have taken part in very different emotional encounters over time, not only because of the different societies and milieus they have tried to study but also because their approaches to feelings have undergone radical shifts. This process of change was especially significant during the twentieth century, when anthropology, until then a semi-professional practice, became a well-defined academic discipline, based on adequate training, participant observation and fieldwork.

The present chapter deals with the history of anthropologists' shifting approaches to emotions and emotional encounters. At the centre of the following pages lies the question of how anthropologists' depictions of emotions both conditioned and reflected the encounters between researchers and their subjects of study. How did these depictions change? Under which conditions and with which effects? What role did emotions play in their encounters with their subjects of study? How did anthropologists' depictions and interpretations of their own feelings differ from their depictions and interpretations of others' feelings? And how did encounters turn other people's emotions into 'other' emotions? In order to answer these questions, the chapter considers a series of key texts that were published in the sixty years stretching roughly from 1920 to 1980. As most of these texts have become part of the canonical literature of anthropology, they can be considered as significant models for the way in which anthropologists conceptualized and experienced feelings in the field. Looking back at these texts, scholars have distinguished between models that treat emotions as natural phenomena and others that treat them as cultural phenomena.[2] This chapter, however, seeks to demonstrate that it might be more helpful to differentiate between those anthropologists who were more interested in different societies and societal structures and those who were more interested in the self and different forms of subjectivation.

While such an approach allows for a concise account of the vast field of anthropology, it also comes with several limitations. Three observations can serve to highlight the approach that animates the present chapter. First, the 'selection of case studies' does not aim at reflecting the history of the entire discipline in all its nuances and variations. While authors have shown that historically distinct strands of the discipline have emerged in different countries, anthropology today has splintered into a variety of highly diverging approaches, with the main line of division being that between social and cultural anthropology.³ The selection of case studies in this chapter is based on the understanding that certain texts can be thought of as having been particularly influential when considered on an international scale.

Second, the 'theories of power' in anthropology have been a topic of controversial debate for a long time. This debate concerns, among other things, such questions as the discipline's relation to colonialism, the agency of local sources and intermediaries, the non-Western origins of anthropology and anthropology's emancipatory potential. While not all of these questions are of immediate relevance to the following analysis, the question of whether anthropology has been chiefly concerned with propagating a specifically 'Western' story of scientific progress is highly relevant to any treatment of the discipline. As part of a global history of encounters, this chapter places anthropology in a global context: it is impossible to imagine the rise of the discipline without taking into account new long-distance interactions and mutual exchange.⁴ In turn, these interactions and exchanges were not simply a projection of European states' power but were also fundamentally shaped by a variety of actors in other parts of the world. The nineteenth century marked a shift in these power relations, as European empires came to occupy an unprecedented position of global hegemony. In this respect, the chapter follows Talal Asad's argument that anthropology:

> emerged as a distinctive discipline at the beginning of the colonial era, that it became a flourishing academic profession towards its close, ... [and] that throughout this period its efforts were devoted to a description and analysis – carried out by Europeans, for a European audience – of non-European societies dominated by European power.⁵

With the rise of national movements and the creation of universities in decolonizing nation states, however, a growing number of non-Western anthropologists began to be active in the field. The following chapter discusses this aspect of the history of anthropology in more detail through a study of the work of the Egyptian anthropologist Hamed Ammar.

Third, the 'definition of the discipline' complicates a long durée account. Who counts as an anthropologist and when and where? Anthropology only developed into a clearly defined field of professional practice during the twentieth century. This process of professionalization was based on the exclusion of 'amateurs' through the insistence on adequate training as well as concrete methodological standards. For the eighteenth and nineteenth centuries in particular, it is rather difficult – if not futile – to try to determine whether authors primarily considered themselves to be anthropologists, philosophers, geographers, travel writers or something altogether different. In fact, these categories become less and less meaningful the further historians research the eras before the professionalization of the discipline in the twentieth century. The texts considered in this chapter are therefore chosen with respect to a genealogy of anthropology that begins in the twentieth century. Yet this approach also necessitates a few reflections on the precursors of professional anthropologists.

'Noble Savages'? Encounters in Anthropology's Precursors

The emergence of anthropology as an academic field in the twentieth century was predicated on at least three dynamics reaching back to the eighteenth century: longer stays of Europeans in non-European societies; detailed published descriptions of these societies; and the formation of a specific understanding of European exceptionalism in which scholars imagined the region as being set apart from the rest of the globe.[6] A variety of authors contributed to descriptions of non-European societies during this earlier period, among them missionaries, travellers and diplomats. The great oceanic voyages of the eighteenth century in particular, along with the literary success of travel literature and natural histories that came out of these voyages, contributed to the formation of anthropological knowledge. These texts often combined zoological with geographical impressions and analyses of foreign places in Africa, Asia, South America or the South Pacific.[7]

An important example of this kind of proto-anthropological research is the work of Georg Forster, a German polymath and humanist, born in 1754.[8] In his popular 1777 scientific travel book, *A Voyage Round the World*, Forster published detailed descriptions of the local people he met on his long journeys to different islands in the South Pacific, which he undertook between 1772 and 1775, together with James Cook.[9] Trying to understand the living conditions, conflict strategies and gender relations of these foreign societies, Forster made a remarkable effort to not prejudge them. While he was clearly reproducing Eurocentric hierarchies by differentiating between 'civilized' and 'barbaric' people, he also modified this distinction.[10]

In this sense, Forster tried to avoid viewing the local population with any prejudices when he and his fellow travellers observed 'cannibalism' in New Zealand. He described not only the disgust and the anger of many 'civilized' European sailors, some of whom were 'so unreasonably incensed' that they planned to kill all of these 'barbarians'. Moreover, he remarked that none of his British fellow travellers had the authority 'to punish the imaginary crime of a people whom they had no right to condemn'. He also directed his readers' attention to the emotions he thought he observed in a local man from the Society Islands, who travelled with him. Only this man 'shone out with superior lustre' because he showed compassion not only with the person killed but also with the 'unhappy parents of the victim', and cried.[11]

Forster's descriptions thus contain much more than just the conventional picture of the 'noble savage'.[12] They shed light on the polyvalence of the 'otherness' that supposedly distinguishes the 'civilized' from the 'barbarians' and the 'barbarians' from the 'noble savages'. Forster's attempt to avoid prejudice clearly premediated his emotional encounters – at least as far as these encounters are explicitly described in his studies. Through this, he foreshadowed the sort of dispassionate approach to the emotions of others that would later become key to professional anthropologists. While Forster was not the first to do this, his efforts to avoid prejudice against native people were quite nuanced and, due to the popularity of his book, widely read. Forster's journey to the South Pacific was thus one of the earliest and most-often cited examples in scientific travel books of Europeans or North Americans with a proto anthropological interest in the understanding of 'primitive', 'exotic' people and their foreign habits, relationships and emotions.[13] While Forster and his contemporaries at the end of the eighteenth century distinguished between 'barbaric' and 'civilized' emotions, they did not see Europe and Europeans as being above comparison with the rest of the world.[14] In this way, authors like Forster paved the way for anthropology as an academic discipline as it emerged at the beginning of the twentieth century.

Different Registers of Emotional Encounter – Bronislaw Malinowski

Introductions to anthropology often portray Bronislaw Malinowski as a key figure of the discipline, who played a great role in the shift from 'armchair anthropology' to an academic discipline largely based on appropriate training, participant observation and fieldwork.[15] Born in 1884 in Krakow, Malinowski spent the formative years of his studies after 1910 at the London School of Economics.[16] London not only proved influential as a new intellectual home for him; the British Empire itself also shaped the young anthropologist's approach when he set out to gather information in the field. In 1914, Malinowski travelled from Britain to Australia in order to conduct research on 'primitive cultures' in Melanesia. This trip ultimately resulted in the book *Argonauts of the Western Pacific*, which became a foundational text in anthropology soon after its first publication in 1922.[17] Malinowski conducted the fieldwork for his book between

1914 and 1917 on a number of islands in the Pacific Southeast of Papua New Guinea, most importantly among them the Trobriand Islands. The choice of this specific region for fieldwork was in part due to imperial and personal ties and in part a matter of coincidence. Malinowski's research was sponsored by funds that his mentor Charles Gabriel Seligman and Alfred Cort Haddon had secured from the British industrialist Robert Mond. Seligman and Haddon had both already conducted fieldwork in Melanesia and shared an interest in further studies of the region. As they provided Malinowski with reference letters to their extensive contacts, he was not only able to draw on the support of the agents of the colonial state but also on a network of missionaries and traders, who helped him establish contacts with local communities.[18]

Emotions played an important role in *Argonauts of the Western Pacific*. In his preface to the first edition, the anthropologist James Frazer praised Malinowski for 'remembering' that 'emotions' were as significant as 'reason'. According to Frazer's reading of the book, Malinowski was 'constantly at pains to discover the emotional as well as the rational basis of human action'.[19] While Frazer referred to the emotions of the subjects studied, the book also included passages on the emotions of the anthropologist in his encounters with the islanders. Nevertheless, a curious split marked Malinowski's writing on his own emotions. His study offered two accounts of his initial arrival on the Trobriand Islands, where he was to conduct his fieldwork: one in the introduction on methodology and another in the book's empirical part. In his introduction, Malinowski describes a 'feeling of hopelessness and despair after many obstinate but futile attempts had entirely failed to bring me into real touch with the natives' during his first visits to the village.[20] This experience led to 'periods of despondency, when I buried myself in the reading of novels, as a man might take to drink in a fit of tropical depression and boredom'.[21] Malinowski's account of this frustrating encounter serves to introduce the 'foundation stones' of the 'ethnographer's magic, by which he is able to evoke the real spirit of the natives, the true picture of tribal life'.[22] Besides pursuing scientific interests, the author urges the anthropologist to apply special methods of 'collecting, manipulating and fixing his evidence' as well as to 'live without other white men, right among the natives'.[23] The book suggests that Malinowski had himself learned 'how to behave' and to live 'in harmony' among the villagers in this way.[24]

Between the introduction and the empirical part of the book, however, the presentation of emotions in the encounter changes. After the remarks on methodology, the anthropologist's 'hopelessness' and 'despair' disappear from the account. What Malinowski describes to his readers in the empirical part as 'our imaginary first visit ashore' rather reads like a smooth promenade. Instead of 'despondency', he notes that '[i]t is difficult to convey the feelings of intense interest and suspense with which an Ethnographer enters for the first time the district that is to be the future scene of his field-work'.[25] Parallel to this change in the presentation of the anthropologist's feelings, the portrayal of the island's inhabitants in the encounter undergoes changes, too. The methodological part of the book highlights the idea that more mutual interaction with the anthropologist can also prompt reactions from native inhabitants. Malinowski informs his readers, for example, that during his second visit to the village he exchanged '[a] few compliments in pidgin-English' and 'some tobacco changing hands', which 'induced an atmosphere of mutual amiability'.[26] In the empirical part, however, the presence of the anthropologist in the encounter is much less prominent. At the same time, the behaviour of the inhabitants of the island is described in more general terms: 'As soon as an interesting stranger arrives, half the village assembles around him, talking loudly and making remarks about him, frequently uncomplimentary, and altogether assuming a tone of jocular familiarity'.[27] In *Argonauts of the Western Pacific*, the depiction of emotions in the encounter thus moves from an ambiguous scene of mutual interaction and potential misunderstanding to a smooth narrative about the general emotional reactions of the villagers.

Other avenues of inquiry provide more detailed information about the encounter between Malinowski and the villagers. Malinowski's posthumously published diary shows, for instance, how much he relied on local informants and demonstrates that he was regularly confronted with problems of language, which clearly hampered his participation in certain emotional practices such as joking.[28] The diary also highlights how Malinowski's ambiguous feelings of interest were often paired with intense frustration. Yet, for the most part, the descriptions of encounters in *Argonauts of the Western Pacific* generally seem to ignore the anthropologist's self. The villagers' active role in emotional communication with him and his own conflicting feelings during fieldwork only play a relevant role insofar as they have to be considered for purposes of methodology. He ascribes emotions mainly to the subjects of his study. During fieldwork, the emotions of the villagers have to be brought up. The anthropologist's emotions, however, need to be reined in, as they risk 'interfering' with the information obtained through observation and statements from 'the natives'.[29] In this context, Malinowski's writing ultimately reflects what some scholars have described as a 'colonial textual practice' that obscures the fragility of European actors in the encounter.[30]

A picture of Malinowski during his stay on the island of Kiriwina in 1918 demonstrates the particular ambiguity of this situation (Figure 3.1).[31]

Figure 3.1 'Malinowski Watching Children at Play, Teyava Village, Kiriwina, May 1918'. Courtesy LSE Library, Malinowski Collection, MALINOWSKI/3/18/10.

Here, the anthropologist is shown as he watches children at play. His presence in the village, his proximity to the villagers and his position as an outside observer are all clearly evident. In this respect, the photo has an almost didactic quality, as if it intended to teach 'objective' behaviour in the field. At second glance, however, the picture seems to raise more questions than it can answer. Who took this picture and why is Malinowski in it at all? It was most likely a pearl trader named Billy Hancock who captured the scene. Hancock, who had taken up photography before Malinowski's arrival, made it possible to show that the anthropologist had been 'there', while at the same time allowing the author to emphasize his seemingly detached presence in a way that might serve as learning material for other anthropologists.[32]

It is telling for the history of the photo and this model of anthropological fieldwork that Malinowski played down the role of intermediaries like Hancock for his own work. The image of an English-Australian pearl trader who organized a photo shoot in a local village did not quite fit the idea of the anthropologist who conducted his fieldwork among the 'natives' without contact to other 'Europeans'. With the erasure of these working conditions and the generalization of 'native' behaviour, this mode of anthropology was interested in the 'group-oriented' rather than the 'personal', the 'formal' rather than the 'informal', as later anthropologists would note.[33] At the same time, this did not mean that emotions were absent from Malinowski's account of the encounter. It only meant that they were considered to be either part of the methodology or part of seemingly objective social structures. The emotions of the 'self' were in this way most present in other registers of knowledge, such as the anthropologist's diary or Malinowski's 'private' dabbling in psychoanalysis.[34] Such a division in two different emotional registers was closely bound up with the idea that a 'dispassionate' and 'objective' methodology should frame the encounters of anthropologists with their subjects of research during the interwar period.[35] The two emotional registers ultimately produced a bifurcation of the encounter into the anthropologist's scholarly interest in social structures and his private interest in the self.

'A Lack of Deep Feelings'? Margret Mead

In this context, it is perhaps no coincidence that some years later, in 1928, another anthropologist put the 'lack' of certain feelings at the centre of her work: Margaret Mead's book *Coming of Age in Samoa: A Psychological Study of Primitive Youth for Western Civilisation* became one of the bestselling field studies of anthropology and its author, born in 1901, one of the most influential anthropologists of the second half of the twentieth century.[36] Before embarking on her first great research stay in the South Pacific, Mead studied at Columbia University in New York under the German anthropologist Franz Boas and the American anthropologist Ruth Benedict, two of the leading figures in the emergence of cultural anthropology in the United States.[37]

Cultural anthropology as Mead pursued it was focused not only on the society of its research subjects but also – and much more than social anthropology – on local people's perception of themselves, their subjectivation and their 'individuality', as she put it.[38] This led Mead to pay close attention to the emotions of others and their seemingly other emotions. At the beginning of her study, she explained that in order to gain insight into these emotions she tried 'to minimize the differences' between herself and her research subjects by 'speaking their language, eating their food, sitting barefoot and cross-legged upon the pebbly floor', conducting interviews and listening to stories.[39]

But Mead not only tried to understand these emotions – she also tried to learn from them. Although she did not offer much insight into her own 'individuality' and her own emotions and encounters, she legitimized and promoted her emotional encounters with local people as liberating and enlightening. In her book on adolescent girls in three villages in the Samoan islands, Mead tried to learn about these girls' development and their seemingly nearly conflict-free passage from childhood to adulthood. Mead – an anti-racist and a feminist – also wanted to learn from these 'primitive', 'exotic' people how adolescence, the family model, gender roles and sexual manners could and should be reformed in North America and Europe.[40]

In comparison to Malinowski, the feelings of these adolescent girls – or their 'lack of deep feelings', as Mead thought she observed – played a much greater role in Mead's work. In contrast to North American or European girls, Mead thought that the 'Samoan girl never tastes the rewards of romantic love as we know it, nor does she suffer as an old maid who has appealed to no lover . . . or as the frustrated wife in a marriage which has not fulfilled her high demands'.[41] Unlike 'our civilisation', the 'simpler civilisation' of the Samoan islands seemed to neither know nor show 'passionate attachment' and 'strong emotions'.[42] Local people always preferred 'a moderate amount of feeling'. Mead was, so it seems, not shocked but fascinated by this way of dealing with emotions and the self, attributing to the local people a great 'emotional stability' and less 'stress' and 'strain'.[43] For Mead, it was this 'moderate amount of feeling' that gave her research subjects the possibility to make 'affectional choices' without having to 'hasten in the choices which they make', allowing them to achieve a kind of tolerance towards different ways of life that Mead thought European or North American societies lacked.[44] But 'there were prices to pay for' this sort of tolerance – namely, 'less individuality'.[45]

According to Mead, cultural anthropology demonstrates 'that neither race nor common humanity can be held responsible for many of the forms which even such basic human emotions as love and fear and anger take under different social conditions', conditions that imply much more than just social structures.[46] In this sense, Mead was not only interested in Samoan society but above all in the Samoan self and Samoans' emotions. This fascination with the Samoan self ultimately premediated her emotional encounters with local people. The Samoan self, she argued, 'shows that it is not necessary to channel so deeply the affection of a child'.[47] Through the American paediatrician Benjamin Spock's 1946 bestselling advice book on baby and child care, this new view of children, emotions and the self also had a considerable impact on reforming child rearing in North America and Europe.[48]

'An Attitude of Detachment'? Claude Lévi-Strauss

While Margret Mead became one of the bestselling anthropologists of the twentieth century as well as one of the leading representatives of cultural anthropology, a very different kind of structural anthropology emerged in the 1940s and 1950s on the other side of the Atlantic. It was Claude Lévi-Strauss, born in 1908, who became the most important representative of this structural anthropology, which paid much less or at times no attention to emotions at all. Rather than being interested in the self, this anthropology sought to study different societies, their social structures and, in particular, their semantics and symbols. Lévi-Strauss, who studied philosophy and law at the Sorbonne in Paris, conducted his first extensive field studies in Brazil in the late 1930s and published his revised notes in 1955 in his book *Tristes Tropiques*.[49] Lévi-Strauss was less interested in the feelings of the local people in the South American rainforest and more interested in their central mythologies, viewing them as complex models of societal order. In doing so, he turned away from the South Pacific and forged the link between anthropology and linguistics.[50] In Lévi-Strauss's account, it wasn't so much the local people who were 'triste' but rather he who had the impression that these people would pass away very soon.

In this sense, Lévi-Strauss was not simply unaware of emotions. In fact, in a way comparable to Malinowski's *Diary*, he began his *Tristes Tropiques* with an emotional lamentation about the 'hunger', 'exhaustion', 'illness' and 'routine duties' involved in such an expedition and spoke very clearly and warmly about his own feelings for the rainforest.[51] Sometimes emotions even made it into his analysis: he observed, for example, that parents of the Nambikwara, a very small society of Amazonian indigenes, 'show . . . the liveliest affection for their children'.[52] But he gave no special place to the concrete emotions of local people or his emotional encounters with them. Moreover, in contrast to cultural anthropologists, structural anthropologists did not seem to depend much on face-to-face interactions. It is, therefore, characteristic that Lévi-Strauss usually spoke about the expression of emotions – thus strictly separating the emotions from their expression – writing that the people 'seem to feel, or at any rate to show' this or that feeling. From the perspective of structural anthropology, what they 'really' feel is not observable and not important.[53]

Even against the background of 'cannibalism, which is of all savage practices the one we find the most horrible and disgusting', he made the challenge of a dispassionate mode of anthropology very clear: if you really want to understand another society, you have to understand that 'no human society is fundamentally good'.[54] He characterized his own professional attitude as 'an attitude of detachment'.[55] In this sense, he claimed some years later that emotions are 'the most obscure side of man', but that they are 'not primary because . . . [they are] incomprehensible'.[56] This claim premediated the negligible importance of emotions and emotional encounters in his studies. In this case, it was not the emotions of other people, or seemingly other emotions that anthropologists encounter during their fieldwork, but only semantics and symbols: 'wild thinking', as Lévi-Strauss put it when distinguishing between two supposedly very different but equally complex and rational kinds of thinking, 'modern' and 'premodern'.[57]

Differences between cultural anthropologists, such as Mead, social anthropologists, such as Malinowski, and structural anthropologists, such as Lévi-Strauss, cannot be explained adequately if we only differentiate between culturalist and particularistic versus naturalistic and universalistic approaches. Scholarship can analyse the different role of emotions and emotional encounters within anthropological research much better if it examines anthropologists' diverging interests, distinguishing between an interest in societies and social structures on the one hand and an interest in the self and subjectivations on the other.

While structural anthropologists did not place emotions at the centre of their research interests, they did pave the way for a new kind of anthropology of emotions that emerged during the 1960s, 1970s and especially the 1980s, for they highlighted the importance of semantics, symbols and language in general. It is also possible to speak about such a new form of anthropology of emotions as it emerged in the context of postcolonialism and an increasing critique of colonialism, Orientalism and racism.[58] Lévi-Strauss thus might be regarded as one of the last researchers among canonical anthropologists of the twentieth century whose fieldwork in the 1930s, 1940s and 1950s was deeply shaped by colonialism and the important role of French academics in Brazil during this period.

Testing Emotions at Home – Hamed Ammar

In the twentieth century, anthropology was not limited to colonial settings or the encounter between the 'West and the Rest'. With the spread of new universities and research institutions in various parts of the world, a growing number of non-Western scholars studied the discipline and identified themselves as anthropologists. Starting in the 1930s at the latest, studies in which authors conducted fieldwork in what they presented as their 'own' societies appeared in regions like South Asia and the Middle East.[59] This dynamic gained further traction through the process of decolonization after the Second World War, when the governments of newly independent countries sought to build on the expertise of local anthropologists to 'reform' and 'develop' their societies.[60]

The work of Hamed Ammar, who is today considered to be among the pioneers of Egyptian anthropology, offers a glimpse into how these non-Western anthropologists conceptualized their fieldwork. During his doctoral studies in London, Ammar returned to Silwa, his native village in the Aswan governorate of Upper Egypt, in order to conduct six months of fieldwork between 1950 and 1951.[61] Based on his fieldwork, he wrote the book *Growing up in an Egyptian Village*, which was published in 1954.[62] Ammar justified the choice of Silwa for fieldwork not because it could be thought of as 'typical' for all Egyptian villages but rather because of his 'personal connection' to the village. He stated that because he was raised there and frequently went back during the holidays, he was 'in close emotional, spiritual and intellectual touch with the villagers, a position which has its merits and demerits for such a study'.[63] Ammar does not spell out these 'merits' and 'demerits' in detail; he only mentions that he did not have to learn the local language or dialect.[64] Yet, his chapter on method offers some insight into how the fieldwork in Silwa was conducted. In this part of the book, Ammar presents his use of different anthropological theories, including the writings of Malinowski and Mead, stressing his interest in a 'psychological' approach that also takes into account feelings, thoughts and motivations.[65]

The methods that Ammar used in order to get at these thoughts and feelings included standardized tests. He conceded that the application of procedures such as the Rorschach test in anthropology was contested, but noted that researchers had demonstrated that 'the principles of the test could be applied with some validity in cross-cultural situations'.[66] Ammar thus used standardized procedures, including the 'Stewart Emotional Response' test. Still, he found it difficult to collect information from the adults of the village, a problem that, as he thought, had no causal relation to the use of such tests. Ammar interpreted this as the villagers being 'reluctant to engage in an activity which might be considered as dangerous gossip'. Yet, the anthropologist found a way to break the villagers' silence. According to Ammar, the inhabitants of Silwa asked him: 'And what is the use of all this to us?'[67] This led him to argue that they might be more willing to cooperate if the anthropologist were to help them with their daily problems and become a useful member of their community. Ammar's approach resonates with stories that the Awlad Ali Bedouins in Egypt's western desert would convey to Lila Abu-Lughod in the late 1970s, namely that researchers before her had mostly handed them questionnaires, which they described as a form of 'exam'.[63] Concerning the emotions of the anthropologist, the dominant mode of Ammar's book is that of the dispassionate and objective observer. This mode can also be found in the work of other early non-Western anthropologists who conducted their fieldwork 'at home'. The future President of Kenya, Jomo Kenyatta, for instance, published an anthropological study of the Kikuyu people in central Kenya in 1938 following his studies at the London School of Economics with Bronislaw Malinowski.[69] Although it was a work with clear political purport, Malinowski praised Kenyatta in the introduction of the book for presenting 'the facts . . . to a large extent without any passion or feeling'.[70]

However, the dispassionate mode of anthropology came under attack in calls for 'non-Western' anthropology 'at home' during the 1970s. In the context of a wider critique of the discipline, scholars had begun to question the notion that anthropologists 'must do . . . [the] utmost to repress' their presence in their fieldwork.[71] In an essay on 'anthropology at home', the Tongan anthropologist Epeli Hau'ofa stressed that it was precisely emotions that allowed the 'indigenous' anthropologist to understand the subjects of his study better than any foreign scholar could. He describes that he 'found it relatively easy to keep fair control over my emotional involvement' during his field work in Trinidad and Papua New Guinea. When he returned to Tonga, however, this 'detachment' became far more difficult. Hau'ofa stressed that although the material (including poetry and fictional essays) he produced during his fieldwork in Tonga as an 'emotional release' was 'nonacademic', he could tap into it as a source 'for more scientific analysis' later. The anthropologist concluded that 'foreign' researchers had largely ignored the 'sentimental dimension of human relationships' and that their studies of the island had thus been 'incomplete and . . . half-meaningful'. From Hau'ofa's perspective, it was up to 'indigenous' anthropologists to fill this void.[72]

The cases of non-Western anthropologists conducting their fieldwork at home are instructive for at least two reasons. First, the figure of the newcomer is replaced by the notion of returning home. Instead of taking on the role of the scholar dropped off on a remote island, anthropologists encounter the subjects of their studies in a place with which they are (or are supposed to be) intimately familiar. This shift also reflects the fact that during the second half of the twentieth century anthropologists worked in the context of nation states, which were based on an ideal of national unity, rather than colonial empires where difference was a foundational aspect of politics and domination.[73] Second, the works of non-Western anthropologists highlight the shifts in perceptions of the role of emotions in these homecomings. As far as Ammar is concerned, the story fits into a narrative that was common in popular representations of the Egyptian middle class (*afandiyya*) in the mid twentieth century.

Receiving a university education in an urban setting functioned as a rite of passage for men from the newly educated middle class. After their studies, these men returned to their rural roots, where they first encountered incomprehension on the part of the local population before they could proceed to reform the village and bring modern improvements to their rural communities.[74] Ammar's study reflects this narrative when he stresses that the villagers lacked an understanding of his scientific mission, in which he used state of the art tests to analyse their emotions and thoughts for a greater good. More than twenty years later, Hau'ofa presented a strikingly different scenario. Here, the return to Tonga opened up the possibility for Hau'ofa to regain a form of emotional authenticity that he had lost after leaving the familiar environment: '[M]y own sentiments have changed from the futility of unconscious imitation of foreign ways to a search for firm roots. That was the main reason for my return to Tonga'.[75] At first sight, these two cases might seem somewhat anecdotal. However, they correspond to a shift that also applies to a number of other anthropologists and ultimately indicates a larger change in the discipline: the increasingly prominent role of anthropologists' emotions and self in depictions of fieldwork.

The Anthropologist's Emotions – Jean Briggs and Renato Rosaldo

In 1970, the American anthropologist Jean L. Briggs published a study that was pioneering for a field that soon came to be known as the 'anthropology of emotions'.[76] Briggs had spent seventeen months between 1963 and 1965 in the Chantrey Inlet on the Arctic coast of Canada with a local tribe called the Utkuhikhalingmiut.[77] Originally, Briggs wanted to conduct a study of shamans, but as it turned out that the tribe consisted of devout Anglicans, she began looking for a different topic. Briggs states that the subjects of her study were not keen on answering inquiries about the past. Under these circumstances, she notes, emotions were the most accessible aspect of local life. What struck her about the Utkuhikhalingmiut was the high value accorded to emotional control.[78] Briggs learned about the importance of emotional control for the group she studied in an incident in which she 'lost her temper' during her fieldwork. The incident arose when a group of visiting sports fishermen wanted to borrow a canoe that Briggs thought was vital for the community. Briggs, who served as the translator between the Utkuhikhalingmiut and the sports fishermen, 'exploded' and told the fishermen 'unsmilingly and in a cold voice . . . a variety of things'.[79] Ultimately, she refused the request, thus going against the accommodating behaviour of the Utkuhikhalingmiut and their ideal of emotional control. As a result, she was ostracized from the community for about three months.[80]

In the introduction to her book, Briggs offers a methodological reflection on the ways in which she sought to understand emotions in the encounters with the subjects of her study. She stresses that she found it necessary not only to observe the 'behavior and feelings' of the local population but also her own emotions:

> I describe the feelings that I myself had in particular situations. My justification for this is that I was an intrinsic part of the research situation. The responses of my hosts to my actions and my feelings, and my own reactions to the situations in which I found myself – my empathy and my experience of contrasts between my feelings and those of my hosts – were all invaluable sources of data.[81]

In practice, for this kind of analysis, Briggs often provided descriptions of her body. She notes, for instance, that the frequency of smiling made her feel 'wooden within and without'.[82] Descriptions and 'readings' of the body are also the means through which she analyses the emotions of the subjects of her study. 'Smiles', 'laughter' or 'gleaming eyes' are the indicators she draws on to attribute the existence of feelings to others. Her formulations suggest that emotions are a presence within the subjects of her study and that they become obvious to her once they 'get out' through conscious or unconscious expression. Not least, her ultimate inability to meet the local expectation of emotional control, which resulted in her being ostracized, seems to stem from a bodily impulse. As she became more and more isolated, Briggs describes that she slipped into a depression, which led her to communicate emotions through her body. From her perspective, this worsened her situation and contributed to her isolation, as it only seemed to confirm the others' perceptions that she would not follow the ideal of emotional control.[83]

Whereas Briggs placed primary focus on the body, later scholars interested in the anthropology of emotions took language as their main point of departure. In the two decades after Briggs' study, authors including Michelle Z. Rosaldo, Catherine Lutz and Lila Abu-Lughod began to argue that anthropologists should direct their energies towards studying the socially determined languages of emotions.[84] These authors shared a self-reflexive mode of observation with Jean Briggs. Yet, from their perspective, the concept of 'inner' emotions that rise to the surface of the body was specific to 'Western' societies and couldn't simply be taken as universal. These authors claimed that the only emotions of a local population accessible to anthropologists were emotions articulated in discourse.[85] At the same time, these authors also had a common interest in the constructions of the self – in the case of Lila Abu-Lughod, for instance, 'a self moved by deep feelings of love and longing'.[86]

Renato Rosaldo's turn to 'experience' to understand others' emotions in his 1989 essay 'Grief and a Headhunter's Rage' represents an ambiguous intervention in this context. After the death of his wife, Michelle, in 1981, Rosaldo began to question the terms borrowed from cultural analysis that he had used to understand the Ilongot practice of headhunting, including 'thick description, multi-vocality, polysemy, richness, and texture'.[87] Much like the arguments about emotions as discourse, these concepts all point to a heavily linguistic understanding of others' emotions. Rosaldo argued, however, that the personal experience of bereavement had helped him understand the practice of the Ilongot in a way that escaped the grasp of these concepts. He claimed that his loss made him feel a similar anger of bereavement, a rage animated by grief. The description of the emotions that Rosaldo now shared with the subjects of his study was very much centred on his body. In the very personal essay, the readers learn about his 'sobs without tears', a 'trembling in my abdomen', or '[p]owerful visceral emotional states' that 'swept over' him.[88] Rosaldo clearly moved from a linguistic mode of understanding others' emotions to a more bodily concept of experience, a sort of common 'affective intensity'.[89] However, his reflection does not correspond to a clear-cut dichotomy of bodily universalism versus cultural constructivism used by many studies. It was not simply a universal body that made him empathize with the Ilongot headhunters but rather something that he described as a shared 'position of the subject', namely the common experience of bereavement. From this perspective, the encounter with others' emotions was as much predicated on 'cultural difference' as it was on differences in 'personal experience'; self and society no longer appeared as separate entities.

Renato Rosaldo's transformed conceptualization of emotions in the encounter reflects a shift that is nowadays evident not only in anthropology. Historians of emotions, for instance, have learned a lot from anthropologists – especially from the new anthropology of emotions as it emerged in the 1970s. In various ways, anthropology was a precursor to historical scholarship that focuses on emotions. Many anthropologists were aware of the importance of emotions much earlier than most historians. They were often confronted with emotions in their daily work on the level of emotional encounters in face-to-face interactions. In the field, anthropologists had to deal with the emotions of others as well as their own emotions. Canonical anthropological texts from Malinowski to Rosaldo illustrate in this context how contemporary knowledge could inform the ways in which anthropologists reflected on feelings in the field.

Whether it be the notion that the researchers' emotions in the encounter can be better expressed in a diary than in the main part of a scientific study, the concept of an emotional authenticity of 'home' in the context of decolonized nation states, or the imperative to provide a detailed account of one's own feelings, historical conjunctures of the place of emotions in knowledge production have exerted a great influence on anthropological fieldwork. This knowledge often premediated the emotional encounters of anthropologists.

At the same time, anthropology evolved into one of the most influential fields for the study of emotion. Anthropologists were not simply the recipients of a coherent body of knowledge about emotions provided by other disciplines, such as psychology or philosophy. Rather, anthropologists frequently pushed for a new understanding of what emotions are or could be, at times even questioning the very existence of emotional categories with cross-cultural validity. This kind of insight was often the result of encounters with what anthropologists understood to be radically different ways of making sense of emotions. In this way, encounters with other, 'barbarian', 'primitive', 'exotic' people mediated a new kind of knowledge about emotions, a dynamic that is probably most obvious in the studies of Margaret Mead and Lila Abu-Lughod.

The shifting interest from society to the self is part of this churning process of premediation and mediation. The texts analysed on the previous pages have shown that it was important for many anthropologists to draw a clear line between society and the self, just as many historians, sociologists or philosophers did. The ways a particular anthropologist viewed the role of emotions in human interactions was often contingent upon whether she or he was primarily interested in emotions as an element of society or as an element of the self. While the self was a topic of psychoanalytic introspection and diary writing for a scholar like Bronislaw Malinowski, it began to occupy a central place in the work of Jane Briggs and other scholars engaged in the new anthropology of emotions that emerged after the 1960s. These diverging interests were simultaneously a component of the premediated understanding about the role of the researcher's self *and* a result of the encounter with the emotions of other people or their seemingly other emotions.

The question as to whether emotions form a part of society or the self also illustrates how anthropologists not only tried to contextualize but also to translate unfamiliar practices and unknown relationships along with their emotional dimensions. While a focus on social structures could lead to a less introspective and detached analysis, as is evident in Malinowski's or Lévi-Strauss' writings, the attempt to understand others' emotions by authors like Briggs or Rosaldo called for quite different translations.

From a historical perspective, it might seem futile to gauge whether such translations necessarily had to fail or to what degree they were even possible.[90] The study of anthropological writing highlights, however, that the conception of emotions as translatable and the impetus to translate them can lead to several pitfalls. The assumption that emotions can be translated often tends to transform others' emotions into other emotions. It is based on the idea – and sometimes maybe the fear – that different cultures produce different emotions. In this sense, emotions can easily become a new stigma of so-called cultural 'otherness'. Moreover, by dealing with emotions from the perspective of cultural studies, scholars also risk treating them as an omnipresent natural feature of human life. This perspective not only implies that every so-called culture supposedly has its own emotions: it also suggests that every culture and every human being has to have emotions. It thus has the tendency to universalize emotions as such, precisely by pointing to their universally assumed particularity. Anthropologists, as much as historians, need to be aware of this paradox.

Today, placing a focus on emotions does not necessarily entail a concentration on society or the self. Historians and anthropologists who are primarily interested in society and social structures focus just as much or as little on emotions as those among their colleagues primarily interested in the self. Just as other dichotomies like nature versus culture or body versus mind have become less rigid and have often proven themselves to be of little use, a strict distinction between society and the self is also no longer convincing. The history of the emotional encounters of anthropologists highlights that this distinction has been conflictual for a while. In this fashion, anthropological scholarship shows that overcoming it might ultimately provide a better understanding of others' or one's own emotions.

Pascal Eitler is a researcher (wissenschaftlicher Mitarbeiter) at the Institute for History, Ethics and Philosophy of Medicine at the Hannover Medical School and currently working in a BMBF-research project on the production and consumption of sexualities and things. He is co-editor of the open access journal *Body Politics*. His most recent book publication is (with Jens Elberfeld) *Zeitgeschichte des Selbst: Therapeutisierung – Politisierung – Emotionalisierung* (Bielefeld: Transcript, 2015).

Joseph Ben Prestel is Assistant Professor (wissenschaftlicher Mitarbeiter) of History at Freie Universität Berlin. Before joining Freie Universität's history department, he held a position at the Center for the History of Emotions at the Max Planck Institute for Human Development in Berlin.

He is the author of *Emotional Cities: Debates on Urban Change in Berlin and Cairo, 1860–1910* (Oxford University Press, 2017) and a co-founder and editor of the *Global Urban History Blog*.

Notes

1. Rosaldo, 'Introduction: Grief and a Headhunter's Rage', 1–21, quotation 1. On emotional practices, see Scheer, 'Are Emotions a Kind of Practice (and Is That What Makes Them Have a History)? A Bourdieuian Approach to Understanding Emotion', 193–220.
2. See, for example, Plamper, *The History of Emotions: An Introduction*.
3. Barth et al., *One Discipline, Four Ways: British, German, French, and American Anthropology*.
4. See, for example, Konishi, Nugent and Shellam, *Indigenous Intermediaries: New Perspectives on Exploration Archives*.
5. Asad, 'Introduction', 14–15.
6. Osterhammel, *Die Entzauberung Asiens: Europa und die asiatischen Reiche im 18. Jahrhundert*.
7. See, for example, Farber, *Finding Order in Nature: The Naturalist Tradition from Linnaeus to E.O. Wilson*.
8. Ackerknecht, 'George Forster, Alexander von Humboldt, and Ethnology', 83–95; Garber and van Hoorn, *Natur—Mensch—Kultur: Georg Forster im Wissenschaftsfeld seiner Zeit*; Heintze, 'Georg Forster (1754–1794)', 69–87, 323–27.
9. Sahlins, *Islands of History*.
10. Forster, *A Voyage Round the World: In His Britannic Majesty's Sloop, Resolution, Commanded by Capt. James Cook, During the Years 1772, 3, 4, and 5*, 211.
11. Forster, *Voyage Round the World*, 513.
12. At this point, see also Plamper, *History of Emotions*, 80–81.
13. See also von Humboldt, *Personal Narrative of Travels to the Equinoctial Regions of the New Continent: During the Years 1799–1804: By Alexander de Humboldt and Aimé Bonpland*; von Kotzebue, *A Voyage of Discovery, into the South Sea and Beering's Straits, for the Purpose of Exploring a North-East Passage, Undertaken in the Years 1815–1818*.
14. Osterhammel, *Entzauberung Asiens*, 375–403.
15. Kenny and Smillie, *Stories of Culture and Place: An Introduction to Anthropology*, 25–50; Kehoe, *Humans: An Introduction to Four-field Anthropology*, 202; Asad, 'Introduction', 9.
16. Young, *Malinowski: Odyssey of an Anthropologist, 1884–1920*, 151–246.
17. Malinowski, *Argonauts of the Western Pacific: An Account of Native Enterprise and Adventure in the Archipelagoes of Melanesian New Guinea*.
18. Malinowski, *Argonauts*, 246, 298–99.
19. Frazer, 'Preface', in Malinowski, *Argonauts*, ix.
20. Malinowski, *Argonauts*, 4.
21. Malinowski, *Argonauts*, 4.
22. Malinowski, *Argonauts*, 6.
23. Malinowski, *Argonauts*, 6.
24. Malinowski, *Argonauts*, 8, 7.
25. Malinowski, *Argonauts*, 55, 51.
26. Malinowski, *Argonauts*, 5.
27. Malinowski, *Argonauts*, 52.
28. Malinowski, *A Diary in the Strict Sense of the Term*, 144–45; on this aspect, see also Plamper, *History of Emotions*, 85.
29. Malinowski, *Argonauts*, 3.

30. See, for example, Konishi, Nugent and Shellam, 'Exploration Archives and Indigenous Histories: An Introduction', 5.
31. On the history of early photography in British New Guinea, see also Lübcke, 'Encounters and the Photographic Record in British New Guinea', 169–87.
32. Young, *Malinowski's Kiriwina: Fieldwork Photography 1915–1918*, 15.
33. Abu-Lughod, *Veiled Sentiments: Honour and Poetry in a Bedouin Society*, 30; on the effects of generalization and abstraction as obscuring the concrete circumstances of early ethnographic encounters, see also: Gascoigne, 'Cross-cultural Knowledge Exchange in the Age of the Enlightenment', 131–45.
34. Young, *Malinowski's Kiriwina*.
35. James, 'The Anthropologist as Reluctant Imperialist', 48.
36. Mead, *Coming of Age in Samoa: A Psychological Study of Primitive Youth for Western Civilisation*.
37. See Darnell, *And Along Came Boas: Continuity and Revolution in Americanist Anthropology*; Geisthövel, *Intelligenz und Rasse: Franz Boas' psychologischer Antirassismus zwischen Amerika und Deutschland, 1920–1942*.
38. Mead, 'Preface to 1973 Edition', unpaginated. On the concept of subjectification and the history of the self, see Foucault, 'The Subject and Power', 777–95.
39. Mead, *Coming*, 10.
40. See also her very influential book on gender constructions in New Guinea: Mead, *Sex and Temperament in Three Primitive Societies*.
41. Mead, *Coming*, 200, 211.
42. Mead, *Coming*, 234, 210.
43. Mead, *Coming*, 128, 231.
44. Mead, *Coming*, 209, 231.
45. Mead, 'Preface', unpaginated.
46. Mead, *Coming*, 4.
47. Mead, *Coming*, 213.
48. Spock, *The Common Sense Book of Baby and Child Care*; Bohannan and van der Elst, *Asking and Listening: Ethnography as Personal Adaptation*, 28.
49. Lévi-Strauss, *World on the Wane*.
50. See, for example, also the work of Georges Dumézil.
51. Lévi-Strauss, *World on the Wane*, 17.
52. Lévi-Strauss, *World on the Wane*, 273–74.
53. Lévi-Strauss, *World on the Wane*, 306.
54. Lévi-Strauss, *World on the Wane*, 385.
55. Lévi-Strauss, *World on the Wane*, 381.
56. Lévi-Strauss, *Totemism*, 68–70. See also Plamper, *History of Emotions*, 99–100.
57. Lévi-Strauss, *The Savage Mind*.
58. See, for example, the works of Edward Said or Talal Asad.
59. Uberoi, Sundar and Deshpande, *Anthropology in the East: Founders of Indian Sociology and Anthropology*; El Shakry, *The Great Social Laboratory: Subjects of Knowledge in Colonial and Postcolonial Egypt*; Hopkins, *Anthropology in Egypt 1900–1967*.
60. Asad, 'Introduction'.
61. Hopkins, *Anthropology in Egypt*, 74–76.
62. Ammar, *Growing up in an Egyptian Village: Silwa, Province of Aswan*.
63. Ammar, *Growing up*, xi.
64. Ammar, *Growing up*, xi.
65. Ammar, *Growing up*, xi.
66. Ammar, *Growing up*, 10.
67. Ammar, *Growing up*, 10.
68. Abu-Lughod, *Veiled Sentiments*, 24.

69. Kenyatta, *Facing Mount Kenya: The Tribal Life of Gikuyu*.
70. Malinowski, 'Introduction', x.
71. Feuchtwang, 'The Colonial Formation of British Social Anthropology', 100.
72. Hau'ofa, 'Anthropology at Home: A South Pacific Islands Experience', 217, 218, 219, 222.
73. On the various uses of difference in empires, see Burbank and Cooper, *Empires in World History: Power and the Politics of Difference*.
74. Ryzova, *The Age of the Efendiyya: Passages to Modernity in National-Colonial Egypt*.
75. Hau'ofa, 'Anthropology at Home', 217.
76. Beatty, 'How Did It Feel for You? Emotion, Narrative and the Limits of Ethnography', 430–31.
77. Briggs, *Never in Anger*.
78. Briggs, *Never in Anger*, 3–4.
79. Briggs, *Never in Anger*, 284.
80. Briggs, *Never in Anger*, 3, 283–99.
81. Briggs, *Never in Anger*, 6.
82. Briggs, *Never in Anger*, 26.
83. Briggs, *Never in Anger*, 285–98.
84. Rosaldo, *Knowledge and Passion: Ilongot Notions of Self and Social Life*; Abu-Lughod, *Veiled Sentiments*; Lutz, *Unnatural Emotions: Everyday Sentiments on a Micronesian Atoll and their Challenge to Western Theory*.
85. See also Plamper, *History of Emotions*, 109–13.
86. Abu-Lughod, *Veiled Sentiments*, 34.
87. Rosaldo, 'Introduction', 2.
88. Rosaldo, 'Introduction', 9.
89. Rosaldo, 'Introduction', 20. For a more substantial discussion on the history of emotions as a history of the body, see Eitler and Scheer, 'Emotionengeschichte als Körpergeschichte: Eine heuristische Perspektive auf religiöse Konversionen im 19. und 20. Jahrhundert', 282–313.
90. See also introduction to this volume.

Bibliography

Abu-Lughod, L. *Veiled Sentiments: Honour and Poetry in a Bedouin Society*. Berkeley: University of California Press, 1986.

Ackerknecht, E.H. 'George Forster, Alexander von Humboldt, and Ethnology'. *Isis* 46(2) (1955), 83–95.

Ammar, H. *Growing up in an Egyptian Village: Silwa, Province of Aswan*. London: Routledge and Kegan Paul, 1954.

Asad, T. 'Introduction', in T. Asad (ed.), *Anthropology & the Colonial Encounter* (New York: Humanities Press, 1973), 9–19.

Barth, F., et al. *One Discipline, Four Ways: British, German, French, and American Anthropology*. Chicago: Chicago University Press, 2005.

Beatty, A. 'How Did It Feel for You? Emotion, Narrative and the Limits of Ethnography'. *American Anthropologist* 112(3) (2010), 430–43, doi: 10.1111/j.1548-1433.2010.01250.x.

Bohannan, P., and D. van der Elst. *Asking and Listening: Ethnography as Personal Adaptation*. Long Grove, IL: Waveland Press, 1998.

Briggs, J.L. *Never in Anger: Portrait of an Eskimo Family*. Cambridge, MA: Harvard University Press, 1970.
Burbank, J., and F. Cooper. *Empires in World History: Power and the Politics of Difference*. Princeton: Princeton University Press, 2010.
Darnell, R. *And Along Came Boas: Continuity and Revolution in Americanist Anthropology*. Amsterdam: Benjamins, 1998.
Eitler, P., and M. Scheer. 'Emotionengeschichte als Körpergeschichte: Eine heuristische Perspektive auf religiöse Konversionen im 19. und 20. Jahrhundert'. *Geschichte und Gesellschaft* 35(2) (2009), 282–313, doi: 10.13109/gege.2009.35.2.282.
El Shakry, O. *The Great Social Laboratory: Subjects of Knowledge in Colonial and Postcolonial Egypt*. Stanford: Stanford University Press, 2007.
Farber, P.L. *Finding Order in Nature: The Naturalist Tradition from Linnaeus to E.O. Wilson*. Baltimore: Johns Hopkins University Press, 2000.
Feuchtwang, S. 'The Colonial Formation of British Social Anthropology', in T. Asad (ed.), *Anthropology & the Colonial Encounter* (New York: Humanities Press, 1973), 71–100.
Forster, G. *A Voyage Round the World: In His Britannic Majesty's Sloop, Resolution, Commanded by Capt. James Cook, During the Years 1772, 3, 4, and 5*, vol. 1. London: B. White et al., 1777.
Foucault, M. 'The Subject and Power'. *Critical Inquiry* 8 (1982), 777–95.
Frazer, J. 'Preface', in B. Malinowski, *Argonauts of the Western Pacific: An Account of Native Enterprise and Adventure in the Archipelagoes of Melanesian New Guinea* (London: Routledge, 1922), vii–xiv.
Garber, J., and T. van Hoorn (eds). *Natur – Mensch – Kultur: Georg Forster im Wissenschaftsfeld seiner Zeit*. Hannover-Laatzen: Wehrhahn, 2006.
Gascoigne, J. 'Cross-cultural Knowledge Exchange in the Age of the Enlightenment', in S. Konishi, M. Nugent and T. Shellam (eds), *Indigenous Intermediaries: New Perspectives on Exploration Archives* (Acton: Australian National University Press, 2015), 131–45.
Geisthövel, A. *Intelligenz und Rasse: Franz Boas' psychologischer Antirassismus zwischen Amerika und Deutschland, 1920–1942*. Bielefeld: Transcript, 2013.
Hau'ofa, E. 'Anthropology at Home: A South Pacific Islands Experience', in H. Fahim (ed.), *Indigenous Anthropology in Non-Western Countries* (Durham: Carolina Academic Press, 1982), 213–22.
Heintze, D. 'Georg Forster (1754–1794)', in W. Marshall (ed.), *Klassiker der Kulturanthropologie: Von Montaigne bis Margaret Mead* (Munich: Beck, 1990), 69–87, 323–27.
Hopkins, N.S. *Anthropology in Egypt 1900–1967*. Cairo: American University in Cairo Press, 2014.
Humboldt, A. von. *Personal Narrative of Travels to the Equinoctial Regions of the New Continent: During the Years 1799–1804: By Alexander de Humboldt and Aimé Bonpland*, trans. Helen Maria Williams. London: Longman et al., 1814–1826 [Fre. orig. *Voyage aux régions équinoxiales du Nouveau Continent: Fait en 1799, 1800, 1801, 1803 et 1804*. Paris: Schoell, 1814–1825].
James, W. 'The Anthropologist as Reluctant Imperialist', in T. Asad (ed.), *Anthropology & the Colonial Encounter* (New York: Humanities Press, 1973), 41–69.

Kehoe, A.B. *Humans: An Introduction to Four-field Anthropology*. New York: Routledge, 1998.
Kenny, M.G., and K. Smillie. *Stories of Culture and Place: An Introduction to Anthropology*. Toronto: University of Toronto Press, 2015.
Kenyatta, J. *Facing Mount Kenya: The Tribal Life of Gikuyu*. London: Secker and Warburg, 1938.
Konishi, S., M. Nugent and T. Shellam. 'Exploration Archives and Indigenous Histories: An Introduction', in S. Konishi, M. Nugent and T. Shellam (eds), *Indigenous Intermediaries: New Perspectives on Exploration Archives* (Acton: Australian National University Press, 2015), 1–10.
Konishi, S., M. Nugent and T. Shellam (eds). *Indigenous Intermediaries: New Perspectives on Exploration Archives*. Acton: Australian National University Press, 2015.
Kotzebue, O. von. *A Voyage of Discovery, into the South Sea and Beering's Straits, for the Purpose of Exploring a North-East Passage, Undertaken in the Years 1815–1818*, 3 vols, trans. H.E. Lloyd. London: Longman et al., 1821 [Ger. orig. *Entdeckungs-Reise in die Süd-See und nach der Berings-Straße zur Erforschung einer nordöstlichen Durchfahrt in den Jahren 1815, 1816, 1817 und 1818*, 3 vols. Weimar: Hoffmann, 1821].
Lévi-Strauss, C. *A World on the Wane*, trans. John Russell. New York: Hutchinson, 1961 [Fre. orig. *Tristes Tropiques*. Paris: Librairie Plon, 1955].
_____. *The Savage Mind*. Chicago: University of Chicago Press, 1966 [Fre. orig. *La Pensée sauvage*. Paris: Librairie Plon, 1962].
_____. *Totemism*, trans. Rodney Needham. Reprint edn. London: Merlin Press, 1991 [Fre. orig. *Le Totémisme aujourd'hui*. Paris: Presses Universitaires de France, 1962].
Lübcke, A. 'Encounters and the Photographic Record in British New Guinea', in S. Konishi, M. Nugent and T. Shellam (eds), *Indigenous Intermediaries: New Perspectives on Exploration Archives* (Acton: Australian National University Press, 2015), 169–87.
Lutz, C.A. *Unnatural Emotions: Everyday Sentiments on a Micronesian Atoll and their Challenge to Western Theory*. Chicago: Chicago University Press, 1988.
Malinowski, B. *Argonauts of the Western Pacific: An Account of Native Enterprise and Adventure in the Archipelagoes of Melanesian New Guinea*. London: Routledge, 1922.
_____. 'Introduction', in J. Kenyatta, *Facing Mount Kenya: The Tribal Life of the Gikuyu* (London: Secker and Warburg, 1938), vii–xiv.
_____. *A Diary in the Strict Sense of the Term*. New York: Harcourt, Brace and World, 1967.
Mead, M. *Coming of Age in Samoa: A Psychological Study of Primitive Youth for Western Civilisation*. New York: Morrow & Company, 1928.
_____. *Sex and Temperament in Three Primitive Societies*. New York: Morrow, 1963.
_____. 'Preface to 1973 Edition', in M. Mead, *Coming of Age in Samoa: A Psychological Study of Primitive Youth for Western Civilisation* (New York: Morrow Quills, 1973), unpaginated.
Osterhammel, J. *Die Entzauberung Asiens: Europa und die asiatischen Reiche im 18. Jahrhundert*. Munich: Beck, 1998.

Plamper, J. *The History of Emotions: An Introduction*. Oxford: Oxford University Press, 2015.

Rosaldo, M.Z. *Knowledge and Passion: Ilongot Notions of Self and Social Life*. Cambridge: Cambridge University Press, 1980.

Rosaldo, R. 'Introduction: Grief and a Headhunter's Rage', in R. Rosaldo, *Culture and Truth: The Remaking of Social Analysis* (Boston: Beacon Press, 1989), 1–21.

Ryzova, L. *The Age of the Efendiyya: Passages to Modernity in National-Colonial Egypt*. Oxford: Oxford University Press, 2014.

Sahlins, M. *Islands of History*. Chicago: University of Chicago Press, 1985.

Scheer, M. 'Are Emotions a Kind of Practice (and Is That What Makes Them Have a History)? A Bourdieuian Approach to Understanding Emotion'. *History and Theory* 51(2) (2012), 193–220, doi: 10.1111/j.1468-2303.2012.00621.x.

Spock, B. *The Common Sense Book of Baby and Child Care*. New York: Duell, Sloan, and Pearce, 1946.

Uberoi, P., N. Sundar and S. Deshpande (eds). *Anthropology in the East: Founders of Indian Sociology and Anthropology*. Ranikhet: Permanent Black, 2007.

Young, M.W. *Malinowski's Kiriwina: Fieldwork Photography 1915–1918*. Chicago: University of Chicago Press, 1998.

———. *Malinowski: Odyssey of an Anthropologist, 1884–1920*. New Haven: Yale University Press, 2004.

Chapter 4

Entrepreneurs
Encountering Trust in Business Relations

Agnes Arndt

'We're meeting today to ask the same questions they asked during Watergate: What did you know and when did you know it?'[1] In the fall of 2015, these words kicked off the juridical interrogations into a scandal that involved the loss of an emotion cultivated with zeal and nourished with care in today's international business world. Along with the U.S. Environmental Protection Agency's (EPA) suspicion that a leading German car producer had manipulated the emissions software of its vehicles, Volkswagen (VW) was also accused of having inflicted lasting damage on the world's trust in German industry and commerce.[2] The press's take on 'Dieselgate' might lead one to believe that pollutants are not the only things being burned in the VW emissions scandal. Emotionally invested 'brands'[3] like the 'Made in Germany' seal and the trust of international business partners and consumers in German companies seem to be going up in smoke too.

But is it really possible for emotions like 'trust' to serve as the single selling point for an entire nation's economic output as the example might have us believe? To reformulate the question: why and since when have emotions such as 'trust', 'honour' and 'fidelity' played a historically significant role in business relations, what purpose have these emotions served and how were they cultivated? What means have been used to communicate these emotions between companies and across borders? What role did various cultural, social, political and economic factors play in shaping them? And how has the meaning of emotions in business relations changed over time?

Notes for this chapter begin on page 124.

Concentrating on the 'feelings'[4] of trust and distrust, this chapter offers a historical perspective on the ways emotions have been generated, communicated and habituated between different business cultures. Specifically, it deals with the ways 'trust'[5] has been expressed, developed, sustained or revoked by business partners in an international context. Like in other historical contexts, such as during wars and occupations, trust has been a particularly prominent and, at the same time, precarious 'emotional disposition'[6] in international business relations.[7] From an economic history perspective, trust implied a 'contract between trust givers and trust recipients',[8] which stabilized expectations and generated social capital.[9] Encounters defined by trust could thus lead to other emotions like loyalty, fidelity, reliability and honour, while relations defined by distrust could give rise to feelings of jealousy, resentment and hate. This chapter seeks at once to grapple with the question of how trust can be cultivated in an intercultural setting and to inquire into which international or transnational processes might foster or hinder its development.

It does so by focusing on face-to-face encounters and by developing the thesis that caught in the tension between economic globalization on the one hand and discourses of political nationalization on the other, the intercultural relations of trust between transnational entrepreneurs underwent fundamental shifts between the eighteenth century and the twenty-first century.

Working with accounts of face-to-face encounters of select entrepreneurs, the chapter links historical research on emotions with research on international companies, attempting to illuminate issues of complexity reduction and information processing in a global economy from an actor perspective.[10] Regarding questions related to what economics refers to as the principal agent problem, the chapter asks whether emotional communication between businesspeople is still possible in today's globalized economy, and it enquires into the historical conditions of its development.

In doing so, it draws on autobiographical writings and published correspondence of members of three German business families whose entrepreneurial activities were from early on geared to internationalization and relied on intercultural face-to-face encounters: Siemens, Stinnes and Thyssen. From the empirical side, letters written by members of business families offer a wide range of perspectives on the various descriptions of face-to-face encounters with both domestic and international business partners and the shapes these contacts can take. The chapter seeks to critically examine them by placing particular focus on encounters between business partners of equal rank. From the methodological perspective, taking up the letters and autobiographical writings of renowned business families makes it possible to analyse how emotions provoked by encounters in the business world have been transformed and changed.

The significance of emotional encounters among businesspeople and entrepreneurs from different countries and cultures goes beyond the effects they had on those immediately involved.[11] Often, the fates of families and entire companies were impacted by the vicissitudes of cross-cultural emotional encounters. In order to ensure a company's survival on the international market, experiences with foreign cultures and business customs had to be shared with other family members so that their emotional content could be both understood and put to strategic use. Family members often took on the role of 'mediators and persons of trust', who had emotional encounters, discussed them with others and made sure that the business family and the business itself adjusted to the lessons learned through these experiences. The chapter reconstructs these earnest attempts to bridge the gap by analysing select case studies on the international expansion of the companies of the families Siemens, Stinnes and Thyssen between the eighteenth and the twenty-first centuries. In doing so, it uses insights from Michael Taussig's *Mimesis and Alterity*.[12]

Yet despite the fact that letters serve as the chapter's key source, the chapter not only focuses on the ways entrepreneurs translated their feelings or the ways they communicated through language. It also places emphasis on the pre-linguistic gestures and symbolic conventions used in the letters' descriptions of encounters. Entrepreneurs used such gestures and symbols to express their attitudes, judgements and feelings about the emotional constitution of their partners or demand that the other explain his comportment, allowing them to adjust their own emotions to the specificity of the encounter. What Taussig understood as a 'yielding' – an opening of the body towards the other – enabled an emotional contact and the production of new emotional expressions and feelings between those who met within a face-to-face-encounter.[13] The chapter analyses the historical shifts undergone by the 'empathy' that businesspeople cultivated with one another through such gestures and symbols and concludes by asking whether this sort of 'empathy' among business partners is still relevant in today's business world.

Practices of Trust in the Eighteenth and Nineteenth Centuries

Founded in Berlin on 1 October 1847 by the engineer and officer Werner Siemens and the master of precision mechanics Johann Georg Halske, the Siemens Company, which today has representatives in 190 countries around the world, always had global ambitions.[14] In an 1887 letter to his brother Carl, Werner Siemens wrote that he had 'enthused since [his] youth about founding a world company à la Fugger'.[15] Having established its London branch in 1850 and its St Petersburg branch in 1855, by 1913 more than 30 per cent of its workforce of eighty thousand was employed abroad.[16] Such expansion not only demanded that corporate representatives acquire good knowledge of the political, social and economic situation of the countries involved in order to enable them to adjust their investment, expansion and restructuring plans accordingly. The need to be able to engage in intercultural communication with European and non-European business partners was also a lesson learned early on. And, as the sources cited in the following show, entrepreneurs came to demand this competence from one another. It was less the personal sensitivity of the entrepreneurs themselves and more the technological advances of the pre-industrial and early industrial period that made the issue of trust so vital. As communications technologies were still in their fledgling years, developing 'trust' was the only effective way for businesspeople to counter their worries of suffering personal and economic losses through trickery, fraud and betrayal of secrets.[17] Thus, 'trust' was more than an emotion. It was a sort of currency – usually given on credit and thus invested with a certain risk – that set the groundwork for business negotiations and dealings, bringing them into the sphere of moral conventions and, ideally, guaranteeing their success.

As Stefan Gorissen has demonstrated, 'relationships of trust'[18] among businesspeople in the pre-industrial era were usually established in one of three ways: through judicially valid contracts, social-moral values or personal and familial relations. With the advent of the industrial revolution and increasing global expansion, however, businesspeople often tried to invest business encounters and relations with some emotional content and tried to bolster productivity through 'emotions work'.[19]

Werner Siemens's letters to his brothers Carl and Wilhelm showcase these concerns. Carl was in charge of operations in St Petersburg; Wilhelm in London. Werner's letters revolve around the questions of how one might learn to read trade partners' feelings, how one could establish trust with them and how one could use this trust to span a bridge to other emotions conducive to good business relations, such as loyalty. Taking a closer look at the face-to-face encounters between Carl and Wilhelm Siemens and their respective Russian and British counterparts, one can reconstruct two distinct ways they grappled with transcultural difference. On the one hand, they attempted to engage in a sort of participatory observation. On the other, they tried to integrate their business relations into their familial relations, thus giving them an endurance that went beyond the spatio-temporal constraints of the brothers' individual work.

Both Carl and Wilhelm married the daughters of their most important business partners in Russia and England, respectively. In 1859, Wilhelm Siemens married Anne Gordon, the sister of Lewis D.B. Gordon, professor of engineering at the University of Glasgow and a co-owner of R.S. Newall & Co., an important business partner of the Siemens Corporation. Similarly, in 1855, Carl married Marie Kap-herr, daughter of Hermann Christian von Kap-herr, a Russian Imperial privy councillor and banker, who secured the Siemens Corporation access to strategically important markets in Russia. Ensuring his short-term support was of great significance for Siemens's success in St Petersburg, but so was ensuring that he did not excessively poke his nose into the company's affairs. In 1855, Werner Siemens wrote to his wife Mathilde that it was 'a joy to see the beautiful young couple', adding that 'the rest of the Kap-herr family has become closer to us through this event'.[20] Just a year later, however, he impelled his brother Carl to 'limit Kap-herr's influence on our business to a very limited sphere'.[21] Like in the eighteenth century, marriages between family members of trade partners served both to curtail business risks and sustain and expand business interests.[22]

When observing and choosing potential trade partners, the Siemens brothers often directed their attention towards certain physical signs and character attributes and tried to discern their relation to their observations on national customs. They then compared their observations with their own customs and tried to translate them into gestures and manners that they thought were universal. As Carl Siemens's experiences in St Petersburg and Wilhelm Siemens's in London show, this could, in extreme cases, be stylized as a transformation of one's own personality, a fact that resonates with Paul Ricoeur's concept of prefiguration, configuration and refiguration.[23]

Cultural differences were both accepted and reflected in the sources presented here – but always in reference to overcoming them wherever it seemed to benefit the economic connections. Finally, 'the mutual transfers in the triangle between St Petersburg, London and Berlin . . . formed the basis for the success of the overall business'.[24] In the long term, the prudent approach of the Siemens brothers towards the differences between themselves and their business partners was a key factor in the successful internationalization of Siemens, unlike other entrepreneurial initiatives in Europe, which, despite favourable starting conditions, failed to enjoy long-lasting success due to the cultural and social isolation of the entrepreneurs in foreign environments.[25]

At the beginning of his time in St Petersburg, Carl Siemens complained that there could be 'no place more boring than Petersburg and no people more boring than the Petersburgers',[26] that he was living 'in a half-cultivated country' and had himself become, 'at least in matters of science, a half-primitive'.[27] In the end, however, this fit well with his character and his preferred lifestyle, and, he claimed, he felt no need to justify this lifestyle to his brothers. However, as far as their relations with their Russian and English trade partners went, Carl and Wilhelm were forced to put up with their brother Werner's tendency to give them directives. Thus, their face-to-face encounters followed certain scripts. Despite the fact that these scripts were – again following Ricoeur – formed by certain assumptions about their Russian and English trade partners, they nevertheless – according to Taussig – motivated the Siemens brothers to cultivate 'empathic' encounters.

These scripts were reflected in the language they used, which often included bodily and sensory metaphors. Of his most important trade partner and later brother-in-law, Lewis D.B. Gordon, Wilhelm Siemens wrote that he was 'really quite a gentleman'. But, he continued, it was 'just part of his nature' that it was difficult to 'get close to him'.[28] At the same time, Werner spoke of how important it was to 'stay on good terms with'[29] Gordon and other trade partners and to respect their 'wishes and needs . . . through personal contact . . . and an open ear'.[30] 'If the people do not speak as a "we" in their business affairs, if they do not feel honoured when the business is honoured, worried when the business has problems, then one can't expect their fidelity when times are tough'.[31] The aim of fostering personal contact and having an open ear for the interests of trade partners and employees was to build up a feeling of 'dedicated fidelity'[32] and 'to liven up the spirits of people who are faithful to us'.[33] Pursuing this aim sometimes required that one adjust one's own comportment, even if one could justify certain behaviours by appealing to the customs and conventions of the other culture – in this case Russian culture. Reflecting on his brother Carl's encounters with his Russian trade partners in an 1857 letter, Werner Siemens wrote: 'I think that you all have allowed the officious tone to become too dominant there [in St Petersburg], which the Russian spirit nevertheless does much to support'.[34] According to him, there were some 'nasty'[35] men in Russia, which made it all the more urgent for the assertion of the company's interests that one engage with the 'simple, just, active people'[36] in a rational, empathic way. Werner told his brother:

> It is my habit to treat all honourable people in my private relations as if they were my equal, and to discuss business affairs that involve them as if they were just as much my interest as theirs – a habit, by the way, that comes completely natural to me and that is thus no particular accomplishment on my part. This habit has always proven its efficacy. A few times a year I treat managers and office workers, etc. This cultivates personal attachment, which makes some other things easier.[37]

Thus, it was not wholly up to Carl and Wilhelm how they structured their face-to-face encounters. Rather, it seemed to be at least partially determined by a familial, corporate code that was reproduced in transcultural exchange and was only slightly modified to adapt to Russian or English conventions ('allowing the officious tone to become too dominant'). The ways they grappled with differences in intercultural or transcultural settings followed a strategy similar to that deployed in intracultural contexts: on the one hand, they clearly perceived differences, while on the other, they tried to smooth them over in order to assert long-term business interests ('treat all honourable people . . . as if they were my equal'). However, considering a longer span of time, one can see that within the company and the family there developed divergent approaches towards cultivating the trust of business partners and thus a shift in the concept of trust itself.

As early as 1863, Werner wrote Wilhelm that the fact that the brothers' approaches to doing business 'are so divergent is natural, because each more or less draws on his own experiences and habits, as well as on his environment'.[38] While Carl and Wilhelm sought to adjust the company's protocols so as to conform with their experiences abroad, Werner, who had remained in Berlin, resisted for a long time. It seems that he believed that the perception of differences should remain in the transcultural context without making an impact on the intracultural climate of the company itself. Wilhelm above all, however, pitted himself against his brother's resistance. 'As to your remarks on the solid German business style and the fanciful British style', Wilhelm wrote to Werner in 1862: 'I am of the opinion that one has to do business in England the English way. . . . The German style of evenly distributing responsibility would never work here in England; just like you all have carried out business in a more speculative (and more lucrative) fashion in Russia'.[39] Wilhelm, who seemed much more influenced by 'Manchester Capitalism' than his brothers, wanted 'blind trust' and 'free dealing' for his management of Siemens's English branch, whereas Werner valued a different sort of trust. He wanted to be constantly informed about, and involved in, business affairs and in no way wanted to be labelled a 'capitalist' whose investments were his only connection to his business.

> It runs counter to our approach [to doing business] that you give us access to the books, but let us not make inquiries about prices or about the way the business is running in general. Maybe it works for the way business is done over there, but it does not work for us. We do not want to have the function of mere shareholders or limited partners (who can at least request a detailed business report every year). Because then we would never be happy and would be demeaned in the eyes of our own people.[40]

Both brothers reproduced the practices of forging trust typical of the national business cultures around them and tried to convince one another of the legitimacy and efficacy of these practices. They borrowed emotions and concepts like trust, loyalty and honour from the business culture of their 'own people', thus trying to bring their own notions in line with the local conventions. Thus, under the conditions of increasing globalization, the brothers' individual understandings of such concepts did not form a universal Siemens-style understanding. Rather, their differences had to be worked through and negotiated. Wilhelm in particular had a tendency to question his identity as a businessman and to adapt to his new environment through intercultural exchange with English trade partners. This tendency reached its apex when he changed his name to 'William' , signed his name with the prefix 'Sir' after having been knighted by Queen Victoria in 1883 shortly before his death and, as a biographer writes, became 'a Brit in lifestyle and worldview'.[41] Carl developed a similar attitude: 'During the decades of entrepreneurial experience in Russia . . ., Carl's initial German national identity evolved into an indeterminate, complex and hybrid self-image'.[42]

When dealing with intercultural disputes, the Siemens brothers tended to appeal to conventions of conflict resolution that had proven themselves in the particular nation, just as they did when dealing with business interests. For instance, in 1855 Werner wrote to Carl: 'The written word is . . . always severe and dangerous, so I've decided to let the matter rest for now'.[43] A year later, as the conflict between Siemens and Kap-herr concerning the distribution of power in the company reached its peak, he mustered up the resolve to write to his trade partner:

> I gather from Carl's letters that you believe I am angry with you or that I have lost my trust in you, and that it is for this reason that I have not continued with our earlier correspondence. As this is the farthest thing from the truth, I have decided to break the silence between us in order to assure you that my sentiments towards you and your family have not changed a bit.[44]

As the letters analysed here show, being 'agitated by abrasiveness'[45] and 'deeply hurt'[46] by the statements of others was not uncommon for leading businessmen in the nineteenth and even at the beginning of the twentieth century. This implied a 'delight in talking openly'[47] that could help re-establish damaged trust. And, if speaking did not help, symbolic gestures like resignations could at least recover the 'honour'[48] of a business.[49] Alongside an increase in intercultural competence, the sources discussed here also seem to evidence an increase in intracultural knowledge about how to treat the emotions of trade partners, family members and, not least of all, one's own emotions.[50] The notion that industry and commerce 'refine manners' and that their very functioning depends on the fact that they support civil forms of conflict resolution seems to find confirmation here.[51]

Discourses on Trust in the Twentieth and Twenty-First Centuries

In 1872, Werner Siemens told his son Wilhelm, who was stationed in Strasbourg, that it was 'natural' and part of the 'school of life' that some things abroad might seem 'foreign and strange ... You have to learn to have friendly contact with people who think and feel differently from you and must go easy on their feelings; of course, you must also ask the same of them'.[52] A few decades later, August Thyssen and Hugo Stinnes were also convinced that 'empathizing'[53] with trade partners was an absolute necessity and tried to pass down this key competency to the younger generations through 'education' and 'upbringing'.[54] Showing trade partners 'a certain trust'[55] seemed essential, as did being 'magnanimous and elegant'[56] and maintaining a 'conciliatory attitude in personal relations'.[57] According to August Thyssen in a 1919 letter, 'feeling'[58] oneself to be an industrialist went hand in hand with the ability to foster business relations by 'empathizing'[59] with important trade partners.

However, as the example of the face-to-face encounters of the entrepreneurial families Thyssen and Stinnes show, at the beginning of the twentieth century, businessmen increasingly distinguished between the forms of trust they developed with domestic trade partners on the one hand and international trade partners on the other. The trust cultivated between closely cooperating domestic entrepreneurs like Thyssen and Stinnes often gave rise to a sort of 'confidence' that helped them to delegate tasks more efficiently and shape business relations both at home and abroad.[60] In the early twentieth century, the social-political discourse on industrialists and merchants and the emotional relations between entrepreneurs were not the only things to undergo such shifts.[61] The ways businessmen developed and shaped their capacity to 'empathize' in intercultural settings also underwent a shift. On the one hand, observing transcultural difference continued to play a key role. On the other, however, the way businessmen were supposed to work through this difference was no longer conceived of as something emotional. Rather, the ability to work through this difference was something that had to be cognitively learned. For its part, what had to be learned was not only determined by business interests but also by other factors, such as political interests.

Traits like 'obstinacy',[62] 'independence',[63] 'openness and honesty',[64] 'energy'[65] and 'desire to do business'[66] could still be decisive factors in whether or not someone could be trusted and, therefore, employed, commissioned or selected as a business partner. This is evidenced by multiple letters exchanged between August Thyssen and Hugo Stinnes in which the two attempt to evaluate the trustworthiness of potential trade partners on the basis of their impressions of physical and psychological traits that they made during personal encounters. They show that top entrepreneurs believed that determining who could be trusted in transnational settings and with whom one should establish business relations could best be done by learning about 'the culture and customs of the country in question',[67] 'taking trips'[68] to experience the country for oneself, learning the 'languages'[69] spoken there and sending high-performing employees to different places.[70] The demands posed on employees abroad and on members of the family business were often reminiscent of older models, such as that of the early modern 'clerk'.[71] As 'men of trust', they were ideally supposed to bring clients from a state of 'blind trust' to a state of 'founded trust'[72] with the aim of spurring the company's growth and ensuring its long-term viability. With the global expansion of corporations and the growing spatial and personal distance between headquarters and regional leaders came an increased risk for loss of trust. As well, the sort of trust in family members that had in many ways been a given over the centuries became more fragile and liable to violation. For these reasons, family members working abroad in the late nineteenth and early twentieth centuries were often paired with employees socialized in the countries where they were stationed. In the twentieth century, the new role played by hired managers not only brought about a transformation of the companies' management structures but also introduced a shift in the way risks were taken and responsibility borne. No doubt these changes went hand in hand with technological advances, in particular those in the sphere of communications. The sources drawn on here also attest to these developments in the ways trust was granted. For instance, in the 1920s, instituting 'men of trust'[73] at Siemens began to gain prevalence, and in the 1990s, 'women of trust' too.[74]

In the early twentieth century, the gradual tendency of German corporations to move towards a more horizontal style of allocating responsibility was accompanied by the vertical intertwining of different companies and corporations. Hugo Stinnes, in particular, did much to advance the idea of combining 'coal mining with the iron and steel industry, energy suppliers, and public transport companies'.[75] Conglomerates based on the Anglo-Saxon model of corporate 'trusts'[76] were supposed to increase efficiency and allow industry and commerce to interact with each other in productive ways.⁷⁷ The restructuring of his industrial holdings during the hyperinflation of 1923 protected Hugo Stinnes from massive losses. However, it also got him the reputation of being an 'insatiable capitalist',⁷⁸ a reputation that preceded him in his face-to-face encounters with international trade partners. 'The "King of Inflation" reminded the British ambassador in Berlin, Viscount D'Abernon, of the American rail tycoon Edward Harriman: "Both had something grubby, unkempt about them, like a Jack Russell terrier that just got finished digging through a pile of trash on the search for the next can."'⁷⁹ As these and other examples show, the lead-up and aftermath of the First World War, the effects of the Treaty of Versailles and the international market crash effected considerable changes in the semantics and strategies used to navigate transcultural difference. In the eighteenth and nineteenth centuries, cultural differences were negotiated through corporeal gestures and sensory objects. In the first third of the twentieth century, however, the negotiation of cultural difference became increasingly more cognitive. At the same time, the differences that businesspeople did perceive were more heavily influenced by predetermined notions of the other, which found their expression in judgements about others' behaviour and, increasingly, in deprecating statements.

Thus, some assessed the trend among German entrepreneurs of adapting a habitus with international and intercultural influences critically. In a 1914 letter to August Thyssen, Hugo Stinnes wrote that 'Rathenau Junior' had always been 'strongly Englandized [sic]', continuing that although 'hardly anyone can resist the attraction of English life & and the pleasant ways of the English in private life', he believed that 'such proclivities' needed to be given up in light of the current situation.⁸⁰ On the other hand, intercultural differences between German and non-German trade partners were given more weight and were sometimes used as an argument against taking up business relations. Perceived intracultural and intercultural differences were used as fodder for racist and, above all, antisemitic prejudices. German Jews were denigrated as culturally inferior and were increasingly avoided in business relations. For instance, in 1923, August Thyssen wrote to his son Heinrich Thyssen-Bornemisza that doing business with 'Jewry' was 'not comfortable' for him but that it 'cannot be avoided', because in some places 'only Jews run the businesses'.⁸¹ Business relations with Russia, however, had to be avoided with resolve. In a 1920 letter, August Thyssen wrote to Heinrich, Margareta and Margit Thyssen-Bornemisza: 'Yesterday Russian Bolshevists who wanted to do business with German industry were in Essen. Krupp, Stinnes . . . and I got together and rejected the Bolshevists' offer, because we don't want to have anything to do with these dangerous people'.⁸² Soon thereafter, he decided that he should also avoid business contacts with the Dutch.

With apparent concern for the trust that his son Heinrich enjoyed with German industrialists, August Thyssen strongly advised him against letting businessmen from Rotterdam sit on the boards of directors of German companies. 'That would do grave injury to German national sentiment', he wrote in a letter from 1924. 'You put in your word for the men from Rotterdam and you become untouchable in the industrial world'.[83]

In the run of the twentieth century, it could be argued that – at least as far as the letters examined here go – the question of how intercultural trust in business relations could be best forged was shifted from a practical to a discursive level and was sometimes tainted by political and national interests. Globalization and the integration of Germany into the European economy and community of values made the national overtones characteristic of discourses on trust in the first half of the twentieth century less significant. At the same time, the competencies necessary to navigate the vicissitudes of intercultural difference in international business relations underwent considerable shifts.

Advice literature played a central role in these shifts, taking on the essential function of reflecting businesspersons' face-to-face encounters abroad and making them into a viable tool for managers' training programmes. In the ideal case, such advice literature served to pave a 'foundation for esteeming the cultural specificities of partners in conversation, negotiation and cooperation', so that the reader might better be able to 'productively interact with these differences', thus avoiding doing damage to his 'potential performance'.[84] In extreme cases, however, advice literature classifies foreign businesspeople according to regional differences and emotional dispositions with claims in the mode of: the north Chinese are 'bawdy ... and soulful', the south Chinese 'just as withdrawn as they are outgoing', the central Chinese are 'persistent, ... intriguing'.[85] By drawing on the sort of nationalization discourses that were prominent in the interwar period, such literature does little more than bolster stereotypes. Thus, while learning to recognize intercultural difference is certainly a stated goal of human resources departments, the ways people are supposed to interact with this difference diverge sharply.

According to the authors of a guide for entrepreneurs who conduct business in Russia, 'the behaviour of others' is usually 'regulated' by cultural standards, which comprise the norms, values, expectations and opinions that one cognitively internalizes in the socialization process. They claim that these standards are often 'inadequately interpreted', and thus draw the conclusion that simply learning the language of the other is not sufficient.[86] Rather, they claim that one has to understand the reasons why the other behaves in a certain way in order 'to be able to grapple with ambiguous situations'.[87] Thus, the authors developed a training programme designed to help managers develop their intercultural competencies. With the help of this 'Culture Assimilator', as they call it, managers 'bolster their cognitive capacity to interpret the reasons for the behaviour of business partners socialized in a foreign culture on the basis of the orientation system of that particular culture'.[88] An 'important step towards understanding the foreign culture' was made when a German businessperson thought to herself during talks with a Russian counterpart: 'If I had grown up in Russia, I would have done the exact same thing in this situation'.[89]

But even if it is focused on training cognitive capacities rather than emotions, the advice book nevertheless claims that the capacity to trust and successfully cooperate with Russian business partners depends to a large extent on one's own openness and flexibility, which recalls Taussig's analyses. In order to gain the trust of their counterparts, managers and entrepreneurs have to be able to empathize with 'the Russian mentality'. The authors of the advice book are not only concerned with teaching businesspeople how to judge the trustworthiness of their Russian counterparts, but also with teaching them how to develop a perspective informed by Russian cultural norms in order to acquire critical distance towards their own behaviour, thus enabling them to cultivate the trust of their foreign partners. The authors advise:

> Bring plenty of patience and understanding, you will not regret it. The people will open their hearts to you, which is the most important thing in Russia. Only then will you be able to experience how warm-hearted Russian people really are, only then will you experience the 'Russian spirit' that one hears so much about. . . . You can see how personally enriching a stay in Russia can be by reading the following anecdote of a German: 'Before my trip to Russia I was happy and satisfied in Germany, where I worked hard and really lived a pretty good life. I had no worries and liked my life. I could not imagine what I could have that would make me any happier. And then I went to Russia, saw life from a completely different perspective, and said to myself: "you could have made your life a lot nicer"'.[90]

Thus, according to the idealized depiction of the advice book, businesses built on such transcultural foundations have more than just an economic benefit for German-Russian business relations.

Conclusion

For the entrepreneurs discussed in this chapter, perceiving intercultural difference and drawing on it to forge business relations based in trust meant using supervision, surveillance and systems of motivation to contain the uncertainties caused by distance and the disadvantages caused by the lags in information common before the advent of new communications technologies.[91] In times when effective supervision and regulation was not always possible – particularly in the pre-industrial and early industrial eras – emotions like trust, loyalty, dependability and business honour played an important role. With 'the transition of face-to-face economic relations in local markets bound by family and kinship towards transregional and international markets',[92] the emotional investment of business relations lost significance. Business relations were 'decoupled from established personal and social relations' and were replaced by 'increasingly fleeting and at times anonymous relations between individual market actors'.[93] For their part, businesspeople began to form networks no longer based on familial relations, such as industrial clubs and interest groups. As the advice manual discussed above and managerial seminars on 'neuro-linguistic programming' (NLP) show, the emotions of other businesspeople have come to be regarded as objects that can supposedly be studied and sometimes even manipulated.[94]

Nevertheless, a number of emotional gestures and styles have survived the period between the eighteenth century and the twenty-first century. Developed by industrialists in the early modern period, they continue to shape the conventions that regulate intracultural and intercultural business encounters and smooth over transcultural differences. Businesspeople of the eighteenth, nineteenth and twentieth centuries and those of today have always striven to win the trust of their counterparts, whether it be in the letter exchanges of the past or e-mail exchanges of today, through congratulations, gifts and flowers,[95] by expressing sympathy in times of personal or professional turmoil[96] or by inviting trade partners to receptions, formal dinners [97] and grand hotels.[98] Through a certain upbringing and attending select schools, boarding schools and universities, a new generation of entrepreneurs are learning to define their emotional capacities and develop their competencies in engaging in emotional and intercultural communication. Since the 2008 financial crisis, researchers have even made a new turn towards studying the global connections between emotions and the economy. Their failure to predict the recession – and their concomitant failure to do anything to stop it – has made John Maynard Keynes' idea of the 'animal spirits'[99] that guide human behaviour on the market attractive again, provoking economists to think about the significance trust has for today's markets.[100] To take up one of this book's fundamental questions, we might say that even if it is impossible to claim that there is a universal understanding of what 'trust' is, it nevertheless seems plausible to claim that economic and cultural adaptation and assimilation have brought about a 'universalized' need for trust in business relations.

Michael Horn, CEO and president of the Volkswagen Group of America, also had to recuperate lost trust by appearing before U.S. Congress, 'admit his guilt' and 'show regret',[101] both in order to dispel the fears of leading economic institutes that the scandal could have negative effects on the German economy as a whole and to help cast away the 'shadow' that had fallen on the reputation of the 'Made in Germany' label.[102] It remains to be seen whether the sort of capacities to engage in intercultural emotional communication that are taught in today's more cognition-based training sessions will be able to compete in the long-term with the forms of 'empathy' that seek to reach trade partners on an emotional level. For the time being, the view of much contemporary advice literature that experiences abroad should be understood on the basis of the particular cultural background in which they occur before they are made useful for one's own culture (in this case one's business) seems to confirm this book's position. As Benno Gammerl, Philipp Nielsen and Margrit Pernau write in the introduction, society and culture can be seen as producers as well as products of translation processes,[103] and business cultures are no exception. It seems that navigating this process of constant translation will remain a part of the challenge facing businesses in their interaction with global diversity.

Agnes Arndt (Max Planck Institute for Human Development) is a historian of modern and contemporary Europe. She was a Gerald D. Feldman Fellow at the German Historical Institutes in London, Paris and Warsaw and has published two award-winning monographs on the political transformation in East Central Europe: *Rote Bürger: Eine Milieu- und Beziehungsgeschichte linker Dissidenz in Polen* (Vandenhoeck & Ruprecht, 2013) and *Intellektuelle in der Opposition: Diskurse zur Zivilgesellschaft in der Volksrepublik Polen* (Campus, 2007). She is currently working on a monograph on the relationship between emotions and capitalism in Germany from the 1840s to the present.

Notes

1. See Lazarovic, 'Kongress grillt VW-USA-Chef', *N-TV.de*. All translations from the German by Adam Bresnahan unless otherwise noted.
2. See 'Volkswagen führt uns besser nicht an der Nase herum', *Handelsblatt* (translation by Agnes Arndt); Doll and Kaiser, 'So wurde der US-Chef von VW vom Kongress gegrillt' (translation by Agnes Arndt); Hulverscheidt and Richter, 'VW hat eine ganze Nation betrogen', *Süddeutsche Zeitung*.

3. See 'Branding', *Gründerszene*.
4. On the history of emotions, see Frevert, 'Defining Emotions: Concepts and Debates over Three Centuries', 1–31; Frevert, 'Was haben Gefühle in der Geschichte zu suchen?', 183–208; Hitzer and Gammerl, 'Wohin mit den Gefühlen? Vergangenheit und Zukunft des Emotional Turn in den Geschichtswissenschaften', 31–40; Scheer, 'Are Emotions a Kind of Practice (and Is That What Makes Them Have a History)? A Bourdieuian Approach to Understanding Emotion', 193–220.
5. On the history of the concept of 'trust', see Frevert, 'Vertrauen—Eine historische Spurensuche', 13–20; Frevert, 'Vertrauen in historischer Perspektive', 39–59.
6. See Frevert, 'Vertrauen: Historische Annäherungen an eine Gefühlshaltung', 178–97; Frevert, *Vertrauensfragen: Eine Obsession der Moderne*, 21–23.
7. See Chapter 6, P. Nielsen, 'Occupiers and Civilians' in this volume.
8. See Lutz, *Siemens im Sowjetgeschäft: Eine Institutionengeschichte der deutsch-sowjetischen Beziehungen 1917–1933*, 64.
9. On the role of trust in business relations, see Berghoff, 'Die Zähmung des entfesselten Prometheus? Die Generierung von Vertrauenskapital und die Konstruktion des Marktes im Industrialisierungs- und Globalisierungsprozess', 43–68; Ripperger, *Ökonomik des Vertrauens: Analyse eines Organisationsprinzips*; Siegenthaler, *Regelvertrauen, Prosperität und Krisen: Die Ungleichmäßigkeit wirtschaftlicher und sozialer Entwicklung als Ergebnis individuellen Handelns und sozialen Lernens*.
10. See Alparslan, *Strukturalistische Prinzipal-Agent-Theorie: Eine Reformulierung der Hidden-Action-Modelle aus der Perspektive des Strukturalismus*; Eisenhardt, 'Agency Theory: An Assessment and Review', 57–74; Jensen and Meckling, 'Theory of the Firm: Managerial Behavior, Agency Costs and Ownership Structure', 305–60.
11. On the history of transnational business, see among others Fernández Pérez and Rose, *Innovation and Entrepreneurial Networks in Europe*; Johnson et al., *Transregional and Transnational Families in Europe and Beyond: Experiences since the Middle Ages*; Jones, *The Multinational Traders*; Lubinski, Fear and Fernández Pérez, *Family Multinationals: Entrepreneurship, Governance, and Pathways to Internationalization*; Trivellato, *The Familiarity of Strangers: The Sephardic Diaspora, Livorno, and Cross-cultural Trade in the Early Modern Period*.
12. See Taussig, *Mimesis and Alterity: A Particular History of the Senses*, 76–78.
13. See introduction to this volume.
14. On the history of the Siemens family in general, see Lutz, *Carl von Siemens: 1829–1906: A Life between Family and World Firm*; Bähr, *Werner von Siemens 1816–1892: A Biography*; Sabean, 'German International Families in the Nineteenth Century: The Siemens Family as a Thought Experiment', 229–52.
15. See Siemens, 'An Karl in St Petersburg', 911.
16. See Lubinski, Fear and Fernández Pérez, 'Family Multinationals: Entrepreneurship, Governance, and Pathways to Internationalization', 1–20.
17. See Gorißen, 'Der Preis des Vertrauens: Unsicherheit, Institutionen und Rationalität im vorindustriellen Fernhandel', 105–6.
18. See Gorißen, 'Preis des Vertrauens', 97–98.
19. See Donauer, 'Emotions at Work—Working on Emotions: The Production of Economic Selves in Twentieth-Century Germany', Ph.D. dissertation.
20. See Heintzenberg, *Aus einem reichen Leben: Werner von Siemens in Briefen an seine Familie und an Freunde*, 107 (to Mathilde Siemens, 31 July 1855).
21. See Heintzenberg, *Aus einem reichen Leben*, 117 (to Carl Siemens, 7 July 1856).
22. See Heintzenberg, *Aus einem reichen Leben*, 97–98 (to Mathilde Siemens, 22 November 1854).
23. See Ricoeur, *Time and Narrative*; chapter 7, P. Vasilyev and G.M. Vidor, 'Prisoners' in this volume.

24. Lutz, 'Carl von Siemens: Vom "Prussky Ingener" zum transnationalen Unternehmer?', 213.
25. See Caglioti, 'Trust, Business Groups and Social Capital: Building a Protestant Entrepreneurial Network in Nineteenth-Century Naples', 219–36.
26. See Lutz, *Carl von Siemens: Ein Leben*, 113.
27. See Ehrenberg, *Unternehmungen*, 453.
28. Ehrenberg, *Unternehmungen*, 142.
29. See Ehrenberg, *Unternehmungen*, 461 (Werner to Carl, 1856).
30. See Ehrenberg, *Unternehmungen*, 461 (Werner to Carl, 1857).
31. See Ehrenberg, *Unternehmungen*, 461 (Werner to Carl, 1857).
32. See Ehrenberg, *Unternehmungen*, 461 (Werner to Carl, 1857).
33. See Ehrenberg, *Unternehmungen*, 461 (Werner to Carl, 1857).
34. See Ehrenberg, *Unternehmungen*, 461 (Werner to Carl, 1857).
35. See Ehrenberg, *Unternehmungen*, 460–61 (William Meyer, 23 October 1855).
36. See Ehrenberg, *Unternehmungen*, 461 (Werner to Carl, 1856).
37. See Ehrenberg, *Unternehmungen*, 461 (Werner to Carl, 1857).
38. See Ehrenberg, *Unternehmungen*, 437 (Werner to Wilhelm, 23 April 1863).
39. See Ehrenberg, *Unternehmungen*, 164 (Wilhelm to Werner, 16 January 1862).
40. See Ehrenberg, *Unternehmungen*, 420–21 (Werner to Wilhelm, 16 April 1863).
41. See Wittendorfer, 'Im Fokus: 16. März 1850—Errichtung einer Siemens-Vertretung in London durch William Siemens'.
42. See Lutz, 'Carl von Siemens', 212.
43. See Heintzenberg, *Aus einem reichen Leben*, 113 (to Carl Siemens, 10 November 1855).
44. See Heintzenberg, *Aus einem reichen Leben*, 116 (to Hermann von Kap-herr, 4 April, 1856).
45. See Rasch and Feldman, *August Thyssen und Hugo Stinnes: Ein Briefwechsel 1898–1922*, 247–48 (A. Thyssen to H. Stinnes, 21 March 1904).
46. See Rasch and Feldman, *Thyssen und Stinnes*, 248–50 (H. Stinnes to A. Thyssen, 21 March 1904).
47. See Rasch and Feldman, *Thyssen und Stinnes*, 269 (A. Thyssen to H. Stinnes, 30 December 1904).
48. See Rasch and Feldman, *Thyssen und Stinnes*, 247–48 (A. Thyssen to H. Stinnes, 21 March 1904).
49. See Rasch and Feldman, *Thyssen und Stinnes*, 247–48 (A. Thyssen to H. Stinnes, 21 March 1904).
50. See Ehrenberg, *Unternehmungen*, 453 (C. Siemens to W. Siemens, 28 February 1867).
51. See Marquis de Condorcet, *Outlines of an Historical View of the Progress of the Human Mind: Being a Posthumous Work of the Late M. de Condorcet*, 184; de Montesquieu, *The Spirit of Laws*, 316. See also Ferguson, *An Essay on the History of Civil Society*; Hegel, *Elements of the Philosophy of Right*, 220–39; Hume, 'Of Commerce', 253–67; Smith, *An Inquiry into the Nature and Causes of the Wealth of Nations*; and, for a good summary, Reichardt, *Soziales Kapital 'im Zeitalter materieller Interessen': Konzeptionelle Überlegungen zum Vertrauen in der Zivil- und Marktgesellschaft des langen 19. Jahrhunderts (1780–1914)*, 3–4.
52. See Heintzenberg, *Aus einem reichen Leben*, 247 (to his son Wilhelm Siemens, 18 November 1872).
53. See Rasch and Feldman, *Thyssen und Stinnes*, 224 (A. Thyssen to H. Stinnes, 10 December 1902).
54. Rasch, *August Thyssen und Heinrich Thyssen-Bornemisza: Briefe einer Industriellenfamilie 1919–1926*, 143 (A. Thyssen to H. Thyssen-Bornemisza, 6 November 1920) and 329 (A. Thyssen to H. Thyssen-Bornemisza, 9 September 1924). On the history of the

Thyssen family in general, see Derix, *Die Thyssens: Familie und Vermögen*; on Hugo Stinnes, see Feldman, *Hugo Stinnes: Biographie eines Industriellen, 1870–1924*.
55. See Rasch, *Thyssen und Thyssen-Bornemisza*, 415 (A. Thyssen to H. Thyssen-Bornemisza, 13 October 1925).
56. See Rasch, *Thyssen und Thyssen-Bornemisza*, 357–58 (A. Thyssen to Heinrich Thyssen-Bornemisza, 23 December 1924).
57. See Rasch, *Thyssen und Thyssen-Bornemisza*, 348 (H. Thyssen-Bornemisza to W. Graf von Arco, 28 November 1924).
58. See Rasch, *Thyssen und Thyssen-Bornemisza*, 404–5 (A. Thyssen to H. Thyssen-Bornemisza, 19 August 1925).
59. See Rasch, *Thyssen und Thyssen-Bornemisza*, 107–8 (A. Thyssen to H. Thyssen-Bornemisza, 30 July 1919), 109 (A. Thyssen to H. Thyssen-Bornemisza, 30 July 1919), 219 (A. Thyssen to H. Thyssen-Bornemisza, 30 July 1923).
60. See Rasch and Feldman, *Thyssen und Stinnes*, 164 (A. Thyssen to H. Stinnes, 8 January 1900), 167 (A. Thyssen to H. Stinnes, 24 January 1900), and, with a similar tenor, 199 (H. Stinnes to A. Thyssen, 10 December 1901), 200 (A. Thyssen to H. Stinnes, 10 January 1902); Rasch, *Thyssen und Thyssen-Bornemisza*, 119–20 (A. Thyssen to H. Thyssen-Bornemisza, 26 October 1919).
61. See Reichardt, *Soziales Kapital*, 5.
62. See Ehrenberg, *Unternehmungen*, 465 (Carl von Siemens, 1902).
63. See Ehrenberg, *Unternehmungen*, 464.
64. See Rasch and Feldman, *Thyssen und Stinnes*, 248–50 (H. Stinnes to A. Thyssen, 21 March 1904).
65. See Rasch and Feldman, *Thyssen und Stinnes*, 188 (A. Thyssen to H. Stinnes, 8 January 1901).
66. See Rasch and Feldman, *Thyssen und Stinnes*, 164 (A. Thyssen to H. Stinnes, 7 January 1900).
67. See Ehrenberg, *Unternehmungen*, 465 (C. von Siemens, 1902).
68. See Rasch, *Thyssen und Thyssen-Bornemisza*, 119–20 (A. Thyssen to H. Thyssen-Bornemisza, 26 October 1919).
69. See Rasch, *Thyssen und Thyssen-Bornemisza*, 309–10 (A. Thyssen to H. Thyssen-Bornemisza, 2 July 1924).
70. See Ehrenberg, *Unternehmungen*, 460–61.
71. See Gorißen, 'Preis des Vertrauens', 92–97; Ludovici, 'Handelsdiener', 158–59, quoted in Gorißen, 'Preis des Vertrauens', 93.
72. See Frevert, 'Vertrauen—Eine historische Spurensuche', 45.
73. See Rasch, *Thyssen und Thyssen-Bornemisza*, 338–39 (A. Thyssen to August Thyssen Mining Union, 26 October 1924), 400 (A. Thyssen to H. Thyssen-Bornemisza, [before 17 August 1925]).
74. See Maier, 'Lisa Davis: Die Frau, die den härtesten Job bei Siemens hat', *Manager Magazin*.
75. See Ullrich, 'Der König der Inflation: Gerald D. Feldman präsentiert den Schwerindustriellen Hugo Stinnes in zeitgemäßem Gewand', *Die Zeit*.
76. See Rasch and Feldman, *Thyssen und Stinnes*, 261 (H. Stinnes to A. Thyssen, 23 August 1904); Rasch, *Thyssen und Thyssen-Bornemisza*, 413–15 (A. Thyssen to H. Thyssen-Bornemisza, 13 October 1925), 421–23 (A. Thyssen an H. Thyssen-Bornemisza, 20 November 1925), 423–26 (A. Thyssen to H. Thyssen-Bornemisza, 23 November 1925).
77. See Feldman, *Hugo Stinnes*, 950.
78. See Ullrich, 'König der Inflation'.
79. See Ullrich, 'König der Inflation'.
80. See Rasch and Feldman, *Thyssen und Stinnes*, 570–71 (H. Stinnes to A. Thyssen, 23 September 1914).

81. See Rasch, *Thyssen und Thyssen-Bornemisza*, 218 (A. Thyssen to H. Thyssen-Bornemisza, 30 July 1923).
82. See Rasch, *Thyssen und Thyssen-Bornemisza*, 130 (A. Thyssen to Heinrich, Margareta and Margit Thyssen-Bornemisza, 22 December 1920).
83. See Rasch, *Thyssen und Thyssen-Bornemisza*, 266–67 (A. Thyssen to H. Thyssen-Bornemisza, 4 January 1924).
84. See Yoosefi and Thomas, *Beruflich in Russland: Trainingsprogramm für Manager, Fach- und Führungskräfte*, 8.
85. See Zürl, *Erfolgreich in China: Ein Reisebuch für Manager*, 40, 41.
86. See Yoosefi and Thomas, *Beruflich in Russland*, 9, 10.
87. See Yoosefi and Thomas, *Beruflich in Russland*, 10.
88. See Yoosefi and Thomas, *Beruflich in Russland*, 10, 11.
89. See Yoosefi and Thomas, *Beruflich in Russland*, 11.
90. See Yoosefi and Thomas, *Beruflich in Russland*, 15.
91. See Gorißen, 'Preis des Vertrauens', 102–3.
92. See Reichardt, *Soziales Kapital*, 16.
93. See Reichardt, *Soziales Kapital*, 16.
94. On the shifts undergone in working life with regard to the emotions, see Donauer, 'Emotions at Work'.
95. See Rasch and Feldman, *Thyssen und Stinnes*, 242 (A. Thyssen to H. Stinnes, 12 February 1904).
96. See Rasch and Feldman, *Thyssen und Stinnes*, 265–66 (A. Thyssen to H. Stinnes, 30 October 1904).
97. See Rasch and Feldman, *Thyssen und Stinnes*, 583–84 (A. Thyssen to H. Stinnes, 22 June 1922).
98. See Rasch and Feldman, *Thyssen und Stinnes*, 161 (A. Thyssen to H. Stinnes, 8 December 1899), 173 (A. Thyssen to H. Stinnes, 14 April 1900), 195 (A. Thyssen to H. Stinnes, 18 October 1901), 197 (A. Thyssen to H. Stinnes, 21 November 1901), 191 (A. Thyssen to H. Stinnes, 22 March 1901), 275 (A. Thyssen to H. Stinnes, 19 March 1905).
99. See Keynes, *The General Theory of Employment, Interest and Money*, 161–62.
100. See Akerlof and Shiller, *Animal Spirits: How Human Psychology Drives the Economy and Why It Matters for Global Capitalism*, 5, 11–18.
101. See Doll and Kaiser, 'So wurde der US-Chef'.
102. See 'Razzia bei Volkswagen – kein Verdacht gegen Winterkorn', *Wirtschaftswoche*.
103. See introduction to this volume.

Bibliography

Akerlof, G.A., and R.J. Shiller. *Animal Spirits: How Human Psychology Drives the Economy and Why It Matters for Global Capitalism*. Princeton, NJ: Princeton University Press, 2009.

Alparslan, A. *Strukturalistische Prinzipal-Agent-Theorie: Eine Reformulierung der Hidden-Action-Modelle aus der Perspektive des Strukturalismus*. Wiesbaden: Deutscher Universitäts-Verlag, 2006.

Bähr, J. *Werner von Siemens 1816–1892: A Biography*, trans. P.C. Sutcliffe. Munich: Beck, 2017 [Ger. orig. *Werner von Siemens 1816–1892: Eine Biographie*. Munich: Beck, 2016].

Berghoff, H. 'Die Zähmung des entfesselten Prometheus? Die Generierung von Vertrauenskapital und die Konstruktion des Marktes im Industrialisierungs-

und Globalisierungsprozess', in H. Berghoff and J. Vogel (eds), *Wirtschaftsgeschichte als Kulturgeschichte: Dimensionen eines Perspektivenwechsels* (Frankfurt am Main: Campus, 2004), 143–68.

'Branding'. *Gründerszene* [online journal]. Retrieved 28 November 2015 from http://www.gruenderszene.de/lexikon/begriffe/branding.

Caglioti, D.L. 'Trust, Business Groups and Social Capital: Building a Protestant Entrepreneurial Network in Nineteenth-Century Naples'. *Journal of Modern Italian Studies* 13(2) (2008), 219–36, doi: 10.1080/13545710802010974.

Condorcet, Marquis de. *Outlines of an Historical View of the Progress of the Human Mind: Being a Posthumous Work of the Late M. de Condorcet*. Philadelphia, PA: Lang and Ustick, 1796 [Fre. orig. *Esquisse d'un tableau historique des progrès de l'esprit humain*. Paris: Chez Agasse, 1795].

Derix, S., *Die Thyssens: Familie und Vermögen*. Paderborn: Schöningh, 2016.

Doll, N., and T. Kaiser. 'So wurde der US-Chef von VW vom Kongress gegrillt'. *Die Welt*, 8 October 2015. Retrieved 28 November 2015 from http://www.welt.de/wirtschaft/article147398686/So-wurde-der-US-Chef-von-VW-vom-Kongress-gegrillt.html.

Donauer, S. 'Emotions at Work – Working on Emotions: The Production of Economic Selves in Twentieth-Century Germany'. Ph.D. dissertation. Berlin: Freie Universität Berlin, 2013.

Ehrenberg, R. *Die Unternehmungen der Brüder Siemens*, vol. 1: *Bis zum Jahre 1870*. Jena: Gustav Fischer, 1906.

Eisenhardt, K.M. 'Agency Theory: An Assessment and Review'. *Academy of Management Review* 14(1) (1989), 57–74.

Feldman, G.D. *Hugo Stinnes: Biographie eines Industriellen, 1870–1924*. Munich: C.H. Beck, 1998.

Ferguson, A. *An Essay on the History of Civil Society*, 8th edn. Philadelphia, PA: Finley, 1819.

Fernández Pérez, P., and M.B. Rose (eds). *Innovation and Entrepreneurial Networks in Europe*. New York: Routledge, 2010.

Frevert, U. 'Vertrauen: Historische Annäherungen an eine Gefühlshaltung', in C. Benthien, A. Fleig and I. Kasten (eds), *Emotionalität: Zur Geschichte der Gefühle* (Cologne: Böhlau, 2000), 178–97.

_____. 'Vertrauen in historischer Perspektive', in R. Schmalz-Bruns and R. Zintl (eds), *Politisches Vertrauen: Soziale Grundlagen reflexiver Kooperation* (Baden-Baden: Nomos, 2002), 39–59.

_____. 'Vertrauen – Eine historische Spurensuche', in U. Frevert (ed.), *Vertrauen: Historische Annäherungen* (Göttingen: Vandenhoeck & Ruprecht, 2003), 7–66.

_____. 'Was haben Gefühle in der Geschichte zu suchen?'. *Geschichte und Gesellschaft* 35(2) (2009), 183–208, doi: 10.13109/gege.2009.35.2.183.

_____. 'Defining Emotions: Concepts and Debates over Three Centuries', in U. Frevert et al., *Emotional Lexicons: Continuity and Change in the Vocabulary of Feeling 1700–2000* (Oxford: Oxford University Press, 2011), 1–31.

_____. *Vertrauensfragen: Eine Obsession der Moderne*. Munich: Beck, 2013.

Gorißen, S. 'Der Preis des Vertrauens: Unsicherheit, Institutionen und Rationalität im vorindustriellen Fernhandel', in U. Frevert (ed.), *Vertrauen: Historische Annäherungen* (Göttingen: Vandenhoeck & Ruprecht, 2003), 90–118.

Hegel, G.W.F. *Elements of the Philosophy of Right*, ed. A.W. Wood, trans. H.B. Nisbet. Cambridge: Cambridge University Press, 1991 [Ger. orig. *Grundlinien der Philosophie des Rechts*. Berlin: Nicolai, 1821].

Heintzenberg, F. (ed.). *Aus einem reichen Leben: Werner von Siemens in Briefen an seine Familie und an Freunde*. Stuttgart: Deutsche Verlags-Anstalt, 1953.

Hitzer, B., and B. Gammerl. 'Wohin mit den Gefühlen? Vergangenheit und Zukunft des Emotional Turn in den Geschichtswissenschaften'. *Berliner Debatte Initial* 24(3) (2013), 31–40.

Hulverscheidt, C., and N. Richter. 'VW hat eine ganze Nation betrogen'. *Süddeutsche Zeitung*, 8 October 2015. Retrieved 28 November 2015 from http://www.sued deutsche.de/wirtschaft/anhoerung-vor-us-kongress-flucht-nach-vorne-1.268 3363.

Hume, D. 'Of Commerce', in D. Hume, *Essays: Moral, Political and Literary*, ed. E.F. Miller rev. edn (Indianapolis, IN: Liberty Fund, 1987), 253–67.

Jensen, M.C., and W.H. Meckling. 'Theory of the Firm: Managerial Behavior, Agency Costs and Ownership Structure'. *Journal of Financial Economics* 3(4) (1976), 305–60, doi: 10.1016/0304-405x(76)90026-x.

Johnson, C.H., et al. (eds). *Transregional and Transnational Families in Europe and Beyond: Experiences since the Middle Ages*. New York: Berghahn, 2011.

Jones, G. (ed.). *The Multinational Traders*. London: Routledge, 1999.

Keynes, J.M. *The General Theory of Employment, Interest and Money*. New York: Harcourt Brace & Co., 1936.

Lazarovic, S. 'Kongress grillt VW-USA-Chef'. *N-TV.de*, 8 October 2015. Retrieved 28 November 2015 from http://www.n-tv.de/wirtschaft/Kongress-grillt-VW-USA-Chef-article16102781.html.

Lubinski, C., J. Fear and P. Fernández Pérez (eds). *Family Multinationals: Entrepreneurship, Governance, and Pathways to Internationalization*. New York: Routledge, 2013.

Lubinski, C., J. Fear and P. Fernández Pérez. 'Family Multinationals: Entrepreneurship, Governance, and Pathways to Internationalization', in C. Lubinski, J. Fear and P. Fernández Pérez, *Family Multinationals: Entrepreneurship, Governance, and Pathways to Internationalization* (New York: Routledge, 2013), 1–20.

Ludovici, C.G. 'Handelsdiener', in *Eröffnete Akademie der Kaufleute oder vollständiges Kaufmanns-Lexicon*, vol. 3 (Leipzig: Bernhard Christoph Breitkopf, 1754), 158–59.

Lutz, M. *Siemens im Sowjetgeschäft: Eine Institutionengeschichte der deutsch-sowjetischen Beziehungen 1917–1933*. Stuttgart: Steiner, 2011.

———. 'Carl von Siemens: Vom "Prussky Ingener" zum transnationalen Unternehmer?'. *Zeitschrift für Unternehmensgeschichte* 58(2) (2013), 197–213, doi: 10.1515/zug-2013-0206.

———. *Carl von Siemens: 1829–1906: A Life between Family and World Firm*, trans. B. Chilcott. Vaduz: Maria-Stiftung, 2017 [Ger. orig. *Carl von Siemens, 1829–1906: Ein Leben zwischen Familie und Weltfirma*. Munich: Beck, 2013].

Maier, A. 'Lisa Davis: Die Frau, die den härtesten Job bei Siemens hat'. *Manager Magazin* (20 April 2015). Retrieved 2 June 2015 from http://

www.manager-magazin.de/magazin/artikel/siemens-lisa-davis-und-das-energiegeschaeft-a-1027545.html.
Montesquieu, C. de. *The Spirit of Laws*, vol. 1, trans. T. Nugent. New York: Colonial Press, 1899 [Fre. orig. *De l'esprit des lois*. Geneve: Barrillot & Fils, 1748].
Rasch, M. (ed.). *August Thyssen und Heinrich Thyssen-Bornemisza: Briefe einer Industriellenfamilie 1919–1926*. Essen: Klartext, 2010.
Rasch, M., and G.D. Feldman (eds). *August Thyssen und Hugo Stinnes: Ein Briefwechsel 1898–1922*. Munich: Beck, 2003.
'Razzia bei Volkswagen – kein Verdacht gegen Winterkorn'. *Wirtschaftswoche*, 8 October 2015. Retrieved 28 November 2015 http://www.wiwo.de/unternehmen/auto/vw-abgas-skandal-razzia-bei-volkswagen-kein-verdacht-gegen-winterkorn/12423756.html.
Reichardt, S. *Soziales Kapital 'im Zeitalter materieller Interessen': Konzeptionelle Überlegungen zum Vertrauen in der Zivil- und Marktgesellschaft des langen 19. Jahrhunderts (1780–1914)*. Berlin: WZB, 2003.
Ricoeur, P. *Time and Narrative*, 3 vols, trans. K. McLaughlin and D. Pellauer. Chicago: University of Chicago Press, 1984–1988 [Fre. orig. *Temps et Récit*. Paris: Editions du Seuil, 1983].
Ripperger, T. *Ökonomik des Vertrauens: Analyse eines Organisationsprinzips*, 2nd edn. Tübingen: Mohr Siebeck, 2003.
Sabean, D.W. 'German International Families in the Nineteenth Century: The Siemens Family as a Thought Experiment', in C.H. Johnson et al., *Transregional and Transnational Families in Europe and Beyond: Experiences since the Middle Ages* (New York: Berghahn, 2011), 229–52.
Scheer, M. 'Are Emotions a Kind of Practice (and Is That What Makes Them Have a History)? A Bourdieuian Approach to Understanding Emotion'. *History and Theory* 51(2) (2012), 193–220, doi: 10.1111/j.1468-2303.2012.00621.x.
Siegenthaler, H. *Regelvertrauen, Prosperität und Krisen: Die Ungleichmäßigkeit wirtschaftlicher und sozialer Entwicklung als Ergebnis individuellen Handelns und sozialen Lernens*. Tübingen: Mohr, 1993.
Siemens, W. 'An Karl in St Petersburg' (25 December 1887), in C. Matschoß (ed.), *Werner Siemens, Ein kurzgefaßtes Lebensbild nebst einer Auswahl seiner Briefe: Aus Anlass der 100. Wiederkehr seines Geburtstages*, vol. 2 (Berlin: Julius Springer, 1916), 911.
Smith, A. *An Inquiry into the Nature and Causes of the Wealth of Nations*, 2 vols. London: Methuen & Co., 1904.
Taussig, M. *Mimesis and Alterity: A Particular History of the Senses*. New York: Routledge, 1993.
Trivellato, F. *The Familiarity of Strangers: The Sephardic Diaspora, Livorno, and Cross-cultural Trade in the Early Modern Period*. New Haven, CT: Yale University Press, 2009.
Ullrich, V. 'Der König der Inflation: Gerald D. Feldman präsentiert den Schwerindustriellen Hugo Stinnes in zeitgemäßem Gewand . *Die Zeit*, 6 May 1999. Retrieved 19 October 2015 from http://www.zeit.de/1999/19/Der_Koenig_der_Inflation/komplettansicht.
'Volkswagen führt uns besser nicht an der Nase herum'. *Handelsblatt*, 7 October 2015. Retrieved 28 November 2015 from http://www.handelsblatt.com/

unternehmen/industrie/us-kongress-prueft-diesel-skandal-volkswagen-fuehrt-uns-besser-nicht-an-der-nase-herum/12422084.html.

Wittendorfer, F. 'Im Fokus: 16. März 1850 – Errichtung einer Siemens-Vertretung in London durch William Siemens'. Retrieved 1 June 2015 from https://www.siemens.com/history/de/aktuelles/1062_vertretung_london.htm.

Yoosefi, T., and A. Thomas. *Beruflich in Russland: Trainingsprogramm für Manager, Fach- und Führungskräfte*, 3rd edn. Göttingen: Vandenhoeck & Ruprecht, 2012.

Zürl, C.-H. *Erfolgreich in China: Ein Reisebuch für Manager*. Berlin: Springer, 1999.

Chapter 5

Diplomats
Kneeling and the Protocol of Humiliation

Ute Frevert

Willy Brandt's Warsaw genuflection on 7 December 1970 made history.[1] It was an emotional gesture that seemed to clearly depart from established practices of negotiating international relations. While the treaty that the West German Chancellor signed on the same day only briefly mentioned the 'great suffering' that the Second World War had inflicted 'on the nations of Europe' and on Poland in particular,[2] his kneeling conveyed sorrow, contrition and self-debasement – and immediately triggered strong emotional reactions. Novelist Günter Grass, who was a member of Brandt's delegation, reported that people looked 'astonished, frightened, ashamed', including 'the Polish hosts who thought that they knew German behaviour; this was new to them'.[3] Poland's Prime Minister József Cyrankiewicz, himself a former prisoner of Auschwitz and Mauthausen, expressed his sincere respect for the Social Democrat: 'Only he could do it. . . . The Poles have certainly understood him'.[4]

On this occasion Cyrankiewicz may have been right. As a general rule, however, it has never been easy to decipher emotional messages within diplomatic exchanges. After all, diplomacy has been known as the art of concealment. Diplomats have always been notorious for withholding emotions and hiding affects, passions and interests under the cloak of polite manners and ceremonial behaviour. As diplomats' manuals advise, the loss of discipline and control could trigger fatal clashes and serious conflicts. Strict adherence to diplomatic rules and conventions, by contrast, could safeguard peace and facilitate communication among international

Notes for this chapter begin on page 149.

players. Indeed, this is the main reason why such rules were established in the first place and, since the seventeenth century, became codified.[5]

Yet, as this chapter argues, even diplomatic encounters guided by 'ceremonial science' have never been devoid of emotions. As much as diplomats have excelled in the art of mastering and silencing individual feelings, they have communicated through an intensely emotional idiom: honour. From the early modern period onward, honour and its opposite, shame, have structured the language of international relations not only within Europe but also between European and non-European states. Language here has not been confined to spoken or written words. In fact, the human body has proved essential for asserting or denying honour. Kneeling is a particularly apt case in point that might help elucidate the role emotional practices have played in communication among states.

Such practices have hitherto been largely overlooked. Although historians of medieval and early modern Europe have recently developed an interest in how rituals and ceremonies contributed to the assertion of political power and the framing of international relations, they have not paid much attention to the languages of emotions.[6] They have thus failed to grasp the dynamics of honour and shame as they played out, for instance, in the refusal to kneel. Interpreted as reducing someone to a lower position, such humiliation caused serious conflicts whose forms and intensity are lost on those who ignore the political implications of shame and shaming.

Analysing emotional practices allows historians to treat diplomacy as more than a field of 'splendid encounters' or an art of negotiating state interests. As the Swiss legal theorist and diplomat Emer de Vattel stated in 1758, princes wanted to be represented 'not only in their rights and in the transactions of their affairs, but also in their dignity, their greatness, and their pre-eminence'.[7] Hence they could fall an easy prey to the politics of humiliation deployed by those who wanted to deliberately deny them greatness and pre-eminence. These politics had a huge impact during the era of European imperialism, with China as their main target. But they also had repercussions in Europe proper, as Willy Brandt's Warsaw genuflection demonstrates.

When the Chancellor fell to his knees in front of Nathan Rapoport's 1948 monument to the Jewish resistance fighters of the Warsaw Ghetto, 48 per cent of West German citizens found his gesture 'exaggerated', while 41 per cent approved.[8] Drawing on the heated domestic controversies over Ostpolitik, conservative opponents were fast to 'twist the genuflection into a kowtow', as Grass had feared and suspected.[9] Already prior to the events of 7 December, the Treaty of Warsaw had been condemned as shameful; no decent, honourable German would sign it, some said.[10] Instead of upholding Germany's claims to her pre-war territory, Brandt had allegedly succumbed to Poland's post-war demands and betrayed national interests. His kneeling was read as an act of deference and subservience that transformed humility (religiously framed or not) into kowtow-like humiliation.

The Kowtow in (Early) Modern European-Chinese Encounters

What did Europeans know about kowtows in the nineteenth and twentieth centuries, and how did they know it? The term entered the English language around 1800, while German speakers were introduced to it a century later.[11] In both countries, the linguistic innovation was the product of a series of diplomatic encounters in which the kowtow had played an important and highly controversial role, raising issues of honour and humiliation.

The first such encounter took place in 1793, when the British envoy George Macartney was received by the Chinese Emperor. Macartney had been ordered by King George III to offer congratulations and gifts on the Qianlong Emperor's birthday and, most importantly, to negotiate for reduced tariffs, fewer restrictions on trade for the British East India Company and a permanent British embassy in Peking. After his arrival, the envoy was instructed by Chinese officials about the customary ceremonial, which included performing the kowtow: he was supposed to kneel three times and touch his head to the ground nine times. The officials brought up the subject frequently, Macartney recalled: 'It seems to be a very serious matter with them, and a point which they have set their hearts upon. They pressed me most earnestly to comply with it'. But Macartney refused, offering instead to treat the Emperor with 'the same obeisance which I did to my own Sovereign'. The etiquette of the English Court dictated kneeling upon one knee and kissing the monarch's hand. If this were not deemed appropriate, the envoy agreed to conform to the Chinese etiquette 'provided a person of equal rank with mine were appointed to perform the same ceremony before my Sovereign's picture'.

After several weeks of tense negotiation, Macartney was finally received by the Qianlong Emperor on his terms. Still, he left China with 'most severe' disappointment. Even though he had managed to avoid the kowtow and 'perform the ceremony after the manner of my own country', he was sent home empty-handed.[12] The Qianlong Emperor let the British King know that he appreciated his 'sincere humility and obedience' and acknowledged the 'tribute articles' (including a planetarium of superb craft and enormous worth). 'Nevertheless', he added, 'we have never valued ingenious articles, nor do we have the slightest need of your Country's manufactures'. He also turned down the British request to establish an official embassy, stating that it 'is not in harmony with the regulations of the Celestial Empire'. Finally, he advised King George III to 'simply act in conformity with our wishes by strengthening your loyalty and swearing perpetual obedience'.[13]

Interestingly, the Imperial Edict had been drafted long before negotiations about kowtowing had even started between Macartney and his Chinese interlocutors. The envoy's refusal to prostrate himself before the Emperor had no impact on the latter's politics and attitude. The Qianlong Emperor was at the height of his power; his Celestial Empire seemed safe and invincible. Vassal states from Central to Southeast Asia offered their tributes and paid him reverence, as weaker powers did to greater powers. A similar asymmetry reigned between China and those countries 'in the Western ocean' that, since the sixteenth century, had sent envoys to solicit trading privileges or other favours. Quite obviously, it was their own (and wholly one-sided) desire to sail across the sea in order to 'be civilized by Chinese culture', as an Imperial Edict put it in 1794.[14] They were therefore well advised to comply with local customs and etiquette. For the ambassadors of the Dutch East India Company, this was a matter of course. Like everyone else, one recorded, '[w]e knelt down' on the street when the Emperor passed on his way to the summer palace. And they happily 'perceived by a look he cast upon us, that we were not unobserved'.[15]

From the Chinese perspective, such compliance was a sign of polished manners.[16] When Macartney stubbornly refused to comply, his hosts found him ignorant, ill-mannered and tiresome but not important enough to waste more time and energy on him. If Korean princes or Tibetan lamas had refused to kowtow, the Chinese would have been concerned. Europeans, however, neither posed a threat to Qing rule in 1793 nor did they have much to offer to the Chinese.[17]

But why did Macartney refuse to kowtow? Considering that his mission was ambitious and mattered greatly to Britain's economic interests, it might seem puzzling that he had taken the risk of upsetting the Chinese. After all, he 'endeavoured always to put the best face upon everything, and to preserve a perfect serenity of countenance upon all occasions', which included shutting his eyes 'upon the flags of our yachts, which were inscribed "The English Ambassador bringing tribute to the Emperor of China"'.[18] So what was so special about kowtowing?

Macartney indeed considered ceremonials to be of great importance, since they communicated power relations. In his opinion, audience etiquette at the Imperial Court had two major flaws: first, it did not conform to the principle of reciprocity, which he believed should govern bilateral communications. Second, and related to the first point, it left no space for distinction 'between the homage of tributary Princes and the ceremony used on the part of a great and independent sovereign'.[19] As his secretary George Staunton described, it rather reflected 'the official style of arrogated superiority' that put everyone else in an inferior position. For the Chinese government, Staunton observed, 'no transaction with foreigners was admissible by it on the ground of reciprocal benefit, but as a grace and condescension from the former to the latter'. Such condescension visibly played out during ceremonial interaction. In Staunton's words, these things 'effect a physical, as well as imply a moral, inequality between the party requiring, and him who pays, such homage'.[20] In the eyes of Macartney's German translator, the kowtow was simply 'humiliating' and incompatible with the 'dignity' of a British envoy.[21]

Interestingly, such strong wording never appeared in the envoy's diary or in his negotiations with Chinese officials. While Englishmen might have been personally appalled by 'this apparent worship of a fellow mortal',[22] they were politically invested in the concept of equality between states and the recognition of British sovereignty. During the early modern period, such concepts had become the foundation of European statehood and were directly translated into diplomatic ceremonies. Sovereignty, that is, political autonomy and independence,[23] was not just stated or claimed but had to be acknowledged by others. As the Dutch diplomat Abraham de Wicquefort wrote in 1676, sovereignty was most illustriously demonstrated by the state's right to send and receive ambassadors.[24] According to Vattel's influential *Droit des gens* of 1758, 'to contest their right in this instance is doing them a very great injury; it is, in fact, contesting their sovereign dignity'.[25]

As Macartney's mission showed, the Chinese neither accepted the principle of sovereignty nor did they subscribe to the notion of equality. Only once had they been forced to deal with such claims, but under different circumstances. In 1720, the Russian envoy Count Ismailof insisted that his monarch Peter the Great 'was on equal terms with the Emperor'. He, as Peter's representative, would thus not perform the customary prostrations but 'would make an obeisance according to the custom of his country'. The Chinese Emperor was profoundly 'displeased' and tried to talk Ismailof out of his 'unreasonable pretensions'.[26] At the same time, he was well aware that Russia and China maintained special relations and ordered his officials and interpreters to assert some measure of reciprocity. Whenever the Emperor

> should send an ambassador to the Czar, he promised that his representative should stand uncovered before him, although in China none but condemned criminals exposed their heads bare, and should perform all the other ceremonies customary at Moscow. No sooner had we [the interpreters] arrived at

these words, than the chief mandarin instantly took off his cap before the ambassador.[27]

This gesture indicated that the promise would be kept and seemed to acknowledge the equal and reciprocal character of mutual relations. Ismailof was immediately 'satisfied' and, on the day of audience, 'prostrated himself before the table'.[28]

Macartney may or may not have known about the incident. His argument, indeed, was the same, although he offered the Chinese a slightly different deal: if the officials kowtowed before his Majesty's portrait, he would reciprocate in the Emperor's presence. The proposal, however, was rejected outright. The Chinese might have been inclined, at least theoretically, to follow Russian rules in Russia, but they were in no way prepared to extend their own practices of reverence to foreign and tributary rulers. Macartney had thus clearly overstretched his search for equality. The fact that he had secured his personal 'dignity' by not going down on both knees did not spare Britain the fate of being denied 'sovereign dignity', as Vattel had put it: Britain was not allowed to establish a permanent embassy in Peking.

It took two wars to gain that right. The 1858 treaties of Tientsin not only granted Britain, France, Russia and the United States favourable trading conditions and opportunities to build independent economic, military and religious infrastructures in China. They also forced the Chinese government to open the country to foreign capital and permit foreign legations. The British undertook a special effort to ensure that no diplomatic representative at the Imperial Court would

> perform any ceremony derogatory to him as representing the sovereign of an independent nation, on a footing of equality with that of China. On the other hand, he shall use the same forms of ceremony and respect to His Majesty the Emperor as are employed by the Ambassadors, Ministers, or Diplomatic Agents of Her Majesty towards the Sovereigns of independent and equal European nations.[29]

In contrast to Macartney, Queen Victoria's plenipotentiary Lord Elgin was no longer willing to negotiate the terms of reciprocity and equality. Instead, British Ministers would treat the Chinese Emperor as they would any other European ruler.[30]

This set a new tone in Chinese-European relations. Due to their increasing economic, technological and military might, Great Britain and other imperialist powers could afford to violate the common diplomatic practice of following local customs in showing reverence and respect.[31] Driven by a new sense of superiority, they forcibly universalized European diplomatic etiquette, thereby stressing their power and openly belittling the recipient. The British, however, did not talk about power but about how they themselves were humiliated by the Chinese policy of refusing parity and demanding that diplomats kowtow before the Emperor. In this vein, Garnet Wolseley, the young Quartermaster General of the British contingent fighting in the Second Opium War, strode upright into the audience hall at Peking's Summer Palace in 1860. He stopped in front of the imperial throne 'before which so many princes and ambassadors of haughty monarchs humbly prostrated themselves, according to the slave-like obeisance customary at the Chinese court'. Those days of humiliation were now gone once and for all.[32]

For the Chinese, the language of humiliation was altogether new and difficult to understand. In their view, ceremonial practices at the Imperial Court had not been designed to humiliate those who performed them. Qing notions of sovereignty differed markedly from those agreed upon by European states and so did the meaning of the kowtow as an act of both humility and privilege.[33] Since the concept of equality was not part of the Chinese political lexicon, the ceremonial could not but reflect unequal power relations. As long as vassal states agreed to their dependent status, they found nothing resentful in showing humility. Only Europeans, obsessed with equality, came to perceive humility as humiliating, but their complaints were bound to fall on deaf ears.

When those ears were forcibly opened, the once mighty and proud Empire quickly learned to speak the language of humiliation on its own terms. Officials and intellectuals frequently referred to 'our humiliation' by 'foreigners' and voiced deep resentment about being 'shamefully humiliated' by 'barbarians' who had forced their way into Chinese territory with 'strong ships and effective guns'.[34] At the same time, the Imperial Court used every opportunity to stop the Europeans from celebrating victory and imposing their own ceremonial etiquette. Although the government could no longer prevent foreign ambassadors from taking up residence in the capital after 1860, the Emperor refused to receive them and recognize their credentials. Ceremonial issues served as the last bastion of resistance to the ever-increasing presence and power of Western 'barbarians'.

The latter, in turn, persisted with their efforts to break the resistance and establish what they claimed were principles of mutual equality. The British in particular insisted that the Emperor should grant audiences and send envoys abroad. When finally, in 1873, the representatives of Britain, France, Russia, the Netherlands, the United States and Japan were received in audience, London's minister was more than content. The ceremony largely followed European standards: upon entering the hall, the diplomats 'bowed to the Emperor, advanced a few paces and bowed again, then advanced a few paces farther bowing again, and halted before a long yellow table'. After delivering the address and credentials, '[w]e then all withdrew in the usual fashion, "à reculons", and bowing'. These gestures were far from trivial, as Sir Thomas Wade acknowledged in a report to the Earl Granville, Secretary of State for Foreign Affairs:

> We must remember the long-standing pretension of the Emperor of China to this act of homage [kowtowing], and the tradition of isolated supremacy on which that pretension had been based. The Empire has, for the first time in its history, broken with the tradition . . . we appeared face to face with the Emperor, standing, because we represented Governments the equal of his own.[35]

Kneeling as an 'Oriental' Custom?

Henceforth, the Eastern world would have to follow the 'usages of the Western world', even though the latter had, for a long time, not known common usages and was still far from displaying unified ceremonial standards that acknowledged the equality of all involved. The Pope, for instance, with his status as a head of state and spiritual leader of all Catholics, continued to observe manners similar to 'Oriental' practices. During his public audiences, people regularly bent down on their knees and kissed the papal ring. In Britain, the King's privy councillors similarly bent their knees while swearing allegiance.[36]

Such practices had their origins in antiquity, both 'Oriental' and 'Occidental'.[37] In the Middle Ages, emperors and princes knelt during anointment, vassals knelt during commendation and homage and knights knelt when receiving the accolade.[38] While in Christian, Jewish and Muslim religions genuflection signalled an act of contrition before God, it had been known since ancient times as a political ritual of submission and was often associated with acts of apology.[39] From the early modern era onwards, however, such gestures of self-debasement were increasingly shunned.[40] In 1734, the Duke of Württemberg ended the practice of supplicants kneeling before him. The Prussian king Frederick II followed suit in 1783, and so did the Austrian Archduke and Holy Roman Emperor in 1787.[41] For 'enlightened' kings and princes, kneeling as a sign of obeisance and reverence was to be reserved exclusively for God and should no longer be part of any secular ceremonial.

The educated public and Protestant circles, in particular, applauded the new policy, especially since the power of princes was increasingly considered to be representational, which rendered gestures of personal subservience inappropriate. Some went on to argue that 'human dignity' was 'humiliated' by the 'slave-like habit' of having to kneel before rulers.

Such 'Oriental' practices did not suit citizens of Christian countries, held to be brothers and free children of God.[42]

Juxtaposing Asia and Europe, despotic and patriotic rule, slavery and freedom, fear and love had become popular tropes of European public discourse by the end of the eighteenth century.[43] Feelings and gestures of homage increasingly served to distinguish the barbarian and cruel 'Orientals' from the civilized and fair-minded Westerners. Civilization was directly translated into bodily postures that were supposed to express respect and reverence without showing submission and adoration. At most European courts, three bows with uncovered head became the common form of paying homage, whereas early modern practices had been much more diverse.[44]

The more European states came to acknowledge each other's sovereign power and accept parity, as codified in 1815/18, the more they resented what Staunton had described as the physical and moral inequality embedded in 'Oriental' customs. This reflected broader changes in society. Even though the French and American revolutions failed to completely overturn and modernize diplomatic ceremonial,[45] they did indeed promote a new sensitivity towards asymmetric power relations. As male citizens pushed for equal political rights and civic honour (for themselves only, ignoring women and people of colour), they came to despise social practices tinged with personal subservience. Questioning allegedly natural hierarchies and God-given inequality were closely linked with emphasizing individual autonomy and dignity. Kneeling counted as undignified behaviour, whereas an erect posture was well suited to self-confident male, white citizens. Nineteenth-century advice books taught men to always keep their body straight: 'Any flexion of the back is to be avoided since it makes a ridiculous figure'.[46] Bending one's knees and tilting the body, as in a curtsey, was now reserved for women, and kneeling came to signal female submission, both in domestic service and in sexual practices.[47]

Hence the reluctance of diplomats to kneel was far from surprising. To be compelled to kowtow meant to forgo one's claim to independence and equality and to succumb to feminine or slave-like postures of subservience and docility. Both stood at odds with how Europeans perceived themselves: as the bearers of sovereign power and the embodiment of masculine prowess in an increasingly imperialist cast.

International Law and the Politics of Apology

In its effort to export and universalize European civilization, high imperialism generously used and reinterpreted international law. Although this law did not cover ceremonial questions, legal scholars alongside politicians and diplomats successfully imposed their own reading of 'Oriental courts' and their offensive 'impositions', which, they claimed, could be reconciled neither with the 'dignity of represented states' nor with the 'dignity of free men'.[48] Furthermore, they persuaded the Chinese to learn and acknowledge the key principles of European diplomatic relations: the 'reciprocal duty' to send and receive public ambassadors as well as the idea that ambassadors represented 'the person and dignity of the sovereign' and were therefore 'entitled to the same honors to which their constituent would be entitled, were he personally present'. They also included the principle of diplomatic immunity: an ambassador represented 'the rights, interests, and dignity of the sovereign or State by whom he is delegated, his person is sacred and inviolable'.[49]

Insulting an envoy was thus tantamount to insulting his monarch and required instant reparation and satisfaction. If satisfaction failed to be granted, a war might ensue.[50] Such conflicts of honour greatly multiplied in scope and number during the late nineteenth century.[51] Once princely honour was transformed into state and national honour, it acquired a far more comprehensive significance and force. In an age of growing political participation, the national public, alerted and informed by the expanding media industry, felt instantly addressed and served as a sounding board for government action. The Franco-Prussian war of 1870, which was initially staged as a conflict of honour in which no side was keen to offer satisfaction, serves as an excellent example.[52]

Among non-European countries, China became the major target of honour politics at around the same time. When the French consulate, cathedral and orphanage at Tientsin were attacked in 1870, the French legation in Peking vehemently protested and called for reparation and satisfaction. In their view, pulling down and destroying the French flag constituted the most serious offense, more serious than the killing of French subjects or the demolition of the house of God. Apart from offering financial compensation for the material damage ('reparation' in international law), the Chinese government was forced to send a mission of apology to Paris. Their only task was to grant satisfaction and soothe the 'feelings hurt' by the assault on national honour.[53]

By the end of the century, such apologies had become common practice between China and European powers.[54] Germany, a newcomer to the imperialist camp, stood out for its particular sensitivity towards violations of its honour. Upon his arrival in Peking in 1896, the German ambassador Edmund von Heyking and his eloquent wife Elisabeth deliberately distanced themselves from an older generation of diplomats, who, as they saw it, had too often acted 'as the advocate of the Chinese'. Subscribing to the 'new, reality-driven' politics, they immediately set out to teach the 'dirty barbarians' a lesson in humiliation: they 'do not need European envoys, but European masters – the sooner, the better'.[55]

The first lesson was given when the German ambassador mistakenly left the Imperial Hall of Audience through the central exit. This was a serious breach of etiquette, as the middle door was reserved for the Emperor and foreign ministers who presented their letters of credence during their first Imperial audience. Once they had turned over the royal document, they were supposed to exit via the door to the left. When Heyking was about to leave through the middle exit, a high-ranking Chinese official pulled him by the sleeve in order to steer him through the side door. Furiously, Heyking complained and demanded an apology, which was denied. According to the U.S. ambassador Charles Denby, who was well versed in the troubled history of imperial audiences, the Chinese had a point. Heyking, however, insisted and threatened that he would not attend a formal lunch organized by the Chinese Foreign Council. A few days later, the official who had touched the ambassador's sleeve, and Li Hongzhang, one of the most influential men in Chinese foreign politics, paid him a formal visit and offered their apologies.[56]

The next lesson came in 1897. When German naval officers were attacked by a Chinese crowd, Heyking immediately demanded 'satisfaction'. The local governor sent a letter of apology and ordered a Chinese warship to hoist and salute the German flag. A few days later, when several German missionaries were killed, Heyking intended to ask all members of the Foreign Council to personally apologize at the embassy. But, in the meantime, Wilhelm II had decided to seize the area of Kiao-chou as 'compensation'.[57] Now it was the Chinese's turn to protest against what they perceived as 'humiliation' and 'rape' – albeit to no avail.[58]

From the 1870s onwards, China was forced to offer apologies at the same pace as she lost ground to foreign powers. Officially, the politics of apology was in line with international law. But when imperialist countries such as France, Great Britain and, increasingly, Japan used the law to play the honour card and demand satisfaction for their hurt feelings, they did more than just observe official protocol. Under the pretence of equality – forcing the Chinese to recognize the 'equality of other governments' as British Minister Wade put it in 1875[59] – they pursued a course of inequality and dominance. Ultimately, their own hurt feelings served the aim of humiliating the inferior party. While apologies among equals were praised as an honourable practice (as in affairs among aristocratic or upper-middle-class men of honour), apologies offered by inferiors to superiors were intended to inflict shame and further debase the inferior party. The message did not fail to get across.

Politics of Humiliation: The 1901 Kowtow Affair

The diplomacy of honour and shame reached its climax, but also its turning point, in 1901. Once again, it was the Germans who delivered the message of humiliation. During the Boxer Rebellion, two diplomats had lost their lives: German Ambassador Clemens von Ketteler and Japanese Legation Chancellor Akira Sugiyama. After the rebellion was crushed by the troops of the Eight-Nation Alliance, the latter compiled a list of demands and presented them to the Imperial Court. While the British were keen on improving trade conditions, the Germans were mainly concerned with honour. The Foreign Office had made it clear from the start that Germany considered it 'a national point of honour' to request 'expiation' and 'satisfaction' for its murdered representative. When Ketteler's successor in Peking communicated this to his European, American and Japanese counterparts they consented unanimously. At the suggestion of the British Minister Sir Ernest Satow, the request was included in the list of demands that were handed over to the Chinese government in December 1900.[60] In an Imperial Decree, the Chinese assented to all terms by conveying 'an idea of the extent to which [they] weigh upon our heart'. According to Satow, this was a highly ambivalent expression that could 'satisfy parties with conflicting views according to the way in which it is read. . . . The words "weigh upon the heart" might mean regret for what has happened; they may, on the other hand, conceal a feeling of resentment with regard to the terms proposed'.[61]

Resentment was not a far cry from what Chinese officials felt when confronted with the dictates of 'the Powers'. In their eyes, the December Protocol complemented the politics of humiliation without leaving them much room for manoeuvre. As early as September 1900, the Emperor had dispatched a telegram to the German Kaiser offering his apologies:

> We have already most deeply lamented and regretted that your Majesty's Minister, Baron von Ketteler, has fallen a victim to the revolt that suddenly broke out in China . . . By Decree of to-day's date we command that sacrifices shall be offered on an altar for the deceased . . . Our grief and our recollection of the deceased will be thus expressed.[62]

In his reply, Wilhelm II 'noted with satisfaction therefrom that your Majesty is striving to expiate according to the usages and precepts of your religion the shameful murder of my Minister in defiance of all the dictates of civilization. Still, as German Emperor and as a Christian, I cannot consider this misdeed as expiated by drink-offerings'.[63] Instead, he urged the Chinese Emperor to bring those responsible 'to their merited punishment' and have them 'atone for their shameful act'.[64]

For about a year, diplomats worked frantically to make this happen. Finally, in July 1901, Prince Chun, brother and 'nearest blood-relation' of the Chinese emperor, embarked on a mission of formal apology that was supposed to resolve the issue once and for all. When the Prince and his interpreter, who later took over as Chinese ambassador in Berlin, were received by the Kaiser in an audience at Potsdam's New Palace, Chun offered his imperial brother's 'sincere regret' for what had happened during the Boxer Rebellion. In a letter to Wilhelm II, the Chinese Emperor confirmed 'how intensely we are now possessed by feelings of shame and remorse'.[65] The German Kaiser accepted the apology and saw the Chinese delegation off with full military honours.

Behind the scenes, however, dramatic events had unfolded prior to the Marble Hall meeting. While the Chinese were on their way to Europe, Wilhelm II thought about how the ceremony might make the encounter a memorable event that would showcase Chinese penitence. Finally, he warmed up to the idea of having the Prince's suite kneel before the imperial throne. Having asked both an eminent sinologist and the German Minister in Peking for advice, the Foreign Office was alarmed. Although Professor Arendt and Minister Mumm unanimously recommended forms of reception that emphasized the expiatory character of the visit, they were opposed to 'oriental ceremonies'. Yet, Wilhelm insisted on the need for the Chinese to kneel 'as is customary before their own Emperor'. The Prince himself would be generously allowed to remain standing and offer the customary three bows while everybody else should be on their knees for the entire duration of the audience.[66]

When the news reached the Prince, he instantly contacted his government. Excusing himself on account of illness, he refused to continue his journey until the affair was settled in his interest. This took longer than expected. For a whole week telegrams were exchanged between Basel and Peking and numerous trips undertaken between Berlin and the Swiss border city. Meanwhile, the media got wind of the conflict. National and international newspapers reported and commented. While the London *Times* 'entirely sympathize[d] with the feeling of the German people that the Chinese envoy should be made to feel the penitential character of his mission' and 'taste the humiliation they have brought upon themselves', they cautioned 'that a kotow in the city where Voltaire was the guest of Frederick the Great would be liable, to say the least of it, to misunderstanding'. The government 'of an enlightened people' should not 'borrow from the servile etiquette of the Far East'.[67] The *New York Times* frequently referred to the 'humiliating ceremony', and so did the *Washington Post* with regard to 'the obsolete custom of kotowing'.[68]

German newspapers were far less critical. They readily quoted Swiss journalists, who ridiculed the Chinese as infantile and effeminate, adding that they lacked humility. Prince Chun's mission to Berlin was likened to Emperor Heinrich's walk to Canossa in 1077, an iconic image of humiliation.[69] Satirical magazines printed caricatures with maids tearing away the Prince's trousers that he had wet after being confronted with the Kaiser's request for a kowtow.[70] The *Berliner Damen-Zeitung* similarly commented on the 'illness of fear' that manifested itself when a person's heart sank into his boots (or, as in the German phrase, into his trousers).[71]

The prolonged 'diplomatic illness' of the Prince put a serious strain on diplomatic relations. German readers were informed that people abroad had started to laugh at the Kaiser's policy, deeming that it was out of touch with the principles of European civilization.[72] In Berlin, the Foreign Office mobilized everyone to change the Emperor's mind. Knowing that the other powers, especially Russia and Japan, considered the kowtow an excessive form of 'humiliation', they were concerned about its 'political disadvantages'.[73] Wilhelm, however, feared losing face, above all to the British, and would have rather sent his fleet to China again than compromise.[74] What finally persuaded him to relent was the experts' argument that kowtowing was a profoundly religious ritual. As such it could or should not be performed for a foreign ruler to avoid hurting religious feelings on both sides.[75]

In his diary, Prince Chun noted that he received a telegram on 2 September 1901 informing him 'that the German Kaiser apparently no longer insists on the kowtow ceremony being performed during the audience' and that he should now 'travel to Germany as quickly as possible'. Upon arriving in Berlin the following day, he was welcomed by the Kaiser's dignitaries and driven to Potsdam, where 'an innumerable number of people lined both sides of the road': 'Young and old people lifted their hats in salute when I went by in my carriage'. On 4 September, Chun delivered the Chinese Emperor's letter, accompanied only by his interpreter.

> In the Great Hall of the New Palace I bowed thrice before the German Kaiser and conveyed to him the letter, after having read its contents aloud. The Kaiser responded with a few words, and the audience was over. The Kaiser offered an escort of 200 riders who guided me back to the Orangery. The Kaiser returned my visit at around 1 o'clock in the afternoon.[76]

There is no direct mention in the diary of the turmoil that had preceded the audience. As a matter of fact, the controversy appears to have been partly and, possibly, intentionally caused by botched communication and messages 'lost in translation'. Initially, the German documents made no mention of the term 'kowtow'. Both Wilhelm and *Oberhofmarschall* August Graf zu Eulenburg, who was responsible for organizing imperial audiences, had spoken of 'kneeling down'. But for the Chinese delegation, the term *Kniefall* (genuflection) amounted to *guikou* (to kneel and perform the kowtow), turning a ceremonial question into a major diplomatic incident.[77] Aware of the fact that the ritual was not part of international diplomatic etiquette, Prince Chun was concerned that he would blemish 'the honour of the country' if he consented to the Kaiser's demands. His government adopted the same view and promptly contacted the German Minister in Peking, who was asked to convince Chancellor von Bülow to omit the kowtow 'because this ceremonial had never been practiced in Europe, did not suit European customs and civilized manners, and was about to be abolished in China in the near future'.[78]

For the German side, performing the whole ritual was obviously out of the question, especially after experts explained its background and proper practice. In accordance with European traditions, kneeling seemed a sufficient gesture of abasement that would convey the message 'you cannot get away with insulting the German Emperor'.[79] Even after he abandoned the plan, Wilhelm made sure that the ceremonial included some derogatory arrangements and expected the Chinese visitors to notice. Escorts and salutes were withheld until the letter of apology had been delivered; during the audience the Kaiser remained seated.[80]

The encounter between Prince Chun and Kaiser Wilhelm was thus riddled with cultural misunderstandings, disinformation and mixed emotions. The Chinese envoy had arrived on a 'hardly enjoyable' mission, as Otto Franke, who served as a translator for the German Foreign Office in Peking and happened to be on the same ship, commented.[81] The task of communicating his Emperor's 'feelings of shame and remorse' was a humiliating act that placed China in an inferior position. Had he complied with the Germans' request for kneeling (or what he understood as kowtowing), the humiliation would have been even more profound. Each side was familiar with the long history of objections to the ritual, which Europeans interpreted as 'derogatory'. So Wilhelm's idea of forcing the Chinese delegation to kneel before him could not but thoroughly offend and debase his visitors.

The Chinese eventually managed to safeguard their country's 'honour' and even gained the upper hand as they found themselves, quite unexpectedly, in a position of power.[82] When Wilhelm conceded and let the audience ceremony follow European protocol, this was generally perceived as a diplomatic victory for China. According to Ernest Satow, the Chinese were 'jubilant' after hearing 'that the Emperor William has given way'.[83] Their non-compliance had shamed the Kaiser and, according to the *Washington Post*, rid the mission 'of all semblance of a national spectacle illustrating German imperial supremacy'.[84]

The turn of the tide did not go unnoticed amidst the German public either. While the Chinese Prince had initially been scorned and ridiculed, he was practically admired by everyone after being received by Wilhelm II. In Berlin, local stores offered a popular piece of merchandise: a small figurine depicting the Prince 'before and after the *Kotau*'. Before, his moustache was drooping, giving the face a melancholy expression. Pulling a paper string, however, produced a different picture: the moustache shot up and the figure looked like a proud and bold character. The item sold well and was said to reflect the feelings of ordinary Berliners, who acknowledged the Prince as the winner rather than the loser in the diplomatic game of humiliation.[85] The Kaiser, by contrast, found himself at the losing end. Having played for high stakes, the result was 'hardly enjoyable'; as Franke bitterly recalled, the affair had turned German diplomacy into 'the laughing stock of the European world'.[86]

* * *

Apart from sardonic laughter, the 'kowtow comedy'[87] also earned the Germans a new word. In 1907, Meyer's *Großes Konversations-Lexikon* for the first time included the lemma *Kotau*, which was translated as: 'Chinese ceremony of deepest subservience'. Readers were informed that such ceremony had been expected of Prince Chun's 1901 expiatory delegation to Berlin but had to be abandoned because it proved 'unacceptable to loyal Chinese'.[88]

Since then, the term has remained in the German vocabulary and can, as evidenced by Günter Grass in 1970, be easily played upon to invoke profoundly negative feelings. To this day, the word kowtow is used as a metaphor to describe a submissive gesture, signalling not simply obedience but capitulation and (self-)humiliation. Consequently, performing the act denigrates a nation's foreign policy as weak, permissive and lacking national honour.[89] Even though the principle of 'sovereign equality' had been acknowledged by the United Nations Charter in 1945, notions of honour and humiliation still resonated in people's hearts and minds. When U.S. President Barack Obama bowed to the Saudi King Abdullah in 2009, he was accused of displaying 'fealty to a foreign potentate' and belittling 'the power and independence' of his own country.[90]

Hence, languages of emotion expressed through performative acts meant to show respect or reverence continue to play an important role in international relations. They gained momentum during the age of imperialism, often serving the aim of humiliating and shaming the inferior party. But they could backfire, as they did in 1901. Or, as in Willy Brandt's case, they could be used to subvert diplomatic protocol. The West German Chancellor found nothing submissive in kneeling at the Warsaw Ghetto memorial. He 'felt that bowing my head was not enough' in order to 'apologize on behalf of our people for the million-fold crime that was committed in the abused name of Germany'. So he did 'what human beings do when speech fails them': he let his body express his feelings of shame and sorrow – a body, however, that held its back erect while bending the knees, thus striking a balance between a traditional gesture of humility and self-humiliation and the posture of self-confident masculine sovereignty.[91]

Ute Frevert is Director at the Max Planck Institute for Human Development and Scientific Member of the Max Planck Society. Between 2003 and 2007 she was professor of German history at Yale University and prior to that she taught History at the Universities of Konstanz, Bielefeld and the Freie Universität Berlin. Her research interests include the history of the emotions, social and cultural history of modern times, gender history and political history. Ute Frevert is honorary professor at the Freie Universität Berlin and a member of several national and international academies.

Notes

1. Gibney and Roxstrom, 'The Status of State Apologies', 911–39, esp. 928; Teitel, 'The Transitional Apology', 101–14, esp. 105; Nobles, *The Politics of Official Apologies*.
2. 'The Treaty of Warsaw (7 December 1970)'.
3. Grass, 'Politisches Tagebuch: Betroffen sein', 81.
4. Behrens, *'Durfte Brandt knien?'*: *Der Kniefall in Warschau und der deutsch-polnische Vertrag: Eine Dokumentation der Meinungen*, 61, 123.
5. Jones, *Splendid Encounters: The Thought and Conduct of Diplomacy*, with special reference to books of advice, see 52–56; Vec, *Zeremonialwissenschaft im Fürstenstaat: Studien zur juristischen und politischen Theorie absolutistischer Herrschaftsrepräsentation*.
6. See, for example, Stollberg-Rilinger, *The Emperor's Old Clothes: Constitutional History and the Symbolic Language of the Holy Roman Empire*. As a counter-example, see Althoff, 'Der König weint: Rituelle Tränen in öffentlicher Kommunikation', 239–52; Althoff, 'Ira Regis: Prolegomena to a History of Royal Anger', 59–74; Althoff, 'Gefühle in der öffentlichen Kommunikation des Mittelalters', 82–99; Althoff, 'Du rire et des larmes: Pourquoi les émotions intéressent-elles les médiévistes?', 27–39.
7. De Vattel, *The Law of Nations or Principles of the Law of Nature, Applied to the Conduct and Affairs of Nations and Sovereigns: From the French of Monsieur de Vattel*, 459.
8. Behrens, *'Durfte Brandt knien?'*, 109.
9. Grass, *Politisches Tagebuch*, 81. See the definition of kowtow (*Kniefall*) in *Brockhaus-Enzyklopädie*, vol 10: *Kat–Kz*, 544.
10. Behrens, *'Durfte Brandt knien?'*, 16–17, 27–28.

11. Chantrell, *The Oxford Dictionary of Word Histories*, 291.
12. Cranmer-Byng, *An Embassy to China: Lord Macartney's Journal, 1793–1794*, vol. 8: *Britain and the China Trade 1635–1842*, 90, 84, 100, 152, 120. As to the later Amherst embassy, see Gao, 'The "Inner Kowtow Controversy" during the Amherst Embassy to China, 1816–1817', 595–614; Gao, 'The Amherst Embassy and British Discoveries in China', 568–87.
13. Cranmer-Byng, 'Lord Macartney's Embassy to Peking in 1793: From Official Chinese Documents', 134, 136–37, 158. See Harrison, 'The Qianlong Emperor's Letter to George III and the Early-Twentieth-Century Origins of Ideas about Traditional China's Foreign Relations', 680–701.
14. Duyvendak, 'The Last Dutch Embassy to the Chinese Court (1794–1795)', 88; Blussé, 'Peeking into the Empires: Dutch Embassies to the Courts of China and Japan', 14–29.
15. Van Braam, *An Authentic Account of the Embassy of the Dutch East-India Company, to the Court of the Emperor of China, in the Years 1794 and 1795*, 285; Duyvendak, 'Last Dutch Embassy', 65.
16. Rockhill, *Diplomatic Audiences at the Court of China*, 29; Pritchard, 'The Kotow in the Macartney Embassy to China in 1793', 197.
17. Hevia, '"The Ultimate Gesture of Deference and Debasement": Kowtowing in China', 233–34.
18. Cranmer-Byng, *Embassy to China*, 88, 90.
19. Cranmer-Byng, *Embassy to China*, 119.
20. Staunton, *An Authentic Account of an Embassy from the King of Great Britain to the Emperor of China*, 80, 72, 79.
21. Hüttner, *Nachricht von der britischen Gesandtschaftsreise nach China 1792–94*, 121.
22. Staunton, *Authentic Account*, 88.
23. Pölitz, *Die Staatswissenschaften im Lichte unsrer Zeit*, 74.
24. De Wiquefort, *L'Ambassadeur et ses Fonctions*, 9 quoted in Stollberg-Rilinger, 'Honores regii: Die Königswürde im zeremoniellen Zeichensystem der Frühen Neuzeit', 12.
25. Vattel, *Law of Nations*, 462.
26. Ripa, *Memoirs of Father Ripa: During Thirteen Years' Residence at the Court of Peking in the Service of the Emperor of China*, 116–21, quotations 116, 118.
27. Ripa, *Memoirs of Father Ripa*, 120.
28. Ripa, *Memoirs of Father Ripa*, 116, 121; see also Hsü, *The Rise of Modern China*, 108–17.
29. Wang, 'The Audience Question: Foreign Representatives and the Emperor of China, 1858–1873', 618. Similar treaties were concluded with France, Russia and the United States. See Hsü, *China's Entrance into the Family of Nations: The Diplomatic Phase, 1858–1880*, esp. chapters 2, 3, 6; Badie, *Humiliation in International Relations: A Pathology of Contemporary International Systems*, 1–3.
30. See the full text of the treaty: 'Treaty of Tientsin [Tianjin] (June 26, 1858)'.
31. Pradier-Fodéré, *Cours de droit diplomatique*, 454; Miruss, *Das Europäische Gesandtschaftsrecht*, 366.
32. Wolseley, *Narrative of the War with China in 1860*, 230, quoted in Hevia, 'Ultimate Gesture', 221–22.
33. As to the different notions of sovereignty (unitary versus hierarchical), see Hevia, 'Sovereignty and Subject: Constituting Relations of Power in Qing Guest Ritual', 181–200; Hevia, *Cherishing Men from Afar: Qing Guest Ritual and the Macartney Embassy of 1793*, 224; with regard to ceremonial acts of obeisance, see Jochim, 'The Imperial Audience Ceremonies of the Ch'ing Dynasty', 88–103; Rawski, *The Last Emperors: A Social History of Qing Imperial Institutions*, 205.
34. Teng and Fairbank, *China's Response to the West: A Documentary Survey 1838–1923*, 105 (quote from 1878); de Bary and Lufrano, *Sources of Chinese Tradition*, vol. 2: *From 1600*

through the Twentieth Century, 235–36; (quotes from the reformer Feng Guifen writing in 1861).
35. Wade, 'Mr. Wade to Earl Granville (Received September 15)', 1–6, quotations 2, 3, 3–4.
36. Hardinge of Penshurst, *Old Diplomacy: The Reminiscences of Lord Hardinge of Penshurst*, 93, 189.
37. Aristotle, *On Rhetoric: A Theory of Civic Discourse*, 59; Marti, 'Proskynesis and Adorare', 272–82.
38. Zakharine, *Von Angesicht zu Angesicht: Der Wandel direkter Kommunikation in der ost- und westeuropäischen Neuzeit*, 407–11.
39. See for historical and anthropological evidence, Spencer, *The Principles of Sociology*, 116–43; Stollberg-Rilinger, 'Knien vor Gott – Knien vor dem Kaiser: Zum Ritualwandel im Konfessionskonflikt', 263–92.
40. Althoff, 'Das Grundvokabular der Rituale: Knien, Küssen, Thronen, Schwören', 149–80, esp. 150–51.
41. 'Knien', in Krünitz, *Oeconomisch-technologische Encyklopädie, oder allgemeines System der Stats- Stadt- Haus- und Land-Wirthschaft, und der Kunst-Geschichte*, 413–19.
42. 'Knien', 417, 419. See Reinders, *Buddhist and Christian Responses to the Kowtow Problem in China*, esp. chapter 5.
43. Osterhammel, *Die Entzauberung Asiens: Europa und die asiatischen Reiche im 18. Jahrhundert*, esp. 375–403; Goody, *The East in the West*, 1–10.
44. Sabatier, 'Les itinéraires des ambassadeurs pour les audiences à Versailles au temps de Louis XIV', 187–211; Volz, 'Eine türkische Gesandtschaft am Hofe Friedrichs des Großen im Winter 1763/64', 17–54, esp. 39; Adelung, *Augustin Freiherr von Meyerberg und seine Reise nach Russland*, 37, 73; Frötschel, 'Mit Handkuss: Die Hand als Gegenstand des Zeremoniells am Wiener Hof im 17. und 18. Jahrhundert', 337–56.
45. Frey and Frey, '"The Reign of the Charlatans is Over": The French Revolutionary Attack on Diplomatic Practice', 706–44.
46. Ebhardt, *Der gute Ton in allen Lebenslagen: Ein Handbuch für den Verkehr in der Familie, in der Gesellschaft und im öffentlichen Leben*, 285. All translations by the author unless otherwise noted. See Döcker, *Die Ordnung der bürgerlichen Welt: Verhaltensideale und soziale Praktiken im 19. Jahrhundert*, 95–100, 179–92.
47. Wildeblood and Brinson, *The Polite World: A Guide to English Manners and Deportment from the Thirteenth to the Nineteenth Century*, 197–98; Davidoff, 'Class and Gender in Victorian England: The Diaries of Arthur J. Munby and Hannah Cullwick', 86–141; Stallybrass and White, *The Politics and Poetics of Transgression*, 153–55.
48. Bluntschli, *Das moderne Völkerrecht der civilisirten Staten als Rechtsbuch dargestellt*, 134–35.
49. Wheaton, *Elements of International Law*, 274, 278, 283. See Frey and Frey, *The History of Diplomatic Immunity*, chapter 9; Xiaomin and Chunfeng, 'The Late Qing Dynasty Diplomatic Transformation: Analysis from an Ideational Perspective', 431; Hsü, *China's Entrance*, chapter 8; Svarverud, *International Law as World Order in Late Imperial China: Translation, Reception and Discourse, 1847–1911*, 88–98; Kroll, *Normgenese durch Re-Interpretation: China und das europäische Völkerrecht im 19. und 20. Jahrhundert*.
50. Von Rohr, *Einleitung zur Ceremoniel-Wissenschafft der Grossen Herren*, 377–414, esp. 412–13.
51. As for a famous early modern case, see Kemmerich, *Grund-Sätze des Völcker-Rechts von der Unverletzlichkeit der Gesandten*; Satow, *A Guide to Diplomatic Practice*, 43.
52. Aschmann, *Preußens Ruhm und Deutschlands Ehre: Zum nationalen Ehrdiskurs im Vorfeld der preußisch-französischen Kriege des 19. Jahrhunderts*, 289–95.
53. Biggerstaff, 'The Ch'ung Hou Mission to France, 1870–1871', 633–47. As for the stipulations of international law, see Triepel, *Völkerrecht und Landesrecht*, 324–48, esp. 335 (on hurt feelings of honour); Vattel, *Law of Nations*, 464; Przetacznik, *Protection of Officials of Foreign States According to International Law*, 217–20.

54. In 1877, the Chinese sent a mission of apology to London in order to express regret for the murder of a British interpreter. See Wang, *The Margary Affair and the Chefoo Agreement*, 70–126; Frodsham, *The First Chinese Embassy to the West: The Journals of Kuo Sung-T'ao, Liu Hsi-Hung and Chang Te-Yi*, 118–21, 155, 187.
55. Von Heyking, *Tagebücher aus vier Welten 1886–1904*, 207, 204–5.
56. Heyking, *Tagebücher aus vier Welten*, 207–9. For the official protocol, see Franke, 'Die Audienz der fremden Gesandten in Peking zur Feier des sechszigsten Geburtstages der Kaiserin Ex-Regentin', 134.
57. Gottschall, *By Order of the Kaiser: Otto von Diederichs and the Rise of the Imperial German Navy, 1865–1902*, 155–80.
58. Heyking, *Tagebücher aus vier Welten*, 232–38.
59. Wang, *Margary Affair*, 70.
60. Lepsius, Mendelssohn Bartholdy and Thimme, *Die Grosse Politik der Europäischen Kabinette 1871–1914: Sammlung der Diplomatischen Akten des Auswärtigen Amtes*, vol. 16: *Die Chinawirren und die Mächte 1900–1902*, 55, 131, 155. Similarly, the Chinese government had to make 'honourable reparations' to the Japanese Emperor and express regret for Sugiyama's assassination – which they did, without further complications. See, for the German case, Fitzpatrick, 'Kowtowing before the Kaiser? Sino-German Relations in the Aftermath of the Boxer Uprising'.
61. Satow, 'Sir E. Satow to the Marquess of Lansdowne – (Received March 16)', 127.
62. Lascelles, 'Lascelles to the Marquess of Salisbury', 16.
63. Lascelles, 'Lascelles to the Marquess of Salisbury', 16.
64. Lascelles, 'Lascelles to the Marquess of Salisbury', 16.
65. 'Prince Chun's Mission: Reception by the Kaiser', 3.
66. 'Memorandum C. Arendt' (15 July 1901); 'Telegram No. 443'; 'Eulenburg to AA' (8 and 19 August 1901), *Politisches Archiv des Auswärtigen Amtes* (PA AA), R 131819; 'Instructions for the Imperial Audience, from 26 August 1901', *Geheimes Staatsarchiv Preußischer Kulturbesitz* (GStA), BPH, Rep. 113, no. 1915, folios 179–182.
67. 'The World is Awaiting with Some Curiosity', 7; 'The Kotow Comedy', *Daily News*.
68. 'Orders to Prince Chun: He Was Told Not to Consent to a Humiliating Ceremony', 1; 'Kaiser Waives Kotowing: Prince Chun Accordingly Proceeds to Berlin to Perform His Mission', 1.
69. 'Die Krankheit des Sühneprinzen' (evening edition, 27 August 1901), 1–2 and 'Die Krankheit des Sühneprinzen' (morning edition, 28 August 1901), 1 (the English equivalent of the proverbial *Kanossagang* being 'eating humble pie'); 'Der Sühneprinz', 1; and 'Ueber die Ankunft des Prinzen Tschun in Basel' (also quoting the Swiss article).
70. 'Die Krankheit Tschuns', [487].
71. Tyll, 'Was man sich in Berlin erzählt' (1 September 1901), 1–2. The same paper later commented on the 'girl-like appearance of the Prince with his strikingly small body'; Tyll, 'Was man sich in Berlin erzählt' (8 September 1901), 1.
72. 'Der kritische Tag', 1; 'Der Sühneakt', 1. See, for example, the Viennese satirical paper *Der Floh*, 35 (1 September 1901).
73. Friedrich von Holstein's letter to Chancellor Bülow (23 August 1901) and Richthofen's telegram to Minister Mumm (29 August 1901) *PA AA*, R 18506. The former consul at Tientsin, Albert von Seckendorff, warned the Chancellor that an 'excessive humiliation' might possibly cost human lives and would be detrimental to 'the further development of our economic interests in the Far East' (Seckendorff to Bülow, 31 August 1901, *PA AA*, R 18506).
74. Heinrich von Tschirschky's telegram to State Secretary von Richthofen (26 August 1901), *PA AA*, R 18506.
75. Richthofen's Pro Memoria (28 August 1901), Richthofen's telegram to Mumm (29 August 1901), evaluations by Max von Brandt and C. Arendt (30 August 1901) as well as by Seckendorff (31 August 1901), *PA AA*, R 18506. To affirm this (questionable)

interpretation, reference was made to Williams, *The Middle Kingdom: A Survey of the Geography, Government, Literature, Social Life, Arts, and History of the Chinese Empire and its Inhabitants*, 801.
76. Zaifeng [Prince Chun], 'Tagebuchaufzeichnungen des Prinzen Chun (September 1901)', 503–4. The diary excerpts only cover the period from 2–10 September 1901.
77. 'Chun qinvang shi De riji' (Diary of Prince Chun's travel to Germany), 151. I would like to thank Professor Angelika Messner and Dr. Zihui Wu for the translation of the Chinese diary and for their expertise. As to the various forms of 'non-verbal salutations', see Wilkinson, *Chinese History: A Manual*, 105–8.
78. Mühlberg to Tschirschky (20 August 1901) (about a meeting with the Chinese envoy) and telegram No. 506 from Mumm, received 23 August 1901, PA AA, R 18506. See also instructions from 26 August 1901, GStA, BPH, Rep. 113, No. 1915, fol. 180.
79. Tschirschky to Mühlberg (23 August 1901) (quoting Kaiser Wilhelm), PA AA, R 18506.
80. Djang, *The Diplomatic Relations between China and Germany since 1898*, 161.
81. Franke, *Erinnerungen aus zwei Welten: Randglossen zur eigenen Lebensgeschichte*, 111.
82. The power was not just symbolic. Only when Prince Chun's expiatory mission was accomplished were all demands of the Powers satisfied and the Final Protocol could be signed. The German Minister in Peking repeatedly urged the other foreign ministers to sign beforehand, which they refused to do. Satow, *The Diaries of Sir Ernest Satow, British Envoy in Peking (1900–06)*, 134–35.
83. Satow, *Diaries*, 135 (4 September 1901); 'China', 3; 'Prince Chun's Mission', 3.
84. 'China's Amend to Germany: Prince Chun to Present Apology to Emperor William To-day', 1.
85. Trilby, 'Was man sich in Berlin erzählt' (29 September 1901), 1–2. See also the satirical covers of *Simplicissimus* 6(27) (1901) and *Kladderadatsch* (1 September 1901), 136.
86. Franke, *Erinnerungen aus zwei Welten*, 111. State Secretary von Richthofen likewise spoke of 'Schadenfreude among the other powers' (Richthofen to Mumm, 29 August 1901, PA AA, R 18506).
87. 'The Kotow Comedy', *Daily News*.
88. 'Kotau', in *Meyers Großes Konversations-Lexikon*, 539.
89. Hevia, 'Sovereignty and Subject', 181–82 about the long-lasting presence of the kowtow in European and U.S. thought. In contemporary Japan, the term 'kowtow diplomacy' (*dogeza gaiko*) is used in order to criticize an accommodative stance in foreign relations, especially with China and Korea.
90. Przetacznik, *Protection of Officials*, 220–23; 'Barack Takes a Bow', *Washington Times*. Obama was also criticized by the conservative press for 'excessively' bowing respectively, 'kowtowing', to the Japanese Emperor in 2009; 'Conservatives Slam Obama for Bow in Japan', *CBS News*; and Edwards, 'Obama in Japan: Not a Bow but a Kotow'.
91. Schreiber, 'Ein Stück Heimkehr', 30; '"Es wird eine Mehrheit dafür geben": Spiegel-Interview mit Bundeskanzler Willy Brandt', 31; Brandt, *My Life in Politics*, 200; Bahr, *Zu meiner Zeit*, 341.

Bibliography

Adelung, F. *Augustin Freiherr von Meyerberg und seine Reise nach Russland*. St Petersburg: Kray, 1827.
Althoff, G. 'Der König weint: Rituelle Tränen in öffentlicher Kommunikation', in J.-D. Müller (ed.), *'Aufführung' und 'Schrift' in Mittelalter und früher Neuzeit* (Stuttgart: Metzler, 1996), 239–52.

_____. 'Ira Regis: Prolegomena to a History of Royal Anger', in B.H. Rosenwein (ed.), *Anger's Past: The Social Uses of an Emotion in the Middle Ages* (Ithaca, NY: Cornell University Press, 1998), 59–74.

_____. 'Gefühle in der öffentlichen Kommunikation des Mittelalters', in C. Benthien, A. Fleig and I. Kasten (eds), *Emotionalität: Zur Geschichte der Gefühle* (Cologne: Böhlau, 2000), 82–99.

_____. 'Das Grundvokabular der Rituale: Knien, Küssen, Thronen, Schwören', in G. Althoff et al. (eds), *Spektakel der Macht: Rituale im Alten Europa 800–1800* (Darmstadt: Wissenschaftliche Buchgesellschaft, 2008), 149–80.

_____. 'Du rire et des larmes: Pourquoi les émotions intéressent-elles les médiévistes?', trans. A. Graceffa. *Ecrire l'histoire* 2 (2008), 27–39.

Aristotle. *On Rhetoric: A Theory of Civic Discourse*, trans. G.A. Kennedy. New York: Oxford University Press, 1991.

Aschmann, B. *Preußens Ruhm und Deutschlands Ehre: Zum nationalen Ehrdiskurs im Vorfeld der preußisch-französischen Kriege des 19. Jahrhunderts*. Munich: Oldenbourg, 2013.

Badie, B. *Humiliation in International Relations: A Pathology of Contemporary International Systems*, trans. J. Lewis. Oxford: Hart, 2017.

Bahr, E. *Zu meiner Zeit*. Munich: Blessing, 1996.

'Barack Takes a Bow'. *Washington Times* (7 April 2009). Retrieved 30 July 2015 from http://www.washingtontimes.com/news/2009/apr/07/barack-takes-a-bow.

Bary, W.T. de, and R. Lufrano (eds). *Sources of Chinese Tradition*, vol. 2: *From 1600 through the Twentieth Century*, 2nd edn. New York: Columbia University Press, 2000.

Behrens, A. (ed.). *'Durfte Brandt knien?': Der Kniefall in Warschau und der deutsch-polnische Vertrag: Eine Dokumentation der Meinungen*. Bonn: Dietz, 2010.

Biggerstaff, K. 'The Ch'ung Hou Mission to France, 1870–1871'. *Nankai Social & Economic Quarterly* 8(3) (1935), 633–47.

Bluntschli, J.C. *Das moderne Völkerrecht der civilisirten Staten als Rechtsbuch dargestellt*. Nördlingen: Beck, 1868.

Blussé, L. 'Peeking into the Empires: Dutch Embassies to the Courts of China and Japan'. *Itinerario* 37(3) (2013), 14–29, doi: 10.1017/S0165115313000776.

Braam, A.E. van. *An Authentic Account of the Embassy of the Dutch East-India Company, to the Court of the Emperor of China, in the Years 1794 and 1795*, vol. 1. London: R. Phillips, 1798.

Brandt, W. *My Life in Politics*, trans. A. Bell. London: Hamish Hamilton Press, 1992 [Ger. orig. *Erinnerungen*. Frankfurt am Main: Propyläen, 1989].

Chantrell, G. (ed.). *The Oxford Dictionary of Word Histories*. Oxford: Oxford University Press, 2002.

'China'. *The Times* (3 September 1901), 3.

'China's Amend to Germany: Prince Chun to Present Apology to Emperor William To-day'. *Washington Post* (4 September 1901), 1.

'Chun qinwang shi De riji' (Diary of Prince Chun's travel to Germany). *Jindaishi ziliao* 73 (1989), 138–68.

'Conservatives Slam Obama for Bow in Japan'. *CBS News* (17 November 2009). Retrieved 30 July 2015 from http://www.cbsnews.com/news/conservatives-slam-obama-for-bow-in-japan/.
Cranmer-Byng, J.L. 'Lord Macartney's Embassy to Peking in 1793: From Official Chinese Documents'. *Journal of Oriental Studies* 4(1/2) (1957/58), 117–87.
_____. *An Embassy to China: Lord Macartney's Journal, 1793–1794*, vol. 8: *Britain and the China Trade 1635–1842*, ed. Patrick Tuck, reprint edn. London: Routledge, 2000.
Davidoff, L. 'Class and Gender in Victorian England: The Diaries of Arthur J. Munby and Hannah Cullwick'. *Feminist Studies* 5(1) (1979), 86–141.
Djang, F.D. [F.-C. Chang]. *The Diplomatic Relations between China and Germany since 1898*. Shanghai: Commercial Press, 1936.
Döcker, U. *Die Ordnung der bürgerlichen Welt: Verhaltensideale und soziale Praktiken im 19. Jahrhundert*. Frankfurt am Main: Campus, 1994.
Duyvendak, J.J.L. 'The Last Dutch Embassy to the Chinese Court (1794–1795)'. *T'oung Pao* 34(1/2) (1938), 1–137.
Ebhardt, F. (ed.). *Der gute Ton in allen Lebenslagen: Ein Handbuch für den Verkehr in der Familie, in der Gesellschaft und im öffentlichen Leben*, 13th edn. Leipzig: Klinkhardt, 1896.
Edwards, L. 'Obama in Japan: Not a Bow but a Kotow'. *Daily Signal* (16 November 2009). Retrieved 30 July 2015 from http://dailysignal.com/2009/11/16/obama-in-japan-not-a-bow-but-a-kowtow/.
'"Es wird eine Mehrheit dafür geben": Spiegel-Interview mit Bundeskanzler Willy Brandt'. *Der Spiegel* 51 (1970), 31.
Fitzpatrick, M.P. 'Kowtowing before the Kaiser? Sino-German Relations in the Aftermath of the Boxer Uprising', *International History Review* (published online 1 March 2018), doi: 10.1080/07075332.2018.1441892.
Der Floh, 35 (1 September 1901).
Franke, O. 'Die Audienz der fremden Gesandten in Peking zur Feier des sechszigsten Geburtstages der Kaiserin Ex-Regentin'. *Der Ostasiatische Lloyd* (23 November 1894), 134.
_____. *Erinnerungen aus zwei Welten: Randglossen zur eigenen Lebensgeschichte*. Berlin: de Gruyter, 1945.
Frey, L., and M. Frey. '"The Reign of the Charlatans is Over": The French Revolutionary Attack on Diplomatic Practice'. *Journal of Modern History* 65(4) (1993), 706–44.
_____. Frey. *The History of Diplomatic Immunity*. Columbus: Ohio State University Press, 1999.
Frodsham, J.D. (ed.). *The First Chinese Embassy to the West: The Journals of Kuo Sung-T'ao, Liu Hsi-Hung and Chang Te-Yi*. Oxford: Clarendon, 1974.
Frötschel, R. 'Mit Handkuss: Die Hand als Gegenstand des Zeremoniells am Wiener Hof im 17. und 18. Jahrhundert', in I. Pangerl, M. Scheutz and T. Winkelbauer (eds), *Der Wiener Hof im Spiegel der Zeremonialprotokolle (1652–1800)* (Innsbruck: Studienverlag, 2007), 337–56.
Gao, H. 'The Amherst Embassy and British Discoveries in China'. *History* 99(337) (2014), 568–87, doi: 10.1111/1468-229X.12069.

———. 'The "Inner Kowtow Controversy" during the Amherst Embassy to China, 1816–1817'. *Diplomacy & Statecraft* 27(4) (2016), 595–614, doi: 10.1080/09592296.2016.1238691.
Gibney, M., and E. Roxstrom. 'The Status of State Apologies'. *Human Rights Quarterly* 23(4) (2001), 911–39.
Goody, J. *The East in the West*. Cambridge: Cambridge University Press, 1996.
Gottschall, T.D. *By Order of the Kaiser: Otto von Diederichs and the Rise of the Imperial German Navy, 1865–1902*. Annapolis, MD: Naval Institute Press, 2003.
Grass, G. 'Politisches Tagebuch: Betroffen sein', in G. Grass, *Werkausgabe*, vol. 15: *Essays und Reden II, 1970–1979*, ed. V. Neuhaus and D. Hermes (Göttingen: Steidl, 1997), 80–82.
Hardinge of Penshurst, C. *Old Diplomacy: The Reminiscences of Lord Hardinge of Penshurst*. London: Murray, 1947.
Harrison, H. 'The Qianlong Emperor's Letter to George III and the Early-Twentieth-Century Origins of Ideas about Traditional China's Foreign Relations'. *American Historical Review* 122(3) (2017), 680–701, doi: 10.1093/ahr/122.3.680.
Hevia, J.L. 'Sovereignty and Subject: Constituting Relations of Power in Qing Guest Ritual', in A. Zito and T.E. Barlow (eds), *Body, Subject & Power in China* (Chicago: University of Chicago Press, 1994), 181–200.
———. *Cherishing Men from Afar: Qing Guest Ritual and the Macartney Embassy of 1793*. Durham, NC: Duke University Press, 1995.
———. '"The Ultimate Gesture of Deference and Debasement": Kowtowing in China'. *Past and Present*, Supplement 4 (2009), 212–34, doi: 10.1093/pastj/gtp010.
Heyking, E. von. *Tagebücher aus vier Welten 1886–1904*, ed. G. Litzmann. Leipzig: Koehler & Amelang, 1926.
Hsü, I.C.Y. *China's Entrance into the Family of Nations: The Diplomatic Phase, 1858–1880*. Cambridge, MA: Harvard University Press, 1960.
———. *The Rise of Modern China*, 6th edn. New York: Oxford University Press, 2000.
Hüttner, J.C. *Nachricht von der britischen Gesandtschaftsreise nach China 1792–94*, ed. S. Dabringhaus. Sigmaringen: Thorbecke, 1996.
Jochim, C. 'The Imperial Audience Ceremonies of the Ch'ing Dynasty'. *Bulletin of the Society for the Study of Chinese Religion* 7 (1979), 88–103.
Jones, D.V. *Splendid Encounters: The Thought and Conduct of Diplomacy*. Chicago: University of Chicago Library, 1984.
'Kaiser Waives Kotowing: Prince Chun Accordingly Proceeds to Berlin to Perform his Mission'. *Washington Post* (3 September 1901), 1.
Kemmerich, D.H. *Grund-Sätze des Völcker-Rechts von der Unverletzlichkeit der Gesandten*. Christian-Erlang: Lorber, 1710.
'Kniefall', in *Brockhaus-Enzyklopädie*, vol 10: *Kat–Kz*, 17th edn (Wiesbaden: Brockhaus, 1970), 544.
'Knien', in J.G. Krünitz, *Oeconomisch-technologische Encyklopädie, oder allgemeines System der Stats- Stadt- Haus- und Land-Wirthschaft, und der Kunst-Geschichte*, vol. 41: *Von Klu bis Knu* (Berlin: Pauli, 1787), 416–20.

'Kotau', in *Meyers Großes Konversations-Lexikon*, vol. 11: *Kimpolung bis Kyzikos*, 6th rev. edn (Leipzig: Bibliographisches Institut, 1907), 539.
'The Kotow Comedy'. *Daily News* (3 September 1901).
'Die Krankheit des Sühneprinzen'. *Berliner Tageblatt* (evening edition, 27 August 1901), 1–2.
'Die Krankheit des Sühneprinzen'. *Berliner Tageblatt* (morning edition, 28 August 1901), 1.
'Die Krankheit Tschuns'. *Kladderadatsch* 54(35) (Zweites Beiblatt, 1 September 1901), [487].
'Der kritische Tag'. *Vossische Zeitung* (evening edition, 2 September 1901), 1.
Kroll, S. *Normgenese durch Re-Interpretation: China und das europäische Völkerrecht im 19. und 20. Jahrhundert*. Baden-Baden: Nomos, 2012.
Lascelles, F.C. 'Sir F. Lascelles to the Marquess of Salisbury – (Received October 8)', in *Houses of Parliament, China: No. 5 (1901): Further Correspondence Respecting the Disturbances in China* (London: Harrison, 1901), 16–17.
Lepsius, J., A. Mendelssohn Bartholdy and F. Thimme (eds). *Die Grosse Politik der Europäischen Kabinette 1871–1914: Sammlung der Diplomatischen Akten des Auswärtigen Amtes*, vol. 16: *Die Chinawirren und die Mächte 1900–1902*. Berlin: Deutsche Verlagsgesellschaft für Politik und Geschichte, 1924.
Marti, B.M. 'Proskynesis and Adorare'. *Language* 12(4) (1936), 272–82, doi: 10.2307/409153.
Miruss, A. (ed.). *Das Europäische Gesandtschaftsrecht*, vol. 1. Leipzig: Engelmann, 1847.
Nobles, M. *The Politics of Official Apologies*. Cambridge: Cambridge University Press, 2008.
'Orders to Prince Chun: He Was Told Not to Consent to a Humiliating Ceremony'. *New York Times* (4 September 1901), 1.
Osterhammel, J. *Die Entzauberung Asiens: Europa und die asiatischen Reiche im 18. Jahrhundert*. Munich: Beck, 1998.
Pölitz, K.H.L. *Die Staatswissenschaften im Lichte unsrer Zeit*, vol. 5. Leipzig: Hinrichs, 1824.
Pradier-Fodéré, P. *Cours de droit diplomatique*, vol 1, 2nd edn. Paris: Pedone, 1899.
'Prince Chun's Mission: Reception by the Kaiser'. *The Times* (5 September 1901), 3.
Pritchard, E.H. 'The Kotow in the Macartney Embassy to China in 1793'. *Far Eastern Quarterly* 2(2) (1943), 163–203, doi: 10.2307/2049496.
Przetacznik, F. *Protection of Officials of Foreign States According to International Law*. The Hague: Nijhoff, 1983.
Rawski, E.S. *The Last Emperors: A Social History of Qing Imperial Institutions*. Berkeley: University of California Press, 1998.
Reinders, E. *Buddhist and Christian Responses to the Kowtow Problem in China*. London: Bloomsbury, 2015.
Ripa, M. *Memoirs of Father Ripa: During Thirteen Years' Residence at the Court of Peking in the Service of the Emperor of China*, selected and trans. F. Prandi. New York: Wiley, 1849.
Rockhill, W.W. *Diplomatic Audiences at the Court of China*. London: Luzac, 1905.

Rohr, J.B. von. *Einleitung zur Ceremoniel-Wissenschafft der Grossen Herren*, ed. M. Schlechte. Berlin: Rüdiger, 1733, reprint Weinheim: VCH, 1990.
Sabatier, G. 'Les itinéraires des ambassadeurs pour les audiences à Versailles au temps de Louis XIV', in R. Kauz, G. Rota and J.P. Niederkorn (eds), *Diplomatisches Zeremoniell in Europa und im Mittleren Osten in der Frühen Neuzeit* (Vienna: Verlag der Österreichischen Akademie der Wissenschaften, 2009), 187–211.
Satow, E. 'Sir E. Satow to the Marquess of Lansdowne – (Received March 16)', in *Houses of Parliament, China: No. 6 (1901): Further Correspondence Respecting the Disturbances in China* (London: Harrison, 1901), 127.
———. *A Guide to Diplomatic Practice*, vol. 1, 2nd rev. edn. London: Longmans, Green and Co., 1922.
———. *The Diaries of Sir Ernest Satow, British Envoy in Peking (1900–06)*, vol. 1: *1900–03*, ed. I.C. Ruxton. Morrisville, NC: Lulu, 2011.
Schreiber, H. 'Ein Stück Heimkehr'. *Der Spiegel* 51 (1970), 29–30.
Spencer, H. *The Principles of Sociology*, vol. 2. New York: Appleton, 1898.
Stallybrass, P., and A. White. *The Politics and Poetics of Transgression*. London: Methuen, 1986.
Staunton, G. *An Authentic Account of an Embassy from the King of Great Britain to the Emperor of China*, vol. 1. Philadelphia, PA: Campbell, 1799.
Stollberg-Rilinger, B. 'Honores regii: Die Königswürde im zeremoniellen Zeichensystem der Frühen Neuzeit', in J. Kunisch (ed.), *Dreihundert Jahre Preußische Königskrönung: Eine Tagungsdokumentation* (Berlin: Duncker und Humblot, 2002), 1–26.
———. 'Knien vor Gott – Knien vor dem Kaiser: Zum Ritualwandel im Konfessionskonflikt', in A. von Hülsen-Esch (ed.), *Inszenierung und Ritual in Mittelalter und Renaissance* (Düsseldorf: Droste, 2005), 263–92.
———. *The Emperor's Old Clothes: Constitutional History and the Symbolic Language of the Holy Roman Empire*, trans. T. Dunlap. New York: Berghahn, 2015 [Ger. orig. *Des Kaisers alte Kleider*. Munich: Beck, 2008].
'Der Sühneakt'. *Berliner Tageblatt* (morning edition, 3 September 1901), 1.
'Der Sühneprinz'. *Vossische Zeitung* (evening edition, 26 August 1901), 1.
Svarverud, R. *International Law as World Order in Late Imperial China: Translation, Reception and Discourse, 1847–1911*. Leiden: Brill, 2007.
Teitel, R. 'The Transitional Apology', in E. Barkan and A. Karn (eds), *Taking Wrongs Seriously: Apologies and Reconciliation* (Stanford, CA: Stanford University Press, 2006), 101–14.
Teng, S.-Y., and J.K. Fairbank. *China's Response to the West: A Documentary Survey 1838–1923*, 5th edn. Cambridge, MA: Harvard University Press, 1979.
'Treaty of Tientsin [Tianjin] (June 26, 1858)'. *China's External Relations: A History*. Retrieved 14 March 2016 from http://www.chinaforeignrelations.net/node/144.
'The Treaty of Warsaw (7 December 1970)'. *Centre Virtuel de la Connaissance sur l'Europe (CVCE)*. Retrieved 11 March 2016 from http://www.cvce.eu/obj/the_treaty_of_warsaw_7_december_1970-en-7f3363b0-2705-472a-b535-c42bd229f9e2.html.
Triepel, H. *Völkerrecht und Landesrecht*. Leipzig: Hirschfeld, 1899.
Trilby. 'Was man sich in Berlin erzählt'. *Berliner Damen-Zeitung* 9(39) (29 September 1901), 1–2.

Tyll. 'Was man sich in Berlin erzählt'. *Berliner Damen-Zeitung* 9(35) (1 September 1901), 1–2.
Tyll. 'Was man sich in Berlin erzählt'. *Berliner Damen-Zeitung* 9(36) (8 September 1901), 1–2.
'Ueber die Ankunft des Prinzen Tschun in Basel'. *Vossische Zeitung* (morning edition, 28 August 1901).
Vattel, E. de. *The Law of Nations or Principles of the Law of Nature, Applied to the Conduct and Affairs of Nations and Sovereigns: From the French of Monsieur de Vattel*, rev. edn. London: G.G. and J. Robinson, 1797.
Vec, M. *Zeremonialwissenschaft im Fürstenstaat: Studien zur juristischen und politischen Theorie absolutistischer Herrschaftsrepräsentation*. Frankfurt am Main: Klostermann, 1995.
Volz, G.B. 'Eine türkische Gesandtschaft am Hofe Friedrichs des Großen im Winter 1763/64'. *Hohenzollern-Jahrbuch* 11 (1907), 17–54.
Wade, T. 'Mr. Wade to Earl Granville (Received September 15)', in Houses of Parliament, *China No. 1 (1874): Correspondence Respecting the Audience Granted to Her Majesty's Minister and the Other Foreign Representatives at Pekin by the Emperor of China* (London: Harrison, 1874), 1–6.
Wang, S.T. *The Margary Affair and the Chefoo Agreement*. London: Oxford University Press, 1940.
Wang, T.-T. 'The Audience Question: Foreign Representatives and the Emperor of China, 1858–1873'. *Historical Journal* 14(3) (1971), 617–26.
Wheaton, H. *Elements of International Law*, 6th edn. Boston: Little Brown and Co., 1855.
Wildeblood, J., and P. Brinson. *The Polite World: A Guide to English Manners and Deportment from the Thirteenth to the Nineteenth Century*. London: Oxford University Press, 1965.
Wilkinson, E. *Chinese History: A Manual*. Cambridge, MA: Harvard University Press, 2000.
Williams, S.W. *The Middle Kingdom: A Survey of the Geography, Government, Literature, Social Life, Arts, and History of the Chinese Empire and its Inhabitants*, vol. 1, rev. edn. New York: Scribner, 1900.
Wiquefort, A. de. *L'Ambassadeur et ses Fonctions*, vol. 1. Amsterdam: Janssons a Waesberge, 1730.
Wolseley, G.J. *Narrative of the War with China in 1860*. London: Longman, Green, Longman, and Roberts, 1862.
'The World is Awaiting with Some Curiosity'. *The Times* (2 September 1901), 7.
Xiaomin, Z., and X. Chunfeng. 'The Late Qing Dynasty Diplomatic Transformation: Analysis from an Ideational Perspective'. *Chinese Journal of International Politics* 1(3) (2007), 405–45, doi: 10.1093/cjip/pom004.
Zaifeng [Prince Chun]. 'Tagebuchaufzeichnungen des Prinzen Chun (September 1901)', in M. Leutner (ed.), *'Musterkolonie Kiautschou': Die Expansion des Deutschen Reiches in China: Deutsch-Chinesische Beziehungen 1897 bis 1914: Eine Quellensammlung* (Berlin: Akademie, 1997), 503–7.
Zakharine, D. *Von Angesicht zu Angesicht: Der Wandel direkter Kommunikation in der ost- und westeuropäischen Neuzeit*. Constance: UVK, 2005.

Chapter 6

Occupiers and Civilians
Facing the Enemy

Philipp Nielsen

> The German youth is a nice looking chap, much like the average fellow you grew up with back home. You may ask yourself how a guy who looks pretty much like one of us could believe and do all the things we know he believed and did.
> —U.S. War Department, *Instructions for American Forces in Germany 1945*

During the Second World War, the United States army published guidebooks for its soldiers on how to behave while abroad, be it in allied, liberated or occupied countries. These instructions, as they were called, were supposed to familiarize the soldiers with, or defamiliarize them from, the other they encountered. Knowing the places they were about to occupy and rule also meant understanding the ways in which the local population would be different from them. Successfully reading the other, key to a government that would rely as little as possible on force, became especially difficult in cases where outer appearance and inner comportment were divorced from each other, where looks suggested similarity yet behaviour revealed difference. Implicit in looking similar was not only race but also gender and age. 'The German' the *Instructions* were concerned about was male, and the most dangerous age group were those 'between the ages of 14 and 28'. Even though they were thought of as civilians, they were roughly the same demographic as the GIs. German women only featured as potential carriers of venereal diseases or romantic interests creating future naturalization problems.[1] Confronted with their deceptive peers,

---

Notes for this chapter begin on page 177.

the U.S. soldiers needed to be taught whom to trust and whom not to trust. At the same time, difference was to be maintained lest one's own soldiers went native and thence became unreliable. A certain amount of suspicion of the other could prove vital for survival. The *Instructions for the American Forces* warned GIs that the German 'will try to make you sorry for him too. Don't fall for it. He is very apt, if he can get to talk to you, to try to plant seeds of disunity, racial intolerance, and discontent, in your mind. If he does, don't fall for it'.[2]

The *Instructions* themselves were the result of a mimetic learning process. Despite the experience of governing the Philippines, Guam and Puerto Rico following the Spanish-American War of 1898, the United States did not think of itself as an occupying or colonial force. The British army, by contrast, had long trained its soldiers in such matters. Thus, in the lead-up to the United States' entry into the Second World War, the U.S. armed forces followed the British model and set up training schools for future occupation administrators.[3] Driven by the belief that understanding was essential to successful occupation regimes, and in light of the fact that few soldiers would know or learn the local language, the body of the other and emotions became as important for interpreting the encounter as words. Misreading the other's emotions and intentions could have fatal consequences, both in the short and long term.

The effects of misreading, both in the German case as well as in such encounters more generally, were not necessarily static. Indeed, they could develop their own, potentially disastrous dynamic. Soldiers needed to be given an interpretative framework as well as advice on how to act – the encounter between occupier and occupied had to be premediated, to use the philosopher Paul Ricoeur's term.[4] This premediation would familiarize and defamiliarize the soldiers from the locals to the extent deemed necessary for a successful occupation. The ambivalence this dual direction introduced into the encounters stands at the heart of this chapter. The U.S. occupation of Germany forms the endpoint of this analysis, which also includes the British colonial regime at the time of the Indian Rebellion of 1857 and the German occupation of Eastern Europe during the First World War. Spread over the course of a century, these cases allow us to assess the changes in the expectations of soldiers as well as the civilian other as armies became increasingly professionalized, nationalized and finally 'ideologized'. They also provide an opportunity to probe the role of emotions in the changing construction of difference sketched in the introduction to this volume: in colonial India from cultural to biological definitions of race, the further 'racialization' of religion in First World War Eastern Europe and finally in the U.S. occupation of Germany of ideology, even more pernicious than the previous two because it was invisible to the naked eye.

The knowledge of and ideas about the other that soldiers had going into the encounter – and the civilians' knowledge of and ideas about the soldiers – shaped their interpretation of the encounter and its dynamic. The way knowledge was produced for and shared among soldiers in turn was influenced fundamentally by developments both within and without the military: conscription and growing literacy standardized the acquisition of knowledge; technology changed the way the other was encountered, both on the battlefield and as part of the growing tourism industry; and the emergence of sciences such as anthropology changed the conceptualization of the other. Moreover, over the course of the nineteenth and twentieth centuries, certain oppositions structuring the encounter became enshrined in law and military doctrine: of ally and enemy, combatant and civilian, the latter frequently gendered and additionally tied to age. None of these dyads was stable within or across conflicts.

The oppositions could be disrupted by markers of commonality, such as race, religion, language and gender, or shared cultural practices. The oppositions as well as the markers of commonality or distinction could also be disrupted by the dynamic emerging from the encounter itself, not least its emotional force. From their induction into the military, soldiers were trained in a highly gendered emotional repertoire – to be a soldier meant to be masculine and to be a masculine soldier meant to be loyal, fearless and at the very least disdainful of the enemy. In and out, camaraderie and hierarchy, were clearly defined not least by emotional practices. Yet in the encounter with opponents, especially close encounters with occupied peoples, the polyvalent nature of feelings held the potential to disrupt the emotional script. The difficulty of gauging the other's emotions is visible in accounts of soldiers as well as the instructions to soldiers that attempt to prevent confusion and hence unpredictability.[5] Frequently lacking a shared language, the body of the other, as well as the place and space in which he or she was encountered, became crucial for reading the other's emotions. Comportment and environment in turn also shaped the emotional disposition of soldiers towards the occupied.

This chapter focuses on the perspective of the soldier and occupier as a way to explore the limits of military power in the encounter and the importance of emotions. Yet where possible and productive, this perspective is supplemented by accounts of the civilian other. In order to analyse the emotions at the level of the face-to-face encounter, the chapter primarily relies on first-person accounts. With the spread of literacy, an increasing number of letters from a variety of social strata were sent between home and the front. These and other ego-documents, such as diaries or retrospective recollections, were published after the war. Each of these source categories has its own advantages and disadvantages.

Taken together and weighed against each other, they provide insight into the dynamic of the encounter.

Of 'Insolents' and 'Infidels': The Indian Rebellion, 1857–58

The historiography on the Indian Rebellion has expanded significantly over the last decade.[6] The renewed emphasis on the place of religion next to socio-economic explanations of the rebellion has also opened up new ways to think about emotions in the construction of the other.[7] Religious sentiment, not least Evangelical Christianity intent on conversion, ran alongside increasingly racial constructions of the Indian other. Together with structural changes in the military as the British government increasingly took control out of the hands of the East India Company, this had the effect of British officers' growing distance from Indian soldiers.[8] Once the rebellion began, the British described the rebels as 'fanatic' to delegitimize their claims and construct them as the 'irrational' other to the rational self.[9] Religion, in the way it was ascribed by the British to the Indians, served the same purpose, while from the rebels' perspective it was precisely religion that gave their actions an overarching rationale and legitimacy.[10]

The rebellion meant that the British encountered the Indian population anew, even when it involved the very same people. William Edwards' account of a long-serving East India Company official accustomed to the idea of close proximity to the local population demonstrates how assumptions about the intercultural readability of emotions were disturbed by the rebellion. William Hodson's diary, by contrast, tracks the experience of the rebellion by a British soldier who arrived in India in the 1840s already with the expectation of racial difference. Yet Hodson, infamous for his violence, also cultivated a large network of Indian spies.[11] The two accounts provide the opportunity to expand on Roy's argument of the importance of emotions in military confrontations and discern patterns intrinsic to the emotional encounter of occupier and occupied, as well as to analyse how the encounter reaffirmed and undermined emotional scripts. Though gender played a crucial role in this encounter, not least the construction of British masculinity on the background of rumours of British women's honour being hurt,[12] the rebel fighters were more likely to be described in derogatory terms derived from class, as children or as animals, rather than being feminized.

To Edwards – a magistrate, judge and collector for the Company in Bareilly, capital of the province of Rohilcund, part of what is today Uttar Pradesh – the 'rebels' were acting beyond their station and 'had become insolent, overbearing and threatening'.[13] These were terms usually reserved for lower classes and unruly children, pointing to the intersectionality of experience.[14] Comportment, and with it feelings, was part and parcel of an orderly society. The 'rebels' standing outside this society were 'excited' and 'insolent'; those siding with the British 'polite' and 'respectful'.[15]

Despite some sympathy for the rebels' grievances, qua his position Edwards soon became a target of the rebellion that affected the region.[16] With his traditional authority gone, Edwards' safety, by his own account, rested on the correct reading of the other's feelings. On several occasions throughout his flight that began in June 1857, body language and comportment became paramount to deciding whom to trust. When he got word about mutiny in his district, for example, 'the excited manner of the sowar and the condition of his panting horse, showed that the tale was too true'.[17] During a heated debate with local notables, his former servant Wuzeer Singh came up behind Edwards and stationed himself there with his gun. As Edwards noted in his diary, Singh's 'entrance was unnoticed, but his quiet and determined demeanour made me for the first time feel an assurance that he was a man I could depend on'.[18] From here on Singh became Edwards' trusted companion and 'brother beloved'.[19]

The local guide who can read people and their intentions correctly is a figure that plays an intrinsic role in occupation regimes and their narratives; the position was often filled by liminal characters, precisely because of their position partly outside of their own society, knowledgeable but also with something to gain from cooperating with the foreigner. Wuzeer Singh was a Sikh in a predominantly Muslim region. Edwards' account of Singh's role is an example of the rise of Sikhs in the esteem of the British as loyal subjects during the rebellion. This culminated in their assignation as a 'martial race' and their preferred recruitment into military service in India after 1858.[20]

Even with Singh on his side, gestures and comportment remained the principal way for Edwards to establish others' trustworthiness over the course of his flight, which lasted until late August 1857. For Edwards, this process was not yet linked to racial or religious characteristics. Even in Singh's case, whom he knew to be religious, he did not make the connection between religion and his confidant's demeanour and trustworthiness.[21] Instead, Edwards described this process in universalist terms. As it transpired, however, demeanour turned out to be less than universally legible. Shortly before Edwards' flight, a sepoy implored him to visit the local guards. His visit would bolster their loyalty. 'The man's earnest and respectful manner quite deceived me: I thought, if ever any one spoke truth it is this person'. It fell to Wuzeer Singh to rectify his impression and warn him of an imminent trap. Singh correctly interpreted the situation because, as he told Edwards, 'he knew these fellows well and that they meant mischief'.[22] Edwards lacked this knowledge despite his long service in India. The other's body could be, or rather was made to be, deceiving.

As the established order in India collapsed, Edwards began to doubt his ability to read the locals, on which he had prided himself. He saw his favourite orderly looting his offices, proudly wearing his former master's dress-sword.[23] On another occasion, Edwards was in 'breathless suspense', uncertain about the intentions of a group of 'insolent' *sowars*.[24] Edwards' loss of certainty was symbolic for a large number of long-serving Company administrators and officers, who had prided themselves on understanding 'the locals'. In 1857, this misplaced certainty often proved fatal.[25] Though not in every case did the 'betrayal' come as a complete surprise.[26]

If Edwards represented the old colonial regime, William Hodson, one of the most infamous British officers during the uprising, stood for the new and was as a military man an outright occupier.[27] Stationed in India from 1846 onwards, even before the uprising his description of villagers in Cashmere as poor, dirty, ugly and as 'beasts of burden' left no room for the sympathy or respect for local customs that Edwards had still voiced.[28] More threateningly, Hodson felt his own English identity challenged through the confrontation with the local population's different customs and indeed feelings:

> I am now writing in his room with the incessant entrances and exits of natives – rajahs, princes, vakeels, &c. &c., and officers civil and military; and the buzz of business and confusion of tongues, black and white, learned and unlearned, on all subjects, political, religious (at this minute they are disputing what 'the Church means'), and military, so that I am tolerably puzzled. . . . Still, I do not let these things annoy me, or weigh down my spirits, but strive, by keeping up English habits, tastes, and feelings, and looking forward to a run home.[29]

Hodson, correspondingly, felt little sympathy for the Company employees who had gone native. 'If I have one feeling stronger than another, it is contempt for a "regular Indian", a man who thinks it fine to adopt a totally different set of habits and morals and fashions, until, in forgetting that he is an Englishman, he usually forgets also that he is a Christian and a gentleman'.[30] Habits, morals and fashions (including emotions) and religion were crucial to maintaining one's identity.

Once the rebellion broke out, Hodson, in contrast to Edwards, did not see any legitimate cause. Instead, he itched to fight the 'rascals' as he usually called them. Like 'insolent', the term linked the rebels' behaviour to the lower classes, if not to petty criminals or at best irresponsible youths.[31] Yet while insolence was an emotional state that could pass, rascal denoted a permanent deformation of character. On another occasion, Hodson described the emotions of the locals as somewhere between childlike and animalistic. And again, these were character traits rather than fleeting feelings. In this instance, it was a positive one, however. During the siege of Delhi, Hodson was reunited with a loyal regiment he had commanded in the early 1850s.

> The Guides came in to-day, . . . cheering and shouting and crowding around me like frantic creatures. . . . They . . . literally threw themselves down before the horse with the tears streaming down their faces. Many officers who were present hardly knew what to make of it, and thought the creatures were mobbing me; and so they were – but for joy, not for mischief.[32]

As opposed to Edwards, the behaviour of Indians during the rebellion did not confound Hodson. Instead, as his brother, who published the letters posthumously, argued, Hodson's 'past experience of Asiatic character, [qualified him] to form a judgment and express an opinion without exposing himself to the charge of presumption'.[33]

Moments of uncertainty, however, appeared in Hodson's dealings with spies. Despite the disdain they felt, the British relied on local troops.[34] Their very ability to adapt and to cross boundaries though occasionally advantageous – for example, when Hodson sent '[o]ne of the native officers of the Guides (you know how ingenious they are at disguise)' into Delhi as a spy[35] – was ultimately problematic. Contrary to Edwards, who still thought to establish trust, for Hodson trust was too elusive a quality. Governing was better when backed up by force and intimidation, something the old and 'faint-hearted' guard did not understand.[36] Difference was to be maintained between rulers and ruled and familiarity should always be viewed with caution. Part of this was their different background, one trained to be a judge, one trained to be a soldier. But a large part was the change in beliefs about the nature of difference, which came to be seen as more absolute and less malleable through contact and education.

Edwards and Hodson agreed, however, that comportment was crucial to the reading and projection of emotions (and thus power). During the Siege of Delhi, Hodson apprehended the Mughal Emperor Bahadur Shah II. One day later, they arrested his sons, and Hodson and his men were, according to them, surrounded and outnumbered by a hostile crowd. To escape, they had to put on a show of calm assurance. One of Hodson's officers described how he smoked incessantly 'to show [that he] was unconcerned'.[37] Another officer later defended Hodson's decision to shoot the princes, by claiming that any moment of hesitation would have been interpreted as weakness.[38]

If Hodson and his men tried to display their actions here as those of calm masculinity, other British soldiers quite openly described their acts as driven by 'divine vengeance'.³⁹ Evangelical Christianity left its mark not only on interpretation but also on action. Fazl-e Haqq, religious scholar, poet and leading member of the rebellion, described the British as 'Christians' and some analogy on the British side exists. For Haqq, though, religion, rather than race or culture, explained all behaviour and feelings, and Christians ruled and operated by deception.⁴⁰ Neither for Edwards nor for Hodson did religion possess quite this absolute explanatory power. Their understanding of the other was more strongly determined by ideas about culture and to some extent race. For Edwards, individual comportment also added an element of flexibility. In Hodson's statements and actions, the hardened attitudes towards difference of the imperial era, a development in which the confrontation in India in 1857 played such an important role, were already visible.

'Playing the German'? Eastern Europe, 1915–18

By the time Germany occupied parts of Eastern Europe during the First World War, race doctrines had hardened further, yet religion and language – quite apart from political expedience – complicated the encounter, especially with the area's large Jewish population. Rendered at once familiar by the proximity of Yiddish to German and unfamiliar by virtue of their customs, dress and above all as a result of antisemitic campaigns in the pre-war period, the encounter itself was a moment of unpredictability. Emotions could run counter to assumptions, sometimes unwillingly, or they could reinforce them. Particularly language could play an ambiguous role in the production of emotions. While the similarity enabled communication and for some created sympathy and feelings of closeness, for others it was precisely the slight differences, the misunderstandings they created, that produced estrangement and hostility.⁴¹ Considering the contested status of Germany's Jewish minority, the perception of Eastern European Jews was always also about German society, but more importantly it was about what kind of regime Germany wanted to establish in Eastern Europe.

Despite a long history of settlement in Eastern Europe, the area had not been a German colony in the sense in which India, even under the Company, had been a British one. Nonetheless, the German presence in the east is frequently described as the country's main colonial project. The 'Wild East' as analogous to 'Wild West' of the United States had become its own trope in the German imagination, disseminated through numerous popular novels.⁴² With the occupation of large parts of this area beginning in 1915 and ending with German defeat in 1918, colonial aspirations of any sort could be put into practice, even if competition within various branches of government and army over the form that German control in the East should take was stiff.⁴³

The British had had their favourite group of natives – high caste Hindus – in India before the rebellion and found new ones – Sikhs and Gurkhas – in its wake; while German soldiers and administrators had no experience of governing the area, they had several potential favourites to choose from. The Jewish population was one of them. Their socio-economic position in commerce and the fact that German soldiers could converse with them made them almost natural allies of the German occupation authorities. Yet the encounter was heavily premediated in a more hostile direction. Though most Germans would not have met Eastern European Jews before the war, they had become a staple in German antisemitic discourse due to their embarkation in German ports on their way to England and the United States and a more limited immigration to the German Empire itself.⁴⁴ Even for German Jews, their Eastern coreligionists had not only been a source of spiritual renewal but also a threat to their own acceptance as Germans.⁴⁵ Thus they had been clearly demarcated as other, even if the otherness was ambiguous, and both Jews and non-Jews in the German forces encountered Eastern European Jews with ambivalence.

The German High Command itself did not issue any specific instructions on how to interpret the Jews' behaviour or on how to behave. There were general guidelines, however. The German government had promised Eastern European Jews liberation, and soldiers were advised to guarantee their equal rights. The heads of the General Government of Warsaw, Germany's largest civil administration in the occupied East, and of Ober Ost, the area of Eastern Europe directly under the army's control, generally stood by this promise, even if occasionally prodded to do so by German Jewish associations.⁴⁶

In the German situation, geographical proximity and technological advances in travel and communication made the connections between national debate and the actions in occupied territories markedly different from the earlier Indian situation. Moreover, in Germany conscription had created a national army that was seen as the 'school of the nation' for the recently created state.⁴⁷ Any lingering differences of class, religion and region were to be set aside in the national effort of the Great War, widely considered to be a defensive act. Yet even in the German case, markers of national identity were not ultimately resolved, and its soldiers now encountered an area of dizzying national complexity and aspirations. And while language and religion held the potential to structure the encounter, the emergence of a pseudo-scientific race discourse that could work in conjunction with and contrast to these factors further complicated the dynamic. Perceived racial difference could reinforce or diminish religious or linguistic markers of identity. The Jewish population, whose national status was contested, and who were at once familiar and strange to German soldiers, were particularly complicated in this regard, and hence particularly interesting for the emotional dynamic of the encounter.

In the second week of January 1915, Otto Köhler, a German Jewish physician in the rank of Aspirant Officer, crossed into Russian Poland. On 15 January, he wrote to Siegmund Feist, head of the Jewish Orphanage in Berlin where Köhler had worked prior to the First World War. Köhler was appalled not only by the state of Polish infrastructure and housing – in this conflict too the perception of space, itself premediated, primed the soldiers for their assessment of the other – but also by the behaviour of the local population: 'A quarter of an hour beyond the border we passed through the small town Jerichow that is mainly populated by Jews. Our co-religionists made a bad impression, the fear and hardship of the last weeks was clear to read in their faces; with unpleasant servility they greeted us and wished us luck and success'.[48] Though in their behaviour they were clearly different – uncomfortably servile – there was no problem in translating or understanding their behaviour or their faces. This dual approach of universalism and difference continued throughout Köhler's letters, also with respect to non-Jews. Though, like many other letters written from Eastern Europe, he disparaged the dirt and low cultural level of the Russians, he never questioned their humanity and fundamental equality.[49] Following a passage on the 'godforsaken, dirty & lice infested Poles' in another letter to Feist, Köhler extolled the charity among soldiers transcending enemy lines. German soldiers would share their last drops of water with wounded Russian captives; a captive Russian would wrap a severely wounded German in his coat.[50]

The subservient attitude of the Jews remained unsettling, however, somehow appearing too excessive to be authentic and thus throwing their true intentions and emotions into question. General Hans Hartwig von Beseler, General Governor of Warsaw, reported similar conflicted sentiments about his encounters with local Jews to his wife. Charmed almost despite himself, he still remained wary of their gratitude and praise of the German administration.[51] 'They play[ed] the German', but he suspected that really they would have liked to have the more corrupt and thus corruptible Russian occupation back.[52]

As in 1857, appearances could be deceiving. The shared language enabled Jews to 'play German', hence both complicating as well as mitigating the dynamic of familiarity and difference between occupier and occupied, for it enabled mimicry.[53] But as problematic as this servile nature seemed, Beseler considered it a historical artefact rather than a natural trait. As a result of centuries of oppression, liberation in Eastern Europe would make it disappear, and Jews would become productive members of any future society.⁵⁴ The history of oppression was also invoked to defend Jews against German soldiers' annoyance at haggling with them at the market. Disgust at the filth could thus be mixed with understanding or even compassion. German soldiers' newspapers, written and published by the different army units, reported on serving in Eastern Europe. In 1916, one paper's story described the encounter with Eastern European Jews in a destroyed Galician village who tried to sell the German soldiers chocolate and cigarettes: 'We happily paid as these poor devils, standing there in front of their houses in long caftans, looked so sad'.⁵⁵ Sadness clearly needed no translation.

The willingness to be empathetic was also a result of the power structure. As opposed to Indians in 1857, Eastern European Jews posed no threat to security (another example of ideology, as by 1939, the same Jews, with no more intention to rise up, were deemed the most diabolic of enemies). In 1915, though, a misreading of emotions was thus not similarly fatal. For Jews, on the other hand, there was a strong incentive to get along with the German occupiers. The onus of reading emotions correctly thus rested more strongly on the occupied, while it was less crucial for the occupying Germans.

Nonetheless, once established in Eastern Europe, the German army had Jewish officers among its ranks, notably military rabbis, give lectures on the history and culture of Eastern European Jews to educate its officers. They tried their best to further the cultural line of thought and to eliminate the perceived link between the outer appearance of Jews and their inner character (and emotions). The centuries-long oppression of Eastern European Jews had created a dual nature. Outwardly, these Jews were servile, dirty and downtrodden, yet inwardly they were deeply believing, authentic and true to god and thus honest and reliable.⁵⁶

German Zionists took this a step further and saw in the deformed body the positive result of inner authenticity, thus in effect coming full circle in linking body and soul. *The Face of East European Jewry* by Arnold Zweig and Hermann Struck, two German Jews serving in the German occupation authority in the east, set out in word and image to show the essence of the Eastern European Jew to his Western brethren – the text, if not the images, were almost exclusively about Jewish men – and to demonstrate his spiritual superiority. His faith and life were inscribed upon his face:

> Nothing is lovelier than the untiring cheerfulness of the Jew. Even if old age and the travails of life have rendered his head bald, left wrinkles in his forehead, carved deep folds beneath his eyes, and molded his cheeks like those of

a woodcut – precisely there, in the corner of his taut mouth, on his nose, and around his eyes, lies a transgression that triumphs.[57]

The difference in corporeality meant that this body was occasionally hard to read for the Western European Jew. Yet precisely the unrefined outward appearance, both in the shape of his body as well as in the lack of manners, proved the inner worth of the Eastern European Jew, even if it shamed his Western brethren.[58]

In his efforts to provide a guide to any future encounter, Zweig acknowledged how the perception and construction of difference were interrelated. The question of Jewish identity, whether confessional or national, had not only preoccupied Jews in Western Europe but also their non-Jewish surrounding. It related to their status in society and state. Encountering other Jews who were quite clearly different from their surrounding society and at the same time somehow related to German Jews (and via language possible Germans) reopened the question of emancipation and assimilation: of how different someone familiar and, conversely, how familiar someone different could be. Even if the German army eventually hoped to cultivate Poles as a reliable (and more important) client group in Eastern Europe and despite increasing antisemitism in Germany, the occupation authorities considered Jews until the end to be sufficiently similar to eventually become Germans or at least outposts of 'Germandom in the East'. Language could instil a sense of familiarity, and education could solidify this familiarity. Negative feelings such as disgust had to be understood as provoked by specific historic constellations, not as a predetermined and justified response to another people's immutable character.

When Germans and Eastern European Jews encountered each other again in the interwar period, Germans regarded themselves not as liberators but as under attack, even if Eastern European Jews fled pogroms and revolutionary violence to settle in Germany's large cities guided by their previous experience of relative safety under German rule. Instead, German antisemites used military metaphors and the language of natural disasters and spoke of floods, attacks and occupation.[59] The benevolent Zionist interpretation, or any other benevolent reading of Eastern European Jews, was increasingly on the defensive in the Weimar period. And when German soldiers advanced into Eastern Europe once more in 1939, the notions that had been instilled in them and that premediated the encounter did not advocate understanding or feelings of similarity but instead only radical, annihilating difference.

'Conquerors Not Oppressors': The Allied Occupation of Germany 1945

'We come as Conquerors not Oppressors' read the signs quoting the U.S. Commander Dwight D. Eisenhower that were erected in the American zone of occupation in the spring and summer of 1945.[60] The message was as simple as it was confusing: Germans should feel defeated but also liberated. While in essence not too different from the promise of liberation the German government had given Eastern European Jews in 1914, the circumstances and the meaning of this statement were very different. This third and final case study investigates the effects of this claim on the encounter between American soldiers and German civilians. Difference now had become not only a matter of nationality, though this still played an important role, but also one of ideology and worldview. Precisely because Germans looked so similar, their difference needed to be explained differently: understanding the emotional disposition of the other became important. The Americans planning the occupation were thus intensely interested in the emotional make-up of the Germans and in structuring their soldiers' response to it. To be effective administrators of the occupied territories, the soldiers needed to understand not only the local language but also the population's customs. One fundamental aspect of this was being able to read the other's emotions and anticipate the opponent's emotional disposition.

While in non-European contexts the difference between American GIs and the local population was supposedly self-evident, this was not the case for European countries, both friendly and not. The instructions for France and Germany, each with different intent, explained the inner difference of the local population to U.S. servicemen. In Germany, as a hostile nation, soldiers needed to 'be aware' – as they were constantly exhorted in the *Instructions* – of German difference primarily for their own safety. Understanding the difference correctly was also of key importance for the future task of re-educating Germans and making them become not only outwardly but also inwardly more like Americans. Particularly dangerous were German youths, who looked so innocent yet had borne the full brunt of National Socialist indoctrination. 'The difference is inside him in his character. For your own safety and the safety of your comrades never for an instant forget that he is the victim of the greatest educational crime in the history of the world'.[61] As the victim of a crime and the key to the country's future, young Germans deserved rehabilitation. To assess where to start and how to go about this, the U.S. authorities upon entering the country were keenly interested in studying the German mind. They ran surveys and had psychologists, not infrequently German émigrés, conduct interviews. One of them was the historian and psychologist Saul Padover, an Austrian-born Jew who had immigrated to the United States in 1920. He served with a psychological warfare division that entered Germany via France and Luxemburg in the spring of 1945.

In his recollections published in 1946, Padover without fail started his description of the Germans he encountered and interviewed with their physical appearance: their gait, shape, gestures and most importantly eyes. These, together with their voice, determined how he regarded and read them, saw them as trustworthy or liars even before they had said a word. Like the writer John Dos Passos, covering the U.S. advance into Germany for *Life*, Padover was particularly galled by what he perceived as the Germans' whining behaviour, the lack of empathy and their complete solipsism.[62] The *Instructions for American Forces in Germany* had warned the soldiers of such behaviour. 'The defeated German enemy may play for sympathy. He displayed this tendency after the last war in 1918, and may be expected to do it again on a larger and grander scale'.[63] The soldiers should not fall for such a ruse.[64] The instructions also provided the soldiers with guidelines on how to react to German arguments. Though in one section it gave them line-by-line rebuttals of German arguments, the greater emphasis was on demeanour and comportment, on displaying and triggering emotions:

> Don't argue with them. Don't try to convince them. Don't get angry. Give them the 'Okay-chum-you'll-find-out-soon-enough' treatment and walk away. By NOT trying to convince them, or to shout them down, by the assumption of a quiet demeanor you can help to create a genuine longing and thirst for the truth and real news in the German people, and break down their resistance to it.[65]

The instruction concluded with a final appeal to emotions. It was not out 'to preach a gospel of hate and revenge' but to set down four guidelines for behaviour:

> be firm, fair, aloof and above all aware of the things this booklet has tried to tell you, so that the honest mistakes of an older generation may not be repeated, and so that, to apply Lincoln's words to the fallen men of our armed forces in this war, 'These dead shall not have died in vain'.[66]

Not only was the German behaviour constructed in a long historical line, but the U.S. aims were also historically premeditated. Knowing that such guidelines were hard to apply, particularly when interaction became more regular, the U.S. army initially laid down a strict fraternization prohibition that included an order not to shake hands with Germans.[67] Over the first few months in Germany, when hostilities had not yet ended, Padover only once ignored this order. In an encounter with an old Social Democrat, his feelings were not what he anticipated:

> Thesen was a surprise, and I still recall him with respect and admiration. He was one of the two Germans I was ever to meet who was not drenched in self-pity, who did not whine, who did not claim to be insignificant and guiltless. Thesen was a man. He was a man rare in Germany. He had a conscience, a sense of public morality, individual courage, and humour. When I found out what manner of man he was, I violated the non-fraternization order and shook his hand. He was a slight individual of forty-seven, with a sensitive face and deliberate speech.[68]

Whether Thesen appreciated the emphatic confirmation of his masculinity and the grandness of the gesture was left unclear. According to Padover, the Germans could be easily duped into misinterpreting the dynamic of the encounter, a few friendly questions was all it needed, so eager were they to please.[69] He, in contrast, thought their behaviour perfectly legible. Even so, reading the emotions correctly did not necessarily predetermine the emotional dynamic. A female schoolteacher Padover interviewed in the town of Roetgen close to the Belgian border recited one National Socialist stereotype after the other. Lacking any self-awareness, she seemed convinced that she had won Padover over. And in fact, she was not entirely wrong. Padover, almost despite himself, was charmed by her demeanour, voice and smile. Her compliments 'had the subtlety of a bazooka shell, but one could not help smiling at her aplomb'.[70] Yet by the end of the meeting when the teacher proposed to shake hands as a sign of friendship, Padover had recovered sufficiently to keep his distance.[71]

On another occasion, Padover had to recognize that even the Germans' behaviour was not quite as clearly readable as he generally assumed. After interviewing a young farm girl at the behest of Roetgen's interim mayor, he was left befuddled. The girl had reluctantly answered his questions, mostly with a simple no, and Padover assumed her to be dumb. Yet when he relayed this impression to the mayor, the latter revealed that the girl in fact had been the head of the town's National Socialist Young Girls' Association and by no means ideologically or otherwise innocent. Struck by this information, Padover had the girl hauled in for questioning again. Understanding that her situation had changed, she altered her demeanour, became teary-eyed and confessional, attempting to establish an emotional connection with Padover.[72] But now, with the help of a trusted local interpreter, the American was warned and the strategy failed. Interestingly, this was exactly the kind of situation the *Instructions* had warned against, except here the deceitful youth was a girl instead of a boy. Even so, Padover would have been duped had it not been for the local, here as in other cases of occupation a relative outsider who had been excluded from the National Socialist order. Another such case was a twelve-year-old boy with a deformed foot, who delighted in identifying the Third Reich's representatives of Roetgen to Padover.[73]

Yet attempting to ingratiate oneself could also arouse suspicion – the disdain for the servile behaviour of the Germans in 1945 is as much an example of this as it was in the case of the Eastern European Jews of 1915. As in the Eastern European case, Americans in general read this as cultural deformation rather than as something natural. The German writer Erich Kästner, who experienced the end of the war in Mayrhofen, a small town in the Austrian Alps, instead viewed it as typical of the German character, not as a deformation of a previous state. In mid May 1945, he commented on a German trying to secure a cigarette from an American soldier: 'No, this wagging of the tail is a German l'art pour l'art'.[74] The efforts of American soldiers, particularly those of German background, to guard themselves against this behaviour seemed heart-warmingly ineffective and naïve to Kästner. The army sergeant who was put in control of Mayrhofen might have desperately tried to hide his German accent. But this distance he tried to put between himself and the villagers did not prevent him from falling for a blonde woman in the village, whose hair was only the beginning of her deception. More importantly, she was an old Nazi. Nonetheless, she had the sergeant 'wrapped around her finger'.[75]

While the non-fraternization order was not as strictly enforced as far as German women were concerned, with regards to German men it could have further unforeseen emotional consequences.[76] At the end of May 1945, a few weeks before the arrival of the above-mentioned army sergeant, another representative of the U.S. army had visited Mayrhofen to question the Germans who were not villagers, including Kästner. When Kästner extended his hand to greet him, the American blushed, barred from reciprocating the gesture. Kästner interpreted the blushing as embarrassment and was in turn himself embarrassed to have placed the American in an awkward position. Reflecting on the emotional dynamic of this encounter however, Kästner was thankful for an occupying power whose representatives could be embarrassed by mere gestures of politeness of those conquered.[77] Kästner's reading was premediated primarily by his experience with German officials rather than by his expectation of American behaviour. The soldier's embarrassment gained its valence through contrast to the norms of National Socialist Germany that served as templates for what to expect from the encounter with the American occupiers.

Emotional norms could be enforced successfully and with the intended effect as well, however. A German-born Counter Intelligence Corps officer questioned Kästner in mid June 1945. According to the writer, the American's distrust permeated the interview's atmosphere. The literal translation of Kästner's description would be that 'you could grasp the distrust of the person leading the questioning, a lieutenant, with your hands'.[78] The German phrase captures the physicality of emotions and the transmission of their effect. Unfortunately, Kästner did not go into greater detail about the lieutenant's comportment to describe how this was effected. He did describe, however, how another officer present manifested intimidation: 'The second one said little, smoked a lot and played with his gun'.[79]

* * *

The United States soon gave up on the prohibition against fraternization. Germans turned out to be different from Americans but not always in the ways imagined by the authors of the *Instructions*. With the onset of the Cold War, ever greater emphasis was placed on similarity rather than difference, at least with regard to West Germans. The familiarity that developed between them and the U.S. occupying forces over time and through repeated interaction played its own part in creating an emotional connection; not unlike the situation in India before 1857 and with its own, though far less fatal, irritations.[80] Yet the way that difference was conceptualized, the concepts that premediated the encounter and the sites of learning had changed significantly over the course of a hundred years.

In 1857–58, generalized cultural assumptions, with religious groups being key to their categorization, provided the basic framework for interpreting the other. In addition to this, however, individual experience rather than training was perceived to be the key for a successful administration of occupied peoples, and thus more familiarity and less difference.

By 1914, the nationalization not only of societies and cultures but also of armies by way of mass conscription created more homogenized experiences and expectations and thus also encounters – despite all individual difference. German Jews were used by the German army to establish a level of familiarity with local customs, at least among officers, but there was no expectation that German soldiers should actively be trained to read Eastern European peoples.

Thirty years later, the U.S. military took the idea of a homogenous national army encountering a clearly defined people one step further. All servicemen were to be at least rudimentarily conversant with the emotional and psychological make-up of the other. The emotions in and of the encounter became sources and tools of power themselves. At the same time, ideology, rather than religion, language and nationality were thought to explain emotional difference, at least in the context of Europe, where, from the American perspective, race was a non-issue. This less obvious and more mutable difference then increased or rather returned worries of going native. Even ideology could be very appealing and ultimately dangerous.

Each of the case studies reveals the unsettling potential of emotions: if one lacked the cultural or even local context they could be misread or deceptive. The honest manner of the Indian guardsmen could in fact be a ruse, the servile Eastern European Jews were perhaps not so grateful and subservient after all, and the young and dumb German girl might actually have been a committed Nazi. While universal or specific assumptions about the other premediated the encounter and created the expectation of clearly intelligible emotions, the dynamic could confound these expectations. The one thing soldiers as well as civilians in all three cases seemed to agree on: smoking a cigarette projected calmness and power.

Philipp Nielsen is Assistant Professor for Modern European History at Sarah Lawrence College and Associated Researcher at the Center for the History of Emotions at the Max Planck Institute for Human Development in Berlin. He received his PhD from Yale University in 2012. His publications include *Between Heimat and Hatred: Jews and the Right in Germany, 1871–1935* (forthcoming with Oxford University Press, 2019) and *Architecture, Democracy and Emotions: The Politics of Feeling after 1945* with Till Großmann (Routledge, 2018). His research interests include Jewish German history, German political and architectural history and the history of emotions.

Notes

1. U.S. War Department, *Instructions for American Forces in Germany 1945*, 398–99.
2. U.S. War Department, *Instructions for American Forces in Germany 1945*, 383–86.
3. Ziemke, *The U.S. Army in the Occupation of Germany, 1944–1946*, 5–8.
4. Ricoeur, *The Course of Recognition*.
5. U.S. War Department, *Instructions for American Forces in Germany 1945*, 383–84. The British *Instructions for British Servicemen in Germany 1944*, 7 carried a very similar warning.
6. See, for example, the seven volumes by Bates, *Mutiny at the Margins: New Perspectives on the Indian Uprising of 1857* and therein especially vol. 5: *Muslim, Dalit and Subaltern Narratives*; Dalrymple, *The Last Mughal: The Fall of a Dynasty: Delhi, 1857*; Farooqui, *Besieged: Voices from Delhi 1857*; Mazumdar, *Insurgent Sepoys: Europe Views the Revolt of 1857*; Pati, *The Great Rebellion of 1857 in India: Exploring Transgressions, Contests and Diversities*; Roy, *The Uprising of 1857: Before and Beyond*.

7. Bates and Carter, 'Holy Warriors: Religion as Military Modus Operandi', 41–43; Dalrymple, *Last Mughal*, 12–13; Maclean, 'Situating the Role of Religion in the Rebellion: The Case of the Prayagwals in the Allahabad Uprising', 149–50; though for a critical perspective, see Farooqui, *Besieged*, 6–7.
8. Callahan, 'From Mornington to the Mutiny: Some Thoughts and Questions about the Company's Army 1805–1857', 58–59, 60; Dalrymple, *Last Mughal*, 60–61, 62; Judd, *The Lion and the Tiger: The Rise and Fall of the British Raj, 1600–1947*, 74–77; Streets, *Martial Races: The Military, Race and Masculinity in British Imperial Culture, 1857–1914*, 23.
9. Roy, 'Combat, Combat Motivation and the Construction of Identities: A Case Study', 28.
10. Maclean, 'Situating the Role of Religion', 163; for religion intersecting with race and an emerging patriotic sentiment, see Chaudhuri and Ray, '"We" and "They" in an Altered Ecumene: The Mutiny from the Mutineers' Mouths', 39–42.
11. On Hodson's role, including his brutality, see, for example, Dalrymple, *Last Mughal*, 187–90, 340–61.
12. On the role of these rumours, see, for example, Roy, 'Combat', 29.
13. Edwards, *Personal Adventures during the Indian Rebellion in Rohilcund, Futtehghur, and Oude*, 92.
14. See introduction to this volume.
15. See, for example, Edwards, *Personal Adventures*, 45.
16. Pati, 'Introduction: The Great Rebellion of 1857', 8; Edwards, *Personal Adventures*, 12–13.
17. Edwards, *Personal Adventures*, 10.
18. Edwards, *Personal Adventures*, 4–5.
19. Edwards, *Personal Adventures*, 5.
20. Streets, *Martial Races*, 62–63.
21. Edwards, *Personal Adventures*, 4–5.
22. Edwards, *Personal Adventures*, 19.
23. Edwards, *Personal Adventures*, 22.
24. Edwards, *Personal Adventures*, 36–37.
25. On misplaced trust and the loss of certainty, see Callahan, 'From Mornington', 64; Judd, *Lion and the Tiger*, 87; Pernau, *Emotions and Modernity in Colonial India: From Balance to Fervor*; Powell, 'Questionable Loyalties: Muslim Government Servants and Rebellion', 82–102; Wagner, *The Great Fear of 1857: Rumours, Conspiracies and the Making of the Indian Uprising*, 151–53.
26. Powell, 'Questionable Loyalties', 89.
27. On Hodson's role, including his brutality, see, for example, Dalrymple, *Last Mughal*, 187–90, 340–61.
28. Hodson, *Twelve Years of a Soldier's Life in India: Being Extracts from the Letters of the Late Major W.S.R. Hodson, B.A*, 37 (6 November 1846).
29. Hodson, *Twelve Years*, 29, 30 (2 and 14 September 1846).
30. Hodson, *Twelve Years*, 30 (14 September 1846).
31. 'rascal, n. and adj'., *OED Online* (June 2016), retrieved 5 July 2016 from http://www.oed.com/view/Entry/158280?isAdvanced=false&result=1&rskey=uuFdFW&.
32. Hodson, *Twelve Years*, 199 (9 June 1857).
33. Hodson, *Twelve Years*, 182.
34. On Hodson's spy network, see Dalrymple, *Last Mughal*, 190–92.
35. Hodson, *Twelve Years*, 219 (25 June 1857).
36. Hodson, *Twelve Years*, 227 (8 July 1857).
37. Hodson, *Twelve Years*, 312 (Lieutenant Macdowell).
38. Hodson, *Twelve Years*, 317 (Sir T. Seaton).
39. Dalrymple, *Last Mughal*, 335–36.

40. Haq, 'The Story of the War of Independence, 1857–58 by "Allamah Fadl-i-Haqq of Khayrabad"', 38. The retroactive and highly stylized nature of Haqq's account would also have played a part in this description; see Malik, 'Letters, Prison Sketches and Autobiographical Literature: The Case of Fadl-e Haqq Khairabaci in the Andaman Penal Colony', 91. For Chaudhuri and Ray emotions are linked to religion, which in turn according to them comes from a racialized understanding of difference by the rebels, though to the authors themselves emotions are 'eternal and universal'; Chaudhuri and Ray, '"We" and "They"', 45–47, quotation 47.
41. See Aschheim, *Brothers and Strangers: The East European Jew in German and German Jewish Conscience, 1800–1923*, 180 and Nelson, *German Soldier Newspapers of the First World War*, 229–35.
42. Kopp, *Germany's Wild East: Constructing Poland as Colonial Space*.
43. On the German occupation in Eastern Europe, see Aschheim, 'Eastern Jews, German Jews and Germany's Ostpolitik in the First World War', 351–68; Liulevicius, *War Land on the Eastern Front: Culture, National Identity, and the German Occupation in World War I*, 126, 191–92; Matthäus, 'German Judenpolitik in Lithuania during the First World War', 155–74; Zechlin, *Die deutsche Politik und die Juden im Ersten Weltkrieg*, 278–84.
44. Aschheim, *Brothers and Strangers*, 58–79.
45. Aschheim, *Brothers and Strangers*, 80–99.
46. See 'An die Juden in Polen', 2; Aschheim, *Brothers and Strangers*, 178–80; Nelson, *German Soldier Newspapers*, 226–27, 236.
47. See Frevert, *A Nation in Barracks: Conscription, Military Service and Civil Society in Modern Germany*, 149–50, 201–2.
48. Köhler, 'Letter to Dr. [Siegmund] Feist (15 January 1915)', 357. All translations from the German by the author unless otherwise noted.
49. Köhler, 'Letter to Dr. Feist (15 January 1915)', 357–58; Jaretzki, 'Letter to Dr. [Siegmund] Feist (23 August 1915)', 294–96; see also Nelson, *German Soldier Newspapers*, 229.
50. Köhler, 'Letter to Dr. [Siegmund] Feist (15 March 1915)', 363.
51. Von Beseler, 'Letter to his wife (20 February 1916)', BArch N 30 (Beseler/Briefe 1915)/54.
52. Von Beseler, 'Letter to his wife (16 October 1915)', BArch N 30 (Beseler/Briefe 1915)/53, Bl. 22.
53. Nelson, *German Soldier Newspapers*, 229–35; see also Nielsen, 'Eastern Promises: Jewish Germans in the German Administration of Eastern Europe during the Great War'.
54. Von Beseler, 'Marginal comments on a pamphlet sent to him by the "Deutsche Vereinigung für die Interessen der osteuropäischen Juden" October (1915)', BArch N 30 (Hans Hartwig von Beseler/Jüdische Angelegenheiten in Polen)/27, Bl. 6–11.
55. Nelson, *German Soldier Newspapers*, 230.
56. Aschheim, *Brothers and Strangers*, 155; Nielsen, 'Eastern Promises'.
57. Zweig, *Face of East European Jewry*, 4.
58. Zweig, *Face of East European Jewry*, 65.
59. Aschheim, *Brothers and Strangers*, 174, 231; see also Blackbourn, *The Conquest of Nature: Water, Landscape, and the Making of Modern Germany*.
60. Grossmann, *Jews, Germans, and Allies: Close Encounters in Occupied Germany*, 25–26.
61. U.S. War Department, *Instructions for American Forces in Germany 1945*, Kindle Locations 294–97.
62. Padover, *Psychologist in Germany: The Story of an American Intelligence Officer*, 29, 51; Dos Passos, *Tour of Duty*, 271.
63. U.S. War Department, *Instructions for American Forces in Germany 1945*, Kindle Locations 329–30.
64. U.S. War Department, *Instructions for American Forces in Germany 1945*, Kindle Locations 383–86.

65. U.S. War Department, *Instructions for American Forces in Germany 1945*, Kindle Locations 432–38.
66. U.S. War Department, *Instructions for American Forces in Germany 1945*, Kindle Locations 580–81.
67. Grossmann, *Jews, Germans, and Allies*, 33.
68. Padover, *Psychologist in Germany*, 53.
69. Padover, *Psychologist in Germany*, 30.
70. Padover, *Psychologist in Germany*, 75
71. Padover, *Psychologist in Germany*, 79.
72. Padover, *Psychologist in Germany*, 66–69.
73. Padover, *Psychologist in Germany*, 65.
74. Kästner, *Notabene*, 159 (19 May 1945).
75. Kästner, *Notabene*, 172 (5 June 1945).
76. Kästner, *Notabene*, 167 (28 May 1945); on heterosexual fraternization, see also Grossmann, *Jews, Germans, and Allies*, 71–77.
77. Kästner, *Notabene*, 166–67 (28 May 1945).
78. Kästner, *Notabene*, 191 (18 June 1945).
79. Kästner, *Notabene*, 190–91 (18 June 1945).
80. For a detailed study of this development, see Höhn, *GIs and Fräuleins: The German-American Encounter in 1950s West Germany*; and also Grossmann, *Jews, Germans, and Allies*; for the emotions in post-war Germany, see also Parkinson, *An Emotional State: The Politics of Emotion in Postwar West German Culture*.

Bibliography

'An die Juden in Polen'. *Berliner Tageblatt und Handelszeitung* 43(442) (Morgenausgabe, 1 September 1914), 2.

Aschheim, S.E. *Brothers and Strangers: The East European Jew in German and German Jewish Conscience, 1800–1923*. Madison: University of Wisconsin Press, 1982.

_____. 'Eastern Jews, German Jews and Germany's Ostpolitik in the First World War'. *Leo Baeck Institute Yearbook* 28(1) (1983), 351–68, doi: 10.1093/leobaeck/28.1.351.

Bates, C. (ed.). *Mutiny at the Margins: New Perspectives on the Indian Uprising of 1857*, 7 vols. New Delhi: Sage, 2013–17.

_____. *Mutiny at the Margins: New Perspectives on the Indian Uprising of 1857*, vol. 5: *Muslim, Dalit and Subaltern Narratives*. New Delhi: Sage, 2014.

Bates, C., and M. Carter. 'Holy Warriors: Religion as Military Modus Operandi', in G. Rand and C. Bates (eds), *Mutiny at the Margins: New Perspectives on the Indian Uprising of 1857*, vol. 4: *Military Aspects of the Indian Uprising* (New Delhi: Sage, 2013), 41–60.

Blackbourn, D. *The Conquest of Nature: Water, Landscape, and the Making of Modern Germany*. London: Cape, 2006.

Callahan, R. 'From Mornington to the Mutiny: Some Thoughts and Questions about the Company's Army 1805–1857', in K. Roy (ed.), *The Uprising of 1857: Before and Beyond* (New Delhi: Manohar, 2010), 47–70.

Chaudhuri, N., and R.K. Ray. '"We" and "They" in an Altered Ecumene: The Mutiny from the Mutineers' Mouths', in C. Bates (ed.), *Mutiny at the Margins:*

New Perspectives on the Indian Uprising of 1857, vol. 5: *Muslim, Dalit and Subaltern Narratives* (New Delhi: Sage, 2014), 36–48.
Dalrymple, W. *The Last Mughal: The Fall of a Dynasty: Delhi, 1857*. New York: Knopf, 2007.
Dos Passos, J. *Tour of Duty*. Boston: Houghton Mifflin, 1946.
Edwards, W. *Personal Adventures during the Indian Rebellion in Rohilcund, Futtehghur, and Oude*, 2nd edn. London: Smith, Elder and Co, 1858.
Farooqui, M. (ed.). *Besieged: Voices from Delhi 1857*. New Delhi: Penguin Viking, 2010.
Frevert, U. *A Nation in Barracks: Conscription, Military Service and Civil Society in Modern Germany*. Oxford: Berg, 2004.
Grossmann, A. *Jews, Germans, and Allies: Close Encounters in Occupied Germany*. Princeton, NJ: Princeton University Press, 2007.
Haq, M.S. 'The Story of the War of Independence, 1857–58 by "Allamah Fadl-i-Haqq of Khayrabad"'. *Journal of the Pakistan Historical Society* 5(1) (1957), 23–57.
Hodson, G.H. (ed.). *Twelve Years of a Soldier's Life in India: Being Extracts from the Letters of the Late Major W.S.R. Hodson, B.A.* London: John W. Parker and Son, 1859.
Höhn, M. *GIs and Fräuleins: The German-American Encounter in 1950s West Germany*. Chapel Hill: University of North Carolina University Press, 2002.
Instructions for British Servicemen in Germany 1944. London: Foreign Office, 1944, repr. edn. Oxford: Bodleian Library, 2007.
Jaretzki, L. 'Letter to Dr. [Siegmund] Feist (23 August 1915)', in S. Hank and H. Simon (eds), *Feldpostbriefe Jüdischer Soldaten 1914–1918*, vol. 1 (Teetz: Hentrich & Hentrich, 2002), 294–96.
Judd, D. *The Lion and the Tiger: The Rise and Fall of the British Raj, 1600–1947*. Oxford: Oxford University Press, 2004.
Kästner, E. *Notabene 45: Ein Tagebuch*. Zurich: Atrium, 1961.
Köhler, O. 'Letter to Dr. [Siegmund] Feist (15 January 1915)', in S. Hank and H. Simon (eds), *Feldpostbriefe Jüdischer Soldaten 1914–1918*, vol. 1 (Teetz: Hentrich & Hentrich, 2002), 356–60.
_____. 'Letter to Dr. [Siegmund] Feist (15 March 1915)', in S. Hank and H. Simon (eds), *Feldpostbriefe Jüdischer Soldaten 1914–1918*, vol. 1 (Teetz: Hentrich & Hentrich, 2002), 361–65.
Kopp, K. *Germany's Wild East: Constructing Poland as Colonial Space*. Ann Arbor: University of Michigan Press, 2012.
Liulevicius, V.G. *War Land on the Eastern Front: Culture, National Identity, and the German Occupation in World War I*. Cambridge: Cambridge University Press, 2000.
Maclean, K. 'Situating the Role of Religion in the Rebellion: The Case of the Prayagwals in the Allahabad Uprising', in C. Bates (ed.), *Mutiny at the Margins: New Perspectives on the Indian Uprising of 1857*, vol. 1: *Anticipations and Experiences in the Locality* (New Delhi: Sage, 2013), 149–68.
Malik, J. 'Letters, Prison Sketches and Autobiographical Literature: The Case of Fadl-e Haqq Khairabadi in the Andaman Penal Colony'. *Indian Economic and Social History Review* 43(1) (2006), 77–100, doi: 10.1177/001946460504300104.

Matthäus, J. 'German Judenpolitik in Lithuania during the First World War'. *Leo Baeck Institute Yearbook* 43(1) (1998), 155–74, doi: 10.1093/leobaeck/43.1.155.

Mazumdar, S. (ed.). *Insurgent Sepoys: Europe Views the Revolt of 1857*. New Delhi: Routledge, 2011.

Nelson, R.L. *German Soldier Newspapers of the First World War*. Cambridge: Cambridge University Press, 2011.

Nielsen, P. 'Eastern Promises: Jewish Germans in the German Administration of Eastern Europe during the Great War', in G. Reuveni and E. Madigan (eds), *The Jewish Experience of the First World War* (London: Palgrave Macmillan, forthcoming).

Padover, S.K. *Psychologist in Germany: The Story of an American Intelligence Officer* (London: Phoenix House, 1946).

Parkinson, A.M. *An Emotional State: The Politics of Emotion in Postwar West German Culture*. Ann Arbor: University of Michigan Press, 2015.

Pati, B. 'Introduction: The Great Rebellion of 1857', in B. Pati (ed.), *The Great Rebellion of 1857 in India: Exploring Transgressions, Contests and Diversities* (London: Routledge, 2010), 1–15.

Pati, B. (ed.). *The Great Rebellion of 1857 in India: Exploring Transgressions, Contests and Diversities*. London: Routledge, 2010.

Pernau, M. *Emotions and Modernity in Colonial India: From Balance to Fervor*. Forthcoming.

Powell, A.A. 'Questionable Loyalties: Muslim Government Servants and Rebellion', in C. Bates (ed.), *Mutiny at the Margins: New Perspectives on the Indian Uprising of 1857*, vol. 5: *Muslim, Dalit and Subaltern Narratives* (New Delhi: Sage, 2014), 82–102.

'rascal, n. and adj'.. *OED Online* (June 2016). Retrieved 5 July 2016 from http://www.oed.com/view/Entry/158280?isAdvanced=false&result=1&rskey=uuFdFW&.

Ricoeur, P. *The Course of Recognition*. Cambridge, MA: Harvard University Press, 2005.

Roy, K. 'Combat, Combat Motivation and the Construction of Identities: A Case Study', in G. Rand and C. Bates (eds), *Mutiny at the Margins: New Perspectives on the Indian Uprising of 1857*, vol. 4: *Military Aspects of the Indian Uprising* (New Delhi: Sage, 2013), 24–40.

Roy, K. (ed.). *The Uprising of 1857: Before and Beyond*. New Delhi: Manohar, 2010.

Streets, H. *Martial Races: The Military, Race and Masculinity in British Imperial Culture, 1857–1914*. Manchester: Manchester University Press, 2004.

U.S. War Department. *Instructions for American Forces in Germany 1945: Official Guidance for American Forces Issued by the United States Army*. n.p.: United States Army, 1945, repr. edn. Kindle Edition, 2012.

Wagner, K.A. *The Great Fear of 1857: Rumours, Conspiracies and the Making of the Indian Uprising*. Oxford: Lang, 2010.

Zechlin, E. *Die deutsche Politik und die Juden im Ersten Weltkrieg*. Göttingen: Vandenhoeck & Ruprecht, 1969.

Ziemke, E.F. *The U.S. Army in the Occupation of Germany, 1944–1946*. Washington, DC: Center for Military History, 1975.

Zweig, A. *The Face of East European Jewry, with Fifty-Two Drawings by Hermann Struck*, ed. and trans. N. Isenburg. Berkeley: University of California Press, 2004 [Ger. orig. *Das ostjüdische Antlitz*. Berlin: Weltverlag, 1920].

Chapter 7

Prisoners
Experiencing the Criminal Other

Pavel Vasilyev and Gian Marco Vidor

> When I first arrived at the Mordovian Corrective Labour Colony #14, Lena took care of me. I used to stand at the end of the lunch line where everyone pushed me out of the way. And I used to step out of the way obediently, just like the rotten intelligentsia. I had just come from the remand prison, and, having spent half a year in a cell, I was not used to the human population. Lena was sitting alone at the time. Not eating. Everyone in the colony knew her, and many loved her, but many envied her . . .
> [Lena:] – Come to me, take a seat. When you go to the canteen, always stick with me and you'll be alright.
> We ate soup with pasta and vegetable fat, and some bread . . .
> – Do you know what her crime is? – they ask me about Lena when she's not around . . .
> [Nadezhda:] – What?
> – She killed her man during orgasm!
> [Nadezhda:] – A beautiful crime.
> Lena never disappoints me.
> That's how I'm doing. These are my friends. These are the crimes.
> —N. Tolokonnikova, blog entry, 29 March 2015

In this Facebook post from 29 March 2015, Nadezhda Tolokonnikova, a Russian artist and political activist, reminisced about her imprisonment following the Pussy Riot trial. This colourful description of an encounter between Tolokonnikova – a former student of the prestigious Department of Philosophy at Moscow State University – and a 'common' criminal illustrates well some of the tensions inherent in the main topic of this

---

Notes for this chapter begin on page 200.

chapter: intracultural encounters between political prisoners and other inmates.

When talking about their time in prison, both Tolokonnikova and another former member of Pussy Riot, Mariia Alekhina, recall having transformative experiences through some of their encounters with other prisoners and describe the emotional and corporeal dimensions of their experiences in detail. Immediately after their release, the two women met in Krasnoyarsk to establish an NGO and a web portal dedicated to prison reform and the fight for the rights of all prisoners (and not just 'politicals'). In explaining their motivations for setting up the NGO, they listed justice, solidarity, humanity and responsibility as their key values, and Tolokonnikova elaborated: 'I have to render this assistance. I will do my best to help the prisoners. I am now linked to the penitentiary system *by the ties of blood* and I will not back down. I will do everything to make it better'.[1]

As powerful as this example is, it is not intended to suggest that encounters between political prisoners and common offenders always end up in harmonious relationships. A different perspective is offered, for example, by Russian nationalist Evgeniia Khasis, who served her sentence in the same corrective labour colony as the left-leaning Tolokonnikova. An adherent of a rigid conservative ideology, Khasis was unable to communicate with her fellow convicts in an emotionally impactful way, and was thus unable to discover new modalities of feeling in her interactions with them. In an interview, she dismissed her fellow inmates as descendants of 'a very poor and antisocial environment, children of drug addicts and alcoholics' and hardly concealed her contempt when talking about prisoners with HIV 'whose life is decaying right in front of your eyes'.[2]

* * *

Prison literature has a long history. It became an important literary genre in the Western world during the nineteenth century.[3] In the twentieth century, the number of novels, diaries and letters recounting prison experiences increased exponentially.[4] It is possible to speak not only of a canon of European prison literature but also of a conscious sense of tradition among prison writers.[5] Prisoners with strong educational backgrounds, in particular, have reflected on, analysed and historicized their experiences. In doing so, they have sometimes consciously placed their own experiences within a literary tradition while at the same time using the narratives of famous prisoners as models for coping with some of the travails of their own imprisonment.

This chapter focuses on two countries that, for both political and cultural reasons, have long traditions of prison literature in the modern period: Italy and Russia. It discusses what have ultimately come to be recognized as canonical texts. Scholars have used these texts to glean biographical information about important political and culture figures or to shed light on social events, political movements and cultural phenomena.[6] Social historians have used them in the framework of the history of justice and punishment,[7] and literary scholars have considered them as part of a specific and complex literary genre.[8] As far as the institution of modern prisons themselves are concerned, much critical research has viewed them as places where the individual is supposed to be morally improved and socially 'rehabilitated', often embracing a Foucauldian perspective that stresses the role of the modern carceral institution in practices of subjectification and self-discipline.[9]

However, in the cases of both Italy and Russia, the relationship between 'intellectual'/'political' convicts and 'common' prisoners has been generally left by the wayside,[10] and the emotional dimensions of this encounter have been almost completely overlooked. This is actually quite surprising given the fact that the experience of meeting the 'common' prisoner is one of the most frequent topoi of narratives of encounter between inmates in prison literature. The prevalence of this narrative is rooted in the fact that most prison memoirs – especially those written before the second half of the twentieth century – were composed by intellectuals or political prisoners writing from a privileged position.

While those involved in the encounters described in this chapter usually belonged to the same broadly defined 'culture' (Italian or Russian) and shared the same language, the often significant divergences in prisoners' upbringing and emotional styles, conditioned by ethnic, religious and, in particular, class differences, justify identifying these prison encounters as 'intercultural', in line with the overall orientation of this volume. To take one example, historians have long argued that, starting in the eighteenth century, the rapid modernization and Westernization of the Russian upper classes led to the co-existence of radically different class cultures within the same country.[11]

But prisons not only bring together people from diverse backgrounds into a confined space. Their very structure is defined by coercion in its many guises. The intracultural encounters that take place within their walls are thus in a category of their own. This chapter focuses on how emotions shape and are shaped by face-to-face encounters and explores the ways in which feelings are communicated across social and cultural divides, both real and perceived. Furthermore, it discusses some instances in which prison encounters deeply transformed the emotional repertoires of those who experienced them.

Drawing on an analysis of a large corpus of published and unpublished sources, this chapter concentrates on four exemplary encounters between 'intellectual' or 'political' convicts and 'common' prisoners. It takes a longue durée perspective that stretches from the early nineteenth century to the present. The diversity of the sources allows the chapter to discuss both male and female 'intellectual' convicts in diverse institutional settings and to consider multiple perspectives on the ways in which the emotions involved in encounters between prisoners shape and are shaped by hierarchies and power structures. The texts analysed here demonstrate that intellectuals have taken a range of different attitudes towards 'common' inmates, from snobbish condescension to a sort of ethnographic curiosity, to attempts to bridge the difference and explore and learn new modalities of feeling that might have been unknown or perceived as impossible in the outside world. At the same time, our analysis concludes that the mostly unchanging coercive framework of the carceral setting has exercised an enormous influence on prison encounters and the outcomes they can have, despite shifting historical circumstances.

The Romantic Prison and the 'Discovery' of a Shared Humanity: The Case of Silvio Pellico

A common trope of many prison narratives is the writer's 'discovery' of the 'shared humanity' that ties them to the other inmates. Silvio Pellico's (1789–1854) memoirs stand out as a typical example of the way in which educated writers have historically portrayed the 'discovery' of a shared humanity in romantic prison literature. Pellico was an Italian patriot and famous dramatist who lived in the Kingdom of Lombardy-Venetia, which was a constituent land (crown land) of the Austrian Empire from 1815 to 1861. In 1822, he was sentenced to death for taking part in the Italian movement for national independence. The sentence was ultimately commuted to life in prison, of which he served eight years in Milan, Venice and in the Špilberk fortress in Brno under very hard conditions. For almost the entire duration of his imprisonment, and, like many other political prisoners, Pellico was placed under heavy surveillance and was kept in solitary confinement. In 1832, he published *Le mie prigioni* (My Prisons). The book rapidly achieved canonical status in Italy and was translated into many languages, enjoying international success.[12] Even though it was read by many as an indictment of the Austrians and as a powerful symbol of the Italian struggle for independence,[13] Pellico explicitly regarded his work as a testimony to the goodness of human nature, as a call for others to 'love all men' and as a book that would console others in times of hardship.[14]

In Pellico's discussion of the common humanity that binds all men, one can certainly hear echoes of the concept of 'fraternity'. Rooted in the revolutionary, philosophical and esoteric thought of the eighteenth century, the concept exerted a powerful influence on the political and cultural life of nineteenth-century Europe and shaped the debate on the relationship between nations and social classes.[15] However, Pellico clearly portrayed his experience as a gradual spiritual reconversion to the 'Christian religion, so rich in humanity'.[16] He interpreted his painful situation as a prisoner through an evangelical lens, viewing it as a unique chance for personal salvation.[17] This successful spiritual journey in and through prison was accented by the author's many failures and shortcomings, which he read as effects of negative emotions such as 'inquietude', 'anger', 'fury' and 'fear'. Pellico's narrative is one of fall and redemption, a classic theme of Romantic literature.[18]

This path of spiritual and moral education was full of encounters that serve both as symbols of and tools for moral improvement. Framed by Pellico's Christian perspective, these encounters allowed him to shed light on the goodness of mankind, underscoring the generally redemptive dimension of prison experience that runs through the narrative. Pellico portrayed the people he encountered in a simplified way, which made it possible for him to use their stories as edificatory *exempla*.[19] Alongside police and prison guards, doctors, other Italian patriots, commissaries and local people he met during transfers from one prison to the other, common offenders played a significant, more complex role in Pellico's image of the essential goodness of humanity shared by each and every person.

In Milan, Pellico's cell was next to the cell of a group of 'degraded women', who argued noisily, sang loudly, talked coarsely and even swore. But among them, he wrote, there was a 'touching voice', that of a certain Magdalen, who talked gently, supportively and religiously and who sometimes sang in verse.[20] During his time in the prison, as he wrote in a long passage, he had a conversation with the leader of a group of male convicts.[21] The encounter had a certain rhythm, articulated by different steps and emotional stages: Pellico first underlined the otherness of the common offenders, stating that none of the '[w]retched men' expressed 'a single tender sentiment, a single thought of religion and of love!'[22]

The leader of the gang later asked Pellico how he could possibly stand this 'cursed life'. The Italian patriot explained that for him, one should continue 'thinking and loving' even in such terrible conditions. When his fellow inmates asked him to explain what he meant, Pellico, a bit hesitant, talked about the tenderness of the voice of Magdalen. The thieves and their boss laughed at him, and he thought he had made a fool of himself. After the thieves mocked him, Pellico once again sought to underscore the difference between himself and the thieves, writing that, both in prison and on the outside, those 'who rest their wisdom upon fretting, complaining and vilifying others, regard as foolishness the feelings of love and pity'. He then sank into a period of silence, refusing to even respond to the thieves when they spoke to him. The leader of the thieves, however, told his gang that they should not laugh at the nobleman but should take what he was saying seriously. This time it was he who drew a strong line between the distinct emotional repertoires of the thieves and Pellico, admonishing the former and admiring the latter. Like '[a]ll detestable scoundrels', the leader said, the thieves only knew how to act like 'madmen'. He continued by saying that Pellico's talk of 'pleasant cheerfulness', 'charity' and the 'confidence in the goodness of Providence' showed that he was less of 'a ruffian' than they were.[23]

Pellico wrote that he felt joy in the fact that such 'degraded men' recognized the importance of cultivating good feelings. This process of configuration led Pellico to hope that his words would provoke a sort of inner change in his fellow inmates. But his expectations were wrong, since, he stated, 'vulgar minds banish serious reflection; if a noble truth breaks upon them, they are capable of applauding it a moment; but they soon turn their attention away from it, and cannot resist the desire of showing their wit, by casting the truth into doubt, or turning it into ridicule'.[24]

The prison guard, 'in a violent rage', interrupted their conversation and told Pellico with the 'gravity of a master' that it was shameful to talk 'with all sorts of people', asking him if he knew that the men were thieves. Pellico 'blushed, and then . . . [he] blushed again for having blushed, for it seemed to . . . [him] that to condescend to converse with all classes of the unhappy, . . . [was] rather an act of kindness than a fault'. In a way, the guard had reminded Pellico of his social status and had put an end to the 'shameful' encounter between what he perceived to be men with wholly divergent moral constitutions. Importantly, Pellico had two distinct bodily and emotional reactions at the end of this encounter. He portrays his first blush as the almost expected automatic reaction of a cultivated and sensitive man told by an authority that he has done something 'wrong'. But he describes his second blush, just a few moments later, as the result of deeper moral reflection. Pellico felt ashamed about having conformed to the prescribed norms of interaction between the social classes, norms that he did not fully embrace.[25]

This encounter has not attracted much scholarly attention,[26] but when viewed together with other examples,[27] it illustrates Pellico's attempt to mediate the gap separating him from the other prisoners. In the end, however, Pellico ultimately ended up reaffirming his view of the otherness of these 'vulgar minds'.[28] Nevertheless, Pellico, through an act of will, strove to overcome this otherness and to bring the common criminals into the circle of those 'souls obedient to the great vocation of man, to love, to pity and to do good'.²⁹ In fact, Pellico explicitly portrayed his prison experience as a spiritual journey guided by philosophy, and, in particular, the teachings of Christianity. In his opinion, both demanded 'energy of will and calmness of judgment' if they were to serve as reliable principles.³⁰ As such, he was able to traverse class differences and engage in emotional communication with 'the common criminal'. Importantly, it was the carceral setting itself that made possible this particular kind of encounter and the transformative process that led Pellico to 'discover' the common humanity he shared with the other prisoners.

Learning to 'Feel the People': Fyodor Dostoyevsky in *The House of the Dead*

Despite the rather different political and social circumstances of the Habsburg and Romanov Empires, a very similar set of moral issues was taken up in arguably the most important 'prison text' of mid-nineteenth century classical Russian literature. In 1849, a young Fyodor Dostoyevsky (1821–1881) was sentenced to execution by firing squad for taking part in an illegal political discussion group. After a mock execution, the death sentence was commuted to a prison sentence in eastern Siberia, where the writer spent the next four years. The authorities deliberately sought to separate political prisoners from one another by placing them with criminal offenders. Because many inmates held rather hostile attitudes towards noblemen like Dostoyevsky and did not shy away from letting them know it, Dostoyevsky originally viewed having to live among other inmates as just as much a part of the punishment as the desolate Siberian environment itself. Immediately after his release in 1854, Dostoyevsky wrote in a letter to his brother that the common offenders were 'rough, angry, embittered men' whose 'hatred for the nobility ... [was] boundless; they regard[ed] all of us who belong to it with hostility and enmity. They would have devoured us if they only could'.³¹ However, this close encounter with 'ordinary people' ultimately exerted a powerful effect on the burgeoning author. It not only turned out to be productive for the writer's work but also helped transform his worldview. In the same letter to his brother, Dostoyevsky also observed: '[M]en everywhere are just – men. Even among the robber-murderers in the prison, I came to know some men. ... [T]here were among them deep, strong, beautiful natures, and it often gave me great joy to find gold under a rough exterior'.³² Furthermore, the writer claimed that he had 'lived into their lives' and 'learnt to know the Russian people as only a few know them'.³³ This was further illustrated in Dostoyevsky's 1876 short story, 'Muzhik Marei' (The

Peasant Marei). In this text, the writer first tells of his frustration and anger during imprisonment. However, he then describes a childhood memory in which a serf comforted the frightened child, writing that the memory set his mind at ease, ameliorated his negative emotions towards the others and helped him see his fellow inmates in a different light.[34]

This personal experience of the cultural differences and conflicts between the educated Russian nobility and the 'ordinary people' was later developed into an important theme in Dostoyevsky's first major publication, *The House of the Dead* (*Zapiski iz mertvogo doma* [1860–1861]). Despite the introduction of an imaginary narrator in the first chapter (probably for the purpose of getting past the censors), many consider the novel to be highly autobiographical: Dostoyevsky scholars have been able to link most of its characters to real-life offenders listed in archival documents and prison memoirs. Importantly, the writer drew on the numerous expressions, proverbs and popular adages that he had collected in his famous 'Siberian notebook', using them in the novel to invoke the rich language of his fellow inmates.[35]

The House of the Dead was an astonishing success and was also one of the first literary works in Russia that dealt openly with prison life. Critics called Dostoyevsky 'a Russian Dante', who gave Russian readers a realistic depiction of his journey through Hell. Indeed, for most of the late nineteenth century, the book was considered to be the writer's best work.[36] *The House of the Dead* thus had a great influence on future Russian prison literature and is referred to in many memoirs of the Stalinist Gulags as well as in the narratives of contemporary Russian political prisoners.

Importantly, Dostoyevsky's political and religious views also underwent a profound transformation as a result of his arrest and imprisonment. Initially interested in Charles Fourier's 'utopian socialism', he had already begun to turn towards political conservatism and Christianity during his pretrial detention in the Peter and Paul Fortress in St Petersburg, his religiosity growing only stronger during his exile and imprisonment in Siberia. Like Pellico's reconversion, this rediscovery of religion certainly informed one of the major themes in *The House of the Dead* – the quest to 'dig out a human being'[37] in every person, no matter how evil, criminal or uneducated. This was definitely not an easy task, since Dostoyevsky felt that the prisoners' hatred for noblemen was indeed omnipresent. Confirming Dostoyevsky's negative first impressions, Akim Akimych, one of the few other prisoners with a noble background, explained:

> Yes, . . . they do not like nobles, above all those who have been condemned for political offences, and they take a pleasure in wounding their feelings. Is it not intelligible? We do not belong to them, we do not suit them. They have all been serfs or soldiers. Tell me what sympathy can they have for us.[38]

Since hatred for the 'men of nobility' was a constant feature of the prison environment that 'poisoned his life', Dostoyevsky even chose to be sent to the hospital on several occasions just in order to escape the atmosphere of 'unrelenting and implacable hostility'.[39] However, it was precisely the unique nature of the prison that set the stage for the destabilization of Dostoyevsky's identity and a reversal of the hierarchies that determined his relation to other prisoners. For their part, the common offenders certainly rejoiced in seeing noble prisoners suffer and even perceived it as a sort of revenge. For instance, some told the writer: 'You nobles have beaks of iron, and you tore us to pieces with your beaks when we were serfs'.[40] It was in this context that Dostoyevsky began to despise his own privilege, even coming to envy 'the people of the lower class', who were seemingly able to quickly and easily integrate themselves into the prison's emotional community when they arrived.[41] Importantly, geographical distance did not play a major role here. In Dostoyevsky's view, even when a peasant convict from Russia's southern provinces was transported to the Empire's eastern outskirts on the Pacific Ocean, he 'finds there Russian peasants like himself; between him and them there can be mutual intelligence; in an hour they will be friends, and live comfortably together'.[42] By contrast, this seemed to be virtually impossible for a nobleman, even for those who had had regular contact with the lower classes as military commanders or administrative workers. As Dostoyevsky put it: '[Y]ou may be his benefactor, all but a father to him – well, you'll never know what is at the bottom of the man's mind or heart. You may think you know something about him, but it is all optical illusion, nothing more'.[43]

Drawing on Alexander Etkind's concept of 'internal colonization', we might view the seemingly intracultural encounter between political prisoners and common offenders as a colonial encounter. It is indisputable that the difference between Dostoyevsky and his fellow inmates was defined by different emotional and linguistic styles and, more importantly, by the long history of hierarchical relations between nobles and 'commoners'. This history not only encompassed explicit violence committed against peasants by the nobility but also nobles' exoticization of 'common people' and their way of life. The prison setting thus brought '[t]he contrast between geographical proximity and cultural distance'[44] to its extreme. However, in Dostoyevsky's case, it also enabled emotional transformation and the discovery of new feelings.

During his time in prison, Dostoyevsky ultimately began to idealize the common offenders, viewing them as naturally kind people with 'pure hearts'. However, it took Dostoyevsky several years before he could be accepted by the emotional community of the prison; indeed, he could never be fully accepted in the way other prisoners might have been.

On the day before his release, he walked around the prison yard and bemoaned the sorrowful fate of 'the strongest' and 'the most gifted of our people' who had been put in prison.⁴⁵ Yet when he was bidding farewell to his fellow inmates the following morning, their emotional and bodily reactions were far more complex than he had expected they would be:

> Many a vigorous, horny hand was held out to me with right good-will. Some grasped and shook my hand as though all their hearts were with the act; but these were the more generous souls. Most of the poor fellows seemed so much to feel that, for them, I was already a man changed by what was coming, that they could feel scarce anything else. They knew that I had friends in the town, that I was going away at once to *gentlemen*, that I should sit at their table as their equal. This the poor fellows felt; and, although they did their best as they took my hand, that hand could not be the hand of an equal. No; I, too, was a gentleman now. Some turned their backs on me, and made no reply to my parting words. I think, too, that I saw looks of aversion on some faces.⁴⁶

As the description above makes clear, Dostoyevsky's emotional transformation was not accepted by the other prisoners on equal terms (as he himself might have wished). Indeed, his fellow inmates perceived his identity and behaviour as something that was conditioned by the prison setting and thought he would go back to acting like a 'gentleman' after his release. In the final scene, this attitude was expressed through body language and emotions in a way that was for the most part tactful and inoffensive yet at the same time clearly perceptible. While Dostoyevsky might have learned to 'feel the people' better as a result of his prison experience, the re-assertion of rigid class boundaries was also a parallel outcome of this encounter.

The Intellectual and the Masses: Eugenia Ginzburg in Stalinist Prisons

This outcome was increasingly mirrored in the prison literature of the twentieth century, when the Stalinist Soviet Union experienced very high rates of incarceration and mass arrests of women and children who happened to be relatives of 'the enemies of the people'. Exemplary of this history is the life of Eugenia Ginzburg (1904–1977), who was a young and enthusiastic communist when she was arrested in Kazan as an alleged member of a 'Trotskyite terrorist organization' in 1937, during the height of the Great Terror. She later spent ten years in prisons and labour camps throughout the Soviet Union and remained in exile in eastern Siberia until de-Stalinization began in the mid 1950s. Her story might thus be considered representative of the experiences undergone by intellectuals imprisoned in the modern totalitarian regimes of the twentieth century. A similar example in the Italian context might be Antonio Gramsci (1891–1937). Gramsci took an almost ethnographic interest in the common convicts he was imprisoned with and made detailed 'psychological and folkloristic observations' of these 'submerged folk strata'.[47]

After Ginzburg was officially rehabilitated in 1955, she went on to write about her prison experience in her memoirs, *Krutoi Marshrut* (1967; published in English in two parts as *Journey into the Whirlwind* [1967] and *Within the Whirlwind* [1981]). The work was not only a significant contribution to the tradition of Russian female prison writing but was also one of the most revelatory texts about the Great Terror when it became available to Soviet readers in the late 1980s. With its strong anti-Stalinist message, the book fit the climate of the glasnost era very well and enjoyed an overwhelmingly positive reception. It remains one of the most influential Gulag narratives.

Like other Soviet prison narratives written by women (for example, Eufrosiniya Kersnovskaya's *What's a Human Being Worth?*),[48] Ginzburg's *Krutoi marshrut* stands out for its focus on the importance of bodily contact (touching, hugging, kissing, stroking) for the communication of feelings. This is evident in her narration of a peculiar encounter that took place in 1937 with Zinaida Abramova, a former 'First Lady' of Tatarstan, who was imprisoned after her husband was accused of being a 'Turkish spy'. In a typical early Soviet success story, Abramova had risen to prominence from a very humble background: a 'peasant girl, selling cigarettes in a village shop' before the Revolution, she married a young Bolshevik, who later went on to become a head of the Council of People's Commissars of Tatarstan.[49] Enjoying the glamorous lifestyle of a Soviet bureaucrat's wife, she cast away her Tatar name and 'rationed [her smiles] in accordance with the social rank of their recipient'.[50] Ginzburg described the sudden change Abramova underwent when she was imprisoned, an experience that not only turned her face into a 'mask of horror' but also 'wiped all the make-believe ... off her face ... leaving the signs of her class and nationality plain for all to see'. She even reassumed the Tatar accent that she had so desperately sought to suppress as part of the Stalinist 'civilizing' project.[51]

Ginzburg had known Abramova before their time together in prison and had not particularly liked her. However, she now put her personal opinions aside, believing that the new inmate 'had to be soothed and comforted as far as lay in our power'.[52] But the feeling of distrust was still there, and Ginzburg's initial attempts to comfort Abramova by hugging and kissing her failed. After Abramova was badly beaten during an interrogation, the glamorous identity she had once adorned was unrecognizable; indeed, Ginzburg writes, she was reduced to a 'classless, ageless, almost sexless' creature, 'a groaning, blood-stained piece of flesh'.[53] Ginzburg once again felt the need to comfort the new inmate, but she changed her strategy slightly. Squatting next to the slop bucket where Abramova was lying, Ginzburg stroked her hair and even tried to talk to her in her native Tatar. This, as the author notes, 'was the right approach', and an emotional connection between the two women was established. The author even states that she was suddenly able to understand the Tatar language much better than she had previously thought she could.[54]

While one can certainly read this story as an example of female solidarity in prison, things are undoubtedly more complex. Indeed, Ginzburg concluded the story of this encounter with the following passage: 'Sleep, poor Zina! You no more deserved those royal suites then, than this filthy cell with its cockroaches and its slop pail now. You should have remained the round-faced peasant girl, Bibi-Zyamal, mowing hay and baking bread'.[55] By referring to Abramova's peasant background and invoking her original Tatar name, Ginzburg clearly insisted on reasserting the class boundaries and difference in emotional styles that separated them. To a certain extent, Ginzburg depicted Abramova's imprisonment as a redemptive and expurgatory experience that laid bare the artificiality of her high social position and returned her to her 'true' identity.

On other occasions, the encounter between inmates in Soviet prisons led to denigrating attitudes and behaviours. For example, Adi Kuntsman has convincingly demonstrated how Ginzburg (as well as another popular Soviet Gulag writer, Varlam Shalamov) discriminated against homosexual prisoners by conflating same-sex relations, belonging to the lower classes, criminality and zoophilia. Kuntsman analysed the role that disgust and related emotions played in this process.[56] Denying other prisoners their status as equals was a product of the failure of emotional communication and the inability to transcend the differences conditioned by education and social status.

Solidarity and Belonging: Goliarda Sapienza and Other Female Prisoners

Increasing rates of female incarceration over the course of the twentieth century and the resulting shifts in prison encounters have also been evident in Italy, where the bi-monthly online journal *Ristretti Orizzonti* has been documenting the perspectives of female offenders in the La Giudecca prison in Venice since 1998.[57] Some of their recollections were compiled in a book published in 2004, while the convicts were still in prison.[58] Some of the women stress the fact that prisoners have to develop and practice a much higher degree of emotional self-control when interacting with fellow inmates than when interacting with other people in the outside world.[59] And in some of the accounts, this view is correlated with the observation made by some prisoners that there is less solidarity among female inmates today than there was in the past.[60] These women describe both heightened emotional self-control and a diminished sense of solidarity as effects of the prisoners' attempts to adapt to the complex system of benefits introduced in the mid 1980s by the so-called 'Gozzini law'.[61] Drafted as an attempt to pacify prisoners after years of dramatic violence, the law set up a system of 'rewards' for good behaviour, such as permission to visit their families and participate in paid work programmes outside prison walls, along with early release programmes.[62] This offered prisoners an incentive to manage their life in prison in a more individualistic way in order to maximize their chances of receiving benefits. This individualistic form of self-management also had an impact on the interpersonal relationships among inmates.[63] The 'Gozzini law' is a clear example of a policy designed to produce what Michel Foucault called 'docile bodies'.[64] Sister Gianna, a nun who has worked at La Giudecca since 1978, has described this change in the relation between convicts in vivid terms: 'I preferred the 1980s, when the women were more quarrelsome, but also more energetic, full of a great desire to create and to fight . . . there was a stronger group feeling, they were very supportive . . . the benefit of one was perceived as the benefit of all. Today [2001] each of them thinks only of herself'.[65] Is this lost 'golden age of solidarity' in female prisons a nostalgic illusion? It is hard to say for sure. However, it should be noted that many female prisoners interviewed in the 1970s did tell a story about the prison experience that is less focused on self-management and more on fostering a sense of community and solidarity. And this despite, or maybe precisely because of, the fact that, as many interviewees note, prison life was charged with an aggressiveness that could easily lead to the use of physical violence by both prisoners and guards.[66]

Sister Gianna also highlighted the role political prisoners played in reinforcing this community feeling.[67] Important here is the historical context in which this sense of community was developed. With the radicalization of political and social conflicts in the 1970s, women accused of political crimes – or crimes with a political connotation – often embraced a culture of transgression and struggle that put the entire dominant social order into question. These women were generally more educated than the majority (90 per cent) of female convicts, many of whom were either illiterate or had only completed primary education.[68] These educated female prisoners became the driving force behind the collective struggle for improved living conditions in female prisons, which were still run by nuns and in many respects resembled those of the nineteenth century.[69] As one of these leftist female activists wrote, in prison intellectuals met 'ordinary' women who were marginalized in three different ways: as women, as proletarians and as convicts.[70] When writing about their encounters with 'common' women, many of the educated women describe their experience as both existentially and politically significant. These women related their empathy for these 'marvellous women' to social criticism and calls for political action.[71]

Goliarda Sapienza's (1924–1996) narrative of her time in prison provides a cogent example of this strong sense of community. Born to a Sicilian family of socialists, she was a screen and stage actress and a writer. In 1980 – that is, before the 'Gozzini law' was passed – she was sent to the female section of the Rebibbia prison in Rome for a few months for stealing jewellery from some of her female acquaintances. Based on this experience, she published the autobiographical novel *L'università di Rebibbia* (The University of Rebibbia) in 1983. She entered the Rome penitentiary at the height of the Italian 'Years of Lead', a time when prisons were at the centre of political and social turmoil. During this period, prisons were attacked by armed leftist groups and were plagued by waves of violence, stormy protests among prisoners and violent police repression.[72] Violent crackdowns on noisy protests, self-harm, the danger of suffering physical violence from other inmates, the pain of depression and hunger strikes all played an important role in Sapienza's narrative. However, she often portrayed them as occasions for building solidarity or as powerful displays of the great vitality of the female prison community, which she described as being at once a 'kingdom', a 'village', a 'zoo' and an 'underground theatre'.

Sapienza's encounters with women who had been sentenced for terrorism, subversive activities, murder, drug addiction, prostitution and theft often had a strong sensory – and sometimes erotic – dimension. For example, during her first visit to the prison yard, she found herself the object of a kind of betting game in which other inmates tried to guess how long she had been in prison by looking to see how clean her hands were, observing her face and clothes and even smelling her.[73]

Constantly engaged in criticizing society outside the prison walls while describing her experiences within them, Sapienza viewed the prison as 'a primitive village where the deepest passions emerge, in all women, even in the most cultivated'.[74] The memoir's title itself makes clear that, for her, the prison was a 'university'. However, it was not a political university in the sense described by Padraic Kenney, where men and women entered as followers and emerged as hardened political activists'.[75] Rather, Sapienza's university taught women what she perceived to be authentic female feelings and solidarity. In prison, she (re)discovered the feeling of being in a community of 'women who still know the art of "caring for others"',[76] which gave her an 'irrepressible joy'. When she was invited to join other inmates at the Sunday lunch prepared by a certain Suzie Wong, she writes:

> The small Chinese woman already knows me. Like all these women she has learned the deep and simple language of emotions, so that languages, dialects, differences of class, and education are swept away as useless masks of the true motives (and needs) of human depths: this makes Rebibbia a great cosmopolitan university where anyone, if she wants, can learn the *primordial language*.[77]

On another occasion, a riot ensued after guards neglected to take a hurt inmate to the hospital. In this case, the common feeling of solidarity not only demanded that the women take care of each other by sharing food or being emotionally supportive. It also demanded that the women be allowed to act out their anger not as individuals but as members of a collective, which they did by specific bodily practices such as screaming, making noise, throwing things, running and fighting against the male police officers who had violently intervened to subdue the protest.

When her body pushed her into the throng almost against her will, Sapienza found herself shouting with the others and suddenly understanding the meaning of what another 'intellectual' prisoner, a young ex-student named Ornella, had told her a few days before: 'Do not hope to leave this place as you were before. You will no longer feel like one of them, and they – those from outside – will not consider you to be one of them anymore'. By participating in the riot, Sapienza felt as if she were part of a collective 'force' and was saluted by one of the inmates as 'one of us' – a recognition that gave her great pride.[78]

However, Sapienza's depiction of prison life was ultimately more complex. In this 'university', overcoming differences was a practice that required hard work and, it seems, something that could only be achieved if every woman held on to her own identity. Sapienza saw Rebibbia as a place where the hierarchies of the outside world were brought together.[79] In prison she discovered that class differences were still there, even if, as she stated, people like her had started to think that the feeling of community among the female prisoners had dissolved them.

She learned this during her first encounter with Giovanella, a teenager from Rome. After they had been talking for a while during a meal, Sapienza addressed Giovanella in Roman dialect. Giovanella responded in her dialect: 'Do not speak Roman, it does not suit you', adding: 'You are more yourself when you speak like you eat'. Sapienza wrote that she stopped talking and thought:

> I should not pretend to have the identity of a prisoner or a proletarian. She is right, and even though I like the Roman so much that I would like to talk like a Roman, I must force myself to go back to my 'class'. You cannot escape your class, I thought bitterly, and my mouth shut itself in humiliation.[80]

Sapienza realized that, in Ornella's words, trying to act like a proletarian only serves to stir up justified hatred and aggression from the 'real proletarians'.[81] The linguistic mimesis, this 'going native' through language, thus turned out to be a false strategy. Solidarity, especially when performed through collective action – like taking part in the riot – could help those involved to overcome class differences, but the differences did not simply disappear for all that, as this one-on-one encounter amply demonstrates.

This chapter has attempted to show that, over the last two hundred years, intellectuals writing about their experiences in modern Italian and Russian prisons have led certain emotional dimensions and dynamics of the encounter to become common topoi of modern narratives of incarceration in both Western and Eastern Europe. By looking closely at encounters between elite prisoners and common convicts, the chapter sought to demonstrate how the prison setting, preconceptions about the other and the emotional strategies that the participants employed all influenced the final outcomes of the encounters. Additionally, it analysed some of the ways in which changes in both society as a whole and in the carceral institution in particular have had an impact on encounters between prisoners and on their feelings towards each other. However, it also stressed that the peculiar coercive nature of the prison setting largely continues to dominate the outcome of these encounters, despite all the enormous changes in the political, social and cultural landscapes that happened outside of the prison walls over the course of the last two centuries.

A close analysis of prison narratives shows that while political prisoners have often perceived the emotional styles of their fellow inmates through the lens of various stereotypes, encounters between prisoners have often occasioned emotional transformations. The success of emotional contact has often ultimately depended on the different strategies that prisoners used. Many claimed that they discovered the common humanity that connected them with other prisoners and had the impression that they could navigate the emotional boundaries that separated the classes. However, in a somewhat paradoxical way, this discovery was always accompanied by the re-establishment of rigid class, cultural and emotional boundaries and by the acknowledgment of the ultimate inability to *become* like the criminal other. Importantly, some political prisoners were unable and/or unwilling to engage in emotional communication with other prisoners, retaining or even reinforcing their preconceptions and thus reaffirming the otherness of the 'common' prisoners. The different ways prison experiences play out can also be linked to the religious, political and ideological orientations of individual prisoners and the inclusiveness of their beliefs. In turn, the prison experience has often compelled prisoners to question or (re)discover these very beliefs. Thus, emotional communication across class and cultural boundaries in modern prisons has not followed a linear pattern of historical change but has rather been constantly performed anew with different results in the various forms of modern incarceration.

Pavel Vasilyev is currently a Polonsky Academy Fellow at the Van Leer Jerusalem Institute, Visiting Researcher at the Hebrew University of Jerusalem and Junior Research Fellow at Siberian State Medical University. He received his doctoral degree in Russian history from the St Petersburg Institute of History of the Russian Academy of Sciences in October 2013. Between 2014 and 2016, he was Postdoctoral Fellow at the Center for the History of Emotions at the Max Planck Institute for Human Development in Berlin. His publications include articles on the history of crime and criminal law in *Historical Research* and *Rechtsgeschichte – Legal History*.

Gian Marco Vidor is a research associate at the institute for Ethics, History and Humanities (iEH2) at the University of Geneva. He was a researcher at the Max Planck Institute for Human Development in Berlin and a MaxNetAging fellow at the Max Planck Institute for Demographic Research in Rostock. His recent publications include a special section 'Law and Emotions' (with Laura Kounine) in the *Journal of Social History* 51(2) (2017) and the article 'Rhetorical Engineering of Emotions in the Courtroom: The Case of Lawyers in Modern France', *Rechtsgeschichte – Legal History* 25 (2017).

Notes

1. 'Tolokonnikovu iz Pussy Riot osvobodili vsled za Alekhinoi' [Pussy Riot's Tolokonnikova Released Shortly after Alekhina], *BBC Russian*, 23 December 2013 (italics added).
2. Levkovich, 'Interv'iu Evgenii Khasis zhurnalu "Rolling Stone"' [Evgeniia Khasis' Interview with Rolling Stone], *Russkii Verdikt*, 15 January 2013.
3. Brombert, *Romantic Prison*; Zanotti, 'Scritture del carcere', 26–33.

4. Sobanet, *Jail Sentences*, 3.
5. Sobanet, *Jail Sentences*, 3.
6. Frank, *Dostoevsky: A Writer in His Time*.
7. Gernet, *Istoriia tsarskoi tiur'my* [The History of Prison under the Tsars]; De Vito, *Camosci e girachiavi: Storia del carcere in Italia; 1943–2007*.
8. Cole, 'Towards a Poetics of Russian Prison Literature: Writings on Prison by Dostoevsky, Chekhov and Solzhenitsyn'; Spila, *Voci da dentro: Itinerari della reclusione nella letteratura italiana*.
9. See esp. Foucault, *Discipline and Punish: The Birth of the Prison* and Perrot, *Les ombres de l'histoire: Crime et châtiment au XIXe siècle*. In the Russian context, see also Engelstein, 'Combined Underdevelopment: Discipline and the Law in Imperial and Soviet Russia', 338–53.
10. For exceptions, see Trombetta, *Punizione e carità: Carceri femminili nell'Italia dell'Ottocento*; Young, 'Knowing Russia's Convicts: The Other in Narratives of Imprisonment and Exile of the Late Imperial Era', 1700–15.
11. Etkind, *Internal Colonization: Russia's Imperial Experience*, 93–122. For a similar perspective on the comparability of racial, gender and class differences in the British colonial context, see Fischer-Tiné, 'Reclaiming Savages in "Darkest England" and "Darkest India": The Salvation Army as Transnational Agent of the Civilizing Mission', 125–64.
12. Diafani, 'Ragionar di sé': Scritture dell'io e romanzo in Italia (1816–1840)', 158; Klopp, *Sentences: The Memoirs and Letters of Italian Political Prisoners from Benvenuto Cellini to Aldo Moro*, 39–40; Panetta, 'Metafore e topoi della letteratura carceraria nella memorialistica di Pellico, Bini e Settembrini', in Spila, *Voci da dentro*, 205; Zanotti, 'Scritture del carcere'; Kaucisvili Melzi d'Eril, 'Montalembert e Pellico', 613–24.
13. Diafani, *'Ragionar di sé'*, 166–67.
14. Pellico, *Memoirs*, 5.
15. Budillon Puma, 'Du Risorgimento à l'Unité: Le roman italien laboratoire d'une fraternité idéale?', 187–205; Conti, 'I fratelli e i profani: La massoneria e l'idea di fratellanza fra Sette e Ottocento', 137–55; on the question of social classes, see Klopp, *Sentences*, esp. 69–70.
16. Pellico, *Memoirs*, 82.
17. Diafani, *'Ragionar di sé'*, 147–92; Mauri, 'Il caso Pellico: La Torino die "santi sociali"', 860–63.
18. Brombert, *Romantic Prison*, 3–17.
19. De Rienzo, 'Introduzione', 5–15.
20. Pellico, *Memoirs*, chapters 11, 12, 18, quotations page 16, 92.
21. Pellico, *Memoirs*, chapters 13, 18.
22. Pellico, *Memoirs*, 17.
23. Pellico, *Memoirs*, 17.
24. Pellico, *Memoirs*, 18.
25. Pellico, *Memoirs*, 18.
26. Not even in the detailed analysis by Diafani, *'Ragionar di sé'*.
27. See the passage about the 'degraded women' in Milan (Pellico, *Memoirs*, chapters 11, 12, 18) and the meeting with some Italian thieves in the courtyard of the Špilberk (Pellico, *Memoirs*, chapter 65).
28. Pellico, *Memoirs*, 18.
29. Pellico, *Memoirs*, 94.
30. Pellico, *Memoirs*, 5. On religious aspects, see also Klopp, *Sentences*, 46 and Kowalska, '"Lasciate ogni speranza voi ch'entrate": Le memorie carcerarie degli eroi del Risorgimento', 275–90.
31. Dostoyevsky, *Letters*, 56.
32. Dostoyevsky, *Letters*, 62.

33. Dostoyevsky, *Letters*, 62.
34. Dostoyevsky, 'The Peasant Marey', 11–15.
35. Dostoyevsky, *Sobranie sochinenii v piatnadtsati tomakh*, 505, 535, 538–44, 546–47.
36. Iakubovich, 'Primechaniia' [comments], 535, 547–50. See also Mirsky, *Contemporary Russian Literature, 1881–1925*.
37. Iakubovich, 'Primechaniia', 537.
38. Dostoïeffsky, *House of the Dead*, 35.
39. Dostoïeffsky, *House of the Dead*, 269.
40. Dostoïeffsky, *House of the Dead*, 269. For more examples of this 'revenge' attitude, see also Dostoïeffsky, *House of the Dead*, 229–30.
41. Dostoïeffsky, *House of the Dead*, 269.
42. Dostoïeffsky, *House of the Dead*, 309.
43. Dostoïeffsky, *House of the Dead*, 309.
44. Etkind, *Internal Colonization*, 109.
45. Dostoïeffsky, *House of the Dead*, 367.
46. Dostoïeffsky, *House of the Dead*, 367 (emphasis in original).
47. Gramsci, *Letters from Prison*, 45–51, 69–72, 94–98, 166. See also Pieroni, 'Antonio Gramsci e il folclore: I contributi gramsciani allo sviluppo dell'antropologia italiana attraverso Lettere e Quaderni'.
48. The form of Kersnovskaya's text is also very interesting because it contains drawings. Retrieved 21 September 2018 from http://www.gulag.su/project/index.php?eng=1&page=0.
49. Ginzburg, *Journey into the Whirlwind*, 121.
50. Ginzburg, *Journey into the Whirlwind*, 122.
51. Ginzburg, *Journey into the Whirlwind*, 121. On the notion of *kul'turnost'* and the politics of identity in the Stalinist 1930s, see Volkov, 'The Concept of *Kul'turnost'*: Notes on the Stalinist Civilizing Process', 210–30.
52. Ginzburg, *Journey into the Whirlwind*, 122.
53. Ginzburg, *Journey into the Whirlwind*, 126.
54. Ginzburg, *Journey into the Whirlwind*, 126–27, quotation 127.
55. Ginzburg, *Journey into the Whirlwind*, 127–28.
56. Kuntsman, '"With a Shade of Disgust": Affective Politics of Sexuality and Class in Memoirs of the Stalinist GULAG', 308–28.
57. *Ristretti Orizzonti*, retrieved 21 September 2018 from www.ristretti.it.
58. *Donne in sospeso: Testimonianze dal carcere femminile della Giudecca e non solo* (Padova: Il granello di senape, 2004).
59. *Donne in sospeso*, 147, 183, 188–89.
60. 'Non ci sono più le detenute di una volta: Sovraffollamento, ma anche tante donne che non sanno "farsi la galera", e poi una convivenza forzata piena di rischi: Discussione nella redazione del carcere femminile della Giudecca', *Ristretti Orizzonti*, November 2005.
61. 'Non ci sono'.
62. De Vito, *Camosci e girachiavi*, 113–14.
63. De Vito, *Camosci e girachiavi*, 113–14.
64. Foucault, *Discipline and Punish*, 135–41.
65. *Donne in sospeso*, 7–11. All Italian sources translated by G.M. Vidor unless otherwise noted.
66. Faré and Spirito, *Mara e le altre: Le donne e la lotta armata: Storie, interviste, riflessioni*, esp. 64–65, 92–97; Parca, *Voci dal carcere femminile*, esp. 62, 137, 240–41, 257.
67. *Donne in sospeso*, 7–11.
68. Parca, *Voci dal carcere femminile*, 14.
69. Anastasia and Gonnella, *Patrie galere: Viaggio nell'Italia dietro le sbarre*, 99; Campelli et al., *Donne in carcere: Ricerca sulla detenzione femminile in Italia*, 17–29; Faccioli, *I soggetti deboli:*

I giovani e le donne nel sistema penale, 111–13. On political female convicts in the 1970s and 1980s, see also Cataldo, *Minima Criminalia: Storie di carcerati e di carcerieri*, 25–30, 59–63.
70. Faré and Spirito, *Mara e le altre*, 93.
71. Faré and Spirito, *Mara e le altre*, 64–65, 92–97.
72. For the history of the institution in the 'Years of Lead', see Calderone, 'L'articolo 41 bis Ord. pen. e altri regimi particolari di detenzione: Aspetti giuridici e sociologici' and De Vito, *Camosci e girachiavi*, 71–100. For an insight into male prison life during this turbulent period, see the memoir by Foschini, *In nome del popolo italiano: Storie di una malavita*.
73. Sapienza, *L'Università di Rebibbia*, 24–25.
74. Centola, 'Orrore e fascinazione di Rebibbia' (interview of Goliarda Sapienza), in Barbarulli, 'Essere o avere il corpo: "L' università di Rebibbia"', 139.
75. Kenney, '"I Felt a Kind of Pleasure in Seeing Them Treat Us Brutally": The Emergence of the Political Prisoner, 1865–1910', 880.
76. Sapienza, *L'Università di Rebibbia*, 90.
77. Sapienza, *L'Università di Rebibbia*, 90 (emphasis in original).
78. Sapienza, *L'Università di Rebibbia*, 129–32.
79. Sapienza, *L'Università di Rebibbia*, 50.
80. Sapienza, *L'Università di Rebibbia*, 29.
81. Sapienza, *L'Università di Rebibbia*, 109–10.

Bibliography

Anastasia, S., and P. Gonnella. *Patrie galere: Viaggio nell'Italia dietro le sbarre*. Rome: Carrocci, 2005.

Barbarulli, C. 'Essere o avere il corpo: "L' università di Rebibbia"', in M. Farnetti (ed.), *Appassionata Sapienza* (Milan: La Tartaruga, 2011), 132–47.

Brombert, V. *The Romantic Prison*. Princeton, NJ: Princeton University Press, 1978 [Fre. orig. *La prison romantique*. Paris: José Corti, 1975].

Budillon Puma, P. 'Du Risorgimento à l'Unité: Le roman italien laboratoire d'une fraternité idéale?', in G. Bertrand, C. Brice and G. Montègre (eds), *Fraternité: Pour une histoire du concept* (Grenoble: Centre de Recherche et d'Histoire de l'Italie et des Pays Alpins, 2012), 187–205.

Calderone, M.R. 'L'articolo 41 bis Ord. pen. e altri regimi particolari di detenzione: Aspetti giuridici e sociologici' (2005). *L'altro diritto: Centro di documentazione su carcere, devianza e marginalità, Università di Firenze*. Retrieved 21 September 2018 from http://www.adir.unifi.it/rivista/2005/calderone/index.htm.

Campelli, E., et al. (eds). *Donne in carcere: Ricerca sulla detenzione femminile in Italia*. Milan: Feltrinelli, 1992.

Cataldo, G. *Minima Criminalia: Storie di carcerati e di carcerieri*, 3rd edn. Rome: Manifesto Libri, 2006.

Centola, G. 'Orrore e fascinazione di Rebibbia' (interview of Goliarda Sapienza). *Il Manifesto* (15 February 1983).

Cole, E.A. 'Towards a Poetics of Russian Prison Literature: Writings on Prison by Dostoevsky, Chekhov and Solzhenitsyn'. PhD dissertation. New Haven, CT: Yale University, 1991.

Conti, F. 'I fratelli e i profani: La massoneria e l'idea di fratellanza fra Sette e Ottocento', in G. Bertrand, C. Brice and G. Montègre (eds), *Fraternité: Pour une histoire du concept* (Grenoble: Centre de Recherche et d'Histoire de l'Italie et des Pays Alpins, 2012), 137–55.

De Rienzo, G. 'Introduzione', in S. Pellico, *Le mie prigioni*, ed. S. Spellanzon (Milan: Rizzoli, 1984), 5–15.

De Vito, C.G. *Camosci e girachiavi: Storia del carcere in Italia; 1943–2007*. Rome: Laterza, 2009.

Diafani, L. *'Ragionar di sé': Scritture dell'io e romanzo in Italia (1816–1840)*. Florence: Società Editrice Fiorentina, 2003.

Donne in sospeso: Testimonianze dal carcere femminile della Giudecca e non solo. Padova: Il granello di senape, 2004.

Dostoïeffsky, F. [F. Dostoyevsky] *The House of the Dead, or Prisoner Life in Siberia*, repr. edn. London: J. M. Dent & Sons, 1914 [Rus. orig. *Zapiski iz mertvogo doma*. St Petersburg: Ogrizko, 1862].

Dostoyevsky, F. *Letters of Fyodor Michailovitch Dostoevsky to his Family and Friends*, trans. Ethel Golburn Mayne, 2nd edn. New York: Macmillan, 1917.

———. *Sobranie sochinenii v piatnadtsati tomakh*, vol. 3. Leningrad: Nauka, 1988.

———. 'The Peasant Marey', in F. Dostoyevsky, *The Heavenly Christmas Tree and Other Stories*, new edn (London: Souvereign, 2013), 11–15 [Rus. orig. 'Muzhik Marei'. *Dnevnik pisatelya* (February 1876)].

Engelstein, L. 'Combined Underdevelopment: Discipline and the Law in Imperial and Soviet Russia'. *American Historical Review* 98(2) (1993), 338–53, doi: 10.2307/2166836.

Etkind, A. *Internal Colonization: Russia's Imperial Experience*. Cambridge: Polity Press, 2011.

Faccioli, F. *I soggetti deboli: I giovani e le donne nel sistema penale*. Milan: Franco Angeli, 1990.

Faré, I., and F. Spirito. *Mara e le altre: Le donne e la lotta armata: Storie, interviste, riflessioni*, 3rd edn. Milan: Feltrinelli, 1979.

Fischer-Tiné, H. 'Reclaiming Savages in "Darkest England" and "Darkest India": The Salvation Army as Transnational Agent of the Civilizing Mission', in C.A. Watt and M. Mann (eds), *Civilizing Missions in Colonial and Postcolonial South Asia: From Improvement to Development* (London: Anthem Press, 2011), 125–64.

Foschini, C. *In nome del popolo italiano: Storie di una malavita*. Bologna: Il Mulino, 2013.

Foucault, M. *Discipline and Punish: The Birth of the Prison*, trans. A. Sheridan. New York: Vintage Books, 1979 [Fre. orig. *Surveiller et punir*. Paris: Gallimard, 1975].

Frank, J. *Dostoevsky: A Writer in His Time*, ed. M. Petrusewicz. Princeton, NJ: Princeton University Press, 2010.

Gernet, M.N. *Istoriia tsarskoi tiur'my* [The History of Prison under the Tsars], 5 vols. Moscow: Goriurizdat, 1951–1956.

Ginzburg, E.S. *Journey into the Whirlwind*, trans. P. Stevenson and M. Hayward. New York: Harcourt, Brace & World, 1967.

Gramsci, A. *Letters from Prison*, vol. 1, ed. F. Rosengarten, trans. R. Rosenthal, 2nd edn. New York: Columbia University Press, 2011.

Iakubovich, I.D. 'Primechaniia' [comments], in F. Dostoyevsky, *Sobranie sochinenii v piatnadtsati tomakh*, vol. 3 (Leningrad: Nauka, 1988), 503–74.
Kaucisvili Melzi d'Eril, F. 'Montalembert e Pellico'. *Vita e Pensiero: Pubblicazioni dell'Università Cattolica del Sacro Cuore* 50(5/6) (1976), 613–24.
Kenney, P. '"I Felt a Kind of Pleasure in Seeing Them Treat Us Brutally": The Emergence of the Political Prisoner, 1865–1910'. *Comparative Studies in Society and History* 54(4) (2012), 863–89, doi: 10.1017/S0010417512000448.
Kersnovskaya, E. *What's a Human Being Worth?* Retrieved 21 September 2018 from http://www.gulag.su/project/index.php?eng=1&page=0.
Klopp, C. *Sentences: The Memoirs and Letters of Italian Political Prisoners from Benvenuto Cellini to Aldo Moro*. Toronto: University of Toronto Press, 1999.
Kowalska, A.T. '"Lasciate ogni speranza voi ch'entrate": Le memorie carcerarie degli eroi del Risorgimento', in G. Traina and N. Zago (eds), *Carceri vere e d'invenzione dal tardo cinquecento al novecento* (Acireale: Bonarno, 2009), 275–90.
Kuntsman, A. '"With a Shade of Disgust": Affective Politics of Sexuality and Class in Memoirs of the Stalinist GULAG'. *Slavic Review* 68(2) (2009), 308–28, doi: 10.2307/27697960.
Levkovich, E. 'Interv'iu Evgenii Khasis zhurnalu "Rolling Stone"' [Evgeniia Khasis' Interview with Rolling Stone]. *Russkii Verdikt*, 15 January 2013. Retrieved 21 September 2018 from http://rusverdict.com/rollingstone/.
Mauri, P. 'Il caso Pellico: La Torino die "santi sociali"', in A. Asor Rosa (ed.), *Letteratura italiana: Storia e geografia*, vol. 2, part 2: *L'età moderna* (Turin: Einaudi, 1988), 860–63.
Mirsky, Prince D.S. *Contemporary Russian Literature, 1881–1925*. New York: Knopf, 1926.
'Non ci sono più le detenute di una volta: Sovraffollamento, ma anche tante donne che non sanno "farsi la galera", e poi una convivenza forzata piena di rischi: Discussione nella redazione del carcere femminile della Giudecca'. *Ristretti Orizzonti*, November 2005. Retrieved 21 September 2018 from http://www.ristretti.it/giornale/numeri/62005/donnedentro.htm.
Panetta, M. 'Metafore e topoi della letteratura carceraria nella memorialistica di Pellico, Bini e Settembrini', in C. Spila (ed.), *Voci da dentro: Itinerari della reclusione nella letteratura italiana* (Rome: Bulzoni, 2008), 203–24.
Parca, G. *Voci dal carcere femminile*. Rome: Editori Riuniti, 1973.
Pellico, S. *Memoirs of Silvio Pellico: Or my Prisons*, trans. M.J. Smead and H.P. Lefebvre. New York: Langley, 1844 [Ita. orig. *Le mie prigioni*. Turin: Bocca, 1832].
Perrot, M. *Les ombres de l'histoire: Crime et châtiment au XIXe siècle*. Paris: Flammarion, 2001.
Pieroni, S. 'Antonio Gramsci e il folclore: I contributi gramsciani allo sviluppo dell'antropologia italiana attraverso Lettere e Quaderni'. *Antrocom: Online Journal of Anthropology* 1(2) (2005), 185–90. Retrieved 21 September 2018 from http://www.antrocom.net/upload/sub/antrocom/010205/07-Antrocom.pdf.
Ristretti Orizzonti. Retrieved 21 September 2018 from www.ristretti.it.
Sapienza, G. *L'Università di Rebibbia*. Turin: Einaudi, 2012.
Sobanet, A. *Jail Sentences: Representing Prison in Twentieth-Century French Fiction*. Lincoln: University of Nebraska Press, 2008.

Spila, C. (ed.). *Voci da dentro: Itinerari della reclusione nella letteratura italiana*. Rome: Bulzoni, 2008.

Tolokonnikova, N. Blog entry, 29 March 2015. Retrieved 21 September 2018 from https://www.facebook.com/tolokno/posts/918705334827019.

'Tolokonnikovu iz Pussy Riot osvobodili vsled za Alekhinoi' [Pussy Riot's Tolokonnikova Released Shortly after Alekhina]. *BBC Russian*, 23 December 2013. Retrieved 21 September 2018 from http://www.bbc.co.uk/russian/russia/2013/12/131223_pussy_riot_tolokonnikova_release.shtml.

Trombetta, S. *Punizione e carità: Carceri femminili nell'Italia dell'Ottocento*. Bologna: Il Mulino, 2004.

Volkov, V. 'The Concept of *Kul'turnost'*: Notes on the Stalinist Civilizing Process', in S. Fitzpatrick (ed.), *Stalinism: New Directions* (London: Routledge, 2000), 210–30.

Young, S.J. 'Knowing Russia's Convicts: The Other in Narratives of Imprisonment and Exile of the Late Imperial Era'. *Europe–Asia Studies* 65(9) (2013), 1700–15, doi: 10.1080/09668136.2013.844509.

Zanotti, P. 'Scritture del carcere', in D. Scarpa (ed.), *Atlante della letteratura italiana*, vol. 3: *Dal romanticismo a oggi* (Turin: Giulio Einaudi, 2012), 26–33.

Chapter 8

'Monsters'
Emotional Incoherence and Familial Murder

Daphne Rozenblatt

On 16 November 1980, French philosopher Louis Althusser strangled his wife Hélène Rytman. In October 1982, he wrote from a psychiatric clinic at Soisy-sur-Seine:

> [I]n the course of a severe, unforeseeable crisis that had left me in a state of mental confusion, I strangled my wife, the woman who was everything in the world to me and who loved me so much that, since living had become impossible, she wanted only to die. In my confusion, not knowing what I was doing, I no doubt rendered her this 'service': she did not defend herself against it, but died of it.[1]

Thus began the *Philosophy of the Encounter*, in which Althusser traced the 'repressed' lineage of events that fell to the earth like rain, sometimes 'swerving' and colliding with one another to form the 'materialism of the encounter'. From this initial encounter others ensue, piling up to cause no less than 'the birth of the world'. It was after the murder of his wife – that 'three-year-long ordeal' – and his departure from the clinic that Althusser wrote one of his last contributions to philosophy. He described it as 'returning to this world that is entirely new to me, and, since I had never encountered it before, full of surprises'.[2]

The autobiographical prologue to the *Philosophy of the Encounter* directly linked the composition of Althusser's philosophy to the events of his life. He expounded upon what he called 'aleatory materialism' with the same cool clarity with which he declared his love for Rytman and explained her death, and just as the encounter Althusser described was unforeseeable

Notes for this chapter begin on page 223.

and unintentional, so was – in Althusser's description – the murder of his wife. Following his almost complete disappearance from public life after the murder, Althusser again became the centre of debate when *The Future Lasts Forever* was published posthumously in 1992.[3] In this memoir, Althusser recounted the uxoricide twice more, beginning the book with a sensational account of that day's events and then describing the lead-up to the murder in detail. The account doubled as a defence in which Althusser attempted to explain his act and vindicate himself: he detailed his hampered mental state at the time of the murder while defending his sanity, and he expressed guilt and remorse for the event while critiquing his psychiatric sentence, which effectively silenced him.

Whether or not we accept Althusser's philosophy, if Althusser's murder of his wife is a kind of encounter, then it is one that must be defined by and understood through emotions. Althusser professed to loving his wife; indeed, that was the central evidence in his defence. But he also described his mania, rage, the difficulties his mental disease placed on his wife, her own suffering, his mourning, his feelings of self-devastation and regret. He also analysed and psychoanalysed himself extensively, providing theoretically informed explanations for his actions. In these ways, the questions of how to understand the emotions of an encounter between an aged husband and wife is a far cry from those encounters usually studied, in which one interacts with someone from a different emotional culture and background for the first time. While such transcultural encounters can offer evidence as to whether feelings can be understood across cultures, the manner in which complex processes can reveal whether emotions are a matter of nature or nurture demonstrates the rule of emotional cultures and emotional learning, along with emotional control, the role of the body and the relationship of emotions to reason and morality.[4] By contrast, encounters that happen intraculturally – indeed within the nuclear family – raise different concerns. Although mediated by shared experiences, education, emotional norms and standards and often decades of lived experience and the closest of personal contact, it would be remiss to describe encounters such as that of Althusser and Rytman as emotional understanding.

But if the Althusser murder is a kind of encounter, can it also be understood historically? Just as transcultural encounters are shaped by the political, social, economic and religious factors that enable contact between disparate people, those same factors also shape significant and consequential encounters that occur within the family. Althusser explained his life, relationship with his wife, the murder and the memoir he wrote through the lens of history. Like the contingency and build-up of events that accounted for the 'birth of the world', Althusser implied that a build-up of events in his personal life and in Rytman's led to her murder.

He detailed his early childhood, his early years in French Algeria, his experiences during the Second World War[5] and admiringly recounted Rytman's own actions as part of the Resistance, as he, 'would never have had the strength or courage to face the physical and life-threatening risks of clandestine armed struggle'.[6] Their personal documents, writings and historical records would surely reflect how notions of marriage, gender, love and sexuality in post-war France, the political and intellectual climate in which Althusser and his wife were deeply entrenched, shaped their self-perception.[7] Furthermore, the influence of Lacanian psychoanalysis and psychoanalytic treatment – which Althusser and his wife both underwent – shaped Althusser's self-understanding and concepts of feeling.[8] He described his feelings for Rytman as modelled on his relationship with his mother, who had 'castrated' him as well as his 'anxious' father:[9] 'the same awful feeling of insensitivity, the feeling that I too was incapable of truly loving another person; nor is it surprising that I projected all this on to Hélène.... It was my, our, destiny to have fulfilled my mother's desires.... I certainly loved Hélène with all my heart'[10] Nonetheless, none of those factors are sufficient to explain the specificities of a murder.

Nevertheless, Althusser also put the murder of his wife, his subsequent treatment and the telling of his tale in historical perspective. He claimed that his 'critical confession' had no precursor besides that of Pierre Rivière, a French peasant who murdered his family in the nineteenth century, whose 'admirable confession' was published by Michel Foucault in 1973. Subsequently translated into English as *I, Pierre Rivière, Having Slaughtered My Mother, My Sister, and My Brother ...*,[11] the dossier pertaining to Rivière's case included not only his statement but also the testimonials of neighbours as to his behaviour and character, news articles, as well as legal and medical opinions. Additionally, the book included several essays by Foucault and his students, who had studied the documents with him in a seminar. Foucault stated that the dossier presented 'a strange contest, a confrontation, a power relation, a battle among discourses and through discourses' and that the purpose of his publication was to 'draw a map ... of those combats, to reconstruct these confrontations and battles, to rediscover the interaction of those discourses as weapons of attack and defense in the relations of power and knowledge .[12] In this reading, Rivière's 'beautiful' account was used as the 'zero benchmark' by which all other discourses – the responses from family and acquaintances, medical and legal opinions – were to be judged.[13] Arguably, Althusser was not so much responding to Rivière's memoir but rather to Foucault's reading of the Rivière case. In doing so, he placed the critiques of his own treatment as a legally condemned/liberated insane person in a long history of misunderstanding, judgement and condemnation.

Scholars have picked up the mantle from Foucault and Althusser, continuing to analyse these cases in which embedded perspectives on human agency, intention, motive and morality within the encounter are unavoidable. But for historians seeking 'natural causes', the episode of murder often places them in the uncomfortable role of being the moral judge and arbiter of guilt or innocence.[14] In the case of Althusser, the publication of the memoir triggered a heated debate among his colleagues, protégés and contemporaries, who questioned the relationship between Althusser's philosophical and political legacy and his personal life and the murder of his wife and dealt with Althusser's emotional self-representation.[15] For opponents, Althusser was either the sick – and perhaps evil – person whose account was the perversion of a true confession, while for his defenders Althusser was the good-hearted but troubled man who suffered from severe psychological disorders. For critics, Althusser's elderly philosophy was a radical shift away from the Marxist philosophy that had made him into a philosophe célèbre, while for others it was the logical outgrowth that contributed to the coherence of the Althusserian oeuvre. Furthermore, these two discussions came together: Althusser was either the 'victim' whose reputation and intellect had to be defended or the villain whose evil acts were symptomatic of a corrupt and immoral philosophical doctrine. Even discussions and commentaries that did not directly problematize emotions often included explicit or implicit moral judgements that called into question the truthfulness of an ego-document. Particularly in relation to feelings, they can express a general disgust and rejection or a merciful empathy for its writer. All of these reactions reflect the moral quagmire of insanity, emotion and will/intent/responsibility.

In the case of Rivière, Foucault's publication of the dossier pertaining to his trial has led to its continued reference and reappraisal in text and discourse.[16] Probing the nature of the documents themselves, they resist as Foucault's publication did, 'involving it in one of the discourses (medical, legal, psychological, criminological) which ... should have brought it within the power relation whose reductive effect [they] wished to show'.[17] Even so, discussions that deal with the difficulties of understanding insanity, agency and culpability in testimonials also contain perspectives on whether the human subject is stable and coherent or changeable and even contradictory, and the assumption of a morally neutral analytical stance is also a moral position. As in the case of Althusser, these discussions tend to take on emotional terms. Foucault, for example, contrasted the stance of his volume to that of Rivière's contemporaries, who sought to 'defuse the terror of a crime committed in their midst and to "preserve the honor of a family"'.[18] Instead, 'owing to a sort of reverence and perhaps, too, terror for a text which was to carry off four corpses along with it, we were unwilling to superimpose our own text on Rivière's memoir. We fell under the spell of the parricide with the reddish-brown eyes'.[19]

A reading of emotions in these encounters offers a different perspective on both how emotions shape encounters and how emotions between the persons involved can be understood, as well as their subsequent narrativizing. Whereas emotions in both the memoirs themselves and within subsequent commentary are usually used descriptively – with a few significant exceptions[20] – this chapter explores the way that emotional discontinuity, incoherence and misunderstanding shape the encounter and can lead to different and unforeseen outcomes, despite the familiarity and intimacy of the persons involved. Instead of common culture and shared lived experience leading to greater emotional understanding, this chapter explores how longstanding relationships and deep emotional connections can go hand in hand with emotional complexities that are often difficult – if indeed impossible – to fully understand, even for the persons involved. This chapter, however, also limits itself to the level of the written text. It deals with the emotions of these documents as part of a one-sided discourse in which the voices of the murdered are understood and presented by a narrator highly motivated in their own defence – whatever that defence may be construed to be. Furthermore, it draws attention to the emotional changes and developments that are expressed by a narrator towards a single event and how conflicting or contrasting emotions towards that event are often presented in the same document and must be understood in terms of momentary reactions, memories, argument and self-defence. These memoirs do not reflect the way a specific emotion shapes an encounter or the emotion- learning processes that shape a person's feelings when meeting someone face-to-face. Rather, they demonstrate how complex and conflicting emotions can be misunderstood within close relations.

Insanity, Emotional Incoherence and Emotional Misapprehension

Thomas Scheff has described human communication as 'intersubjective guessing' in which speech is always 'fragmented and contextualized', requiring humans to interpret communications partly by taking on the role – or perspective – of the other person in the exchange.[21] Just as the complexities of communication along with possibilities for miscommunication are compounded by differences of culture, they are also complicated by mental difference. As James Russell underscored, different understandings of emotion contribute to 'intergroup conflict, cross-cultural mental health, and ethnic misunderstanding. A group's conceptualization of emotion is a part of a much larger pattern that is that group's behaviour and thought'.[22] Complementarily, different understandings of emotions also contribute to intragroup conflicts, mental health issues and misunderstandings. Such circumstances in which a person's understanding of emotion or manifest emotions is so drastically different from social and cultural norms or difficult to understand for other persons, even within the family, are often understood in terms of mental illness.

The questions raised by sociologists and psychologists regarding the nature of mental illness and how to understand it – particularly in relation to emotions – differ from historical questions. For historians, definitions of insanity, which often say more about theoretical approaches taken to concrete phenomena than the phenomena themselves, must be understood in time; the judgement of mental illness, let alone its juxtaposition across space and time, can lead to the perpetuation of historical perceptions or understandings rather than their analysis. While mental illness offers perspectives on the nature-nurture scale of emotions, historical analyses tend to focus on the nurture end. Since the publication of two watershed studies on the asylum as a site in which power dynamics affected the experience and treatment of patients/inmates, which was arguably not medicinal or curative in nature, historians have eschewed biological or synchronic explanations of mental illness, focusing on 'top-down' analyses of how asylum practices controlled and shaped the 'modern soul', or how the 'bottom-up' relational patterns of 'total institutions' created patterned interactions and emotional responses.[23] Furthermore, historians of science have further deconstructed the 'nature' of mental illness by examining it in terms of 'making up people', in which 'interactions between classifications of people and the people classified' have a 'looping effect' and have also historicized seemingly 'natural scientific objects' such as the 'self'.[24] More recently, social historians interested in madness and the family have removed insanity from its institutional setting entirely, exploring caregiving within the community,[25] how families scaled the 'impenetrable' walls of the asylum and played decisive roles in the care of relatives[26] and the emotional relationships between the insane and their families.[27] Whether tending towards biomedical essentialism on the one end and cultural relativism on the other, definitions of madness, insanity and mental illness describe a variety of intracultural mental, emotional and psychosomatic manifestations often so different as to tend towards mutual exclusivity. In describing two discrete historical instances in which the very applicability of these terms has been called into question and from which generalizations about insanity cannot be made, this chapter aims at case-specific examinations of the ways in which emotions are expressed or understood in instances in which manifest psychological difference falls outside the norms of social and cultural explanatory frameworks within interfamilial encounters.

Necessarily taking a synchronic stance towards instances of 'insanity', the approach of this chapter is nonetheless informed by research into mental illness outside the asylum context. The initial recognition of insanity within the household is well documented in the autobiographies and memoirs of the insane, their families and in clinical files.[28] On a microinteractional scale, these encounters have been discussed by sociologists and psychologists in terms of labelling (how a set of behaviours comes to be understood as mental illness) and interaction (taking insanity as a behaviour always 'involving a pattern of exchange ... between individuals'[29]). With the important exception of August Hollingshead and Frederick Redlich's identification of 'lay appraisal' as the way that 'nonprofessionals' determine who is labelled and what the label is,[30] label theory tends to focus on the nominal power of insanity separate from an analysis of the behaviour itself. Thomas Scheff, for example, analysed labelling as the way in which certain behaviours or 'residual rule breaking' are related to or reaffirmed as insane through ordinary social interaction, leading to the reinforcement of stereotypes and the strategic use of the label by those giving and receiving it.[31] By contrast, interaction-based analyses have emphasized 'family patterns and processes that are precursors, concomitants, and consequences of disordered behavior' and their relationship to genetic, sociocultural and personality factors in psychopathology.[32] Drawing on Ernest Burgess' description of family as a group of 'interacting personalities',[33] this approach describes insanity as the product and substance of familial social relations, placing primacy on the 'interactional context' and making the interaction the smallest unit of analysis.[34]

Understood as specific patterns of translation or intersubjective guessing, this chapter combines an emphasis on domestic labelling and interaction together with an emphasis on emotions to understand instances of emotional incoherence, misapprehension or misunderstanding. In such encounters, the way one person manifests emotions is either misapprehended or misunderstood, affecting the reactions of the other person or persons. Allan Horwitz explored such instances, arguing that when the 'categories observers use to comprehend behavior do not yield any socially understandable reasons for the behavior', lay persons label someone as mentally ill.[35] Furthermore, he suggested that such behaviours are more likely perceived as 'incomprehensible' when the observer is relationally and culturally different from the person observed.[36] Similarly, this chapter describes the emotional patterns surrounding the recognition of psychological difference in terms of emotional incoherence and emotional misapprehension. However, it demonstrates how incomprehensibility occurs in relational and cultural intimacy.

Emotional incoherence describes emotions that contrast with the social, cultural or familial expectations, even when taking into account the particularities of a person's character or life experiences. This is a matter of degree: incoherence is not exclusive to mental illness but becomes a sign of psychological difference, though this does not negate its role as a symptom of medical power.[37] Instead, this chapter emphasizes the emotions of insanity in encounters that are not 'managed' or disobey the 'feeling rules' of a given society, culture or family and which cannot be redressed or translated through normal social explanations.[38] Emotions that do not cohere with presumed norms are witnessed by persons that cannot make sense of them within familial social, cultural or medical frameworks. Again, the difference is relational, not categorical: emotions are observed and misapprehended when they are starkly different from those of previous social exchanges or because changing contexts alter the perception of a longstanding emotional pattern. Unlike linguistic miscommunication, which emphasizes communicative failure of conscious efforts to fully convey intention or meaning,[39] and unlike cultural misunderstanding, often used to explain intergroup dynamics and usually conflicts,[40] this chapter uses misapprehension to emphasize the hindered or failed recognition or transmission of nonconscious and nonverbal as well as conscious and verbal emotional cues.[41] In these cases, familiarity does not necessarily enable increased emotional apprehension in face-to-face encounters and can even hinder it.

Emotional incoherence and misapprehension contribute to social and familial conflict and, in the cases evaluated here, lead to violence. Randall Collins argued that micro-interactional behaviour is usually emotionally motivated, that 'microsituational cognition' is partly shaped by the amount of 'emotional energy' in an exchange[42] and this emotional energy can result in violent action.[43] In other words, emotions not only shape the perception of another's behaviours or feelings but also the response. While such family dynamics are often shaped by socioeconomic relationships and other structures of power in which rational motives to clear ends may sometimes be discerned, emotions as well as their incoherence and misapprehension are also shaped by socioemotional dynamics in which a family's description of 'illness' emerges.[44] In the family context wherein relationships rely on emotions or their misunderstanding in order to structure, perpetuate or undermine 'rational' behaviours, the emotional as opposed to rational actor can explain the often surprising outcomes of an encounter.

The emotions surrounding mental illness are also mediated and remediated by popular, medical and legal notions of mental difference. Thus, memoirs, testimonials and other accounts demand a nuanced consideration of remediation, in particular the effects of medical power on emotional understanding. After a domestic encounter that manifests emotional difference understood in terms of illness, both sides of the dyad seek ways to reinterpret emotions in relation to events and personality. In memoirs, these layers of emotions and emotional reinterpretation demonstrate how 'manifold experiences which contribute to the process of socialization (co) exist in one and the same body'.[45] Likewise, emotions that lead up to or constitute an encounter (co)exist in the same text for personal and strategic reasons. Therefore, such ego-documents establish a benchmark into which multiple discourses are already embedded, just as multiple dispositions exist within a single mind and body.

The Rivière Encounter

In 1835, Pierre Rivière murdered his pregnant mother, eighteen-year-old sister and seven-year-old brother with a sharpened hook. After living off the land for about a month, Rivière was arrested. He began the memoir he subsequently wrote as follows:

> I, Pierre Rivière, having slaughtered my mother, my sister, and my brother, and wishing to make known the motives which led me to this deed, have written down the whole of the life which my father and my mother led together since their marriage.... I shall then tell how I resolved to commit this crime, what my thoughts were at the time, and what was my intention. I shall also say what went on in my mind after doing this deed, ... and what were the resolutions I took.[46]

So began the testimonial in which Rivière explained his feelings towards his father and his mother, Marie Anne Victoire Brion Rivière, the main target of the attack. In the legal proceedings and psychiatric investigation that followed, his family, fellow villagers and Rivière himself were questioned and Rivière underwent psychiatric evaluation. While some psychiatric experts argued that the defendant was insane, which would condemn him to a life of confinement, others argued that he was sane and deserved the death penalty. But after initially feigning religious mania, Rivière claimed that he was sane. After the trial, his death sentence was commuted to life imprisonment. After five years in prison, Rivière committed suicide.

If we take Rivière at his word, then the motive for the murder was the 'tribulations and afflictions which [his] father suffered at the hands of [his] mother'.[47] Rivière professed love and devotion to his father and hatred for his mother. But he also expressed his inner conflict and his sympathies for his brother, as well as regret. Rivière substantiated the reasons for his feelings by telling the story of his parents and recounting the many ways in which his mother had humiliated his father and made their family suffer, his own nervous excitement leading up to the crime, as well as his feelings afterward. If the Rivière murders can be understood in terms of an encounter, then it is not only one shaped by emotions; it is one in which emotional misapprehension among relatives had deadly results, and emotional incoherence must be taken into account in understanding motive.

The case of Pierre Rivière became the subject of extensive historical analysis and subsequent debate when Michel Foucault published the documents together with a collection of essays, in which he emphasized that the case of parricide was not particularly noteworthy at the time and that Rivière's memoir did not change the interpretation of the crime: 'the fact of killing and the fact of writing, the deeds done and the things narrated, coincided since they were elements of a like nature'.[48] Setting aside Rivière's temporary plea of insanity, Foucault underscored Rivière's intentions in committing the crime as seeking 'glory'.[49] In Foucault's reading, the text was neither a 'confession (in the judicial sense) nor [a] defense or justification; nor is it the starting point for begging for reprieve or reconciliation'.[50] Undisciplined by law or medicine, the murderer did not try to justify his acts after the fact.[51] However, despite this interpretation of Rivière as a parricide who resisted the psychiatric gaze and whose confession reflected his resistance to or defiance of the moral norms that surrounded him, the emotions that Rivière professed reflect complex relationships within his nuclear family, internal conflicts prior to, during and after the murder, as well as regret.

The conflicts within the Rivière family that shaped Pierre's feelings towards them were at least partly structured by France's early nineteenth-century agricultural society. While 'one cannot speak of the French example [of the family] before the unification of the country', the general thesis developed by social historians regarding the ties of family relations to property and labour holds true for the Rivière family.[52] The effects of the Napoleonic Wars laid the groundwork for Pierre's complaints. His parents' marriage was founded on relative equality: both contributed material goods at the time of their union, although Rivière's father's contribution was valued at a hundred francs more, and if either partner were to die, the surviving partner would be the sole heir. However, their marriage also took place when rural families such as the Rivières tried to increase their land and wealth after the extreme poverty following 1789 and as men from the families of both husband and wife were called up to serve in the Napoleonic War.[53] Rivière's father was advised to marry, as he was the second of three brothers. Both Rivière's maternal uncles were killed in the war, leaving his mother the sole heir of the Victoire family.[54] Although inferior according to the law, Rivière's mother was part of a rural society in which wives were active and sometimes domineering forces in family life.[55] What Rivière described as the 'tyranny' of his mother continued throughout the couple's marriage. She threatened to slander, refused to live with her husband and divided her children's loyalties.

In the memoir he wrote after he was imprisoned, Rivière described his motives in terms of his hatred for his mother and love of his father, emotions that were expressed through the day-to-day conflicts of agricultural labour and material disputes of the household. Rivière justified his hatred for his mother by describing her cruelty towards his father as well as the emotional and economic hardship she had inflicted since their marriage and throughout their lives together. He described her as a greedy, lazy and cruel woman who had lied about her marriage dowry, refused to come to live with Rivière senior, demanded he leave to work as a day labourer and ate lavish and expensive food that she could hardly afford.[56] Furthermore, she symbolically and literally divided the family. Rivière describes one instance in which his father insisted on naming their child after his side of the family, and his mother reacted by refusing to provide the child with proper clothes or care for it. These familial divides were also reiterated in the murders: Rivière killed the sister and brother, who were loyal to his mother.

While Rivière's description of his family history focused on the wrongdoings of his mother, he argued that his real motive was his love for his father. He described his father as a kind, gentle and hardworking man who had done his best for his family. Rivière argued that his father had tolerated his wife for too long, a wife who accused him of being 'lewd', a 'wastrel', of keeping harlots and feigning religious devotion, while his father 'displayed only his usual mood at all these reproaches, always mild and seeking to justify himself by explaining the truth'.[57] Rivière was 'sorely affected' by his father's troubles and saw his mother's murder as an act of 'glory' inspired by Roman law and resolved to 'immortalize' himself by dying for his father. He died to 'restore ... peace and quiet' to his grandmother and his father,[58] and he purportedly stated after the murder to two persons he met, 'I have just delivered my father, now he will no longer be unhappy'.[59]

While they had long since noted Rivière's peculiar behaviour, fellow villagers generally agreed with Rivière's complaints about his family, but they did not see these as justifying Rivière's emotional response. Instead, they understood the murders in terms of Rivière's longstanding history of abnormal behaviour and described him as an idiot, mad or as one local newspaper put it, a 'maniac' who was 'not to be in full possession of his mental faculties'.[60] Emotions marked Rivière's psychological difference, specifically his pleasure in the pain of others. He tortured animals, created difficulties for his father and threatened children and his siblings.[61] He had imaginary conversations and battles in the woods, sometimes letting out 'terrifying cries' or outbursts of laughter.[62] In particular, his 'strange laugh' was seen as a sign of idiocy because it had no perceivable cause.[63] Specifically, Rivière's professions of love did not match his family and community's description of his emotional disposition towards his father. Discord in relationships was expressed through agricultural labour. One village witness recounted a story in which Rivière intentionally made work harder for his father, who 'said it was a great misfortune to have a son like that',[64] and on the day that Rivière did not go out to the fields but stayed at home (to murder his family), his grandmother complained to him that he 'would have done better to go this morning instead of his father who is sick'.[65] Even Rivière's cruelty towards animals was sometimes an affront to farm life. Mistreating a horse that ploughed the land threatened the family's well-being. Using their own vocabulary, the villagers who witnessed Rivière's behaviour prior to the murders characterized his emotions in terms of psychological difference.

This misapprehension of Rivière's emotions endured all the way up to the murders. Prior to the murders, Rivière's family did not fully apprehend Rivière's emotional disposition. Although they were aware of his 'bizarre behaviour', which they purportedly tried to conceal, and testified that he had always been a misfit and a burden, they did not apprehend what Rivière's emotions could lead to. Despite the difficulties he caused, Rivière's family relied on him. As the eldest son, Rivière worked the land alongside his father. Even just prior to the murder, when Rivière's behaviour grew increasingly strange, no one noticed but his maternal grandmother. Rivière describes his interaction with his sister, Aimee, who asked to read his diary but did not appear to suspect anything, and his father went to work the fields as usual. His grandmother, however, became deeply worried when Rivière wore his Sunday clothes:

> I went into my g-m's house and found her weeping; where do you want to go to, she said to me, if you do not think you are earning enough with your father and want to go elsewhere, say so, without going off like that and saying nothing to anyone . . . why do you do it, your father offered you all the advantages he could, when you were little he said he would sacrifice part of his property to make you a priest, he offered to have you taught a trade if you wished, if you want to leave him, he still will not let you go without money . . . ah he is not backward in helping you do your work, he can be happy with all of you if

he wants to. . . . if he leaves him, that will be yet another forceful argument his mother will have against his father in her suit, she will tell the judges: he is so bad that his children will not stay with him; yet if he wishes to go, his father will not hold him back; let him tell us and we shall not be worried about where he is.[66]

Familial conflicts and affects were described in economic terms. Rivière's grandmother reminded Rivière of his father's desire to secure him a good occupation, and she believed that Rivière's behaviour was the consequence of his dissatisfaction with his earnings. Moreover, Rivière's discontent and departure could further break up the family. Rivière's grandmother was greatly concerned; she could not apprehend her grandson's hatred or love that would result in the 'fearful crime'.[67]

Despite the clarity with which he explained that hatred, love and even glory were the motives for his actions, Rivière's strongest feelings following the murders were horror and regret, ultimately rejecting his own feelings and actions and describing himself as a monster. After he fled into the woods outside Aunay, he described his emotions as follows:

> As I went I felt this courage and this idea of glory that inspired me weaken, and when I had gone farther and came into the woods I regained my full senses, ah, can it be so, I asked myself, monster that I am! Hapless victims! can I possibly have done that, no it is but a dream! ah but it is all too true! chasms gape beneath my feet, earth swallow me; I wept, I fell to the ground . . . poor mother, poor sister, guilty maybe in some sort, but never did they have ideas so unworthy as mine, poor unhappy child.[68]

In the month after his crime, Rivière's 'ideas changed more than once', he was 'aching with regret', and fell into 'despairing thoughts'. It was after he decided that he 'could not go on in this fashion, and feeling that it could only have been an aberration that had brought [him] to commit this crime' that he resolved to be arrested. While Rivière confessed to manipulating his own testimony to lessen his punishment, he continued to express regret: 'now that I have made known all my monstrosity . . . I accept it in expiation of my faults; alas if only I could see the hapless victims of my cruelty alive once more, even if for that I must suffer the utmost torments'.[69] Rivière might have clearly understood the emotions motivating his actions, but he would later criticize and disavow his own feelings. He came to see himself, his 'cruelty' and his own psychological aberrance as 'monstrosity'. In the wake of the murders, Rivière remediated his own understanding of the events and his feelings, a process that would continue after his arrest. While Rivière may have protested his psychiatric assessment and pled for his own sanity, the way in which he describes and explains his own emotions in his memoir reflects not only his hatred of his mother and love for his father but also a judgement of his own actions. Rivière's memoir pled his case, a confession with intention. Rivière remediated his own feelings and shaped them, extreme as they might be, to gain what sympathies he could from others. Part of this was recognizing his own psychological difference, seeing himself as a 'monster'.

The Althusser Encounter

Althusser described his account, *The Future Lasts Forever*, as 'not a diary, not [his] memoirs, not an autobiography'. Rather, he wrote, 'I simply wanted to remember those emotional experiences which had an impact on me and helped shape my life'. It was, he stated, the 'crucial and marked similarity of those emotional experiences which occurred at different points in my life and made me what I am'.[70] In this account of emotional experiences, Althusser connected his relationship with Rytman to his early childhood years and his relationship with both his mother and his father. Like the memoir of Pierre Rivière, Louis Althusser's emotional professions were a dominant feature of his tale. However, despite his desire not to confuse any further the events of his life but to clarify them, Althusser's emotions feature as a contradictory aspect of his account. Contrasting starkly with the calm lucidity of his writing were powerful feelings that were strategically presented. On the one hand, Althusser took care to emphasize the love, admiration and sympathy he had for Rytman. On the other, Althusser also revealed anger, rage and hatred for his wife, whether wittingly or unwittingly. However, in his presentation of his feelings, Althusser discussed his true feelings in terms of love and affection while his diseased feelings were those of anger and hatred.

If Althusser loved and admired his wife, how could he have intended to kill her? Insisting upon his devotion to his wife as well as the act of murder itself as an act of 'kindness', Althusser attempted to argue and demonstrate how he could have unintentionally murdered someone he loved. Indeed, his text is both romantic and hagiographic, both characterizing his wife as a kindred lost soul as well as describing her as a political hero. Filled with affection, sympathy and admiration, Althusser set their romance within the heated political and intellectual climate of postwar France. In December 1946, when Althusser met Rytman, a Jewish Lithuanian who had participated in the Resistance against fascism, they were both 'lonely people, both in the depths of despair'.[71] He described the instinctive moment when he reached for her hand, foreseeing his loving devotion: 'From that moment on I was filled with a powerful desire to serve her: to save her and help her live! Throughout our life together, right to the very end, I never abandoned this supreme mission which gave my life its meaning until the final moment'.[72] Althusser described Rytman with appreciation of her patience and unending support as his wife. Particularly during his psychotic episodes when he was hospitalized, he described not only her unconditional love but her advocacy for his betterment and release. At the same time, Althusser acknowledged her own psychological difficulties and sufferings inflicted by his intellectual celebrity. She was continually contacted by friends curious to know about Althusser's own health, and in her final days, 'no one ever asked how she was, about her own unhappy mental state'.[73] In the text, the love and admiration Althusser professed for his wife align with his presentation of the murder as a 'service'. At the same time, he also expressed his shock and horror at the death of his wife, after which he reportedly ran out in the streets yelling, 'I killed my wife, I strangled her, I've killed her'.[74] His horror and sadness at her death seem to be meant to show that he was innocent.

At the same time, Althusser's account included glimpses of other feelings towards his wife that seem to contradict the narrative he presented. Despite his portrayal of extreme love and respect for his wife, Althusser's memoir is also peppered with signs of negative emotions. While Althusser expressed admiration and almost reverence for his wife's pain and tolerance for his romantic interludes with other women, he described his own actions and emotions as 'hypomanic states' when he was 'truly unbearable'.[75] At other moments, Althusser only alluded to the worst of his emotions and behaviour toward Hélène, which became 'constantly aggressive and provocative'.[76] At times his provocations were 'of a different order'. He described bringing home his 'new woman friends as soon as possible' for her approval, and her reactions.[77] For Althusser, these negative emotions towards Rytman were either forgotten or cast as part of hallucinatory or manic episodes. Although he did not remember 'exactly' what he put Hélène through, he seemed to ignore that he was 'truly capable of the most terrible things'.[78] Additionally, Althusser suffered 'terrible nightmares which went on for a long time when I was awake', and this '"pathological" pattern was accompanied by ... suicidal tendencies' in which, a friend reminded him, he also wanted to murder Hélène. He wrote,

> I imagined all sorts of possible ways of dying and, in addition, wanted not only to destroy myself physically but also to destroy all traces of my existence: in particular by destroying every one of my books, all my notes, by burning down the École as well, and 'if possible', while I was at it, by getting rid of Hélène herself.[79]

At these moments when Althusser described his own cruelty towards Rytman, he avoided explicit emotional terms, reverting to the medicalized emotional language that he used to describe his general condition. Instead of describing his cruelty and terrible behaviour towards his wife through emotions like hate or anger, he used delusions, hallucinations and perceptions veiled in madness to explain his actions. What followed was a period in which they 'were shut up together in [their] own private Hell'.[80]

At the same time that Althusser described his negative emotions towards Rytman through the language of mental illness, he also characterized himself as a victim of these emotions, especially during the events leading up to the murder. Specifically, he described the murder in terms of terror. However, the terrorized individual was Althusser. He alluded to her unhappiness and troubles on the days leading up to the murder, when she 'terrified' Althusser by saying she would leave him and telling him that he was a 'monster'.[81] He described Rytman's emotions and behaviour as increasingly aggressive. She ignored him, slammed doors and would not eat with him or stay in the same room with him, which he found 'unbearable'. Although he claimed he was trying to help her, Althusser reiterated that she threatened to kill herself. For Althusser, this thought 'was both unthinkable and unbearably awful' and made him 'tremble'.[82] In Althusser's account, Rytman did not resist and did not have any emotional reaction except for a serene expression in death.

By tracing the direct lineage of his memoir to that of Pierre Rivière, Althusser placed his critiques of his own treatment in the wake of the murder in an historical perspective. Althusser detailed the 'negative affects' of having been declared insane – and therefore going without a trial or prison sentence – as the experience of being one of the living dead (*Lebenstodt*).[83] Being saved from a legal trial also deprived him of having a voice, and it did not save him from the social condemnation or judgement of others who saw him as an enduring threat or danger or simply as a guilty man. In this discussion, Foucault – Althusser's former student and colleague who visited him twice after the murder – was Althusser's touchstone. Foucault had described the hospitalized insane as 'simply missing'. It was the possibility of 'reappearing' that 'gives rise to a sense of unease and disquiet in relation to him'.[84] Both he and Rivière, Althusser argued, were victims of the medical-legal machinery that used notions of insanity to oppress their voices and autonomy. Accordingly, scholars have continued to examine Rivière and Althusser's works together.

* * *

However different the cases may be despite their intertextual connection, both Rivière and Althusser's memoirs demonstrate the importance of evaluating complex, contradictory emotions within a domestic setting in understanding the outcomes of an encounter. The aim of the chapter has not been to examine emotional experiences as lived by the persons involved or to perform a complete reading of these texts, historical or otherwise. Rather, it has been to analyse the role of emotions in representations of such encounters and to show how emotions can meaningfully contribute to such understandings. At the risk of capitalizing on the sufferings of others, this chapter has taken two instances of murder precisely because they demonstrate how emotional incoherence (emotions that do not cohere with a socially or culturally accepted narrative) and emotional misapprehension (the inability to understand the layers of another person's feelings for whatever reasons) shape encounters of great consequence.

Daphne Rozenblatt is currently Research Fellow at the Center for the History of Emotions at the Max Planck Institute for Human Development in Berlin. She completed her PhD in history at the University of California, Los Angeles, in 2014, where she wrote her dissertation on the social history of modern Italian psychiatry. Her current research focuses on the role of emotions in trials of political crime in Europe during the long nineteenth century. Her recent scholarship will be published in *Social History of Medicine*, *History of Human Sciences* and *Rechtsgeschichte*.

Notes

1. Althusser, *Philosophy of the Encounter*, 164.
2. Althusser, *Philosophy of the Encounter*, 165–69, quotation 165.
3. Originally published as Althusser, *L'Avenir dure longtemps: Suivi de Les faits*.
4. See introduction to this volume.
5. Althusser, *Philosophy of the Encounter*, 31–114.
6. Althusser, *The Future Lasts Forever: A Memoir*, 115–32, quotation 132.
7. See Boutang, *Louis Althusser: Une biographie, vol. 1: La Formation du mythe (1918–1956)*; Kaplan and Sprinker, *The Althusserian Legacy*; Lewis, *Louis Althusser and the Traditions of French Marxism*; Montag, *Althusser and His Contemporaries: Philosophy's Perpetual War*; Resch, *Althusser and the Renewal of Marxist Social Theory*.
8. See Althusser, *Writings on Psychoanalysis: Freud and Lacan*; Illouz, *Saving the Modern Soul: Therapy, Emotions, and the Culture of Self-Help*; Rieff, *The Triumph of the Therapeutic: Uses of Faith after Freud*.
9. Althusser, *Future Lasts Forever*, 138, 139.
10. Althusser, *Future Lasts Forever*, 139–40.

11. Foucault, *I, Pierre Rivière, Having Slaughtered my Mother, my Sister, and my Brother . . .: A Case of Parricide in the 19th Century*.
12. Foucault, 'Foreword', x, xi.
13. Foucault, 'Foreword', x, xiii.
14. Ginzburg, 'Checking the Evidence: The Judge and the Historian', 80.
15. See, for example, Deniker and Olié, 'La mort d'Hélène Althusser: Un cas d'homicide altruiste rapporté par le mélancolique', 389–92; Finn, *Why Althusser Killed His Wife: Essays on Discourse and Violence*; Judt, 'Elucubrations: The "Marxism" of Louis Althusser', 106–15; Sprinker, 'The Legacies of Althusser', 201–25; Sturrock, 'The Paris Strangler', 6–7.
16. See, for example, Gilmore, 'Bastard Testimony: Illegitimacy and Incest in Dorothy Allison's *Bastard Out of Carolina*', 45–70.
17. Foucault, 'Foreword', xiii.
18. Foucault, 'Foreword', x–xi.
19. Foucault, 'Foreword', xiii.
20. For recent work on emotions and the case of Pierre Rivière, see Davies and Speedy, *Pierre Rivière*.
21. Scheff, 'A Social/Emotional Theory of "Mental Illness"', 87.
22. Russell, 'Preface', ix.
23. Foucault, *Madness and Civilization: A History of Insanity in the Age of Reason*; Goffman, *Asylums: Essays on the Social Situation of Mental Patients and Other Inmates*.
24. See, for example, Daston, 'The Coming into Being of Scientific Objects', 6–12; Hacking, 'Between Michel Foucault and Erving Goffman: Between Discourse in the Abstract and Face-to-Face-Interaction', 279, 285.
25. See, for example, Melling and Forsythe, 'Community, Friends and Family: Asylum, Lunatics and the Social Environment, 1845–1914', 99–124; Rosenkrantz and Vinovskis, 'Caring for the Insane in Ante-Bellum Massachusetts: Family, Community, and State Participation', 187–218; Suzuki, *Madness at Home: The Psychiatrist, the Patient, and the Family in England, 1820–1860*.
26. See, for example, Bartlett and Wright, *Outside the Walls of the Asylum: The History of Care in the Community 1750–2000*; Coleborne, 'Challenging Institutional Hegemony: Family Visitors to Hospitals for the Insane in Australia and New Zealand, 1880s–1910s', 289–308; Coleborne, *Madness in the Family: Insanity and Institutions in the Australasian Colonial World, 1860–1914*; Finnane, 'Asylums, Families and the State', 134–48; Wright, 'Family Strategies and the Institutional Confinement of "Idiot" Children in Victorian England', 190–208.
27. Coleborne, 'Families, Patients and Emotions: Asylums for the Insane in Colonial Australia and New Zealand, c. 1880–1910', 425–42.
28. See, for example, Berkenkotter, *Patient Tales: Case Histories and the Uses of Narrative in Psychiatry*; Eghigian, *From Madness to Mental Health: Psychiatric Disorder and Its Treatment in Western Civilization*; Hodgkin, *Madness in Seventeenth-Century Autobiography*; Homberger, 'Insanity and Life Writing', 469–71; Peterson, *A Mad People's History of Madness*; Porter, *A Social History of Madness: Stories of the Insane*. See also Coleborne, 'Families, Patients and Emotions'.
29. Jacob, 'Family Interaction and Psychopathology: Historical Overview', 11.
30. Phelan and Link, 'The Labeling Theory of Mental Disorder (I): The Role of Social Contingencies in the Application of Psychiatric Labels', 144.
31. Scheff, *Being Mentally Ill: A Sociological Theory*.
32. Jacob, 'Family Interaction and Psychopathology', 5.
33. Burgess, 'The Family as a Unit of Interacting Personalities', 3–9.
34. Jacob, 'Family Interaction and Psychopathology', 11.
35. Horwitz, *The Social Control of Mental Illness*, 16.

36. Horwitz, *Social Control*, 36, 47.
37. See Goffman, *Encounters: Two Studies in the Sociology of Interaction*; Foucault, *Madness and Civilization*.
38. Hochschild, 'Emotion Work, Feeling Rules, and Social Structure', 551–75.
39. Mortensen and Ayres, *Miscommunication*.
40. Demoulin, Leyens and Dovidio, *Intergroup Misunderstandings: Impact of Divergent Social Realities*.
41. See discussions of mimesis and transmission in the introduction to this volume.
42. Collins, 'Emotional Energy as the Common Denominator of Rational Action', 205–6.
43. Collins, *Violence: A Micro-Sociological Theory*, 19–20.
44. Bhattacahrjee et al., 'Sociological Understanding of Psychiatric Illness: An Appraisal', 54–62; Kleinman, *The Illness Narratives: Suffering, Healing, and the Human Condition*.
45. Lahire, 'From the Habitus to an Individual Heritage of Dispositions: Toward a Sociology at the Level of the Individual', 332.
46. Foucault, *I, Pierre Rivière*, 54–55.
47. Foucault, *I, Pierre Rivière*, 55.
48. Foucault, 'Tales of Murder', 200.
49. Foucault, 'Tales of Murder', 210.
50. Foucault, 'Tales of Murder', 208.
51. See also Foucault, 'About the Concept of the "Dangerous Individual" in 19th-Century Legal Psychiatry', 1–18.
52. See Goubert, 'Family and Province: A Contribution to the Knowledge of Family Structures in Early Modern France', 179; Medick and Sabean, *Interest and Emotion: Essays on the Study of Family and Kinship*; Poitrineau, *La vie rurale en Basse-Auvergne au XVIIIe siècle*.
53. Peter and Favret, 'The Animal, the Madman, and Death', 177–80.
54. Foucault, *I, Pierre Rivière*, 55–57.
55. See Segalen, *Love and Power in the Peasant Family: Rural France in the Nineteenth Century*.
56. Foucault, *I, Pierre Rivière*, 104.
57. Foucault, *I, Pierre Rivière*, 64.
58. Foucault, *I, Pierre Rivière*, 104, 105, 112.
59. Foucault, *I, Pierre Rivière*, 11.
60. Foucault, *I, Pierre Rivière*, 16 (article in *Pilote du Calvados*, 16 July 1835), 26 ('Gabriel-Pierre Retout, Sixty-three, Property Owner and Farmer'), 28–30 ('Marguerite Colleville, Fifty-eight, Wife of Louis Hébert, Known as Laviolette, Farmer'), 32 ('Michel Nativel, Thirty-eight, Tow Maker'), 34 ('Charles Grelley, Forty-nine, Merchant'), 33 ('Louis Hamel, Fifty-eight, Pumphand'), 25 ('Zéphyr Théodore Morin, Thirty-one, Doctor of Medicine'), 25.
61. Foucault, *I, Pierre Rivière*, 31 ('Geneviève Rivière, Thirty-six, Widow of Jean Quesnel, Housewife').
62. Foucault, *I, Pierre Rivière*, 30 ('Geneviève Rivière, Thirty-six, Widow of Jean Quesnel, Housewife').
63. Foucault, *I, Pierre Rivière*, 32 ('Michel Nativel, Thirty-eight, Tow Maker').
64. Foucault, *I, Pierre Rivière*, 28 ('Pierre, Known as Lami Binet, Fifty-nine, Day Labourer').
65. Foucault, *I, Pierre Rivière*, 111.
66. Foucault, *I, Pierre Rivière*, 111–12.
67. Foucault, *I, Pierre Rivière*, 112.
68. Foucault, *I, Pierre Rivière*, 112–13.
69. Foucault, *I, Pierre Rivière*, 113, 115, 121.
70. Althusser, *Future Lasts Forever*, 29.
71. Althusser, *Future Lasts Forever*, 116.
72. Althusser, *Future Lasts Forever*, 116.

73. Althusser, *Future Lasts Forever*, 248, 203.
74. Johnson, 'Introduction: Louis Althusser 1918–1990', vi.
75. Althusser, *Future Lasts Forever*, 248.
76. Althusser, *Future Lasts Forever*, 248.
77. Althusser, *Future Lasts Forever*, 154.
78. Althusser, *Future Lasts Forever*, 251.
79. Althusser, *Future Lasts Forever*, 249, 250.
80. Althusser, *Future Lasts Forever*, 252.
81. Althusser, *Future Lasts Forever*, 251.
82. Althusser, *Future Lasts Forever*, 252.
83. Althusser, *Future Lasts Forever*, 22, 23.
84. Althusser, *Future Lasts Forever*, 23.

Bibliography

Althusser, L. *L'Avenir dure longtemps: Suivi de Les faits*, ed. O. Corpet and Y.M. Boutang. Paris: Stock, 1992.
_____. *The Future Lasts Forever: A Memoir*, ed. O. Corpet and Y.M. Boutang, trans. R. Veasey. New York: New Press, 1993.
_____. *Writings on Psychoanalysis: Freud and Lacan*, ed. O. Corpet and F. Matheron. New York: Columbia University Press, 1996.
_____. *Philosophy of the Encounter: Later Writings, 1978–87*, ed. F. Matheron and O. Corpet, trans. G.M. Goshgarian. London: Verso, 2006 [Fre. orig. *Sur la philosophie*. Paris: Gallimard, 1994].
Bartlett, P., and D. Wright (eds). *Outside the Walls of the Asylum: The History of Care in the Community 1750–2000*. London: Athlone Press, 1999.
Berkenkotter, C. *Patient Tales: Case Histories and the Uses of Narrative in Psychiatry*. Columbia: University of South Carolina Press, 2008.
Bhattacahrjee, D., et al. 'Sociological Understanding of Psychiatric Illness: An Appraisal'. *Delhi Psychiatry Journal* 14(1) (2011), 54–62.
Boutang, Y.M. *Louis Althusser: Une biographie*, vol. 1: *La Formation du mythe (1918–1956)*. Paris: Grasset, 1992.
Burgess, E. 'The Family as a Unit of Interacting Personalities'. *The Family* 7 (1926), 3–9.
Coleborne, C. 'Families, Patients and Emotions: Asylums for the Insane in Colonial Australia and New Zealand, c. 1880–1910'. *Social History of Medicine* 19(3) (2006), 425–42, doi: 10.1093/shm/hkl042.
_____. 'Challenging Institutional Hegemony: Family Visitors to Hospitals for the Insane in Australia and New Zealand, 1880s–1910s', in G. Mooney and J. Reinarz (eds), *Permeable Walls: Historical Perspectives on Hospital and Asylum Visiting* (Amsterdam: Rodopi, 2009), 289–308.
_____. *Madness in the Family: Insanity and Institutions in the Australasian Colonial World, 1860–1914*. Basingstoke: Palgrave Macmillan, 2010.
Collins, R. 'Emotional Energy as the Common Denominator of Rational Action'. *Rationality and Society* 5(2) (1993), 203–30, doi: 10.1177/1043463193005002005.
_____. *Violence: A Micro-Sociological Theory*. Princeton, NJ: Princeton University Press, 2008.

Daston, L. 'The Coming into Being of Scientific Objects', in L. Daston (ed.), *Biographies of Scientific Objects* (Chicago: University of Chicago Press, 2000), 1–14.
Davies, B., and J. Speedy (eds). *Pierre Rivière*. Oxford: Elsevier, 2012 [*Emotion, Space and Society* 5(4, special issue) (2012)].
Demoulin, S., J.-P. Leyens and J.F. Dovidio. *Intergroup Misunderstandings: Impact of Divergent Social Realities*. New York: Psychology Press, 2009.
Deniker, P., and J.P. Olié. 'La mort d'Hélène Althusser: Un cas d'homicide altruiste rapporté par le mélancolique'. *Annales Medico-Psychologiques* 152(6) (1994), 389–92.
Eghigian, G. (ed.). *From Madness to Mental Health: Psychiatric Disorder and Its Treatment in Western Civilization*. New Brunswick, NJ: Rutgers University Press, 2010.
Finn, G. *Why Althusser Killed His Wife: Essays on Discourse and Violence*. Atlantic Highlands, NJ: Humanities Press, 1996.
Finnane, M. 'Asylums, Families and the State'. *History Workshop Journal* 20(1) (1985), 134–48.
Foucault, M. 'Foreword', in M. Foucault (ed.), *I, Pierre Rivière, Having Slaughtered My Mother, My Sister, and My Brother . . .: A Case of Parricide in the 19th Century*, trans. F. Jellinek (Lincoln: University of Nebraska Press, 1975), vii–xiv.
_____. 'Tales of Murder', in M. Foucault (ed.), *I, Pierre Rivière, Having Slaughtered My Mother, My Sister, and My Brother . . .: A Case of Parricide in the 19th Century*, trans. F. Jellinek (Lincoln: University of Nebraska Press, 1975), 199–212.
_____. 'About the Concept of the "Dangerous Individual" in 19th-Century Legal Psychiatry', trans. A. Baudot and J. Couchman. *International Journal of Law and Psychiatry* 1(1) (1978), 1–18, doi: 10.1016/0160-2527(78)90020-2.
_____. *Madness and Civilization: A History of Insanity in the Age of Reason*, trans. R. Howard. New York: Routledge, 2007 [Fre. orig. *Folie et déraison*. Paris: Plon, 1961].
Foucault, M. (ed.). *I, Pierre Rivière, Having Slaughtered My Mother, My Sister, and My Brother . . .: A Case of Parricide in the 19th Century*, trans. F Jellinek. Lincoln: University of Nebraska Press, 1975 [Fre. orig. *Moi, Pierre Rivière ayant égorgé ma mère, ma soeur et mon frère . . .* Paris: Gallimard, 1973].
Gilmore, L. 'Bastard Testimony: Illegitimacy and Incest in Dorothy Allison's *Bastard Out of Carolina*', in L. Gilmore, *The Limits of Autobiography: Trauma and Testimony* (Ithaca, NY: Cornell University Press, 2001), 45–70.
Ginzburg, C. 'Checking the Evidence: The Judge and the Historian'. *Critical Inquiry* 18(1) (1991), 79–92.
Goffman, E. *Asylums: Essays on the Social Situation of Mental Patients and Other Inmates*. New York: Doubleday, 1961.
_____. *Encounters: Two Studies in the Sociology of Interaction*. Indianapolis, IN: Bobbs-Merill, 1961.
Goubert, P. 'Family and Province: A Contribution to the Knowledge of Family Structures in Early Modern France'. *Journal of Family History* 2(3) (1977), 179–95, doi: 10.1177/036319907700200302.

Hacking, I. 'Between Michel Foucault and Erving Goffman: Between Discourse in the Abstract and Face-to-Face-Interaction'. *Economy and Society* 33(3) (2004), 277–302, doi: 10.1080/0308514042000225671.

Hochschild, A.R. 'Emotion Work, Feeling Rules, and Social Structure'. *American Journal of Sociology* 85(3) (1979), 551–75, doi: 10.1086/227049.

Hodgkin, K. *Madness in Seventeenth-Century Autobiography*. Basingstoke: Palgrave Macmillan, 2006.

Homberger, M. 'Insanity and Life Writing', in M. Jolly (ed.), *Encyclopedia of Life Writing: Autobiographical and Biographical Forms*, vol. 1: *A–K* (London: Fitzroy Dearborn, 2001), 469–71.

Horwitz, A.V. *The Social Control of Mental Illness*. New York: Academic Press, 1982.

Illouz, E. *Saving the Modern Soul: Therapy, Emotions, and the Culture of Self-Help*. Berkeley: University of California Press, 2008.

Jacob, T. 'Family Interaction and Psychopathology: Historical Overview', in T. Jacob (ed.), *Family Interaction and Psychopathology: Theories, Methods, and Findings* (New York: Plenum Press, 1987), 3–22.

Johnson, D. 'Introduction: Louis Althusser 1918–1990', in L. Althusser, *The Future Lasts Forever: A Memoir*, ed. O. Corpet and Y.M. Boutang, trans. R. Veasey. New York: New Press, 1993, vi–xviii.

Judt, T. 'Elucubrations: The "Marxism" of Louis Althusser', in T. Judt, *Reappraisals: Reflections on the Forgotten Twentieth Century* (London: Vintage Books, 2009), 106–15.

Kaplan, E.A., and M. Sprinker (eds). *The Althusserian Legacy*. London: Verso, 1993.

Kleinman, A. *The Illness Narratives: Suffering, Healing, and the Human Condition*. New York: Basic Books, 1988.

Lahire, B. 'From the Habitus to an Individual Heritage of Dispositions: Toward a Sociology at the Level of the Individual'. *Poetics* 31(5/6) (2003), 329–55, doi: 10.1016/j.poetic.2003.08.002.

Lewis, W.S. *Louis Althusser and the Traditions of French Marxism*. Lanham, MD: Lexington Books, 2005.

Medick, H., and D.W. Sabean (eds). *Interest and Emotion: Essays on the Study of Family and Kinship*. Cambridge: Cambridge University Press, 1988.

Melling, J., and B. Forsythe. 'Community, Friends and Family: Asylum, Lunatics and the Social Environment, 1845–1914', in J. Melling and B. Forsythe, *The Politics of Madness: The State, Insanity and Society in England, 1845–1914* (New York: Routledge, 2006), 99–124.

Montag, W. *Althusser and His Contemporaries: Philosophy's Perpetual War*. Durham, NC: Duke University Press, 2013.

Mortensen, C.D., and C.M. Ayres. *Miscommunication*. Thousand Oaks, CA: Sage Publications, 1997.

Peter, J.-P., and J. Favret. 'The Animal, the Madman, and Death', in M. Foucault (ed.), *I, Pierre Rivière, Having Slaughtered My Mother, My Sister, and My Brother. . .: A Case of Parricide in the 19th Century*, trans. F. Jellinek (Lincoln: University of Nebraska Press, 1975), 175–99.

Peterson, D. (ed.). *A Mad People's History of Madness*. Pittsburgh, PA: University of Pittsburgh Press, 1982.

Phelan, J.C., and B.G. Link. 'The Labeling Theory of Mental Disorder (I): The Role of Social Contingencies in the Application of Psychiatric Labels', in A.V. Horwitz and T.L. Scheid (eds), *A Handbook for the Study of Mental Health: Social Contexts, Theories, and Systems* (Cambridge: Cambridge University Press, 1999), 139–49.

Poitrineau, A. *La vie rurale en Basse-Auvergne au XVIIIe siècle*, 2 vols. Paris: Presse Universitaires de France, 1965.

Porter, R. *A Social History of Madness: Stories of the Insane*. London: Weidenfeld and Nicolson, 1987.

Resch, R.P. *Althusser and the Renewal of Marxist Social Theory*. Berkeley: University of California Press, 1992.

Rieff, P. *The Triumph of the Therapeutic: Uses of Faith after Freud*. Chicago: University of Chicago Press, 1987.

Rosenkrantz, B.G., and M.A. Vinovskis. 'Caring for the Insane in Ante-Bellum Massachusetts: Family, Community, and State Participation', in A.J. Lichtman and J.R. Challinor, *Kin and Communities: Families in America* (Washington, DC: Smithsonian Institution Press, 1979), 187–218.

Russell, J.A. 'Preface', in J.A. Russell et al. (eds), *Everyday Conceptions of Emotion: An Introduction to the Psychology, Anthropology and Linguistics of Emotion* (Dordrecht: Kluwer Academic, 1995), ix–xi.

Scheff, T.J. *Being Mentally Ill: A Sociological Theory*. Chicago: Aldine, 1966.

———. 'A Social/Emotional Theory of "Mental Illness"', *International Journal of Social Psychiatry* 59(1) (2013), 87–92, doi: 10.1177/0020764012445004.

Segalen, M. *Love and Power in the Peasant Family: Rural France in the Nineteenth Century*. Oxford: Blackwell, 1983.

Sprinker, M. 'The Legacies of Althusser'. *Yale French Studies* 88 (1995), 201–25, doi: 10.2307/2930108.

Sturrock, J. 'The Paris Strangler'. *London Review of Books* 14(24) (1992), 6–7.

Suzuki, A. *Madness at Home: The Psychiatrist, the Patient, and the Family in England, 1820–1860*. Berkeley: University of California Press, 2006.

Wright, D. 'Family Strategies and the Institutional Confinement of "Idiot" Children in Victorian England'. *Journal of Family History* 23(2) (1998), 190–208.

Chapter 9

Performers
From 'Courtesans' to *Kathakali King Lear*

Kedar A. Kulkarni

In 1989, the dance artist Annette Leday worked with senior Kathakali artists and an Australian collaborator to produce a Kathakali dance drama version of *King Lear*. Kathakali is a highly stylized, costumed, non-naturalistic form of drama that emerged in courtly settings in southwestern India in the seventeenth century (see Figure 9.3 below). The production of a *Kathakali King Lear* (in the following simply KKL) was staged more than seventy times over the following decade in front of audiences in India and around Europe. It was widely acknowledged as having an 'integrity hard to find in a number of other intercultural experiments', which, according to Phillip Zarrilli, are often marked by cultural insensitivity and arrogance.[1] In rehearsal, KKL circumvented such criticism. Critics who viewed performances of KKL, however, provided a different set of responses. Some found it boring, 'monotonous' and 'frustrating', while others said that the performance spoke across cultures by way of emotion and that it pulled at one's heart strings.[2] These reactions were complex but seemingly divided into two camps: those who saw absolute cultural difference and those who saw value in cross-cultural artistic work.[3] This tension masks something crucial about KKL: the staging had created a new relationship between the Kathakali repertoire and *King Lear*. In other words, the intercultural production broke each – Western realist drama and Kathakali – free of its predetermined emotional scripts and expanded their emotional repertoire.

Cross-cultural (which I use interchangeably with 'intercultural') encounters all have a performative element – of viewing and being

---

Notes for this chapter begin on page 251.

viewed, of deploying or resisting the theatrical registers of exoticism and spectacle. When intercultural performance itself is the encounter, these dynamics are intentionally heightened. Similar experiences in the past, 'cultural' scripts such as genre, and expectations generated by the press and other media are necessary parts of the encounter, as is the instability of performance itself. Performers and audiences both know that it is not simply enough for the performance to meet expectations but rather that it has to purposefully expand horizons by offering something new.[4]

The case studies presented in this chapter range from the encounter with female performers in early colonial India to pioneers of modern dance such as Ruth St Denis, up to contemporary dance-theatre artist Annette Leday. In taking up examples from a long period of time, the chapter explores the effects and affects of cross-cultural performances over the longue durée. For their part, the case studies mark artistic interventions that were singularly resonant within their own artistic milieu and have been frequent topics of scholarly work. The basic argument here is that each intercultural performance-encounter expanded the emotional repertoires of those involved (performers and audiences) by augmenting the range of emotions associated with a particular genre or medium. Often, these performance-encounters destabilized roles of performer and audience, as each emulated the other for specific ends within and without the performance. Sometimes, historical changes signalled the end of certain performance practices, as is evident from the first case study of female performers in colonial India, departing from certain emotional practices while creating others. In all cases, intercultural performance became a heightened, self-conscious site for negotiating emotional scripts that had implications beyond the performance itself.

The first part of this chapter moves from the interest in female performance traditions in the late 1700s to the beginnings of modern dance in the 1920s. It details overlapping thematic concerns about the inner and outer worlds of the performance, between the encounter within performance and its larger social functions, and the status of performer as artist. From the late nineteenth century onwards, female performers in India were dubbed 'courtesans', both because the performance often involved sexual transactions and because of the importation of Victorian ideology. Initially, all personal memoirs and other published accounts indicated the ubiquity of female performers in cultural life well beyond any specific sexual-transactional role implied by the word 'courtesan'. While ubiquitous, however, female performers were nonetheless socially marginal.[5] The first case studies analyse these multiple sites of performance and their interpretations in some colonial memoirs, before attitudes towards female performers soured and created the image of the seductive 'courtesan' who irked Victorian sensibilities. These descriptions are punctuated by the writings of the actress Binodini Dasi, herself from a female performance community. Her rich descriptions of relationships with various patrons demonstrate the epochal shift in the way the public viewed female performance traditions as sexually deviant, views that Dasi had internalized. At the same time, well-connected American dancers such as Ruth St Denis invented modern dance in the United States by drawing inspiration from Indian dancers such as Dasi. St Denis's projects were highly collaborative at home and overseas, and yet they were fraught with all the Orientalist trappings of her era. The second section analyses the work of Annette Leday and specifically the performance of KKL. None of these 'intercultural' encounters are absent of politics – colonial and postcolonial dynamics are often the condition of their possibility – but these conditions can be overcome. Leday's own work has been exemplary in this regard.

Private and Political Emotions in Performance

Prior to the mid 1800s, there was no single identity coterminous with 'courtesan' for female performers in South Asia. Perhaps this is because of the ubiquity of female performers in South Asia: one of the most visible communities in colonial memoirs, they were present to adorn every occasion, and for the wealthy, no occasion was complete without them. Births, marriages, coronations, many major festivals such as Durga Puja and Ganesh Chaturthi; formal dinners, aspects of diplomacy, the general cultural life of a city – these occasions all engaged female performers. In engaging female performers, rulers and wealthy patrons showcased their cultivation and authority in the public sphere. For high-ranking female performers, such as the *tawa'ifs* of Lucknow, prestige depended upon such public appearances.[6] Early European traders and later company officials found themselves in a milieu where female performers were present at almost all official events and specialized in the kinds of events at which they would perform. I pause here to note the difference between these performance traditions and the association of actresses with prostitution in Britain, where actresses were often denounced as women of ill repute, despite (or because of) the connection between the Restoration stage and the crown. These associations persisted well into the eighteenth century.[7] Company officials thus entered an unfamiliar situation and struggled to appreciate the comparatively less marginal position of female performers in South Asia.

The earliest memoirs of travellers retain a sense of fascination with female performance traditions while also engaging in various attempts to translate the scenes they saw for audiences back home. The memoirs of James Forbes (1749–1819) are typical in this regard. He writes: 'All the large cities in Hindostan contain sets of musicians and dancing-girls, under the care of their respective duennas ... at weddings, and other festivities; or to finish the evening entertainment of the Europeans and natives; and many of them accompany the Asiatic armies to the field'. To this straightforward note, Forbes appends a set of comparisons about dancing women in biblical scenes of David and Saul: 'The women of Israel came out to meet David and Saul dancing to instruments of music ... The choristers of Palestine resembled those in India'.[8] Forbes also offers more details and a sketch titled 'Dancing Girls with Musicians' (Figure 9.1) that attempts to recreate the perspective of the spectator as he is 'seduced' by the performers.

Forbes discerns training and skill as well as purpose in the performer's actions:

> Many of the dancing-girls are extremely delicate in their persons, soft and regular in their features, with a form of perfect symmetry; ... they ... preserve a decency and modesty in their demeanor, which is more likely to allure, than the shameless effrontery of similar characters in other countries. Their dances require great attention, from the dancer's feet being hung with small bells, which act in concert with the music. Two girls usually perform at the same time; their steps are not so mazy or active as ours, but much more into resting; as the song, the music, and the motions of the dance, combine to express love, hope, jealousy, despair, and the passions so well known to lovers, and very easily to be understood by those who are ignorant of other languages. The Indians are extremely fond of this entertainment and lavish large sums on their favourites.[9]

With a few deft strokes, Forbes locates the performers in a temporal (akin to biblical) and non-linguistic (understood despite language barriers) space. The performers are similar, but not identical, to European dancers. Though Forbes' readers are 'ignorant', he glibly insists that the motions of the dance 'combine' to express emotions within the performance that are easily understood. Despite this, Forbes writes that the 'dances require great attention' and are not 'shameless effrontery', which suggests that Forbes took part in Indian codes of connoisseurship, which were different from those of female performers in Britain. While we do not have an account from the performers themselves here, Forbes' encounter evinces a nuanced tension, carefully delineating what performance is and what it is not – alluring and modest, not shameless.

Forbes' description and descriptive tensions reveal the uncomfortable complicity of East India Company officials, who similarly lavished large sums of money on performers for various political and scientific endeavours and for the cultural life of Europeans. Warren Hastings, the

Figure 9.1 'Dancing Girls and Musicians'. J. Forbes, *Oriental Memoirs: Selected from a Series of Familiar Letters Written during Seventeen Years Residence in India*, vol. 1 (London: White, Cochrane, and Co., 1813), after 84 (plate xv).

first governor general of the Bengal Presidency (1773–1785), for example, encouraged Europeans to patronize such performers in order to become more efficacious in diplomacy.[10] Addressing the wife of another company official, he wrote:

Hope that you will have contributed by it [the program] to convey to the people of Hindostan an Opinion that our Meetings of Festivity were always conducted with the same Taste and Decorum as that in which you condescended to gratify the Prince's Curiosity by shewing him what they were at Benares.[11]

Much as Chinese and European diplomats performed various social codes in the presence of kings and emperors,[12] here too we see that the performance has political consequences, serving as a vehicle for East India Company officials to demonstrate their own acculturation to kings and other potentates. Similarly, employing a munshi or pandit (an expert, often in language) to help translate the lyrics from songs so that Europeans could understand the lyrics was relatively common practice. For instance, the early Orientalist William Jones had lyrics from many songs translated from Braj into Persian, which he then translated into English and sent them along to satisfy the curiosity and interests of the wives of company officials, some of whom were also in touch with Warren Hastings.[13]

Ian Woodfield's account of the ways in which political and 'scientific' interests (of documenting lyrics and music) intermingled with ideals of sociability describes encounters between company officials and performers. Replicating the domestic music culture from Britain required certain adaptations in India, where most company officials lacked the musical skills to provide decent entertainment. Female performers were an antidote to boredom as well as a balm for political intrigue. In response to boredom and the exigencies of diplomacy, amateur enthusiasts actively had lyrics from female performers' songs translated and transcribed into Western notation for their amusement. Woodfield provides five different musical arrangements used for the same song, evincing the many complications of translation. Few in colonial India of the 1730s were capable of tuning harpsichords, the instrument most often used for transcription. The inability to reproduce the 'original' was often blamed on a lack of skill. Woodfield relates the ways transcribers were caught between a desire to preserve the 'wildness' of the original and to somehow contain any dissonance that would be fundamentally unacceptable to the 'cultivated' ear; indeed, this tension continues even in some reviews of *Kathakali King Lear*, given below.[14] Amateurs also engaged in some semblance of performance, and one Sophia Plowden even imitated a nautch, or dance, for a masquerade, going to great lengths to find an appropriate dress, studded with the requisite diamonds, emeralds and rubies.[15] Plowden's description of herself with three musicians and an accompanying dancer seems to have been the most typical arrangement, akin to Figure 9.1 above. Memoirs also tell of the Gummer nautch – a dance with over a hundred performers – as well as an individual's 'egg' dance. In addition to these, we read of popular songs and the more famous *tawa'ifs*, such as Begum Sumroo, who amassed a fortune through performance, married wealthy, became a potentate and even led armies.[16] Another *tawa'if*, Gauhar Jaan, was the first recorded artist in India, permitting the encounter of performance to have a mechanical afterlife through the phonograph. All told, Woodfield's account describes the various attempts made by company officials to understand, analyse and replicate the performances, thus making them into performer-connoisseurs who sought to alleviate boredom and engage in the interconnected practice of demonstrating political power.

Audience and occasion dictated the kinds of nautch performed, given that the dance served a variety of social functions. On an everyday, social level, one Miss Roberts notes that in the presence of European ladies, the dance is 'dull and decorous: but when the audience is exclusively masculine, it is said to assume a different character'.[17] Details of the 'different character' of the nautch (female performance) for all-male audiences implied here refer to the way the inner and outer worlds of the nautch often intermingled. Through their numerous gifts and exchanges, patrons often engaged with the performer as she approached them during the dance and afterwards in encounters of a more personal nature, as kept women and lovers. Forbes' sketch (Figure 9.1 above) illustrates these dynamics by positioning the viewer as the recipient of the dancers' overtures, as one of the dancers exposes her breast to the viewer.

Even though the performance-encounter functioned in multiple ways, such depictions – in which the performers came to be seen exclusively as peddlers of sexuality – became increasingly common during the course of the nineteenth century. Diplomacy became less of a process of negotiation as the East India Company consolidated its power and had less of a need to engage in the diplomatic practices of connoisseurship and their performative symbolism in India. Combined with this, the increasing tendency of women to accompany their husbands to India also enabled a wholesale importation of preconceived notions of sexuality, especially of kept women, which were largely determined by debates in Europe.[18] Additionally, the 1857 revolt displaced thousands of female performers who had been in the employ of regional elites after the demise of the Mughal Empire. Many displaced performers made their way to expanding colonial cities such as Calcutta, where the red light district grew substantially in the early 1860s and performance was denuded of its prior association with connoisseurship, civility and public functions.[19] Others increasingly accompanied company (and not only the 'Asiatic') armies and in doing so became cause for concern for leaders of military campaigns.[20] Curtailing the spread of venereal disease and gonorrhoea through performers who had turned to more common prostitution became the cause of legislation from the 1860s onwards as well, further eroding their status in society.²¹ These factors proved to disrupt female performance traditions and contract the emotional repertoires of the performance-encounter so that by the late nineteenth century female performers were on the defensive about their own status. However, for the better part of the eighteenth and early nineteenth centuries, female performance played a role in expanding the emotional horizons of its participants. If one thinks about recent work on romantic movements in Europe, then these encounters were hugely influential when figures such as William Jones transferred (exported) them overseas, where they were endlessly imitated – especially the poetic vocabularies ('lyric' poetry) of the performance.²²

Binodini Dasi (1862–1941), however, was born towards the end of an era that witnessed the decline of female performance. She learned to sing from a *baiji*, or female singer-performer. Baijis were neither as sophisticated nor as highly esteemed as *tawa'ifs*, and Dasi recounts that she was born to a humble family comprised only of her mother and grandmother.²³ In her autobiography, Dasi is preoccupied with processing emergent negative attitudes of audiences towards performing women, and she often directly confronts the portrayals of performing women as 'immoral'. Far from the expanded social and diplomatic function of performing women seen in the early colonial accounts, Dasi's writings seek to modestly reframe the morality of performing woman.

The most poignant moments of Dasi's autobiography occur when she inverts portrayals of performing women and patrons. For example, she writes:

> Although it has been our practice to move from the protection of one man to that of another ... our deceptions cost us much agony.... There is no lack of those who come greedily to talk to us of love, hoping all the while to seduce us.... Has anyone ever sought to know whether it was we who first deceived or whether we learnt deception only after we were ourselves deceived?²⁴

Such descriptions highlight the complicity of those who participated in the increasingly illicit forms of female performance and makes one wonder whether Forbes' sketch (Figure 9.1 above) would have been different if he had taken performers' views into account. How many men would there be leering at her? Rather than attributing to her performance some irresistible and enchanting power, Dasi writes that the opposite was true, namely that her patrons seduced her, greedily searching for love. 'Deception' too seems to be an overt reference to the inauthenticity of performed emotions and their inapplicability outside the world of performance. These moments in Dasi's autobiography are a direct response to popular discourses about prostitutes acquiring wealth by ruining the lives of respectable men.[25] Dasi's autobiography, written as a series of letters to her teacher, is permeated with moments of role reversals in the encounter, posing questions like: who is seducing whom, who is the performer and who is the audience?

The autobiography also prompts an examination of 'authenticity' in emotions, especially in her comment about 'deception' above. 'Authenticity' is bound up in the pedagogic project of her tutor, Girish C. Ghosh, a Brahmin man who is regarded as a key figure in Bengali theatre and literary history.[26] For many early actresses in Bengal, such mentorship was indispensable to their success and prestige, serving both to provide them access to the stage and develop their careers but also to give them training in theatre, play analysis and acting. Ghosh, for example, encouraged Dasi to go and see other plays and then questioned and critiqued her opinions of those plays.[27] More importantly, Ghosh taught Dasi about bhāvas, or emotional states, in order to help her play them on stage, and Dasi often played more than one role (five on one occasion), which required her to quickly change her bhāvas.[28] Dasi's autobiography provides insight into the threat that actresses allegedly posed to society because they crossed social class and caste on stage, thus publicly revealing the artificiality of those divisions. In some ways, this speaks of a more vernacular version of 'the rule of colonial difference', marked less by race and overt bodily visibility. That is, even in her intracultural performances, she reveals the performative nature of class, caste and respectability. She blurs distinctions of 'authenticity' and 'inauthenticity', requiring those distinctions to be even more closely policed.

Role reversal, authenticity and seduction – Dasi's experiences are important because they attest most fully to new emotional regimes. Audiences and performers themselves envision a break between the inner and outer frames of the performance, gradually distancing the associated (outer) sexual economy from the emotional repertoire of the performance. Indeed, these are also associated with the development of the idea of an author-performer-artist. Labelling a work 'art' is a way to police the social boundaries that performance, by crossing boundaries, implicitly questions; it prevents the overflow from art and affects into society that was so essential for earlier colonial and pre-colonial governance.

Expressing through the Body: Ruth St Denis

Female performance never completely disappeared, even as a new intelligentsia consciously pushed it towards the edges of the emerging modern

Indian nation.[29] The early twentieth century witnessed a transformation of traditional female performers into professional artists, like Dasi herself. These transformations were (often) antithetical to the Indian milieu. Earlier female performance communities transferred their performance knowledges within 'different contexts of ownership and belonging' than the 'liberal logic of creative autonomy and authorial independence' that Rustom Bharucha has described for a different context.[30] The female performer, dubbed 'nautch girl', had become a topic of fiction and fantasy for Americans and Europeans during the course of the nineteenth century, and that fantasy often became a cause for Europeans and Americans to embark on their own, liberal, authorially independent projects.[31] In the Unites States of the early twentieth century, all classes were drawn to 'India' in the same manner as in the 1960s, namely as a 'collective fantasy'.[32] These fantasies and liberal-artistic appropriations were at the centre of Ruth St Denis' (1879–1968) oeuvre and the emergence of modern American dance. The purpose of this brief section is twofold: to place St Denis' work back into a long history of colonial contingency as well as to foreground what the 'Oriental' dance offered a Euro-American dancer in terms of bodily 'expressivity'.

Like many women of her time, St Denis had been trained in the Delsarte system of 'expression', a kind of manual of bodily posturing that was popular among middle- and upper-class white women in the late nineteenth century.[33] St Denis mentions that her mother occasionally gave her lessons in the technique, that a group of musicians dubbed her 'Delsarte', and that her first public performance (at age twelve) was billed as 'Lessons from Delsarte' rather than a 'dance'.[34] Why? St Denis writes: 'Outside of the perfunctory and at this time moribund ballet at the Metropolitan Opera, dancing consisted solely in the number of cartwheels, roll-overs and splits, kicks and other agilities that a dancer could achieve. Artists like Genevieve Stebbins appeared only occasionally'.[35] Such remarks casually indicate her frustration with a dance culture whose primary focus was on the mechanical, physical aspects of the body, rather than on any emotionally expressive potential, unlike Genevieve Stebbins, who had written about Delsarte. St Denis' entire practice seems to search for expressive potential through the body, rather than mechanical reproduction.[36] Briefly, 'mechanical' in this sense is akin to 'inauthentic' and performed, rather than authentic and sincere.

From such a background, Ruth St Denis saw Indian nautch in the Delhi Durbar exhibit at Coney Island, New York, in 1904/1905 and soon after followed a well-trod trail reaching all the way back to Sophia Plowden (see above). She writes: 'my whole attention was not captured until I came to an East Indian village.... Here, for the first time, I saw ... Nautch dancers ... the remarkable fascination of India caught hold of me. ... I had determined to create one or two Nautch dances, in imitation of these whirling skirted damsels'.[37] To be sure, these descriptions seem like clichés, but they were otherwise for St Denis. At the library, St Denis eventually stumbled upon devadasis – temple dancers, literally 'servants of the Gods' – and from there to Radha, the devotee and lover of Krishna. 'The beautiful symbology of Radha fascinated me.... [L]egends of Radha showed her sometimes in great ecstasy standing on the same lotus with her beloved and at other times wandering in a night of doubt and pride', writes St Denis.[38] She collected an assortment of people: 'Hindus, Moslems, Buddhists. Some were clerks from shops, some were students at Columbia, and one or two were unmistakable ne'er-do-wells', who all gave her feedback on her project.[39]

It is difficult to view St Denis' oeuvre outside of the paradigm of hegemonic intercultural theatre, 'a specific artistic genre and state of mind that combines First World capital and brainpower with Third World raw material and labor', and see her as anything other than an early practitioner of such theatre.[40] Her Indian collaborators recede into the background, literally and figuratively. Even though she toured with Inayat Khan, an eminent Sufi mystic, during her 1910–1911 tour from New York to San Francisco, he is never mentioned in her autobiography, just like the 'Hindus, Moslems, Buddhists' above (see Figure 9.2).[41]

Indeed, her intercultural encounters are premised on her imagination (state of mind) and appropriation (brainpower), with a cadre of 'Orientals' to lend her work an authentic air, similar to critiques levelled at contemporary directors like Robert Wilson.[42] These intercultural encounters, however, are not so different than the kinds of worlds inhabited by figures such as Anna Pavlova, Uday Shankar and Rukmini Devi – this international collaboration is the topic of at least a few recent volumes.[43] With St Denis, it is difficult to imagine her Radha, with all the details, without the assistance of those in the background and, as I have attempted to show here, the background and long history of performance in colonial India. Here, St Denis effectively transformed her experience as a spectator into a career as a performer, blurring the boundary between the audience and performer.

St Denis' travels to India in the 1920s with her husband, dancer Ted Shawn, reveal their real encounter with performers and traditions hitherto only imagined. Unlike Forbes' colonial memoirs, St Denis and Shawn were quite ignorant of nautch. Shawn writes:

> The *incongruity* of her getup was quickly overlooked when she [the dancer] did her bell tricks, playing any number up to ten separate from the rest. We

Figure 9.2 'Ruth St Denis with Native Hindus in Radha' (1906). Jerome Robbins Dance Division, The New York Public Library for the Performing Arts, Astor, Lenox and Tilden Foundations.

> requested that she play just three bells and *listened incredulous* to three separate and distinct bells chiming from ankles loaded with hundreds.[44]

Similarly, St Denis writes,

> It was all a *mystery* to us, but fascinating. Then, as we gazed at her in rapt attention, we fascinatedly watched those flying black swallows – her brows – carrying out in *some interior rhythm* the story of pursuit, retreat, and capture from the immortal Radha and Krishna love theme. Then dozens of little bells on her feet began a perfect cascade of sound as she did turns and half turns. Her whole body became an exclamation point to climax the preceding part of her tale, which she had been telling with her brows.[45]

Both of these descriptions from 18 January 1926 are neither as appreciative as early colonial memoirs nor as knowledgeable, even though her lack of understanding is not a barrier, as with Forbes's memoir above. With his comment about 'incongruity', one wonders what Shawn thought of St Denis' own 'getup'! More to the point, Shawn sees it as incongruous because it is new and real. St Denis' observations are contradictory too. How does she know the theme if it is all a 'mystery' with 'some' interior rhythm? Instead, these are encounters where her twenty-year Orientalist fascination supplies emotionally scripted content to compensate for the incomprehension of real encounter. Their training also seems insufficient to actually reproduce the dance. Shawn remarks that they tried 'unsuccessfully' to copy the nautch turns of a bazaar dancer, whom they tried to hire for a movie.[46] St Denis and Shawn also seem arrogant in the way they, as liberal-minded artists, expect to easily replicate the nautch, as though one kind of training easily translates in other contexts. In fact, in the many images of St Denis as Radha, it is clear that she wears bells on her feet – but in early videos, it is obvious that her movements lack a sophisticated use of them, music notwithstanding.[47] St Denis' relationship to Indian dance is a complex mix of actual and imaginary encounter, weighted towards the latter: before seeing the nautch described above, she wrote of the crowds along the Ganga: 'If twenty years before I had seen any such sight there would have been no *Radha*, and perhaps no career'.[48] While she began her career with the (by then) cliché trope of imagining India and Indian dance, her work and travels brought her into contact with actual artists of Indian dance, leaving her unsettled and confused about her earlier inspiration. Large portions of St Denis' encounter were about the way emotions were transformed as she attempted to comprehend a reality that she had previously only imagined.

Intercultural Performance after Postcolonialism?

Thus far, the narrative arc points towards contraction and then again expansion – a transfer of emotional knowledges – in the artists of Ruth St Denis' generation. The career of dance theatre artist Annette Leday (active since 1983) seems quite distant from the contexts above. However, Leday models the ways in which intercultural performance can be done in culturally sensitive, creative and exciting ways. Within the dance theatre world, Leday's jointly produced *Kathakali King Lear* (1989; KKL hereafter) comes towards the end of several important developments in intercultural performance, including the work of practitioners like Ruth St Denis. Many theatre personalities of the era after the Second World War were explicitly interested in and channelled not just Kathakali but various South, East and Southeast Asian forms to inspire their own work.[49] Eugenio Barba, Jerzy Grotowski, Peter Brook, Ariane Mnouchkine, Robert Wilson and others are the most well known of these practitioners, and all have been roundly critiqued for their mercenary use of other traditions, which has been labelled 'hegemonic intercultural theatre'.[50] The purpose here is not to repeat these critiques, but rather to offer an analysis of what happens when the encounter is less mercenary and designed to be open to exchange.[51]

Given the fact that Leday needed two to three years to complete each project, her work lends itself to deep exploration of cultural difference and cannot be called 'experimental' – a label she rejects.[52] For her, the process is a prolonged encounter, one that remains open to emotional transformations over a longer time period; indeed, she has worked with the same artists for several decades now. These lengthy projects lend themselves to the development of mutual trust and affection, both between French and Malayali performers, as well as between men and women.[53] For Leday, these elements are incredibly important during the rehearsal and research process. In particular, trust is important for her when dealing with the physicality of theatre. She points out: 'a sense of deep freedom to just be in contact, both looking and touching, for me is extraordinary . . . respect. These are the real emotions that help to enhance the artificial ones that come out in the performance, like anger, or love or desire'.[54]

Leday inaugurated her career with a now famous and much discussed staging of a Kathakali dance drama with the plot of *King Lear*, after having trained as a Kathakali artist for over four years with artists at two institutions in Kerala. KKL was a huge collaboration with David McRuvie and was 'realized under the guidance' of her two Kathakali teachers, Keezhpadam Kumaran Nair and C. Padmanabhan Nair.[55] It was initially staged in Thiruvananthapuram (Trivandrum), Kerala, and then in various locations in the Netherlands, France, Spain and the U.K. and was performed over seventy times. It received mixed reviews (some of which were mentioned at the beginning of this chapter). It was revived in 1999. However, perhaps the best proof of its success has been its ongoing ability to produce discussion, and its popular success has inspired similar productions of *Othello, Julius Caesar, Macbeth* and *El Cid*, among others.[56] Leday's work, however, is not limited to KKL. Over the past three decades, she has repeatedly collaborated with several artists who were part of KKL, most recently in *Mithuna*, or 'Gemini' (2015), a piece about the encounter of dance. This final case study revisits some of the responses and scholarship about KKL while also discussing Leday's theorizing of *Mithuna*. Leday's inaugural KKL explicitly demonstrates some of the challenges of translating emotions in the intercultural encounter. The adaptation of plot and character are particularly noteworthy, in addition to the actual rehearsal process and final staging.

Elements of plot and character present some of the most radical instances of the formal difficulties involved in staging the play, which was chosen, in part, because the 'great themes of *King Lear* – kingship and succession, marriage and the dowry, exile and renunciation of the world, the relation of man to man, man to nature and man to death – are already central to the Kathakali universe'. Furthermore, according to the artists, only in *Lear* does Shakespeare 'draw on a much earlier dramatic tradition of character-types. Lear is violent and vulnerable. . . . Goneril and Regan are evil and scheming; Cordelia is sensitive and virtuous'.[57] The similarities, however, end there. While both *Lear* and the form Kathakali are broadly contemporary – written/originating in the seventeenth century – the latter eschews complicated plots and 'human' drama, choosing to instead focus on the development of a simple (short) plot from a larger epic, elaborated through an expansive gestural vocabulary. Adapting the plot, therefore, was a complicated process, because it necessitated dealing with the nature of language and syntax and the demands of the genre.

David McRuvie prepared the script in accordance with Kathakali by completely removing the subplot with Gloucester and his two sons and reducing the action to nine scenes deemed 'essential'.[58] Lear's reconciliation with Cordelia and his death are most topical for this chapter. A substantial difficulty came in the fact that in Kathakali, actors do not speak: they elaborate the dialogue that is spoken or sung by two singers who are present on the stage. So the script not only had to be translated into Malayalam with the assistance of Kathakali dramatist Iyyamkode Sreedharan, its language also had to be adapted for singing and declamation. And, it had to be highly compressed. For instance, the Fool's singing 'has to sum up the whole discourse of the Fool', notes McRuvie.[59] Thus, with the plot redacted and the language simplified to give the 'sum' of the discursive potentialities, the script was ready for the actor-driven process of expanding the text through performance.

Expansion, too, proved tricky. From one point of view, the entire premise of King Lear seems like a farce: should not an aged king act with more dignity and know better? And if not, why is that tragic and not the workings of something more light-hearted?[60] These concerns seeped into actual character portrayals, and Lear, though a king, could not be the eponymous hero of the play, according to Kathakali formalism. As a result, France was cast as the traditional hero, while Lear's emotional instability gave him less than perfect royal attributes (such as violence and vulnerability), which found themselves represented by red face paint in addition to the traditional green reserved for heroic characters – a demotion of character that was clearly visible and comprehensible to the Malayali audiences. Similarly, the closest analogy for Goneril and Regan were demonesses, but actors viewed these two as 'selfish human beings capable of monstrous behavior, not as true demonesses', the result being that the portrayal turned them both into objects of humour in their overdetermined sexual overtures to France and of mock ferocity.[61] In many ways, these changes in plot and character undermined Shakespearean textual authority and privileged the virtuosity of performance instead. They also reached beyond a colonial episteme, in which Shakespeare, especially Shakespearean language, was fundamental to the creation of civilized (read: disciplined) subjects in the empire as well as in the United Kingdom.[62]

For the actors encountering *Lear* for the first time, developing the characters for KKL was vexing in yet another way, especially with regards to Kathakali actor training. During normal training (which requires four years), actors train in each and every role of the regular Kathakali repertoire of over twenty plays. They learn multiple characters inside out and are ready on short notice to stage any of those plays and play any character. Since the vocalists sing sections and create the dialogue, the actors playing characters 'only' improvise using their gestural vocabulary. But KKL was a completely new plot: in Kathakali, kings do not go mad and do not disgrace themselves, and there are no such characters as the Fool. Moreover, while characters grieve, and actors portray that grief, no character dies of grief alone. In Kathakali, characters only die when others kill them. How does one represent such a consuming grief within a repertoire that has no prior models to draw upon for it? If one has trained by learning all the parts in every play in order to easily step into a role without too much preparation, then one does not need to rehearse – and indeed, the concept of a rehearsal as such was new to actors at the Kerala Kalamandalam.[63]

As a new concept, rehearsing upset the normal hierarchies of the Kalamandalam, at least in some ways. Instead of senior artists elaborating roles in basic ways while students watched, Leday mentions that it was quite the reverse. David McRuvie had to give extensive notes and information to artists on the background of the play, its history and sources, and its context within the Shakespearean repertoire and canonical Western literature. The problems of the play had to be explained and understood. Indeed, actors had to render the alien, illogical plot into something that could be represented and understood. Leday mentions that to begin with, the junior artists began to elaborate the characters while many senior artists watched and commented. More than that, all the artists had to become students – a humbling reversion indeed, which would have been impossible without the time required to gain trust and develop affection and respect. The junior artists framed the many characters for most of the rehearsal process, giving the senior artists a sense of their characters. It was only later that many senior artists began to rehearse their own parts, and it was only then that the characters started to take on their 'full dimension'.[64] But this role reversal had yet another interesting effect: it quickly enabled junior artists to make KKL part of their newly expanded repertoire.

Reactions to these productions also evince a kind of tension, akin to the kinds mentioned above with music and Forbes' memoirs. Zarrilli, citing Ronald Inden, suggests that much like the Orientalists and Romanticists of the nineteenth century, the 'Western' responses to KKL primarily conformed to one of two standard Orientalist tropes – the other as absolutely different/unchangeable, or the other as spiritual/ideal.[65] Malayali and other Indian connoisseurs, meanwhile, emphasized the unsuitability of human drama for a form that is based on epic characters that only exist in the imagination.[66] Suresh Awasthi, former chair of the National School of Drama, seemed at least slightly miffed by the vacuous reviews of the production before he launched into his own view of 'The Aesthetic Violations in *King Lear*'.[67] However, Zarrilli suggests that two scenes were easily registered for multiple audiences, suggesting that not all of it was about the absolute differences between the two traditions and that there was some aspect that was translatable and communicable. First, scene seven, in which Lear and Cordelia reconcile, was a moment during which for the Malayali audience Lear successfully 'remembered' and awoke from his 'dreamlike state of forgetfulness' to Cordelia and the Fool, remembering his status as a king and once again donning his crown.[68] The contrast with the fully costumed Cordelia is significant – only a character fully conscious of his kingly self can fully be a king and represent himself as such with all the symbolic external appurtenances of costume. With the Fool, class marks him differently than Lear and Cordelia. Lear's grief over Cordelia dying was the second scenario, which one (Western) critic described as 'a frightening and uninterrupted moment of agonized theatrical communication', even though that same critic had been coolly distant for the rest of the production.[69] In the first case, the reconciliation of Cordelia and Lear functioned along the lines of classical Indian aesthetics, in which memory is 'an act of reception that resonates long beyond the immediate apprehension of the five senses'. Since the senses leave latent impressions on the mind, and memory 'awakens' those latent impressions, the seventh scene enabled an imaginative process of relating. Moreover, it reminded the Malayali audience of a similar scenario of reflection from the Kathakali repertoire. For the Western audience, this scene makes tragedy possible because Lear finally recognizes his loss.[70]

As mentioned earlier, Kathakali actors do not speak but elaborate the spoken text of the singers through their extensive gestural vocabulary, which includes *hastamudras* (hand-gestures) and *abhinayas* (facial expressions). In addition to gestures with a 'theatrical dimension' (hugging, begging, rejection, protection, etc.), the hastamudras include imitation of the thing itself (tears, animals, weapons), abstract concepts (kingdom, lie, life, death) and even grammatical structures (pronouns, the past, the future, the conditional, belonging, causality, etc.). These take the place of speech, and certainly for high-ranking characters, gesture supplants speech. In Kathakali, gesture is a highly coded system of communication with a closer analogy to sign language than 'normative' concepts of gesture. And yet, Lear has already shown himself disgraced – even from the beginning he has red face paint in addition to green. Thus, he is neither the hero of the play, nor of the stature of a 'true' king. The actor who played him, C.P. Nair, used this demoted position of Lear to utter a cry and break gestural representation, which (apparently) resounded across the Kathakali form and into the ears of Western audiences: a frightening moment of agonized theatrical communication, wherein a character hitherto silent cried his swan song. Raw visceral grief extended between the two forms, successfully legible for multiple audiences.

Other reviewers had still different opinions, but one seems especially significant because it demonstrates an epistemic failure. One reviewer mentioned that KKL strips Lear of his 'Western psychology' (characters lose their 'depth'), which is ironically analogous to Kathakali actors and critics who complained that Shakespeare's characters are shallow![71] Such remarks register at the heart of the problem of translating the performance aesthetics: what is professed as psychological and emotional depth in one context is taken to be shallow in another. What gives characters their depth? Rachel Halliburton suggests that Kathakali 'deviates from Western concepts by ignoring character development and instead creating a striking theatre of types'.[72] Halliburton thinks Western character development is incompatible with the 'extreme moods of Lear' in the KKL production, though I think even any high school student would readily submit that Lear is Lear precisely because of his extreme moods, and it is precisely an extreme mood that sets off the action of the play. But Kathakali artists suggested that these characters are shallow precisely because they do not have background stories – that they occur only once or twice in literature and are not 'types'! That is, according to the Kathakali artists, how can a character have psychological depth if she/he is only part of one text rather than endlessly discussed as with the recurrent characters in Indian epic traditions? In other words, from an Indian perspective, purported 'originality' is precisely what makes the characters in *Lear* 'shallow'. And furthermore, given that Lear was drawn by Shakespeare from a historical source, how can characters with a known real existence have depth? Only characters known to be from and of the imagination (epic characters) can be successfully and completely developed, giving the artist free reign to interpret for two hours – or twenty![73] Western reviews demonstrate epistemological blind spots, as do the responses of the Kathakali artists to Western aesthetic forms. The performance itself tackles these blind spots through the two aforementioned moments when emotions registered across multiple audiences.

Costuming above, in Figure 9.3, raises one more question that is not discussed in the literature elsewhere. Not only did the production forge new interpretations of *Lear* (and Kathakali). It also expanded who could play Lear, rejecting the stale and standard casting of Lear. For example, a persistent way to stage Lear has been with an actor in his fifties or sixties – the role demands a lot. But as spectators, we are to imagine that Lear is eighty-four years old. Being the right age is crucial – but the right age is not, certainly, Lear's age, as Jonathan Bate and Elinor Fuchs have pointed out.[74] Laurence Olivier, for example, 'tried both too soon and too late: on the stage in 1946, still in his thirties, he seemed to be impersonating a whimsical old tyrant rather than actually being one, while on television in 1983, he was too frail for the rage'.[75] By contrast, Kathakali actors have an entirely different relation to their bodies. Leday notes that 'age' has become a topic of interest for dance in the past few years, but elderly actors have always been part of the Kathakali repertoire.[76] In fact, in the first few productions, two actors played Lear, one in his late seventies (C. Padmanabhan Nair) and one in his mid eighties (K. Kumaran Nair), with the 'younger' of the two taking over for the entire show as they travelled. Indeed, the facticity of old bodies staging old characters asks us to rethink our assumptions about realist theatre as a form: Kathakali is non-realist, and yet its casting is; Shakespeare is often not realistic and yet is staged predominantly in realistic ways. How do formal staging techniques mask or reveal bodies to alter our emotional responses? Are we allergic to actual elderly performers playing Lear? Perhaps realist drama does not do formal justice to old bodies.

Ultimately, KKL was an incredibly generative production, with critics, scholars, audiences and actors all tested through the intercultural performance-encounter. These conversations tackled many aspects of the production, some of which are presented above. W.B. Worthen's academic response needs mentioning: he says that the production simply confirmed the hierarchies of 'authority and authorization' by pointing to the absent original – *King Lear* or Kathakali – rather than testing these hierarchies.[77] This position – convincingly critiqued by many scholars – fundamentally seems to omit the long history of colonial intercultural practices that has been elucidated above. The displacement of the colonial text – Shakespeare and language, in this case – is especially significant in this regard.[78] KKL created a truly 'bi-lingual' performance using multiple grammars of performance that were not always compatible, replacing the 'scripts' of colonialism with bi-directional flows.

Figure 9.3 'Before Lear's Death'. Courtesy of Annette Leday.

One reviewer writes candidly: 'Having seen King Lear in an oriental transformation, I looked forward to seeing the Renaissance Theatre Company's *King Lear* in the same week. But alas, comparisons are odorous. Kenneth Branagh's production is brisk, old-fashioned, and dreary'.[79] Moments such as these, placed back within the context of spectatorial response and the difficulties of staging, instead suggest that with KKL, both *King Lear* and Kathakali saw their repertoires expanded – audiences were broken out of their culturally scripted emotional straightjackets. While certain 'universals' could be communicated, the majority of the production 'tested the condition[s] of performance'.[80] By testing, it ultimately changed them too. It hardly seems fitting to say that a silent Lear, who breaks only in the final scene, is 'conservative'. Rather than pointing to the absent authorities of *King Lear* and Kathakali, this production pointed to an absence within those authorities – the absent relationship. In making that connection, this encounter thus expanded the possibilities of *King Lear* and Kathakali. Reflecting on her career and on the recent *Mithuna*, Leday mentions:

> encounter cannot go without separation because we are definitely separated, we are culturally, linguistically, geographically, you name it, separated. We are completely from different horizons, different types of bodies, different techniques, different approaches and mentalities, emotional approaches. . . . And the singularity of this company is that even though we are definitely separated, in terms of geography, but also in terms of time – sometimes we have a long gaps – so for me encounter is the moment where we get together out of this separation, for me encounters are unique moments where we get together to create, to create meaning out of strange entities and strange separated entities . . . and I suppose in a situation like this, when separation is the basic background, encounters take more importance and more emphasis, and more meaning.[81]

The many ways in which these meanings are highly emotional for both performers and audiences – in the rehearsal room (how can grief and madness be portrayed, who is the student, who is the master? Trust, affection, respect), in the audience (a silent Lear cries but once, how can grief be communicated, what gives characters psychological depth?) – is what the descriptions above have sought to portray.

* * *

Performance, as a supramundane form of encounter, is indeed intimately invested in all forms of encounter, certainly during the colonial era and often as a form of soft diplomacy after. In roughly contemporary practice, cross-cultural performances offer aesthetic (affective/emotional) possibilities not commonly found within one's home 'culture' and participate in an economy of expanding emotional repertoires, sometimes jarring but also often from within relatively safe, contained spaces. These are sites that are no less or no more artificial than diplomatic protocols, the considerations of military occupants, or the way even missionaries, lovers and others may plan out their encounters, often to no avail as the actual event may take an unexpected turn. And so too we cannot perfectly anticipate how the performance will play out, so to speak, and offer, still, less than perfect hindsight on matters related to performers, their performances and the many emotions in circulation at different sites of encounter. Officials for the East India Company adopted the connoisseurship practices of Indian princes and aristocrats out of political and social necessity and deployed them for diplomatic leverage; Ruth St Denis sought a spiritual – though highly Orientalist and unselfconscious – version of dance for her career. In doing so, both parties were able to move beyond the limitations of their own social positions and limited artistic exposure, as in St Denis' case. At the same time, Annette Leday's practice undoes some of the colonial and Orientalist baggage that is present in the history of intercultural performance. Her collaborators are collaborators as such, and there is a sense of an equal give and take that avoids practices of cultural appropriation, especially given the different contexts of 'ownership and belonging' that were described above. It also creates new interpretations for *Lear* and makes available new repertoires for Kathakali. The intercultural performance-encounter thus seeks, at its best, an expansion in emotional scripts: in 'Lapis Lazuli', W.B. Yeats writes that tragedy is wrought to its uttermost, and 'Though Hamlet rambles and Lear rages, / And all the drop scenes drop at once / Upon a hundred thousand stages, / It cannot grow by an inch or an ounce'.[82] And yet, as we see, when *Lear* meets Kathakali, both grow in unexpected and stimulating ways.

Kedar A. Kulkarni is Assistant Professor of Literary and Cultural Studies at FLAME, in Pune, India. Recently, he co-edited a special issue of *Nineteenth Century Theatre and Film*, 'Beyond the Playhouse: Travelling Theatre in the Long Nineteenth Century' that considers multiple theatrical networks in light of recent work on world literature and global history.

Notes

1. Harding, *The Ghosts of the Avant-Garde(s): Exorcising Experimental Theater and Performance*, 116; Zarrilli, 'For Whom is the King a King? Issues of Intercultural Production, Perception, and Reception in a Kathakali King Lear', 128.

2. Billington, 'Empty Gestures of a Frustrating Lear: Michael Billington Welcomes a Kathakali Shakespeare but Wonders about the Meaning behind the Spectacle', 28; Gardner, 'Courting Monotony; Kathakali King Lear, Globe, London', A19; Kingston, 'India's Lear is Green and Dotty', 41; Zarrilli, 'For Whom', 126.
3. Zarrilli, 'For Whom', 119.
4. Zarrilli notes that there are four different ways a performance can be perceived: via a spectator's cultural assumptions, through similar performance experiences in the past, expectation created by publicity and what happens in the frame of the performance itself, during the performance itself; Zarrilli, 'For Whom', 116.
5. Butler Brown, 'The Social Liminality of Musicians: Case Studies from the Mughal India and Beyond', 13–49; Ghosh, 'Decoding the Nameless: Gender, Subjectivity, and Historical Methodologies in Reading the Archives of Colonial India', 297–316.
6. Sachdeva, 'In Search of the Tawa'if in History: Courtesans, Nautch Girls and Celebrity Entertainers in India', 72, 139–40.
7. Straub, *Sexual Suspects: Eighteenth-Century Players and Sexual Ideology*.
8. Forbes, *Oriental Memoirs: Selected from a Series of Familiar Letters Written during Seventeen Years Residence in India*, 82.
9. Forbes, *Oriental Memoirs*, 81.
10. Woodfield, *Music of the Raj: A Social and Economic History of Music in Late Eighteenth-Century Anglo-Indian Society*, 175.
11. Woodfield, *Music of the Raj*, 174 (Warren Hastings to Margaret Fowke, 9 January 1785).
12. See Chapter 5, Frevert, 'Diplomats' in this volume.
13. Woodfield, *Music of the Raj*, 170.
14. Woodfield, *Music of the Raj*, 149–80.
15. British Library, OIOC Plowden MS B187.
16. Nevile, *Nautch Girls of the Raj*, 33.
17. Kushari Dyson, *A Various Universe: A Study of the Journals and Memoirs of British Men and Women in the Indian Subcontinent, 1765–1856*, 348; Ghose, *Women Travellers in Colonial India: The Power of the Female Gaze*.
18. Teltscher, *India Inscribed: European and British Writing on India, 1600–1800*, 35–39; Butler Brown, 'Social Liminality of Musicians', 13–49; Ghosh, *Sex and the Family in Colonial India: The Making of Empire*.
19. Banerjee, 'The "Beshya" and the "Babu": Prostitute and Her Clientele in 19th Century Bengal', 2464.
20. Postans, *Western India in 1838: In Two Volumes*, 198. See also Chapter 6, P. Nielsen, 'Occupiers and Civilians' in this volume.
21. See, for example, Dang, 'Prostitutes, Patrons and the State: Nineteenth Century Awadh', 173–96; Levine, 'Venereal Disease, Prostitution, and the Politics of Empire: The Case of British India', 579–602; Levine, 'Orientalist Sociology and the Creation of Colonial Sexualities', 5–21. Some of these themes are also covered in Chapter 10, M. Pernau, 'Lovers and Friends' in this volume.
22. See Aamir Mufti, via M.H. Abram and Raymond Schwab, on William Jones and Johann Gottfried Herder: Mufti, *Forget English! Orientalisms and World Literatures*, 56–145.
23. Dāsī, *My Story*, 61.
24. Dāsī, *My Story*, 85–86.
25. Banerjee, '"Beshya" and the "Babu"', 2467–69.
26. Chatterjee, *The Colonial Staged: Theatre in Colonial Calcutta*.
27. Bhattacharya, '"Public Women": Early Actresses of the Bengali Stage – Role and Reality', 152.
28. Bhattacharya, 'Public Women', 154.
29. Morcom, *Illicit Worlds of Indian Dance: Cultures of Exclusion*, 1–30.

30. Bharucha, 'Hauntings of the Intercultural: Enigmas and Lessons on the Borders of Failure', 191.
31. Coorlawala, 'Ruth St. Denis and India's Dance Renaissance', 123–52; Erdman, 'Dance Discourses: Rethinking the History of the "Oriental Dance"', 288–305; Sherman, *Denishawn: The Enduring Influence*; Spear and Meduri, 'Knowing the Dancer: East Meets West', 435–48; Teo, 'Women's Travel, Dance, and British Metropolitan Anxieties, 1890–1939', 366–400.
32. Bald, *Bengali Harlem and the Lost Histories of South Asian America*, 16–19.
33. Suter, 'Living Pictures, Living Memory: Women's Rhetorical Silence within the American Delsarte Movement', 94.
34. St Denis, *Ruth St. Denis*, 7–14.
35. St Denis, *Ruth St. Denis*, 21.
36. Miller, *Wisdom Comes Dancing: Selected Writings of Ruth St. Denis on Dance, Spirituality, and the Body*, 19; Shelton, *Divine Dancer: A Biography of Ruth St. Denis*, 11.
37. St Denis, *Ruth St. Denis*, 55.
38. St Denis, *Ruth St. Denis*, 57.
39. St Denis, *Ruth St. Denis*, 56.
40. Lei, 'Interruption, Intervention, Interculturalism: Robert Wilson's HIT Productions in Taiwan', 571.
41. De Jong-Keesing, *Inayat Khan: A Biography*, 91–95; Schlundt, *The Professional Appearances of Ruth St. Denis & Ted Shawn: A Chronology and an Index of Dances, 1906–1932*, 15–16; St Denis, *Ruth St. Denis*, 131–55.
42. Lei, 'Interruption, Intervention, Interculturalism', 571–86.
43. See, for example, Purkayastha, *Indian Modern Dance, Feminism and Transnationalism*; Srinivasan, *Sweating Saris: Indian Dance as Transnational Labor*.
44. Shawn and Poole, *One Thousand and One Night Stands*, 181, emphasis added.
45. St Denis, *Ruth St. Denis*, 286, emphasis added.
46. Shawn and Poole, *One Thousand*, 182.
47. 'Ruth St Denis in the *East Indian Nautch Dance* (1932)'.
48. St Denis, *Ruth St. Denis*, 286.
49. Pavis, *The Intercultural Performance Reader*.
50. I cite two examples here: Bharucha, *Theatre and the World: Performance and the Politics of Culture*; Lei, 'Interruption, Intervention, Interculturalism', 571–86
51. See Fischer-Lichte, 'Introduction: Interweaving Performing Cultures – Rethinking "Intercultural Theatre": Toward an Experience and Theory of Performance beyond Postcolonialism', 1–21.
52. Annette Leday, interview by the author (23 June 2015).
53. Annette Leday, interview by the author (29 June 2015).
54. Annette Leday, interview by the author (29 June 2015).
55. Daugherty, 'The Pendulum of Intercultural Performance: Kathakali King Lear at Shakespeare's Globe', 57.
56. Daugherty, 'Pendulum of Intercultural Performance', 67.
57. McRuvie, *Kathakali – King Lear, William Shakespeare*, 7.
58. McRuvie, *Kathakali – King Lear*, 21.
59. Daugherty, 'Pendulum of Intercultural Performance', 58.
60. Zarrilli, 'For Whom', 128.
61. Daugherty, 'Pendulum of Intercultural Performance', 60–61.
62. Macaulay, 'Indian Education: Minute of the 2nd of February, 1835', 719–30; Viswanathan, *Masks of Conquest: Literary Study and British Rule in India*.
63. Annette Leday, interview by the author (23 June 2015).
64. Annette Leday, interview by the author (23 June 2015).
65. Zarrilli, 'For Whom', 119.

66. See Zarrilli, 'For Whom', 121–24. Zarrilli provides one view from the noted critic Appakoothann Nayar that contains an extended explanation of his displeasure.
67. Awasthi, 'The Intercultural Experience and the Kathakali "King Lear"', 172, 176–77.
68. Zarrilli, 'For Whom', 127; Daugherty, 'Pendulum of Intercultural Performance', 65.
69. Zarrilli, 'For Whom', 126.
70. Zarrilli, 'For Whom', 122.
71. Daugherty, 'Pendulum of Intercultural Performance', 65; Gardner, 'Courting Monotony', A19; Halliburton, 'Theatre: India Plays England at the Globe: A Kathakali Company is Staging King Lear', *Independent* (7 July 1999).
72. Halliburton, 'Theatre'.
73. Zarrilli, 'For Whom', 124.
74. Bate, 'What Makes a Great King Lear?', *The Telegraph* (8 December 2010); Fuchs, 'Interdisciplinary Performance Studies at Yale: December 3 – Elinor Fuchs'.
75. Bate, 'What Makes a Great King Lear?'.
76. Annette Leday, interview by the author (29 June 2015).
77. Worthen, 'Disciplines of the Text/Sites of Performance', *TDR* 39(1) (1995), 20.
78. See note 62.
79. Peter, 'A Ritual Lear through an Eastern Eye', *Sunday Times* (19 August 1990).
80. Worthen, Disciplines of the Text/Sites of Performance', 20.
81. Annette Leday, interview by the author (29 June 2015).
82. Yeats, 'Lapis Lazuli', 179.

Bibliography

Awasthi, S. 'The Intercultural Experience and the Kathakali "King Lear"'. *New Theatre Quarterly* 9(34) (1993), 172–78, doi: 10.1017/S0266464X00007752.

Bald, V. *Bengali Harlem and the Lost Histories of South Asian America*. Cambridge, MA: Harvard University Press, 2013.

Banerjee, S. 'The "Beshya" and the "Babu": Prostitute and Her Clientele in 19th Century Bengal'. *Economic and Political Weekly* 28(45) (1993), 2461–72.

Bate, J. 'What Makes a Great King Lear?'. *The Telegraph* (8 December 2010). Retrieved 1 August 2016 from http://www.telegraph.co.uk/culture/theatre/8189890/What-makes-a-great-King-Lear.html.

Bharucha, R. *Theatre and the World: Performance and the Politics of Culture*. London: Routledge, 1993.

———. 'Hauntings of the Intercultural: Enigmas and Lessons on the Borders of Failure', in E. Fischer-Lichte, T. Jost and S.I. Jain (eds), *The Politics of Interweaving Performance Cultures: Beyond Postcolonialism* (New York: Routledge, 2014), 179–200.

Bhattacharya, R. '"Public Women": Early Actresses of the Bengali Stage – Role and Reality'. *India International Centre Quarterly*, 17(3/4) (1990), 142–69.

Billington, M. 'Empty Gestures of a Frustrating Lear: Michael Billington Welcomes a Kathakali Shakespeare but Wonders about the Meaning behind the Spectacle'. *The Guardian* (17 August 1990), 28.

Butler Brown, K. 'The Social Liminality of Musicians: Case Studies from the Mughal India and Beyond'. *Twentieth-Century Music* 3(1) (2006), 13–49, doi: 10.1017/S147857220700031X.

Chatterjee, S. *The Colonial Staged: Theatre in Colonial Calcutta*. London: Seagull Books, 2007.
Coorlawala, U.A. 'Ruth St. Denis and India's Dance Renaissance'. *Dance Chronicle* 15(2) (1992), 123–52.
Dang, K. 'Prostitutes, Patrons and the State: Nineteenth Century Awadh'. *Social Scientist* 21(9/11) (1993), 173–96, doi: 10.2307/3520432.
Dāsī, B. *My Story and My Life as an Actress*, ed. and trans. R. Bhattacharya. New Delhi: Kali for Women, 1998.
Daugherty, D. 'The Pendulum of Intercultural Performance: Kathakali King Lear at Shakespeare's Globe'. *Asian Theatre Journal* 22(1) (2005), 52–72.
De Jong-Keesing, E. *Inayat Khan: A Biography*. The Hague: East-West Publications Fonds B.V., 1974.
Erdman, J.L. 'Dance Discourses: Rethinking the History of the "Oriental Dance"', in G. Morris (ed.), *Moving Words: Re-Writing Dance* (London: Routledge, 1996), 288–305.
Fischer-Lichte, E. 'Introduction: Interweaving Performing Cultures – Rethinking "Intercultural Theatre": Toward an Experience and Theory of Performance beyond Postcolonialism', in E. Fischer-Lichte, T. Jost and S.I. Jain (eds), *The Politics of Interweaving Performance Cultures: Beyond Postcolonialism* (New York: Routledge, 2014), 1–21.
Forbes, J. *Oriental Memoirs: Selected from a Series of Familiar Letters Written during Seventeen Years Residence in India*, Vol. 1. Delhi: Gian, 1988.
Fuchs, E. 'Interdisciplinary Performance Studies at Yale: December 3 – Elinor Fuchs'. *Interdisciplinary Performance Studies at Yale*. Retrieved 10 March 2016 from http://campuspress.yale.edu/ipsy/december-3-elinor-fuchs/.
Gardner, L. 'Courting Monotony; Kathakali King Lear, Globe, London'. *The Guardian* (8 July 1999), A19.
Ghose, I. *Women Travellers in Colonial India: The Power of the Female Gaze*. Delhi: Oxford University Press, 1998.
Ghosh, D. 'Decoding the Nameless: Gender, Subjectivity, and Historical Methodologies in Reading the Archives of Colonial India', in K. Wilson (ed.), *A New Imperial History: Culture, Identity, and Modernity in Britain and the Empire, 1660–1840* (Cambridge: Cambridge University Press, 2004), 297–316.
_____. *Sex and the Family in Colonial India: The Making of Empire*. Cambridge: Cambridge University Press, 2006.
Halliburton, R. 'Theatre: India Plays England at the Globe: A Kathakali Company is Staging King Lear'. *Independent* (7 July 1999). Retrieved 17 February 2016 from http://www.independent.co.uk/arts-entertainment/theatre-india-plays-england-at-the-globe-1104785.html.
Harding, J.M. *The Ghosts of the Avant-Garde(s): Exorcising Experimental Theater and Performance*. Ann Arbor: University of Michigan Press, 2013.
Kingston, J. 'India's Lear is Green and Dotty'. *The Times* (13 July 1999), 41.
Kushari Dyson, K. *A Various Universe: A Study of the Journals and Memoirs of British Men and Women in the Indian Subcontinent, 1765–1856*. New Delhi: Oxford University Press, 2006.

Lei, D.P. 'Interruption, Intervention, Interculturalism: Robert Wilson's HIT Productions in Taiwan'. *Theatre Journal* 63(4) (2011), 571–86, doi: 10.1353/tj.2011.0118.

Levine, P. 'Venereal Disease, Prostitution, and the Politics of Empire: The Case of British India'. *Journal of the History of Sexuality* 4(4) (1994), 579–602.

_____. 'Orientalist Sociology and the Creation of Colonial Sexualities'. *Feminist Review* 65 (2000), 5–21.

Macaulay, T.B. 'Indian Education: Minute of the 2nd of February, 1835', in T.B. Macaulay, *Prose and Poetry*, selected by G.M. Young (Cambridge, MA: Harvard University Press, 1952), 719–30.

McRuvie, D. *Kathakali – King Lear, William Shakespeare*. Paris: Association Keli, 1989.

Miller, K.A. *Wisdom Comes Dancing: Selected Writings of Ruth St. Denis on Dance, Spirituality, and the Body*. Seattle, WA: PeaceWorks, 1997.

Morcom, A. *Illicit Worlds of Indian Dance: Cultures of Exclusion*. Oxford: Oxford University Press, 2013.

Mufti, A.R. *Forget English! Orientalisms and World Literatures*. Cambridge, MA: Harvard University Press, 2016.

Nevile, P. *Nautch Girls of the Raj*. New Delhi: Penguin Books, 2009.

Pavis, P. (ed.). *The Intercultural Performance Reader*. London: Routledge, 1996.

Peter, J. 'A Ritual Lear through an Eastern Eye'. *Sunday Times* (19 August 1990).

Postans, Mrs. [M.]. *Western India in 1838: In Two Volumes*. London: Saunders & Otley, 1839.

Purkayastha, P. *Indian Modern Dance, Feminism and Transnationalism*. Houndsmills: Palgrave Macmillan, 2014.

'Ruth St Denis in the *East Indian Nautch Dance* (1932)'. Retrieved 28 July 2016 from https://www.youtube.com/watch?v=T8mVKL4RHxg&index=1&list=PLbdTnx8lvyebK0W9l-Nd49EihtE9ApYNF.

Sachdeva, S. 'In Search of the Tawa'if in History: Courtesans, Nautch Girls and Celebrity Entertainers in India'. Ph.D. dissertation. London: School of Oriental and African Studies, University of London, 2008.

Schlundt, C.L. *The Professional Appearances of Ruth St. Denis & Ted Shawn: A Chronology and an Index of Dances, 1906–1932*. New York: New York Public Library, 1962.

Shawn, T., and G. Poole. *One Thousand and One Night Stands*. Garden City, NJ: Doubleday, 1960.

Shelton, S. *Divine Dancer: A Biography of Ruth St. Denis*. Garden City: Doubleday, 1981.

Sherman, J. *Denishawn: The Enduring Influence*. Boston: Twayne, 1983.

Spear, J.L., and A. Meduri. 'Knowing the Dancer: East Meets West'. *Victorian Literature and Culture* 32(2) (2004), 435–48, doi: 10.1017.s1060150304000580.

Srinivasan, P. *Sweating Saris: Indian Dance as Transnational Labor*. Philadelphia, PA: Temple University Press, 2012.

St Denis, R. *Ruth St. Denis, an Unfinished Life: An Autobiography*. London: Harrap, [1940].

Straub, K. *Sexual Suspects: Eighteenth-Century Players and Sexual Ideology*. Princeton, NJ: Princeton University Press, 1992.

Suter, L. 'Living Pictures, Living Memory: Women's Rhetorical Silence within the American Delsarte Movement', in C. Glenn and K. Ratcliffe (eds), *Silence and Listening as Rhetorical Arts* (Carbondale: Southern Illinois University Press, 2011), 94–110.

Teltscher, K. *India Inscribed: European and British Writing on India, 1600–1800*. Delhi: Oxford University Press, 1995.

Teo, H.-M. 'Women's Travel, Dance, and British Metropolitan Anxieties, 1890–1939'. *Gender & History* 12(2) (2000), 366–400, doi: 10.1111/1468-0424.00188.

Viswanathan, G. *Masks of Conquest: Literary Study and British Rule in India*. New York: Columbia University Press, 1989.

Woodfield, I. *Music of the Raj: A Social and Economic History of Music in Late Eighteenth-Century Anglo-Indian Society*. Oxford: Oxford University Press, 2000.

Worthen, W.B. 'Disciplines of the Text/Sites of Performance'. *TDR* 39(1) (1995), 13–28, doi: 10.2307/1146399.

Yeats, W.B. 'Lapis Lazuli', in W.B. Yeats, *Selected Poems and Four Plays of William Butler Yeats*, ed. M. L. Rosenthal, 4th edn (New York: Scribner, 1996), 179–80.

Zarrilli, P.B. 'For Whom is the King a King? Issues of Intercultural Production, Perception, and Reception in a Kathakali King Lear', in J.G. Reinelt and J.R. Roach (eds), *Critical Theory and Performance*, rev. and enl. edn (Ann Arbor: University of Michigan Press, 2010), 108–33.

Chapter 10

Lovers and Friends
Encounters of Hearts and Bodies

Margrit Pernau

> My name is Lauren Mokasdar and I left my life in England and moved to India to be with the man I love, a man I met online. Since moving to India, I have become stronger, healthier and more aware of my spirituality. It hasn't always been easy but I hope sharing my experiences, epiphanies and failures will help and/or entertain you, maybe even inspire you to follow your own heart.
> —L. Mokasdar, *English Wife, Indian Life*

Since 2013, Lauren Mokasdar has been posting a weekly blog on her encounter with the man she married three months after meeting him on an internet platform on vegetarianism. Although their first encounter was as mediated as could be – they were separated by several thousand kilometres distance, could neither see nor hear each other and communicated only by typing – theirs was an immediate connection: 'Instantly my heart started to beat faster and we were discussing everything about our lives in detail. It just felt as if we had known each other since the beginning of time'.[1] Communication between the spouses continued to be unproblematic, a fact that Lauren Mokasdar gratefully attributes to their divine partnership being ordained by fate. The feeling of bliss India first evoked in her, however, became much more nuanced over time. Upon her arrival in India, she modelled herself on the image of the dutiful Indian wife, from dressing in a sari to participating in all the religious festivals and living with her in-laws. Her certitude that this had earned her the unconditional love of her mother-in-law broke down during her wedding, when

---

Notes for this chapter begin on page 278.

the mehndi painters, providing henna decorations for festive occasions, revealed that they had been instructed to give her only an ordinary and not a bridal painting and said that her mother-in-law spoke of her with hate. The lovers' effortless reading of emotions across the cultural divide apparently did not extend to their families. By 2015, the young couple had moved out of the parental home, and Lauren has also become the centre of a whole internet circle of young women with similar experiences and is currently writing a book on the topic.

This vignette brings to the fore three central claims advanced in this chapter: first, the script for love and encounter premediates the first meeting and forms the basis for its interpretation. In Lauren Mokasdar's case, this would be the notion of love at first sight (or rather at first mouse click), of spouses meeting again incarnation after incarnation, of the power of love to overcome all differences, but also of India as a place of deep spirituality and healing power. Second, encounters use intersectionality in their negotiation of difference.[2] Not every category of difference points in the same direction; and not all are endowed with the same importance by the lovers: the cultural difference between an English wife and her Indian husband is bridged by a common spirituality and shared religious practices, from vegetarianism to visits to temples and a veneration of the same gods. Third, the romantic interpretation of love focuses on two individuals and their emotions for each other. These emotions, however, do not occur in a world apart: family, friends, neighbours and colleagues form part of a network of emotions, which are intertwined with the lovers' feelings and shape them.

This chapter's aim is to complicate the category of love. To limit its scope to heterosexual relations leading to sex and marriage would presuppose a stability of emotions, practices and institutions, which does not take into account the much messier and plural realities of encounters between the hearts and bodies of Europeans and Indians since the eighteenth century. The chapter therefore begins with the relation of Englishmen and their Indian companions in eighteenth-century Calcutta, which often began as a negotiated contract for sex and housekeeping but in a number of cases ended in a lifelong affective engagement. While mixed-race relations were ostracized in the nineteenth century, at the turn of the twentieth century marriages of white women to Oriental princes became a glamorous topic, equally taken up by the press, films and novels, the topic of the second section. At the same time, male friendships – marked by erotic desire or not – began crossing the racial divide; this will be discussed in the third section. It is only in the second half of the twentieth century, the time frame of the last section, that love came to mean a relationship that necessarily brought together romance and sex, involving both hearts and bodies but no longer always ending in marriage.

Each section will encompass a central and a minor and contrasting case study, to bring out the wide range of possibilities even the same type of love at the same time and place still allowed for. Taking up approaches that have brought together intimacy and colonialism in the last fifteen years, the aim of the chapter is to move beyond unidirectional claims of social context, power relations and emotions. Premediation and social structures impacted the possibilities for emotions of love and friendship to be played out and even felt, but they did not determine them; feelings of love and intimacy, however, were not only private and individual but also central for the creation of colonial and postcolonial categories of difference and their enactment.[3]

Colonial Officers and Their *Bibis*

When Richard Blechynden, an architect who had since 1782 mostly worked for the East India Company in Calcutta, took an evening ride in early 1800, he saw a Eurasian girl who walked 'like one who had learnt to dance' and who 'attracted him greatly'.[4] He followed her, but it took several attempts and finally the intervention of his groom to elicit a reply from the girl. After he had made sure that she was neither married nor anyone's mistress, he invited her to live with him. Her name was Mary Walker, she informed him. She had attended school for some years and spoke English, though it does not seem to have been the language in which she communicated with Blechynden. She lived with her mother but had already once been the mistress of an Irish captain and was now under the protection of an English trader, who trained her for a job. Mary Walker agreed to become Blechynden's *bibi*, his concubine and housekeeper, though not without setting her conditions: the former *bibi* had to be dismissed immediately and she herself was to be set up in Blechynden's town house, apparently with at least some authority to command the servants and with monetary allocations both for herself and her mother.[5]

Mary Walker was but one episode in the love life of Blechynden. His relations to his *bibis* were as varied as the women themselves. They were Indians, poor Europeans, but mostly Indo-Europeans, offspring from earlier encounters between European men and their concubines. Some of these relations lasted over several years, closely resembling family life, while others ended after some weeks. His affair with Mary was one of the shorter ones but probably the most passionate (on his side) and the one which evoked the most contradictory emotions (on both sides).

Blechynden recorded a detailed daily account of all his actions and emotions in his diary, covering eighty volumes for the period between 1791 and 1822, allowing us to closely follow his navigation of feelings.

Blechynden was not exceptional in India at the turn of the century in preferring to keep a *bibi* than marry a British woman. Leaving aside the fact that there were fewer than 250 British women in Calcutta for over four thousand men (and the ratio was even more disparate upcountry), the *East India Vade-Mecum* also pointed out that the expenses of wedlock and providing children with the appropriate education were simply beyond the means of most men.[6] In the days before British rule established regular access to local information, 'carnal knowledge' moreover often opened the way to other forms of knowledge – linguistic at the most basic level but also political, especially when British officers married ladies from high-ranking Indian families.[7] Since the publication of William Dalrymple's bestselling *White Mughals* in 2002,[8] the debate on the emotions men like Blechynden felt for their companions and what it reveals about the character of early British colonialism has picked up momentum. However, the question whether men like James Kirkpatrick, the British resident at the court of Hyderabad, 'really' loved Khair un Nissa, a young girl from the highest nobility of the state, can only be answered if the concept and feeling of love is presumed to be stable over time. Rather than measuring the evidence against a pregiven yardstick, for this chapter it seems more interesting to follow Blechynden's diaries in a close reading, which shows his attempts to understand both Mary's and his own emotions and to navigate between passion, the call for reasonableness and what he perceived as his moral duties.

Only a few weeks after she had settled in, Mary Walker announced that she wanted to organize a nautch party, a performance with dancing girls, in honour of her mother. Blechynden did not care for the entertainment but allowed her to proceed on her own. The next morning, he not only received reports from his servants that the event had turned into a revelry 'of man-servants with tom-toms' but, worse, that one of them, named Buxoo, had spent the night with Mary Walker. Blechynden passed a sleepless night, identified his mood as angry and depressed, and summed up his verdict that this was 'one of the most unfortunate connexions I ever formed'.[9] This may seem a rather subdued reaction. Even when Mary Walker admitted that Buxoo had long since been her lover, he was not yet sure how he should react. 'I shall be miserable if I let her go and despise myself if I keep her. I wish I had never set eyes upon her'.[10] The next days were spent in negotiations – first Blechynden wanted to dismiss her and she refused to go, then he wanted to keep her and she explored alternatives. Finally, Mary Walker left and joined the captain of a country ship.¹¹ What again looked like a closure was but a step in the negotiations, which by now involved not only Blechynden's servants and a number of his friends but also the servants of the captain and his friends, as well as Mary's mother. Feelings were exacerbated by the news that Mary Walker had attempted an abortion with the help of her new patron, which raised even more questions – was the pregnancy the reason why she left Blechynden? Was she even aware of the intended effect of the medication the captain had given her? And had the abortion been successful or not? Blechynden was thrown into a vortex of contradictory emotions:

> Great God! and is it for such a Woman as this (for such a Monster rather) that I make all this lamentation – is this the *being* I wished to receive back to my Arms! Whilst I write this, Pity is the Predominant passion in my Breast, at others Love, Hatred – Rage – Malice – Pity & Contempt have taken possession of it by turns and sometimes the whole of them together, so as nearly to extinguish my Reason.¹²

During the entire month, while it was not yet clear whether Mary Walker would return to him or not, Blechynden closely observed his own emotions, taking his body as an indicator of the strength of his passions. He recorded in detail his sleepless nights, the dryness of his mouth that made it difficult to swallow and the bouts of fever that forced him to rest during the day.¹³ Mary Walker's bodily expressions of emotions did not receive the same attention, perhaps simply because her emotions mattered less in this situation. Blechynden did worry about whether she would be treated well and what fate had in store for her; he reproached himself for enticing her away from a situation that might have provided her with other means of earning her living. But neither her feelings for him, the captain or for Buxoo nor any desires she might have for her future entered his observations.

Even before meeting Mary Walker for the first time, Blechynden had developed fairly detailed expectations of how a relationship with a *bibi* should and would be played out, drawn from his previous experiences but also from ways of interacting that were deemed moral or immoral in the Calcutta of his time. These rules and expectations were stable enough to form a chapter of their own in Thomas Williamson's *Vade-Mecum* for newly arrived Europeans. In the best scenario, a companion would allow Blechynden to 'have all the comforts of marriage without its plagues',¹⁴ but he knew this happened only rarely and was, therefore, willing to put up with behaviour he deemed inappropriate – not only Mary Walker's infidelity but also other *bibis*' alcoholism and the instances where they beat either his children or attacked him physically.¹⁵ These relations certainly were not based on any form of equality, but, as the tolerance for this behaviour shows, they were perhaps less unequal than the ordinary British middle-class marriage of the Georgian age. Gender and class were defining categories of difference and hierarchy; race much less so, though Blechynden compared Mary Walker's fairness favourably to her predecessor's 'blackness'.[16] Blechynden had Indian, Indo-European and even European companions (he spoke Portuguese with Mary Walker's mother, which may indicate that she was the offspring of an Indo-Portuguese relationship), without treating them differently; the fact that Mary Walker had an Indian lover was not commented upon more negatively than her leaving him for another white man.

Not every European in Calcutta at that time worried so excessively about his own emotions and so little about the feelings of his companion. William Hickey has left behind four large volumes of memoirs in which he not only gives a frank depiction of his professional life but also of his love life. His many affairs and his riotous lifestyle in Britain were the despair of his parents, he confessed. After he had embezzled a considerable sum from his father's office, he was sent to India to work as a lawyer in the service of the East India Company. The companion he brought with

Figure 10.1 Thomas Hickey (Irish 1741–1824), *An Indian Lady, perhaps 'Jemdanee', Bibi of William Hickey* (1787), oil on canvas, 102 × 127 cm. Photo © National Gallery of Ireland. Used with permission.

him died, and he settled down with the 'kind-hearted and interesting favourite native woman Jemdanee'.[17] She was a stabilizing influence on his life and much cherished by all his friends, who fondly remembered her in their letters to Hickey and never forgot to send their 'love to Fatty'.[18] The memoirs convey the image not so much of passion as of loving companionship. Hickey arranged a 'very large and commodious residence' for Jemdanee, a little outside the city, where she might have some privacy with her female attendants. She greatly enjoyed the place in the beginning but discovered that it did not suit her health, whereupon Hickey set her up at another place they had discovered during a boat outing and visited her there every weekend, happy that she had become 'as stout and healthy as she had ever been'.[19] The importance of her place in his life was also acknowledged by the commission of a portrait by the Irish artist Thomas Hickey. Unfortunately, we do not know whether the two Hickeys were related.

When Jemdanee died in childbirth, Hickey was devastated: 'Thus did I lose as gentle and affectionately attached a girl as ever man was blessed with. She possessed a strong natural understanding, with more acuteness and wit than is usually to be found amongst native women of Hindostan'.[20]

As mentioned earlier, rules existed on the comportment admissible towards a *bibi*. Enticing a woman away from her current patron was as much condemned as dismissing her without adequate provision, at least if she had not given a serious and unprovoked cause. The presence of *bibis* was admissible and customary in the circle of male friends, but they were barred from all occasions when British ladies were present and from all official functions. At the same time, these rules left ample room for the navigation of individual relationships, allowing for all kinds of arrangements across racial divides and ranging from official marriages involving the conversion either of the Indian woman or of the British officer to short-time pecuniary arrangements. Premediation certainly influenced these relations. But they in turn contributed to the corpus of knowledge on India, a knowledge that was permeated by the experiences through which it was created – sometimes loving, sometimes cruel, but always unequal.

The Glamour of the Oriental Prince

From the end of the eighteenth century onwards, racial boundaries continuously hardened. While sons from mixed couples had been able to look for a career with the East India Company, they were increasingly barred from its service after 1780,[21] long before Evangelicals clamped down on the sinfulness of sexual relations out of wedlock and British ladies started to arrive in India in greater numbers (the reasons usually given for the increasing distance between rulers and ruled). In the 1820s, it was still possible – if rare – for a British lady from a good family to marry into an Indian aristocratic household without being shunned by British society.[22] The revolt of 1857 increased the segregating tendencies of the previous decades: the moral panic linked to reports about the rape of white ladies by mutinous Indians barred intimate relations (or pushed them into clandestineness) for almost half a century. The only sexual contact across races took place in the domain of prostitution, which was still condoned, at least for soldiers, but increasingly policed.[23]

For the two thirds of India under direct British administration, these forms of racial segregation could be enforced. The case was more difficult in the rest of India, formally under the sovereignty of Indian princes and controlled by the British through various mechanisms of indirect rule. In the last decade of the nineteenth century, these princes became increasingly visible in Europe – an unforeseen result of their Western education – where they displayed their dazzling wealth and became the projection screen of Orientalizing fantasies.[24] Class, in their case, mitigated the effect of race and allowed them access to European women, at least usually from a status markedly below their own.

Anita Delgado came from a poor Spanish family with alleged aristocratic origins, making it incumbent for her and her sister to earn their living as varieté dancers from an early age in the Kursaal of Madrid. Watching the public festivities of the wedding of King Alfonso to Princess Victoria in 1905,

> an enormous silver carriage catches the astonished gaze of . . . Anita. It contains an exotic figure who might have stepped from the pages of the Arabian Nights. He is wearing a huge turquoise turban and silk robes of an eccentric cut. As Anita takes in his rather heavy build, his strange beard, she realises his penetrating gaze is fixed upon her. For an instant as he smiles at her astonishment, Anita has a fleeting impression of an abundance of brooches, strings of pearls, diamonds and emeralds.[25]

The Maharaja became a regular visitor to the Kursaal, showering presents upon Anita Delgado, but she refused his advances until he asked for her hand in marriage. She agreed after consulting with her family and friends, knowing that he already had several wives and children, but relying on his promise that she would not be forced to live in the harem.

What followed was a Pygmalion story, in which the Maharaja took it upon himself to educate his bride into the European, preferably French, woman of his dreams. The seventeen-year-old girl and he did not even share a language. Therefore, he set her up with her family in Paris, where she was not only taught French but also learnt to wear long dresses, be coiffed à la mode and move in society. She followed his instructions to the letter, dazzled by his wealth and his attention, but was also frightened and lonely – the present of 'a wonderful doll the size of a five year old girl!'[26] excited her almost as much as precious jewellery. Once she reached India and was married to the Maharaja according to Sikh rites, she had to negotiate her life between European and Indian culture. She dressed up as a princess and played with Oriental images, if the fancy took her, but usually she held on to her European identity (by now a mix between Spanish, French and English) in dress, in the Versailles-like palace the Maharaja

Figure 10.2 'Anita Delgado Posed at the Age of 22 Years with Indian Attire'. Photo by Rita Martin in her atelier in 29 Baker Street, London, 1912. Courtesy Elisa Vázquez de Gey.

had allocated her and in refusing to interact with the other women of the family, claiming her husband for herself.

The emotional encounter is difficult to read, not only because there is no account from the Maharaja's side but also because Anita Delgado's memoirs or diary (which is only available in quotation) seems heavily edited and not necessarily written by herself: she was apparently almost illiterate when the Maharaja met her. She learnt French and English, which became her main languages, but the few surviving letters show that she was not very fluent in writing. Even from her own description of their meeting, it becomes clear that it was the possibility of escaping the poverty of her upbringing – ideally without compromising her honour – that tempted her the most. Not by chance did her description of their first gaze dwell longer on his jewellery than on his person. It was only after her education in Paris, when the couple separated in preparation of the wedding, that she admitted: 'I think that by then I already loved him a bit'.[27] The feelings of the Maharaja can only be guessed. Beyond the erotic attraction, the fact of inverting colonialism through the appropriation of not only European knowledge but also a European woman may have played a central role, allowing him to mimic European relations. But unlike the English-educated clerks and assistants to the colonial bureaucracy, who are usually cited as instances for mimicry,[28] he retained control over the variety – French rather than English – and the extent of the mimicry. Anita Delgado remained a segregated part of his life, and he separated from her when she went through a phase of depression after her second son was stillborn. She was quickly replaced by a succession of European women. Indirect rule made a direct British intervention into princely love affairs impossible, but British Indian society never recognized these relations, and European women who married outside the fold were never invited to any official (or for that matter even unofficial) function. If they also refused to integrate into the Indian context, they could and often did end up in a no man's land between cultures.[29]

Similar structural constraints and similar premediations and fantasies about the Oriental prince, however, could also allow for very different love stories. Morag Murray first set eyes on Syed Abdullah, son of a Pathan chieftain, who had just finished his studies in medicine in Edinburgh, at a dance shortly after the end of the First World War.

> Suddenly an Eastern student appeared at the entrance. His appearance was different from the others. . . . I followed the chieftain's son with my eyes as he crossed the room. He walked so erectly and looked like the popular idea of a handsome sheikh. He was tall, with finely chiselled features . . . He seemed defiant and yet devil-may-care, and I could look at no one else.[30]

From the first moment on, she played with the image of the sheikh, which the films of Rudolph Valentino had made available to Western audiences as a female erotic fantasy,[31] acknowledging how this script had shaped her perceptions (and even more those of her readers') but simultaneously smiling at them once she started to know and to love Syed: 'He did not now seem like the Eastern sheikhs at the cinema! He said none of the things the picture hero had said'.[32]

The intersectionality that from the beginning marked their relationship was not premised on race but based on their shared love for the mountains and their common position as offspring of mountain chieftains, which made the difference between a Highlander and a Pathan seem much less important. Still, they had to fight a hard battle to obtain the consent of both families for their marriage – Syed's father agreed only after his son had cabled him: 'I belonged to a Highland clan and was willing to become Muslim, and he took it upon himself to vouch for my ability to guard any fort!'[33] Two and a half years later the couple and their small daughter left for the Pathan country beyond the north-western border of India. Unlike Anita Delgado, Morag Abdullah was from the start willing to conform to the norms of local culture and quickly learnt the language. In spite of her adventurous spirit, she had been apprehensive to meet her in-laws and her husband's clan, but their first meeting dispelled her fears: '[w]hat a welcome to give a foreigner, I thought! The hospitality of the hills is the same everywhere. My heart warmed to these people, many of whom . . . had come long distances to greet me'.[34] She struck up a close friendship with her sisters-in-law and mother-in-law. Deep and mutual affection also developed between her and her father-in-law, and she heartily embraced her position as the senior daughter-in-law of the chieftain's family and hence her leading position among the clanswomen. She took to the Pathans' sincerity, which struck a chord with what she saw as Highland identity: 'these were plain people who could not hide their feelings. I felt glad they had received me so generously in the "Free Land", for the past was past. I was now one of the clanswomen'.[35] She quickly learnt what was expected of her and took to her role, be it in arranging marriages or, as she had promised, defending the fort at gun point in the absence of the men.

Her memoirs are an explicit attempt at remediation of what she saw as British prejudices, in the light of her own encounters: 'The East is not a land of sweet-do-nothing inhabited by handsome, wealthy sheikhs lying in wait to lay hands on white women, load them with jewels, and loll away the sunny hours round lotus-ponds'.[36] Instead, the same standards of decency and respectability applied as in Britain, and her experience showed that 'the East is no more lurid than the West'.[37] Her memoirs end on a note of hope for an understanding crossing the lines of culture, extending the encounter with emotions from her personal life to a reconfiguration of the relations among nations to a future in which, quoting the Scottish poet Robert Burns, 'Man to man the world o'er shall brothers be'.[38]

Male Lovers and Friends

The ideal of romantic love, as it was developed as an increasingly global norm in the nineteenth and twentieth centuries, brought together emotions, the body and institutional validation in a seemingly seamless whole of heterosexual love, sexuality and marriage. Encounters with emotions, however, continued to elude these neat classifications. Western European traditions after the end of the age of sentimentality had introduced an unequivocal distinction between love and friendship, particularly for men, premised on the presence of erotic attraction and sexual relations or the lack thereof. The South Asian, notably the Indo-Persianate, tradition remained much more fluid well into the twentieth century. Not only was the gender of the beloved notoriously ambiguous in love poetry, but male friends also wrote about their feelings for each other in vocabulary ranging from measured love (*muhabbat*) to unrestrained passion (*'ishq*).[39] Hyperbolic images from poetry easily flowed into these descriptions and constituted the pre-mediation marking the experience of both friendship and love.

The negotiations and navigations between friendship, passion and homosexual desire were at the core of the relationship between E.M. Forster and Syed Ross Masood. When they first met in 1906, Forster was already well known as a novelist – *Where Angels Fear to Tread* had been published, *Room with a View* and *Howards End* were to come out soon.[40] Masood was the grandson of Syed Ahmad Khan, the founder of the Aligarh College and a famous Indo-Muslim reformer. He later went on to become the Director of Public Instruction in Hyderabad, Vice Chancellor of Aligarh and Minister of Education in the Princely State of Bhopal.[41] Forster quickly fell in love with the young student he was coaching for his Latin entrance examination at Oxford, and Masood responded with passion. They engaged in a stormy friendship that survived both Masood's return to India, where Forster visited him twice, and his marriage. But increasingly it became clear that there was no space in which such a relationship could be lived out. *A Passage to India* is rightly regarded as a *roman à clef*, Fielding and Aziz, the Beloved, being modelled on Forster and Masood and incorporating many incidents that had originally left their traces in Forster's letters and diaries.[42]

While in their letters they used emotional language and expressed their love for each other, the question as to what these ardent expressions meant and how feelings should be voiced held an important place during their England years. Early on, Forster was open about his love and desire for a sexual relation. Masood responded with a passion that might have been taken out of a Persian ghazal, but like the ghazal, it remained equivocal how these images were to be translated into everyday life. The question whether their love included sexual encounters cannot be answered definitely (there are indications that it never did), but it is probably also not the most interesting question that this relationship provokes.

The negotiation of passion and passionate expression came to a head when at the parting after an intensely joyful holiday in Paris Masood expressed his despair at their parting as if 'all happiness was over until the world ended'.[43] Forster reproached him, commenting that such a display of emotions on such a slight occasion was out of place. Masood then asked: 'Do you measure out your emotions as if they were potatoes?' to which Forster agreed 'it is better than slopping them about like water from a pail, which is what you did'.[44] This dialogue was taken up again and further developed in *A Passage to India*:

> 'Your emotions never seem in proportion to their objects, Aziz'.
> 'Is emotion a sack of potatoes, so much to the pound, to be measured out? Am I a machine? I shall be told I can use up my emotions by using them, next'.
> 'I should have thought you could. It sounds common sense. You can't eat your cake and have it, even in the world of the spirit'.
> 'If you are right, there is no point in any friendship; it all comes down to give and take, or give and return, which is disgusting'.[45]

The fact that Forster reused the incident more than ten years later seems to indicate that he indeed held fast to his own feeling rules, yet he also reflected on their embeddedness in their two cultures: 'I spoke as a member of a prudent middle-class nation. . . . But my friend spoke as an Oriental, and the Oriental has behind him a tradition, not of middle-class prudence, but of kingly munificence and splendour . . . The emotions may be endless'.[46]

Emotions were read back into their respective cultures, and the continually refined knowledge about the other to a certain extent contributed to their readability. Friendship opened up a space to transcend communitarian boundaries.[47] But in the end, this space was too narrow to sustain a living relationship, and it was their communitarian anchoring that pulled them apart. They played with cultural differences in the beginning, Masood adopting an excessively Oriental persona in some of his letters, addressing the 'worthy and highly esteemed Forster' in the guise of a 'humble and like-unto-the-dust-beneath-thy-feet scribe'.[48] Forster jokingly embodied an imperial officer, writing his letter 'from Forster, member of the Ruling Race to Masood, a nigger'.[49] But in the end, neither humour nor passion, nor a playful adoption of an Oriental persona, bridged the gap that colonialism had dug between the two cultures, and the final scene of *A Passage to India* is a desperate farewell between Fielding and Aziz:

> '[W]e shall drive every blasted Englishman into the sea, and then' – he [Aziz] rode against him [Fielding] furiously – 'and then', he concluded, half kissing him, 'you and I shall be friends'. 'Why can't we be friends now?' said the other, holding him affectionately. 'It's what I want. It's what you want'. But the horses didn't want it – they swerved apart; the earth didn't want it sending up rocks through which riders must pass single-file; the temples, the tank, the jail, the palace, the birds, the carrion, the Guest House, that came into view as they issued from the gap and saw Mau beneath: they didn't want it, they said in their hundred voices, 'No, not yet', and the sky said, 'No, not there'.[50]

But not all relations failed, and the friendships Charles Freer Andrews developed throughout his lifetime showed that private emotions could well transcend the colonial binaries and generate a transformative power that went far beyond the individuals involved. Andrews came out to India as a missionary in 1906 and taught at Delhi's St Stephen College for almost a decade. In accordance with the theology of the Cambridge Brotherhood, to which he belonged, from the beginning he viewed his mission not as a spreading of a pre-set truth, but as an encounter, to which both sides contributed. In this view, Islam and Hinduism were regarded as steps on the way to an ultimate truth. While this was still held to be Christianity for the Cambridge Brotherhood, Andrews successively widened the framework and in the end arrived at a position in which each religion and belief brought out what was best in the other. In his eyes, friendship, the loving encounter between two individuals, was the path leading to this mutual transformation. From the beginning, therefore, friendship was an experience and a practice that was at the same time emotional, religious and political. It was the means to overcome divisions between the races: praying for friends 'with the longing prayer of love' was what was required, 'younger missionaries forming a "true and deep Christian friendship with at least one fellow Christian Communicant of another race"' and pouring into that friendship 'all the longing affection and intercession which God in his great Love may bestow'.[51] While in the beginning his thoughts were directed towards Christian friendship,[52] soon his quest for friends went beyond these boundaries.[53]

Andrews first met Tagore in London in 1912, on the evening that saw the latter's first recitation of *Gitanjali*, the collection of poems that were to earn him the Nobel Prize in Literature the following year. The missionary and the poet knew of each other and had been wanting to meet for a long time. Andrews described their encounter:

> I knew by the beautiful face (which I had seen in portraits) that it was Rabindra Babu himself. I should like to have made obeisance to the poet, who has so raised his nation by his songs, but in a moment he had clasped my hand and said to me – 'Oh! Mr. Andrews, I have so longed to see you, I cannot tell you how I have longed to see you'.[54]

Andrews continued to reflect on what this instantaneous affection, which developed into a lifelong friendship, meant. The fact that this emotional encounter took place between an Englishman and a Bengali was supremely important: in the eyes of Andrews, but also of Tagore, this was not only an encounter between two individuals but also between the nations, cultures and religions that they represented. If they could meet in friendship and love; their relationship would transform not only the two persons encountering each other but ultimately also the communities they represented.

> The Englishman, who possesses this instinct of attraction for India, is not less English on that account. The best sides of his English nature expand, rather than contract. In the same way the Indian who learns to appreciate England to the full, by sympathy and love, does not become less Indian, but rather the reverse.[55]

Unlike Forster, Andrews never seemed to have had to struggle with the interpretation of Tagore's emotions. For him 'Rabindra needed no interpreter' because his language was universal, 'appealing direct [sic] to the heart'.[56] Crossing the gap was neither an impossibility nor a process that required sustained efforts to learn new emotional expressions and new emotions. Based on his theology of encounter, in which human encounters were always already prefigured and mediated through the encounter with God, he could claim love as a universal notion, which had only to be recognized as such.

Soon after their first encounter, Tagore invited Andrews to settle with him in Santiniketan. Over the next two and a half decades, until Andrews' death, he helped develop the school and later the college, founded to provide a space for the meeting of the East and the West and the unfolding of a new generation of individuals who would carry this message of possible encounters forward. The few photographs that are available of Andrews show how the emotional bond over the years not only transformed his character but also his exterior, making him look more and more like Tagore.

Figure 10.3 Left to right: Young Andrews, Tagore, Old Andrews. Photos of C.F. Andrews from S. Bose (ed.), *C.F. Andrews: Centenary Volume 1871–1971* (Calcutta: Deenabandhu Andrews Centenary Committee, 1972), after page 40 and 48. © Tagore Archives, Visva-Bharati University, Santiniketan. Photo of R. Tagore: © John Vanderpant (1929) / Library and Archives Canada / a195928. Used with permission.

Love in the Time of Globalization

The last decades of the twentieth century saw a significant increase in geographical mobility. Quicker and cheaper modes of transport made it possible for an ever-growing number of people to move from one continent to another; be it for education, professional careers or tourism and self-discovery.[57] This not only led to more frequent encounters and hence increased the probability of falling in love. It also multiplied the number and diversity of available prescripts. The Hippie and related movements of the 1960s had led to a revival of certain Orientalist stereotypes, keeping the trope of fundamental difference but using it to turn India into a space for critique of – and salvation from – modernity. At the same time, the multiplication of encounters had also led to a script that placed Indian differences in a context of multiple differences – Indians were different, but not extraordinarily so. A similar movement can be observed in the transformation of the image of the West (and notably Western women and Western forms of intimacy) in India, where even in popular media clichés of female immorality and sexual availability since the 1990s gave way to a new normality – the West was no longer the shocking other against which Indian values had to be reaffirmed but gained a familiarity as the place to go to for studies or holidays, or the permanent domicile of part of the extended family.

Simultaneously, the end of formal colonialism meant that racial boundaries and hierarchies were no longer policed by the state. This did not lead to a disappearance of power structures or their impact on emotions, but power was played out in different and increasingly diverse ways, leading to a whole multitude of possible encounters. In the following paragraphs, this field will be explored through two novels: one openly autobiographical and the other providing no indications of a possible intercultural experience other than the name of the author.

India was not the first country that Sarah Lloyd, a young British woman from an upper-class background, had explored since the late 1970s, but little is known about her except through her diary recounting her travels in India. After travelling across India for some months, a man belonging to the Nihang sect of the Sikh community caught her gaze: 'He sat cross-legged on a brown blanket. It was a powerful face that instantly registered: high forehead, long nose, fine mouth and skin the colour of almonds; but it was a face that suggested sadness'. As she was 'going through a being-charitable-to-Nihangs phase', she bought him milk, sweets and fruit, and they spent some time together.[58] Sarah Lloyd was attracted to the young man with whom she had not yet spoken a single word, assuming that he could not speak English. 'I was moved by his tenderness, his simplicity and his beautiful eyes. Beauty is a great robber of my common sense'.[59] She travelled on, but returned to Amritsar where she had first met him, after some weeks, this time to accompany him to his village and live with him and his family. She wondered only briefly about the consequences of her actions; any thought about the future was engulfed in the present feeling for Jungli (as she had renamed her lover) and the joy of finding 'rural life, the real India, the one I had come to find'.[60]

Though all of this – the claiming through the erotic gaze, the refiguration of her lover as a creature of the wilderness, the refusal to consider what moving in with the family might mean for him and for them – might be read as an almost colonial appropriation, though with a reversal of gender roles; she slipped into the role of Jungli's wife quite willingly and easily. The present was all that mattered. Her past did not count; it had not provided her any prescripts: 'A handful of films had been my introduction to India. I knew no Indians; I had read nothing. To arrive in a country with the minimum of preconceived notions is to explore it through the medium of one's own experience'.[61] Nevertheless, she had enough of a precise idea of the 'real India' to recognize it when she encountered it, and the language of her descriptions, too, did show continuities to the colonial imagery. From the beginning, she had felt drawn to Sikhs, describing them as 'manly in a country where men lean towards effeminacy, they were proud and dignified, fearless and determined, passionate and warm-hearted ... everything I liked and admired and wanted to be'. To her, Jungli embodied all these qualities: 'he was the soul of my India'.[62]

Her introduction into this new world was through the bodily senses only, she claimed. 'I saw, I smelt, I touched, I heard, but I lived in a world of my own'.[63] The impossibility of communication through language not only did not take away from the depth of their emotional encounter but even added to it: 'Our inability to converse was the one thing we shared. Had we spoken the same tongue, we might have found our differences too great. Had I understood what Jungli was saying, the words might have dimmed his aura of romance'.[64] By the time she learnt Punjabi, they were already so used to each other that the differences they discovered were less significant.

What remained an irreconcilable difference was the temporality within which they perceived their emotions. From the first 'I love you', Jungli seemed to have had no doubt that their relation was there to stay (if it is possible, that is, to gauge his feelings at all, as he appears only through the mediation of Sarah's writings).

> The force of Jungli's feelings made subtle and invisible demands on me. He seemed to have no doubt but that they were returned in like strength, as if love automatically created an equal response in the object of its attention. I was very much attracted by Jungli, but whereas his emotions were blind and unlimited, my feelings for him could be rationalized. And they were finite.[65]

Although Sarah refused to think about the future, she knew from the beginning that she would be moving on after some weeks, months or even years. The bodily and sensory experiences as an immediate access to an emotional reality, which had fascinated her so much in the beginning, proved insufficient in the long run, once it became clear that they shared no language and never would be able to negotiate and navigate the meanings of these experiences together.

Power structures played out in imbricated and contradictory ways in this encounter with emotions. Sarah Lloyd adapted to the local cultural expectations to an extent that once they moved to their next home at a Sikh shrine where Jungli had found work, no one realized that they were not married. They lived in a tiny room, in poverty and with no privacy, and she fulfilled all the duties expected in a patriarchal setting from the wife of an officeholder at the shrine. At the same time, her knowledge of other worlds, of other ways of living and of the possibility to return to them made this a matter of choice, which would hardly be the case for the Sikh wife she was mimicking. Her class background and education and the access to material and intellectual resources they provided her with, criss-crossed with her gender identity. Even within her submissive role, she had the option to evaluate whether her experiences contributed to her own goals, and if not, to leave. She was self-reflective enough to concede:

'We could never have made each other happy, but my guilt still gnawed at my stomach. I knew with absolute certainty that Jungli would love me until his death'.[66]

Unlike the other texts, Valerie Anand's book *To a Native Shore* is fiction. As there is no biographical information available on the author, it is impossible to tell which experiences could be at the basis of the novel (the author's name might point to a British Indian marriage). If this does not give an indication of the possibility of successful love stories in real life, they have at least entered the collective imaginary since the 1980s. Melanie and Avtar, the couple at the centre of the novel, meet at an exhibition of Indian art in London, where Avtar has gone to gain extra medical experience as a doctor and Melanie has been working as a designer.[67] After their first gaze, they start 'a trivial conversation which was no more than a means of remaining side by side while each of them secretly put the other's face and voice and aura against some private master image'.[68] Three weeks later they are engaged, and when Avtar finishes his training Melanie travels to India with him and they get married. Her mother-in-law from the start makes her feel welcome and she finds a friend in her sister-in-law but nevertheless finds it hard to adjust to some members of the extended family. When her grandfather dies and leaves her the family home, she travels back to England against the advice of her husband, who is afraid of losing her. Going back to the place where she has her emotional roots brings the question of belonging to a point of crisis, which is exacerbated when she realizes that she is pregnant and discovers that her grandfather and most of her family had secretly hoped for the failure of her marriage and for her return to her own culture. She accepts the challenge of belonging to two cultures and is ready to do what it takes to convince her husband that these are not mutually exclusive – for the sake of their love and even more that of their child: 'She must not let herself be made to choose between them. Such a loss would be a bad thing not only for her but for her child. The child would belong to both far more thoroughly than Melanie herself did. . . . Can't have both? She must!'[69]

As in Sarah Lloyd's *An Indian Attachment*, the body and the senses are important during the extended period of the first encounter, allowing for an affective engagement beyond cultural differences and for a reading and translating of the emotions involved, not only between the lovers but involving their surroundings, their families, friends and colleagues. This affective engagement is a precondition, albeit insufficient, for a long-term relationship. In this situation, the body does not disappear but language, the explicit processing of questions of identity and meaning and their cultural mooring become of central relevance, to the point of deciding on the possibility of a shared future for the lovers. It is here that the protagonists in Lloyd's and Anand's book part on different trajectories – the books end too early to tell about final success or failure.

* * *

At first glance, it seems counter-intuitive to attempt a cultural history of encounters between lovers. If there are emotions that are immediately widely believed to be linked to the body and recognizable across boundaries, sexual desire would certainly count among them. However, this chapter has argued that even desire is embedded in cultural scripts. Moreover, it is only one of the many emotions that penetrate the relations between lovers and friends. However close to the body they may be, emotions in cross-cultural encounters are therefore embedded in culture(s) that shape the expectations of lovers and friends and provide the patterns along which they interpret their encounters. The experience of the encounter in turn can spark a remediation and reinterpretation of the previous patterns. As argued in the introduction, nature and culture are intimately linked in the way they shape and are shaped by encounters.

The chapter has further shown that power relations have been of central importance throughout the historical trajectory – the difference in power between lovers but also the power structures into which their relationship has been embedded. The juxtaposition of case studies for each area, however, has also shown that these power structures did not completely determine the course of the relationship but left an open space in which the partners could (unequally) negotiate their emotions, the place given to love, desire, romantic understanding and the merging of horizons but also to pride, the wish for adventure and exoticism, greed or simply the desire to overcome poverty and to provide for oneself and one's family.

Finally, the chapter has shown that cross-cultural differences backed by power structures need not be the most important category for the way male and female lovers and friends experience their relationship. Not all differences point in the same direction and reinforce each other – rather the case studies have shown how racial, national or cultural differences, multiple in themselves, intersect with a shared spirituality, artistic sensibility, political goals or love for the mountains.

Margrit Pernau is Senior Researcher at the Center for the History of Emotions at the Max Planck Institute for Human Development in Berlin. She has been Research Fellow at the Social Science Research Center Berlin, the Modern Orient Centre in Berlin, the Institute of Advanced Studies in Freiburg and the EHESS in Paris. Among her publications are

The Delhi College: Traditional Elites, the Colonial State and Education before 1857 (Oxford University Press, 2006), *Ashraf into Middle Classes: Muslims in 19th Century Delhi* (Oxford University Press, 2013), *Civilizing Emotions: Concepts in Nineteenth Century Asia and Europe* (with Helge Jordheim et al., Oxford University Press, 2015). She has also written numerous articles on the history of emotions, modern Indian history and historical semantics.

Notes

1. Mokasdar, 'Love Story'.
2. For more detail on the concepts of premediation and intersectionality, see the introduction to this volume.
3. Ballantyne and Burton, *Moving Subjects: Gender, Mobility, and Intimacy in an Age of Global Empire*; Stoler, *Carnal Knowledge and Imperial Power: Race and the Intimate in Colonial Rule*.
4. Robb, *Sex and Sensibility*, 1.
5. Robb, *Sex and Sensibility*, 1–3, 70.
6. Williamson, *The East India Vade-Mecum: Or Complete Guide to Gentlemen Intended for the Civil, Military, or Naval Service of the Hon. East India Company*, 453–57.
7. For a balanced discussion of this argument, see Ghosh, *Sex and the Family in Colonial India: The Making of Empire*, 6.
8. Dalrymple, *White Mughals: Love and Betrayal in Eighteenth-Century India*.
9. Robb, *Sex and Sensibility*, 71.
10. Robb, *Sex and Sensibility*, 73.
11. Robb, *Sex and Sensibility*, 76.
12. Robb, *Sex and Sensibility*, 83.
13. Robb, *Sex and Sensibility*, 99.
14. Robb, *Sex and Sensibility*, 71.
15. Robb, *Sex and Sensibility*, 124, 65, 194.
16. Robb, *Sex and Sensibility*, 1–2.
17. Spencer, *Memoirs of William Hickey*, 6.
18. Spencer, *Memoirs of William Hickey*, 105, passim.
19. Spencer, *Memoirs of William Hickey*, 26, 29.
20. Spencer, *Memoirs of William Hickey*, 141.
21. For a case study on James Skinner, son of a Rajput mother and a British father, see Alavi, 'The Makings of Company Power: James Skinner in the Ceded and Conquered Provinces, 1802–1840', 437–66.
22. Meer Hasan Ali, *Observations on the Mussulmauns of India: Descriptive of their Manners, Customs, Habits, and Religious Opinions*. Though this ethnography contained respectful and loving depictions of her father-in-law, the emotions of the spouses could not be voiced in this context.
23. Levine, *Prostitution, Race, and Politics: Policing Venereal Disease in the British Empire*.
24. See Chapter 2, Cabanas, Khan and Marjanen, 'Travellers' in this volume on the Indian princes as travellers.
25. Vázquez de Gey, *Anita Delgado: Maharani of Kapurthala*, 24. For the parts of her biography that have been left out in this tale, see Moro, *Passion India: The Story of the Spanish Princess of Kapurthala*.
26. Vázquez de Gey, *Anita Delgado*, 24.
27. Vázquez de Gey, *Anita Delgado*, 48.
28. Bhabha, 'Of Mimicry and Man: The Ambivalence of Colonial Discourse', 85–92.

29. Younger, *Wicked Women of the Raj: European Women Who Broke Society's Rules and Married Indian Princes*.
30. Abdullah, *My Khyber Marriage: Experiences of a Scotswoman as the Wife of a Pathan Chieftain's Son*, 10.
31. Hansen, 'Pleasure, Ambivalence, Identification: Valentino and Female Spectatorship', 6–32; Teo, 'Historicizing the Sheikh: Comparisons of the British Novel and the American Film'.
32. Abdullah, *My Khyber Marriage*, 14.
33. Abdullah, *My Khyber Marriage*, 18.
34. Abdullah, *My Khyber Marriage*, 50.
35. Abdullah, *My Khyber Marriage*, 61.
36. Abdullah, *My Khyber Marriage*, 269.
37. Abdullah, *My Khyber Marriage*, 272.
38. Abdullah, *My Khyber Marriage*, 272 [quotation from a poem by Robert Burns].
39. Kia, 'Contours of Persianate Community, 1722–1835', Ph.D. dissertation (Cambridge, MA: Harvard University, 2011), Chapter 4.
40. Saunders, 'Forster's Life and Life-Writing', 8–31.
41. Kidwai, *Khayaban-e-masood*, 10–11.
42. Forster, *Passage to India*; Childs, 'Passage to India', 188–208; Shaheen, *E.M. Forster and the Politics of Imperialism*.
43. Noble, 'Dearest Forster', 62.
44. Noble, 'Dearest Forster', 64.
45. Forster, *Passage to India*, 255.
46. Noble, 'Dearest Forster', 64.
47. Gandhi, *Affective Communities: Anticolonial Thought, Fin-de-Siècle Radicalism, and the Politics of Friendship*, 23–26.
48. Kidwai, *Forster-Masood Letters*, 98.
49. Kidwai, *Forster-Masood Letters*, 58.
50. Forster, *Passage to India*, 324–25.
51. O'Connor, *A Clear Star: C.F. Andrews and India, 1904–1914*, 64.
52. Viswanathan, 'S.K. Rudra, C.F. Andrews and M.K. Gandhi: Friendship, Dialogue and Interiority in the Question of Indian Nationalism', 3532–41.
53. Pernau, 'Preparing a Meeting-Ground: C.F. Andrews, St. Stephen's, and the Delhi College: An Introduction', xlvii–lxxv. See also Chapter 1. Cummins and Lee, 'Missionaries' in this volume on missionary encounters.
54. Andrews, 'An Evening with Rabindra', 227.
55. Andrews, 'With Rabindra in England', 74.
56. Andrews, 'With Rabindra in England', 71.
57. See also Chapter 2, Cabanas, Khan and Marjanen, 'Travellers' in this volume.
58. Lloyd, *An Indian Attachment: An Englishwoman's Unforgettable Two-Year Encounter with Indian Village Life among the Sikhs*, 1.
59. Lloyd, *Indian Attachment*, 4.
60. Lloyd, *Indian Attachment*, 9.
61. Lloyd, *Indian Attachment*, 16. One might wonder what in this case enabled her to recognize the 'real' India and to distinguish it from the day-to-day, but supposedly 'fake', version.
62. Lloyd, *Indian Attachment*, 16.
63. Lloyd, *Indian Attachment*, 18.
64. Lloyd, *Indian Attachment*, 33.
65. Lloyd, *Indian Attachment*, 14.
66. Lloyd, *Indian Attachment*, 244.
67. Anand, *To a Native Shore: A Novel of India*.

68. Anand, *To a Native Shore*, 50.
69. Anand, *To a Native Shore*, 261.

Bibliography

Abdullah, M.M. *My Khyber Marriage: Experiences of a Scotswoman as the Wife of a Pathan Chieftain's Son*. London: Harrap, 1934.

Alavi, S. 'The Makings of Company Power: James Skinner in the Ceded and Conquered Provinces, 1802–1840'. *Indian Economic and Social History Review* 30(4) (1993), 437–66, doi: 10.1177/001946469303000403.

Anand, V. *To a Native Shore: A Novel of India*. London: Piatkus, 1985.

Andrews, C.F. 'An Evening with Rabindra'. *Modern Review* 12(2) (1912), 225–28.

_____. 'With Rabindra in England'. *Modern Review* 13(1) (1913), 70–75.

Ballantyne, T., and A. Burton (eds). *Moving Subjects: Gender, Mobility, and Intimacy in an Age of Global Empire*. Urbana: University of Illinois Press, 2009.

Bhabha, H. 'Of Mimicry and Man: The Ambivalence of Colonial Discourse', in H. Bhabha, *The Location of Culture* (New York: Routledge, 1994), 85–92.

Childs, P. 'A Passage to India', in D. Bradshaw (ed.), *The Cambridge Companion to E.M. Forster* (Cambridge: Cambridge University Press, 2007), 188–208.

Dalrymple, W. *White Mughals: Love and Betrayal in Eighteenth-Century India*. London: HarperCollins, 2002.

Forster, E.M. *A Passage to India*. London: Arnold, 1924.

Gandhi, L. *Affective Communities: Anticolonial Thought, Fin-de-Siècle Radicalism, and the Politics of Friendship*. Durham, NC: Duke University Press, 2006.

Ghosh, D. *Sex and the Family in Colonial India: The Making of Empire*. Cambridge: Cambridge University Press, 2006.

Hansen, M. 'Pleasure, Ambivalence, Identification: Valentino and Female Spectatorship'. *Cinema Journal* 25(4) (1986), 6–32, doi: 10.2307/1225080.

Kia, M. 'Contours of Persianate Community, 1722–1835'. Ph.D. dissertation. Cambridge, MA: Harvard University, 2011.

Kidwai, J.A. (ed.). *Khayaban-e-masood*. Karachi: Ross Masood Education and Culture Society of Pakistan, 1970.

_____. *Forster-Masood Letters*. Karachi: Ross Masood Education and Culture Society of Pakistan, 1984.

Levine, P. *Prostitution, Race, and Politics: Policing Venereal Disease in the British Empire*. New York: Routledge, 2003.

Lloyd, S. *An Indian Attachment: An Englishwoman's Unforgettable Two-Year Encounter with Indian Village Life among the Sikhs*. New York: Quill, 1984.

Meer Hasan Ali, Mrs. *Observations on the Mussulmauns of India: Descriptive of their Manners, Customs, Habits, and Religious Opinions*, 2 vols. London: Parbury, Allen, 1832.

Mokasdar, L. *English Wife, Indian Life* (30 August 2013). Retrieved 15 June 2015 from http://www.englishwifeindianlife.com.

_____. 'Love Story'. *English Wife, Indian Life*. Retrieved 11 November 2015 from http://englishwifeindianlife.com/love-story.

Moro, J. *Passion India: The Story of the Spanish Princess of Kapurthala*, trans. P.J. Hearn. New Delhi: Full Circle, 2006 [Spa. orig. *Pasión india*. Barcelona: Seix Barral, 2005].

Noble, R.W. '"Dearest Forster" – "Dearest Masood": An East-West Friendship'. *Encounter* 56(6) (1981), 61–72.

O'Connor, D. *A Clear Star: C.F. Andrews and India, 1904–1914*, new edn. New Delhi: Chronicle Books, 2005.

Pernau, M. 'Preparing a Meeting-Ground: C.F. Andrews, St. Stephen's, and the Delhi College: An Introduction', in C.F. Andrews, *Zaka Ullah of Delhi* (New Delhi: Oxford University Press, 2003), xlvii–lxxv.

Robb, P. *Sex and Sensibility: Richard Blechynden's Calcutta Diaries, 1791–1822*. New Delhi: Oxford University Press, 2011.

Saunders, M. 'Forster's Life and Life-Writing', in D. Bradshaw (ed.), *The Cambridge Companion to E.M. Forster* (Cambridge: Cambridge University Press, 2007), 8–31.

Shaheen, M. *E.M. Forster and the Politics of Imperialism*. Basingstoke: Palgrave Macmillan, 2004.

Spencer, A. (ed.). *Memoirs of William Hickey*, vol. 4: *1790–1809*, 3rd edn. London: Hurst & Blackett, 1925.

Stoler, A.L. *Carnal Knowledge and Imperial Power: Race and the Intimate in Colonial Rule*. Berkeley: University of California Press, 2002.

Teo, H.-M. 'Historicizing the Sheikh: Comparisons of the British Novel and the American Film'. *Journal of Popular Romance Studies* 1(1) (2010). Retrieved 11 September 2018 from http://www.jprstudies.org.

Vázquez de Gey, E. *Anita Delgado: Maharani of Kapurthala*, trans. À. Gimeno-Balonwu. New Delhi: Hemkunt, 2002.

Viswanathan, S. 'S.K. Rudra, C.F. Andrews and M.K. Gandhi: Friendship, Dialogue and Interiority in the Question of Indian Nationalism'. *Economic and Political Weekly* 37(34) (2002), 3532–41.

Williamson, T. *The East India Vade-Mecum: Or Complete Guide to Gentlemen Intended for the Civil, Military, or Naval Service of the Hon. East India Company*, vol. 1. London: Black, Perry, and Kingsbury, 1810.

Younger, C. *Wicked Women of the Raj: European Women Who Broke Society's Rules and Married Indian Princes*. New Delhi: Harper Collins India, 2003.

Conclusion
After Encounters with Feelings
Outcomes and Further Issues

Benno Gammerl

Elliot wanted to introduce a very special new friend to his brother Michael, asking the latter to open his eyes only when told. At Elliot's signal, the two saw each other for the first time. While Michael's grin vanished slowly from his face, the new friend tried to perform an amiable smile. Then their sister Gertie entered the room and started shrieking at the shocking sight, prompting the others to scream as well and a neck to extend. It took quite an effort to calm the emotional turmoil caused by the encounter, which is hardly surprising when one considers that this was the moment when Elliot introduced E.T. to his siblings. This scene can serve as a prime example of an encounter with emotion: while the terrestrials and the alien initially lacked a shared language that would have allowed them to communicate verbally, bodily expressions like E.T.'s neck extension, and, later on, the direct transmission of emotional and physiological states between 'it' and Elliot, established an intense interaction that triggered a succession of unforeseen events. Steven Spielberg's 1982 film further demonstrates how vital science fiction has been for negotiating ways of dealing with emotional difference, not only on an intra- or intercultural but also on an interplanetary level.[1]

Building on this encounter that involves more than 'just' human participants, the conclusion summarizes the most significant insights of the preceding chapters in light of the questions raised in the introduction. As it cannot possibly do justice to the rich case studies that have been examined, the conclusion focuses on certain aspects. The first three sections

---

Notes for this chapter begin on page 293.

highlight crucial findings about the emotional dynamics of transcultural encounters and the final two discuss the ways in which these dynamics have themselves changed across time. Along the way, the conclusion will also suggest how the analyses presented here can be fruitfully linked with debates in other fields and will identify some avenues of research that deserve further exploration.

Between the Particular and the Universal

The analyses collected in this volume highlight the ambiguous position of emotions, which straddle, on the one hand, particular, culturally specific and, on the other, universal supra-cultural dimensions. The case studies do so by showing how specific sociocultural frames shape emotional practices while, at the same time, bodily affects cut across such frames, transcending boundaries of class, race, religion and gender. The studies thus contribute to a reconsideration of the dichotomies between languages and bodies or nurture and nature that have haunted emotion research since its beginnings. On the one hand, the case studies discuss instances where actors claimed that expressing their feelings through the body has helped them when language failed them.[2] A similarly universal understanding of emotional communication is revealed when it is described as reaching directly to the heart and thus as transcending cultural boundaries.[3] At the same time, however, emotional interactions are not relegated to a realm totally beyond the semiotic. Rather, feelings are themselves at times described as a language.[4] Emotions thus do not necessarily constitute a universally transparent alternative to the exchange of linguistic signs. Nevertheless, they comprise a bodily surplus that transcends individual cultures and languages. This surplus opens up a space where sensorial registers, like scent and touch, are privileged and which, at the same time, is adjacent to and interconnected with speech.

The cultural specificity of emotions also becomes apparent when bodily signs and gestures are closely linked to certain social positions, when feelings rely on specific frames of understanding, and when they are linked with particular political structures. Actors of differing occupations have thus, in some instances, favoured very specific emotional behaviours, as the chapter on entrepreneurs aptly demonstrates. Simultaneously, specific conceptual frameworks were decisive in shaping the outcomes of emotional encounters; for example, when the effects of pain or empathy varied depending on whether actors viewed them through a Christian lens or from the perspective of social criticism.[5] Moreover, the political implications of emotional gestures transpire from the controversies around kneeling and from the doubts cast upon the love expressed by subalterns for persons of power.[6] Yet constructionist perspectives highlighting cultural specificities alone do not suffice to comprehensively grasp – let alone explain – the dynamics of emotional encounters. In particular, they tend to lose sight of the multilayered and polysemous character of feelings that have often been accompanied by a multiplicity of contradictory meanings. The chapter on missionaries demonstrates this by highlighting the confusion that the converts' laughter caused among missionaries, making it impossible for the latter to interpret their flock's feelings in a clear-cut fashion.

These ambiguities become particularly pronounced when one brings the question of intentionality into play. Clearly, emotional interactions sometimes involve certain aims, the collaborative coordination of the communicative process being one of them. This is most clearly the case among diplomats but also between occupying forces and occupied populations. In other instances, travellers have explicitly sought out emotional encounters in order to experience self-transformation or to enhance their emotional self-control. But even in cases involving very specific intentions, these could be considerably thrown off track in the course of the emotional interaction. The chapter on occupiers demonstrates this by telling the story of a U.S. officer who fell for a blonde Nazi woman in spite of his attempts to maintain a distance between himself and the local population.[7] Emotional communication can also take place without those involved intentionally trying to have an effect on one another at all. The dynamics triggered by Jean Briggs' loss of temper, as described in the chapter on anthropologists, aptly illustrates this. Emotional encounters have not always been primarily determined by cognitive deliberations and intentional actions but also by involuntary gestures, utterances and other signals.

Thus, neither nurture nor nature can alone entirely account for the emotional dynamics triggered by transcultural encounters – neither on a theoretical level nor on the level of the actors' own accounts. The book hence highlights the intersections and interstices between both dimensions. Accordingly, we might view language not only as a culturally shaped system of intelligibility that imposes certain fixed meanings and interpretative frameworks upon its speakers. Rather, we should consider the fact that language itself has the potential to harbour affective dynamism and immediacy, properties that are usually ascribed exclusively to the body.[8] The encounter between divergent semiotic traditions can therefore also engender transformative effects and linguistic creativity, thus destabilizing performative usages, extending their horizons and allowing for something new to emerge.[9]

While modifying our understanding of language, arguing against the sharp distinction between nature and nurture also compels us to dispute conceptualizations of the body as a natural entity that is resistant to sociocultural disciplining. The physiological aspects of corporeality – for example, the body's reactions to pharmaceutical stimuli in the chapter on the mentally ill or its extreme reduction to a mere piece of flesh through torture – should not be hypostasized to encompass it as a whole. The body itself is a historically specific construct with malleable boundaries that are, in part, informed by culturally specific conventions.[10] This becomes apparent when 'civilizing processes' promote certain bodily postures or when bodies gendered as feminine prefer to communicate their feelings through physical contact.[11] Drawing a clear line between these cultural aspects of the body and its physical dimension is therefore ultimately misleading. Thus, historical research on emotions should not limit itself to the supposedly safe ground of constructionist paradigms that focus on how prescribed rules shape bodily behaviours. Rather, research on the history of emotions should also pay attention to how bodies themselves can impact the dynamics of emotional encounters in unexpected ways.

Maintaining such a twofold perspective makes it possible for us to take an approach that emphasizes the unruly features of the corporeal and at the same time avoids the danger of unintentionally reintroducing a universal understanding of emotions. In this respect, the analysis of transcultural emotional encounters can also contribute to other strands of research, like the study of queer migrations, where sexuality is often viewed as something that oscillates between universal bodily desires and particular sociocultural scripts. As the approach advocated here offers alternative routes for analysing the interstices between bodies and languages, it ties in with explorations of migratory and queer disidentifications that shift boundaries and positions in an often unpredictable fashion.[12] It simultaneously opens up new perspectives on the spatial imaginaries of 'home/away, proximity/distance, and absence/presence taking place both at home and in transnational settings'.[13]

Spatial Dimensions between the Local and the Global

The previous observation hints at a second point that deserves special attention, namely the significance of space in general and the interaction between global and local processes in particular. The spatial settings within which transcultural encounters unfold can have a decisive impact on the emotional dynamics they engender. This is why, as the chapter on travellers argues, Persian accounts about journeys to England in the late eighteenth and early nineteenth century carefully noted the divergences between the emotional styles prevalent in the street and those prevalent in the more exclusive setting of clubs. At the same time, the distinct emotional connotations of dance performances in all-male as opposed to hetero-social environments did not escape the attention of British authors writing about their experiences in colonial India. In the chapter on lovers, the emotional effects of spatial surroundings are shown to have been caused by the familiar chord the mountainous Pathan country struck within Morag Murray, who was raised in the Scottish Highlands. They are also evidenced by the ways in which the perception of certain landscapes and cityscapes influenced the encounters between advancing military forces and local populations.[14]

Beyond such intimate links between spaces and feelings, the preceding chapters also enable broader insights into how global transformations impacted on local emotional events and vice versa. In this sense, the establishment of ever more clear-cut racist and imperialist hierarchies in the second half of the nineteenth century contributed to a shift in the feelings that informed the gaze with which Indian travellers viewed the spectacles of London and other European cities. Wondering curiosity was increasingly replaced by envy and an ambition to emulate what was now coming to be considered the metropolitan standard.[15] Later on, the shift from colonialism proper to more complex and diverse postcolonial asymmetries in the course of the twentieth century decisively changed the emotional experiences of anthropologists in the field and enabled encounters among lovers that would have been unlikely before.

Conversely, local dynamics could also have effects on a global level. The far-reaching revision of missionary models for appropriate religious feelings occasioned by the transition from individual to mass conversions in colonial locales illustrates this, as do the ways in which the feelings of tourists at a local level shaped the commodification of the exotic and rising fears about immigration in a globalizing world.[16] One would definitely overstretch the book's findings, however, if one were to claim that local and global developments have always interacted with one another, not to mention the even less tenable contention that their interaction followed a clearly defined pattern. In contrast to linear narratives about neo-imperialism, globalization or neo-liberalization, the present analyses emphasize uneven combinations of sometimes contradictory developments. This is because they link micro- and macro-perspectives and consider enduring as well as fleeting, ritualized as well as spontaneous encounters.

Similarly, the chapters' discussions of the emotional conditions and effects of globalization point in multiple directions, thus avoiding overly clear-cut conclusions. Insecurity, anxiety and trust might at first seem to be among the primary emotions that either inhibited or accelerated globalizing dynamics. Yet a closer look reveals that insecurity is too broad a notion to serve as a meaningful category for analysing historical case studies. The mechanisms actors have employed for building trust ultimately have proved to be too unreliable and have generated results too inconsistent for trust to function as the emotional foundation upon which globalization could thrive, at least if one perceives the latter as a continuous process of increasing global interconnectedness.[17]

A history of emotions perspective, therefore, highlights globalization's discontinuous and ambiguous features.[18] The multitude of emotions evoked by transcultural encounters – ranging from curiosity, fear and disgust to contempt, longing and solidarity – supports this claim. If processes of globalization have a distinct emotional effect at all, this consists in the intensification of these ambiguities. Thus, historically feelings have had the capacity to facilitate as well as obstruct the establishment of links and communication across spatial distances. They could amplify as well as attenuate cultural gaps and boundaries.[19]

From this vantage point, attending to emotional dynamics in transcultural encounters contributes significantly to current debates within global history by exposing the equivocality of globalizing processes. While the postcolonial emphasis on notions of equality granted actors more leeway in emotionally navigating transcultural encounters and thus eased the establishment of global interconnections, the emotional celebration of diversity could also camouflage intensifications of global inequalities. An all too naïve reliance on the liaising force of feelings may thus prevent actors and scholars from appropriately addressing the challenges posed by surges in global emotional disconnection and alienation.

The Open-Ended Features of Translation and Mimesis

This ambiguity is closely linked to the third point worth highlighting, namely the open-ended nature of transcultural encounters. Focusing on the role feelings have played in such interactions, the analyses have drawn attention to their unpredictable effects. The chapter on performers demonstrates that even in cases where the encounter was intentionally staged in order to expand the emotional repertoires of all parties involved its actual outcomes ultimately remained beyond the control of those staging it. Throughout, encounters have had the potential to destabilize as well as restabilize pre-existing categories. This point is amply illustrated by the chapter on prisoners, which discusses how Dostoyevsky's prison experience reversed classist hierarchies and, at the same time, reaffirmed rigid boundaries. The case studies thus testify to the limits and the strengths of encounters' transformative potential.

In analysing this open-endedness of communication and the production of meaning within transcultural constellations, the notions of translation and mimesis have proven particularly useful, less so the concept of affective transmission. This might be due to the fact that it draws too sharp a division between bodily affect and the cognitive dimensions of thought and meaning. For this reason, the concept can hardly be applied in historical analyses of sources that do not allow for such a separation. Furthermore, drawing such a sharp distinction ultimately runs counter to insights into the biocultural character of emotions. The concept of translation, on the other hand, implies that the alleged opposites are always already intertwined with each other, without, however, merging into one another.[20] Similarly, one can describe the correlations that translation establishes between different languages as the unfolding of an in-between space in which connections emerge and meanings shift. In this vein, the case studies emphasize the crucial role of intermediaries such as missionaries, diplomats and travellers, who move between diverse semiotic codes, thereby negotiating difference, transforming linguistic practices, familiarizing strange idioms and denaturalizing familiar expressions. Furthermore, translation can be regarded as an ongoing process that continues to operate beyond the moment of encounter itself: it also shapes retrospective accounts of the encounter as well as these accounts' own translation into different languages and genres, which may – like poetry – themselves be particularly emotional and difficult to translate.[21]

These points underscore the productive aspects of translation. However, they also hint at its problematic aspects. For various historical actors, moving between different codes and languages has been accompanied by the risk of misunderstandings, especially in situations involving highly formalized performative and literary genres. The danger of such misapprehensions alarmed some actors to an exceptional degree.[22] Misunderstandings have led to international complications and have had fatal consequences, even in cases where the process of translation did not have to bridge different languages.[23] At the same time, misunderstandings have also harboured the potential to enhance communication, contribute to the creation of new meanings and thus to foster emotional closeness and understanding.[24]

Beyond such dynamics that played out – not exclusively but predominantly – at the level of signification, the concept of mimesis enabled the chapters to discuss the bodily dimensions involved in transcultural encounters. In doing so, the chapters reveal how the re-enactment of displays of emotion could enable people to embody the other and defamiliarize the self, as happened with European missionaries when they took part in funerary rituals at the imperial court in Beijing. Yet far from being played out by bodies completely devoid of any pre-existing cultural formation, such mimetic processes involved prefigurations or premediations that rendered the respective practices knowable. In some instances, explicit instructions tried to ensure that actors were informed about the other emotional culture before they entered into the encounter.[25] These examples demonstrate that researchers have to take preconceptions of historical actors into account if they want to fully understand the cross-cultural dynamics at play in an encounter. At the same time, they have to be careful not to allow their own presumptions to impact the results of the analysis. Yet while mimesis always involves pre-existing ideas and habits, its outcomes cannot be determined in advance, as mimetic performances also provoke remediations and refigurations that potentially trigger a rewriting of previous emotional scripts. Even if actors engage in mimetic behaviour of their own volition, it often still has the potential to generate unpredictable effects.[26]

Uneven Historical Trajectories

Having emphasized the open-ended character of emotional encounters, it is hardly surprising that the attempt to tease out historical trajectories does not yield any clear-cut results. The changing conditions for and effects of transcultural interactions did not follow a linear narrative leading from struggle and discrimination to harmonious recognition and the resolution of all conflicts. Nevertheless, three observations might prove helpful for charting this uneven terrain from a historical point of view. The first concerns historical shifts in the evaluation of mimetic behaviour; the second deals with historical actors' increasingly nuanced attempts to reflect on the emotional intricacies of transcultural encounters; and the third links their shifting dynamics with historically specific notions of the self.

In the eighteenth century, attempts at mimetic re-enactment were – at least in some cases – viewed as proof that 'civilized Europeans' had advanced skills that allowed them to master unfamiliar codes so successfully that they could 'blend in' among the locals without – so they thought – being noticed.[27] In other cases, mimesis was viewed as a poor substitute for appropriate forms of understanding, a method used by 'barbaric' others, who supposedly lacked the cognitive abilities necessary for 'proper' communication. This negative evaluation of mimesis can be witnessed in the distrust with which missionaries faced the mimicking of religious emotions by converted Dalits in the nineteenth century. In another context, the refusal to mimetically re-enact local habits was seen as demonstrating international prestige among European envoys in Beijing, or as an indispensable means for maintaining control and guaranteeing the safety of occupying troops in Germany after 1945. These findings are not sufficient to produce a concrete narrative about how 'Europeans' despised mimesis at first and then gradually came to cherish it or the other way round. Nevertheless, they make clear that the evaluation of mimetic practices depended on who engaged in mimesis and how groups or individuals perceived the relationship between the people providing the model and the people mimetically emulating it. While less nuanced hierarchies did not necessarily hinder people from disdaining mimetic practices, we can nevertheless claim that the more relationships were informed by hierarchies and an unequal distribution of power, the more mimesis was regarded as dubious and disreputable.

The growing number of books offering advice on the emotional dynamics of transcultural encounters was, in part, aimed at helping people to avoid questionable and above all ignorant forms of mimetic behaviour. These books were intended to enable all sorts of transnationally mobile actors to properly understand the intricacies of the encounter and to manage their emotional comportment accordingly. Such attempts at promoting certain kinds of knowledge about emotions range from instructions issued to soldiers deployed in foreign countries to advice books for employees of transnational corporations; from advertisements marketing tourist destinations to internet blogs discussing the problems of intercultural relationships; from missionary training preparing candidates for different cultures to anthropological research making the anthropologist's feelings themselves the object of enquiry. Such projects also increasingly exposed the relation between assumptions about different emotional cultures and their embeddedness in imperialist hierarchies or neo-liberal policies of development. Although these forms of knowledge production were not entirely new in the second half of the twentieth century, they became accessible to an unprecedented number of people following the advent and spread of various media. These bodies of knowledge thus contributed to a shift in the primary way individuals learned about transcultural emotional differences, away from personal contacts and relationships and towards the sphere of sociological or behaviourist generalizations.[28] At the same time, the increased medial exhibition of encounters with emotions has made efforts to intentionally regulate or even manipulate their dynamics ever more likely. But due to the fact that transcultural encounters with emotions are inherently open-ended, attempts at regulating and manipulating them have not relieved – let alone resolved – the issues permeating them. Instead, efforts to regulate encounters only intensified participants' ambition to successfully work through them, which ultimately increased the unpredictability of their outcomes.

People thus increasingly strove in a self-optimizing fashion to excel in the navigation of transcultural encounters. This observation links the shifting emotional dynamics of the encounter with the history of the self.[29] Roughly speaking, this history runs from early modern notions of porous selfhood to modern conceptions of the sovereign subject who takes pride in independence and steadfastness, all the way to postmodern or avant-garde forms of subjectivity that might be described as being decentred, potentially self-contradictory and engaged in an ongoing project of experimentation.[30] These transitions have also had an impact on emotional encounters. While from the modern perspective a rupture in the self was typically considered to be an indication of mental illness,[31] avant-garde subjectivity has often entailed a desire for shocking experiences and encountering the alien, which would optimally enable the self to transcend its own limits.[32] This trajectory is certainly in need of more nuanced historical differentiation and should be complemented by perspectives that consider cultural varieties of selfhood. Nevertheless, these preliminary observations should suffice to demonstrate that diverse perceptions of the self have had a strong impact on the ways in which transcultural differences have been historically negotiated in face-to-face encounters.

The Changing Evaluation of Differences

The shift from the modern emphasis on sovereign identity and self-sameness to the postmodern striving for experimental self-alteration also points towards decisive changes in the ways difference has been historically perceived. These changes were intimately intertwined with shifting regimes of power and logics of racial distinction. While the latter allowed for permeability in the seventeenth and eighteenth centuries, they privileged closures and hierarchies in the nineteenth, which in turn gave way to reopenings and complex asymmetries in the twentieth century. Whereas ideas about equality inspired by religious beliefs or legal discourse informed the emotional dynamics of transcultural encounters in the early phase, racist disdain felt by 'Westerners' towards their 'non-Western' counterparts gained prevalence later on, increasing the gap between rulers and ruled and barring intimate encounters between them.[33] Alongside colonial racism, processes of nationalization played an important role in spurring the emotional production of distance and closeness, strangeness and familiarity well into the twentieth century. At the same time, notions of universal humanness and solidarity continued to influence face-to-face encounters, even if attempts to overcome differences often, paradoxically, went hand in hand with a re-establishment of rigid boundaries.

Thus, changes in the potential of emotions to cross various boundaries, such as distinctions of race or class, did not follow a clear-cut historical trajectory. Rather, the historical analyses show a coincidence of conflicting ideas and practices. In the twentieth century, this tangle was further complicated by the rise of discourses and practices that celebrated diversity. Sympathy towards and a will to understand different cultures gained in prominence, as did longings for the exotic other, which further complicated the relationship between universal sameness and universal differences.[34] Yet, while its effects remained ambiguous, this trend once more illustrates how feelings influenced the construction, perception and treatment of differences, and vice versa.

One particularly interesting observation in this respect concerns the increasing relevance of multipolar differentiations and subtle distinctions in the twentieth century that replaced the previously prevalent, stark and mostly binary oppositions of race, class or other differences. This trend can be inferred from the increasingly precarious nature of the distinction between familiarity and strangeness, as well as from the blurred boundaries between sanity and insanity.[35] While several institutions have continued to uphold this opposition, individuals have increasingly come to perceive themselves as nodes in complex networks that bring together different kinds of relationships and distinctions; this has led to an uneven distribution of emotional normalcy and aberration within such networks, where the two are no longer categorically separated. Similar tendencies towards valuing 'multiple differences' informed the negotiation of love and sexuality in transcultural settings towards the end of the twentieth century.[36] Highlighting these multipolar forms of differentiation, the analysis of emotional encounters can also make a significant contribution to current debates on migration, where emotional patterns and practices play a prominent role.[37] All too often these debates revolve around overly simple notions of integration that presuppose the existence of a monolithic host society into which newcomers are then supposed to assimilate. In this context, the emphasis on complex, multipolar relations between closeness and distance, and familiarity and foreignness, offers much more appropriate ways of thinking regarding the emotional negotiation of cultural and other differences.

* * *

One of the advantages of the enquiry into the emotional dynamics of transcultural encounters is the attention it draws to these multipolar patterns of differentiation. Moreover, it opens up fresh and, considering the recent upsurge in emotional alienation from transnational solidarity, also timely perspectives on the ambiguous ways in which feelings at once facilitate and obstruct global interconnections. The preceding chapters have also shed light on the intriguing interstices between universalizing supra-cultural and particularizing culturally relative approaches and tendencies. These tensions between the universal and the particular might ultimately help us better understand interactions not only within the human sphere, which is the focus of most strands of emotion research: it might also shed light on other, less anthropocentric understandings of encounter that involve different forms of life, as the example discussed at the outset of the conclusion demonstrates. Further research might thus extend its scope to include extraterrestrials as well as other non-human beings, like the puppet that figured as E.T. in Steven Spielberg's 1982 film. On the film set, the director urged actresses and actors to emotionally interact with this manufactured creature in order to increase the authenticity of their on-screen encounters. This hints at the multitude of different kinds of emotional encounters that further research might explore by building on the analyses and the arguments proposed by this book.

Benno Gammerl is DAAD Lecturer in queer history at Goldsmiths, University of London and Associate Researcher at the Max Planck Institute for Human Development's Center for the History of Emotions in Berlin. He published (with Jan S. Hutta and Monique Scheer) 'Feeling Differently: Approaches and their Politics', in *Emotion, Space and Society* (2017) and *Subjects, Citizens and Others: Administering Ethnic Heterogeneity in the British and Habsburg Empires, 1867–1918* (Berghahn, 2018).

Notes

1. See, for example, Grady and Hemstrom, 'Nostalgia for Empire, 1963–1974', 125–41; Vettel-Becker, 'Space and the Single Girl: Star Trek, Aesthetics, and 1960s Femininity', 143–78.
2. Chapter 5, Frevert, 'Diplomats' in this volume.
3. Chapter 10, Pernau, 'Lovers and Friends' in this volume.
4. Chapter 7, Vasilyev and Vidor, 'Prisoners' in this volume.
5. Chapter 7, Vasilyev and Vidor, 'Prisoners' in this volume.
6. See Chapter 6, Nielsen, 'Occupiers and Civilians' in this volume. On kneeling, see Chapters 1, Cummins and Lee, 'Missionaries' and 5, Frevert, 'Diplomats' in this volume.
7. Chapter 6, Nielsen, 'Occupiers and Civilians' in this volume.
8. Such a concept of language or semiotics at large is proposed by Brinkema, *The Forms of the Affects*; Hutta, 'The Affective Life of Semiotics', 295–309; Riley, *Impersonal Passion: Language as Affect*.

9. Chapter 9, Kulkarni, 'Performers' in this volume.
10. See, for example, the debate on cyborgs: Haraway, 'A Manifesto for Cyborgs: Science, Technology, and Socialist Feminism in the 1980s', 65–107; Puar, '"I Would Rather Be a Cyborg than a Goddess"': Becoming-Intersectional in Assemblage Theory', 49–66.
11. Chapters 5, Frevert, 'Diplomats' and 7, Vasilyev and Vidor, 'Prisoners' in this volume.
12. On the centrality of the threshold between body and language in this respect, see Cantú, *The Sexuality of Migration: Border Crossings and Mexican Immigrant Men*, 171–72. On the emotional and affective dimensions of migratory processes, see Mai and King, 'Introduction: Love, Sexuality and Migration: Mapping the Issue(s)', 295–307. On queer migrations in general, see Luibhéid, 'Queer/Migration: An Unruly Body of Scholarship', 169–90. On disidentification, see Muñoz, *Disidentifications: Queers of Color and the Performance of Politics*.
13. Mai and King, 'Introduction', 304.
14. Chapters 6, Nielsen, 'Occupiers and Civilians' and 10, Pernau, 'Lovers and Friends' in this volume. On the interplay between spaces and emotions, see also Anderson, 'Affective Atmospheres', 77–81; Gammerl and Herrn, 'Gefühlsräume – Raumgefühle: Perspektiven auf die Verschränkung von emotionalen Praktiken und Topografien der Moderne', 7–22; Pile, 'Emotions and Affect in Recent Human Geography', 5–20; Reckwitz, 'Affective Spaces: A Praxeological Outlook', 241–58.
15. See Chapter 2, Cabanas, Khan and Marjanen, 'Travellers' in this volume.
16. Chapter 1, Cummins and Lee, 'Missionaries' in this volume. See also Chapter 2, Cabanas, Khan and Marjanen, 'Travellers' in this volume.
17. See Chapters 4, Arndt, 'Entrepreneurs' and 6, Nielsen, 'Occupiers and Civilians' in this volume.
18. For discussions criticizing unidirectional and simplifying understandings of globalization from different points of view, see, among many others, Sassen, *Expulsions: Brutality and Complexity in the Global Economy*; Steger and James, 'Levels of Subjective Globalization: Ideologies, Imaginaries, Ontologies', 17–40.
19. Chapter 2, Cabanas, Khan and Marjanen, 'Travellers' in this volume. The ambivalent emotional effects of globalizing processes are also emphasized in Svašek and Skrbiš, 'Passions and Powers: Emotions and Globalisation', 367–83. See also Pain, 'Globalized Fear? Towards an Emotional Geopolitics', 466–86; Pedwell, 'Affect at the Margins: Alternative Empathies in a Small Place', 18–26; Seyd, 'Gegenwart des Unbehagens: Gefühle und Globalisierung'.
20. On how translation and the related concepts of feedback and resonance are used in research on affect and emotions in order to describe the complex interplay between the different dimensions of these phenomena, see Pernau and Rajamani, 'Emotional Translations: Conceptual History beyond Language', 46–65; Massumi, *Parables for the Virtual: Movement, Affect, Sensation*, 12; Reddy, *The Navigation of Feeling: A Framework for the History of Emotions*, 64, 84; Russell, 'Core Affect and the Psychological Construction of Emotion', 150, 165.
21. See Chapter 2, Cabanas, Khan and Marjanen, 'Travellers' in this volume.
22. Chapter 1, Cummins and Lee, 'Missionaries' in this volume.
23. See Chapters 5, Frevert, 'Diplomats' and 8, Rozenblatt, 'Monsters' in this volume.
24. Chapter 2, Cabanas, Khan and Marjanen, 'Travellers' in this volume.
25. See Chapter 6, Nielsen, 'Occupiers and Civilians' in this volume.
26. Chapter 9, Kulkarni, 'Performers' in this volume. See also Chapters 2, Cabanas, Khan and Marjanen, 'Travellers' and 10, Pernau, 'Lovers and Friends' in this volume.
27. See Chapter 2, Cabanas, Khan and Marjanen, 'Travellers' in this volume.
28. Chapter 4, Arndt, 'Entrepreneurs' in this volume.
29. For discussions about emotions in this field, see Eitler and Elberfeld, *Zeitgeschichte des Selbst: Therapeutisierung – Politisierung – Emotionalisierung*; Illouz, *Saving the Modern Soul:*

Therapy, Emotions, and the Culture of Self-Help; Lupton, *The Emotional Self: A Sociocultural Exploration*.
30. See, for example, Reckwitz, *Das hybride Subjekt: Eine Theorie der Subjektkulturen von der bürgerlichen Moderne zur Postmoderne*; Rose, *Inventing Our Selves: Psychology, Power, and Personhood*. On porous selfhood, see Taylor, *A Secular Age*.
31. Chapter 8, Rozenblatt, 'Monsters' in this volume.
32. Chapter 2, Cabanas, Khan and Marjanen, 'Travellers' in this volume.
33. Chapter 10, Pernau, 'Lovers and Friends' in this volume. See also Chapters 1, Cummins and Lee, 'Missionaries' and 5, Frevert, 'Diplomats' in this volume.
34. Chapter 2, Cabanas, Khan and Marjanen, 'Travellers' in this volume
35. See Chapters 6, Nielsen, 'Occupiers and Civilians' and 8, Rozenblatt. 'Monsters' in this volume.
36. Chapter 10, Pernau, 'Lovers and Friends' in this volume.
37. See Boccagni and Baldassar, 'Emotions on the Move: Mapping the Emergent Field of Emotion and Migration', 73–80.

Bibliography

Anderson, B. 'Affective Atmospheres'. *Emotion, Space and Society* 2(2) (2009), 77–81, doi: 10.1016/j.emospa.2009.08.005.
Boccagni, P., and L. Baldassar. 'Emotions on the Move: Mapping the Emergent Field of Emotion and Migration'. *Emotion, Space and Society* 16 (2015), 73–80, doi: 10.1016/j.emospa.2015.06.009.
Brinkema, E. *The Forms of the Affects*. Durham, NC: Duke University Press, 2014.
Cantú, Jr., L. *The Sexuality of Migration: Border Crossings and Mexican Immigrant Men*, ed. N.A. Naples and S. Vidal-Ortiz. New York: New York University Press, 2009.
Eitler, P., and J. Elberfeld (eds). *Zeitgeschichte des Selbst: Therapeutisierung – Politisierung – Emotionalisierung*. Bielefeld: Transcript, 2015.
Gammerl, B., and R. Herrn. 'Gefühlsräume – Raumgefühle: Perspektiven auf die Verschränkung von emotionalen Praktiken und Topografien der Moderne'. *sub\urban* 3(2) (2015), 7–22.
Grady, M., and C. Hemstrom. 'Nostalgia for Empire, 1963–1974'. in G.I. Leitch (ed.), *Doctor Who in Time and Space: Essays on Themes, Characters, History and Fandom, 1963–2012* (Jefferson, NC: McFarland, 2013), 125–41.
Haraway, D. 'A Manifesto for Cyborgs: Science, Technology, and Socialist Feminism in the 1980s'. *Socialist Review* 15(2) (1985), 65–107.
Hutta, J.S. 'The Affective Life of Semiotics'. *Geographica Helvetica* 70(4) (2015), 295–309, doi: 10.5194/gh-70-295-2015.
Illouz, E. *Saving the Modern Soul: Therapy, Emotions, and the Culture of Self-Help*. Berkeley: University of California Press, 2008.
Luibhéid, E. 'Queer/Migration: An Unruly Body of Scholarship'. *GLQ: A Journal of Lesbian and Gay Studies* 14(2/3) (2008), 169–90, doi: 10.1215/10642684-2007-029.
Lupton, D. *The Emotional Self: A Sociocultural Exploration*. London: Sage, 1998.
Mai, N., and R. King. 'Introduction: Love, Sexuality and Migration: Mapping the Issue(s)'. *Mobilities* 4(3) (2009), 295–307, doi: 10.1080/17450100903195318.

Massumi, B. *Parables for the Virtual: Movement, Affect, Sensation*. Durham, NC: Duke University Press, 2002.
Muñoz, J.E. *Disidentifications: Queers of Color and the Performance of Politics*. Minneapolis: University of Minnesota Press, 1999.
Pain, R. 'Globalized Fear? Towards an Emotional Geopolitics'. *Progress in Human Geography* 33(4) (2009), 466–86, doi: 10.1177/0309132508104994.
Pedwell, C. 'Affect at the Margins: Alternative Empathies in a Small Place'. *Emotion, Space and Society* 8 (2013), 18–26, doi: 10.1016/j.emospa.2012.07.001.
Pernau, M., and I. Rajamani. 'Emotional Translations: Conceptual History beyond Language'. *History and Theory* 55(1) (2016), 46–65, doi: 10.1111/hith.10787.
Pile, S. 'Emotions and Affect in Recent Human Geography'. *Transactions of the Institute of British Geographers* 35(1) (2010), 5–20, doi: 10.1111/j.1475-5661.2009.00368.x.
Puar, J.K. '"I Would Rather Be a Cyborg than a Goddess": Becoming-Intersectional in Assemblage Theory'. *philoSOPHIA* 2(1) (2012), 49–66.
Reckwitz, A. *Das hybride Subjekt: Eine Theorie der Subjektkulturen von der bürgerlichen Moderne zur Postmoderne*. Weilerswist: Velbrück Wissenschaft, 2006.
———. 'Affective Spaces: A Praxeological Outlook'. *Rethinking History* 16(2) (2012), 241–58, doi: 10.1080/13642529.2012.681193.
Reddy, W.M. *The Navigation of Feeling: A Framework for the History of Emotions*. Cambridge: Cambridge University Press, 2001.
Riley, D. *Impersonal Passion: Language as Affect*. Durham, NC: Duke University Press, 2005.
Rose, N. *Inventing Our Selves: Psychology, Power, and Personhood*. Cambridge: Cambridge University Press, 1998.
Russell, J.A. 'Core Affect and the Psychological Construction of Emotion'. *Psychological Review* 110(1) (2003), 145–72, doi: 10.1037/0033-295X.110.1.145.
Sassen, S. *Expulsions: Brutality and Complexity in the Global Economy*. Cambridge, MA: Belknap Press of Harvard University Press, 2014.
Seyd, B.C. 'Gegenwart des Unbehagens: Gefühle und Globalisierung'. *Aus Politik und Zeitgeschichte* (2013). Retrieved 11 September 2018 from http://www.bpb.de/apuz/165749/gegenwart-des-unbehagens-gefuehle-und-globalisierung?p=all.
Steger, M.B., and P. James. 'Levels of Subjective Globalization: Ideologies, Imaginaries, Ontologies'. *Perspectives on Global Development and Technology* 12(1/2) (2013), 17–40, doi: 10.1163/15691497-12341240.
Svašek, M., and Z. Skrbiš. 'Passions and Powers: Emotions and Globalisation'. *Identities: Global Studies in Power and Culture* 14(4) (2007), 367–83, doi: 10.1080/10702890701578415.
Taylor, C. *A Secular Age*. Cambridge, MA: Harvard University Press, 2007.
Vettel-Becker, P. 'Space and the Single Girl: Star Trek, Aesthetics, and 1960s Femininity'. *Frontiers: A Journal of Women Studies* 35(2) (2014), 143–78.

Index of Subjects

adaptation, 10, 12, 15, 41, 44, 53, 63, 68, 75, 112–13, 115–17, 120, 124, 135, 166, 171, 189, 196, 235, 268, 275–76, 292
admiration, 47, 62, 69–70, 72, 148, 174, 189, 209, 220–21, 274
adoration, 141
advice literature, 9, 94, 121–24, 141, 149n5, 290
affect, 7, 17, 39-40, 48, 52, 101, 133, 217, 219, 222, 231, 238, 250, 283–84, 288, 294n12, 194n20; theory, 7, 12, 24n16, 25n34
affection, 6, 94–95, 220, 243, 245, 250, 259, 264, 268, 271–72, 276
age, 13–14, 22, 25n41, 66, 160, 162, 195, 239, 248, 265–66
alienation, 37, 287, 293
alterity, 12, 16, 70, 115–22, 213–14. *See also* otherness
amazement, 70
anger, 40, 65, 88, 94, 101, 117, 173, 188, 190–91, 198, 220, 222, 243, 261
annoyance, 65, 165, 170
anthropologist, 3, 19–20, 62, 74, 76, 85–106, 284, 286, 290
anthropology, 6, 11–12, 38, 85–106, 162, 290

antisemitism, 120, 167–68, 171
anxiety, 39, 50, 73, 133, 209, 287
apology, 65, 89–91, 140–43, 145–49, 152n54
arrogance, 230, 242
asylum, 212–13
astonishment, 74, 133, 265
attachment, 94, 115, 264
authenticity, 39, 62, 67, 74, 78–79, 90, 99, 102, 169–70, 198, 237–40, 293
autobiography, 47, 111, 191, 197, 207, 213, 220, 237–38, 240, 274
avant-garde, 16, 291
awe, 62–63, 69, 72, 78

barbarian, 88–89, 102, 139, 141, 143, 289
belonging, 190–91, 195–99, 239, 247, 251, 268, 271, 274, 276
bereavement, 85, 101
body, 2–4, 6–7, 12–13, 19–20, 43–44, 100–1, 106n89, 134, 165, 170–71, 194, 198, 238–42, 248, 262, 272–73, 277, 283–85, 289, 294n12: language, 2, 4, 12, 54, 70, 75, 100, 120, 141, 149, 164, 193, 244–47, 282–83
boredom/boring, 90, 114, 230, 235–36
Buddhism/Buddhist, 10, 42, 240

business, 122, 124, 165; culture, 111, 117, 116–17, 124; -people, 111–13, 117–18, 120–23

camaraderie, 61, 162
cannibalism, 88, 95
caste, 40, 48, 50–51, 53, 168, 238
Catholicism/Catholic, 22, 39–42, 45, 47, 54, 140
Chinese Foreign Council, 143
Chinese Rites controversy, 40–42, 44-47
Christianity/Christian, 22, 37–57, 140–41, 144, 163, 165, 167, 188, 190–91, 271, 283
civility, 43, 68–73, 78, 236
class, 15–16, 26n51, 40, 69, 74, 79, 98–99, 163–65, 186, 189, 192, 194, 198–200, 201n11, 201n15, 238, 263, 265, 275, 292
clothing/dress, 22, 43, 46, 70, 77, 167, 170, 197, 217–18, 230, 235, 246, 248, 258, 265–66
coercion, 15, 186
colonial encounter, 12–14, 17, 68–73, 79, 91, 192, 240–41
colonialism, 15–16, 40, 71–72, 74, 87, 96, 98, 165, 238, 248, 260–65, 267, 271, 273, 286
communication, 3–5, 13, 41, 45, 54, 75, 91, 110–13, 119, 123–24, 133–34, 136–37, 144, 146–47, 167–68, 185–86, 190, 194–95, 200, 211, 214, 282–85, 287
company, 110–17, 119, 121, 136, 250. *See also* East India Company
compassion, 89, 170
comportment, 51, 54, 112, 115, 160, 162, 164, 166–67, 173, 176, 264, 290
condemnation, 44–45, 88, 134, 137, 191, 209, 264
condescension, 53, 137, 187, 189, 235
Confucianism, 42
contempt, 15, 76, 165, 185, 262, 287
conversion, 17, 22, 38–40, 43, 47–53, 163, 264, 284, 286, 290
corporeal. *See under* body
criminal, 137, 165, 184, 189–91, 195, 200

cruelty, 20, 141, 217–19, 222, 264
curiosity, 5, 17, 22, 63, 65, 69–71, 76, 78, 90, 187, 235, 286–87
custom, 42–44, 54, 112, 114–15, 119, 135–41, 145, 147, 165, 167, 172, 176, 264

Dalit, 39–40, 48–53, 290
dance, 230–54, 260–61, 267, 286
Daoism, 42
David and Saul, 233
decency, 134, 233, 235, 268
deception, 11, 49, 51, 113, 160, 164–65, 167, 169, 174–75, 177, 237–38, 261–62
defamiliarization, 160–61, 289
dependence, 15, 39, 61, 139
depression, 90, 100, 197, 261, 267
despair, 90–91, 219, 220, 233, 263, 270
detachment, 95–96, 98
development, stages of, 14–15
devil, 10, 44, 70, 170, 267
devotion, 216–17, 220, 240
diary, 63, 67–68, 91, 93, 102, 137, 146, 162–64, 185, 218, 220, 261, 267, 269, 274
dignity, 134, 138, 140–42, 244, 274
diplomacy, 19–20, 40, 65, 88, 133–53, 232, 234–37, 250–51, 284, 288
disgust, 5, 15, 17, 62–63, 70–71, 74, 78, 88, 95, 170–71, 195, 210, 270, 287
dispassion, 89, 93, 95, 97–98, 120
distrust, 39, 111, 176, 194, 289

East India Company, 5, 135, 163, 165, 167, 232–36, 251, 260, 263–64
economy, 14, 17–18, 65, 77, 110, 136, 152n73
education, 4, 7, 48, 61, 64–65, 72–73, 80n10, 99, 118, 166, 171–72, 195–97, 261, 265–67, 275
ego-documents, 9, 38, 63, 162, 209–10, 215
embarrassment, 65, 175
emotional code, 10, 13, 65
emotional community, 192, 198
emotion, concept of, 6–7, 20, 38, 45, 63, 86, 89, 95, 283, 285

emotional control/self-control, 6, 76, 98–100, 186, 196, 208, 270, 284
emotional dynamics, 7, 9, 43, 45, 63, 169, 174–75, 283–85, 287, 289–92
emotional incoherence, 207–26
emotional misapprehension, 39–40, 75, 161, 170, 177, 211–16, 218, 223, 288. *See also* misunderstanding
emotional practice, 3, 10, 38–39, 62, 78–79, 85, 91, 101, 104n1, 112–18, 134, 162, 196, 212, 231, 283
emotional repertoires, 22, 39, 162, 186, 189, 230–31, 237–38, 251, 287
emotional script, 40, 47–48, 50–53, 62–64, 66, 68, 162–63, 230–31, 242, 251, 270, 277, 289
emotional strategy, 5, 15, 199
emotional style, 5, 13–14, 16, 52, 69–70, 76, 94, 123, 172, 186, 192, 195, 199, 286
empathy, 72, 85, 100–1, 112, 115, 118, 122, 124, 170, 173–74, 197, 210–11, 283
entrepreneur, 19, 110–28, 283
envy, 12, 184, 192, 286
equality, 16–17, 111, 115–16, 135, 137–41, 143, 148, 169, 193, 195, 216, 262–64, 287, 291
ethnicity, 3, 8, 15, 26n52, 67, 186, 212
Europology, 13, 16, 18, 69, 73, 87–88
evangelization, 41–43
exotic/exoticism, 13, 16, 86, 89, 94, 102, 192, 231, 265, 277, 286, 292
expiation, 144–45, 148, 153n82, 219

facial expression, 3, 10, 67, 133, 148, 170–71, 241, 246, 282
faith, 37–38, 41, 43, 53, 170
familiarization, 160–61, 288
familiarity, 7, 8, 37, 62, 70, 91, 166–67, 169, 171, 176, 211, 214, 273, 291–92
family, 13–15, 25n41, 94, 111–14, 116, 119, 123, 208–9, 212–19, 259, 265, 268, 276
fascination, 63–64, 71, 74, 94, 232, 240–42, 275
fashion, 70, 165

fear, 5, 16, 61, 63, 67–68, 70–71, 74, 76–77, 94, 103, 124, 134, 141, 146, 169, 188, 219, 268, 286–87
female performance traditions, 231–39. *See also* dance
feminization, 15, 16, 47, 70, 141, 146, 163, 274, 285
fidelity, 110–11, 115
film, 248, 259, 268, 274, 282, 293
fraternity, 187
fraternization, 173–76, 180n76, 192
friendliness, 69–70, 118, 174, 221
friendship, 14, 42–43, 67–68, 174, 184, 192–93, 268–72, 282
frustration, 40, 90–91, 94, 191, 230, 239
Fugger, 113
funeral practice, 44–47
fury, 2, 143, 188, 271

gender, 9, 13–16, 19, 25n41, 26n51, 50, 53, 69, 71, 73, 88, 94, 105n40, 160, 162–63, 201n11, 209, 263, 269, 274–75, 283, 285
General Government of Warsaw, 168
genuflection, 133–34, 140, 147. *See also* kneeling, prostration
geographer, 87
German Foreign Office, 144–47
German High Command, 168
global history, 4, 24n10, 40, 87, 287
globalization, 4, 14–15, 17, 20, 78, 111, 117, 121, 124, 269, 273–77, 285–87, 293, 294nn18–19
grace, 39, 137
Grand Tour, 62, 64–65, 68, 73
gratitude, 40, 169, 258
Great Terror, 193–94
grief, 45–46, 85, 101, 144, 245–47, 250
guide(book), 64, 77, 121, 160, 171. *See also* instructions
guilt, 71, 124, 208, 276
Gulag, 191, 193–95

habit(us), 5, 40, 49–52, 66, 69, 89, 111, 115–16, 120, 140, 165, 289–90
happiness, 37, 122, 136, 218, 264, 270, 276

hate, 17, 111, 173, 190–92, 199, 216–17, 219–20, 222, 259, 262
headhunting, 85, 101
heterosexuality, 180n76, 259, 269
hierarchy, 14–16, 18, 43, 88, 141, 150n33, 162, 187, 192, 198, 245–46, 248, 263, 273, 286, 288, 290–91
Hindu, 22, 48–49, 52, 168, 240
homosexuality, 195, 259, 269. *See also* queer
honour, 65, 78, 110–11, 115–17, 123, 134–35, 141–44, 147–48, 151n53, 163, 210, 261, 267
hope, 65, 72–73, 76, 171, 189, 198, 233, 235, 237, 258, 269, 276
hopelessness, 90
hospitality, 17, 22, 70, 268
hostility, 166–68, 172–73, 190, 192
humanity, 67, 94, 169, 185, 187–90, 199, 292
humiliation, 1–2, 47, 61, 116, 133–35, 137, 139–40, 143–49, 152n73, 197, 199, 216
humility, 50, 135, 139, 146, 149
humour, 52, 174, 244, 271
hyperinflation of 1923, 120

idolatry, 41, 44–46, 54
imitation, 12, 25n33, 99, 235–37, 240, 242, 246
Imperial Court, 136, 138–39, 144, 289
Imperialism, 15, 68, 81n28, 134, 141, 148, 286, 290
independence, 97, 137, 141, 148, 187, 239, 291
Indian Rebellion of 1857, 72, 161, 163–67, 176, 236, 265
infantilization, 68, 76, 146, 163–64, 166
inquietude, 188
insecurity, 287
insensitivity, 209, 230
insolence, 49–50, 52, 163–65
instructions (governmental record), 9, 133–34, 160, 162, 168, 172–73, 289–90. *See also* guide(book)
integration, 8, 15, 42, 113, 121, 192, 267, 292. *See also* adaptation

intellectual, 39, 45, 63, 89, 97, 139, 186–87, 193–95, 209, 220–21, 275
intelligentsia, 184, 238
interiority, 38
internationalization, 111, 114
intersectionality, 9, 13–17, 164, 178n10, 186, 195, 230, 247–48, 259, 268–71, 277, 278n2, 284, 289–92
intimacy, 16–17, 98, 250, 260, 265, 273, 286, 291
intimidation, 166, 176
intracultural, 9, 13, 19, 116–17, 120, 123, 185–86, 192, 208, 211–12, 238, 282
irreverence, 1–2, 37–57, 76
Islam, 5, 73, 140, 271

jealousy, 43, 111, 233
Jesuit, 40, 42, 44–45
Jew, 22, 120, 134, 167–73, 175–77, 220
joking, 91, 271
joy, 47, 51, 65, 114, 166, 189–90, 198, 270, 274
Judaism, 140
judgement, 112, 120, 122, 166, 190, 209–10, 212, 220, 222
justice, 11, 185, 248, 282

kneeling, 43-44, 46, 56n41, 133–36, 140–41, 145, 147, 149, 284, 293n6
kowtow, 47, 134–41, 144–48, 149n9, 153nn89–90
Krishna, 240–41

labelling, 86, 116, 213, 238, 242–43
language, 4, 6, 72, 77, 121, 135, 162, 169, 172, 176, 186, 195, 244–45, 274, 276, 284–85, 288, 293n8, 294n12; barriers, 1, 91, 167, 198–99, 265, 275, 282; learning of, 115, 119, 161, 267–68; of emotion, 11, 65, 71, 100, 134, 139, 148, 198, 222, 233, 270, 272, 283; sign, 247
laughter, 37, 43, 45, 50, 52, 75, 100, 146, 148, 188–89, 218, 284
leisure, 63, 77–78
letter, 45, 49, 67, 72, 80n25, 90, 111–13, 115, 117–21, 123, 143, 145–47, 162,

166, 169, 185, 190, 238, 264, 267, 269–71
linguistics, 95, 101, 135, 169, 247, 261, 288
literary, 11, 88, 185–86, 238, 288
literature, 39, 47, 50, 67, 77, 86, 190, 245, 247–48; prison, 185–88, 191, 193–94; travel, 62–64, 66, 69, 72–74, 77–79, 88–89
longing, 5, 101, 173, 271, 287, 292
love, 3, 20, 38, 40, 49, 66–67, 94, 101, 141, 184, 187–89, 207–9, 216–21, 233, 237, 240–41, 243, 258–80, 284, 292
lover, 19–20, 94, 233, 236, 240, 251, 258–80, 286
loyalty, 20, 66, 72, 111, 113, 117, 123, 136, 148, 162, 164, 166, 217

Malayali, 243–44, 246
Manchu dynasty, 43
mania/maniac, 208, 215, 218, 221
marriage, 94, 114, 194, 209, 215–17, 232, 236, 243, 258–69, 276
masculinity, 15, 23n2, 141, 149, 162–63, 166, 174, 236, 274
masquerade, 69–70, 235
mass movement, 40, 48, 50, 52, 54
media, 3, 142, 145, 231, 248, 273, 290. *See also* newspaper
mediation, 8, 10, 22, 54, 102, 189, 208, 215, 258, 272, 275
medicine, 6, 216, 267, 276
melancholy, 42, 148
memoir, 42–44, 186–87, 191, 194–95, 197, 203n72, 208–11, 213, 215–17, 219–23, 231–32, 235, 240–41, 246, 263–64, 267–68
mentally ill, 19–20, 207–22, 285, 291–92
migration, 3, 5, 61, 168, 173, 285–86, 292, 294n12
mimesis, 9, 12, 75, 114–22, 161, 199, 213–14, 225n41, 287–90
mimicry, 12, 67–68, 70–71, 169, 267, 275, 289
Ming dynasty, 42, 45
missionary, 5, 19–20, 22, 37–57, 62, 88, 90, 143, 251, 271–72, 284, 286, 288–90

misunderstanding, 1, 4, 6, 63, 70, 75–76, 91, 145, 147, 167, 209, 211–14, 240–42, 288. *See also* emotional misapprehension
moral/morals/morality. 6, 71–72, 113, 137, 141, 165, 174, 188–90, 208, 210, 216, 237, 261–62, 265, 273
Muslim, 22, 47–48, 52, 62, 67–68, 72–73, 79, 164, 240, 268–69

nationality, 16, 66, 79, 117, 168–69, 172, 176, 194
nationalization, 87, 98, 111, 121, 161, 168, 176, 291
National Socialist, 172, 174–75, 177, 284
nature and nurture/culture, 3–4, 7, 10, 20, 22, 103, 208, 212, 277, 283–85
neuro-linguistic programming (NLP), 123
neurosciences, 3, 7, 12
newspaper/press, 3, 145–46, 152n71, 170, 218, 231, 259
nobility, 64–65, 69, 72, 189–93, 261
noble savage, 88–89
novel, 9, 74, 77, 90, 167, 185, 191, 197, 259, 269, 274, 276

obedience, 50, 135–36, 148, 184, 189
obeisance, 47, 135, 137, 139, 272
Occidental, 140
occupier, 19, 87, 160–80, 251, 284, 290
Oriental, 16, 47, 140–41, 145, 239–40, 250, 259, 264, 266–67, 270–71
Orientalism, 11, 73, 96
orientalist, 19, 62, 67, 232, 235, 242, 246, 251, 265, 273
otherness, 19, 62–63, 66, 69, 77, 86, 89, 103, 160, 162, 168, 188–89, 200, 212, 246, 273, 289

pain, 75, 78, 90, 188, 197, 218, 221, 283
passion, 1, 6, 72, 76, 94, 98, 133, 197, 233, 261–62, 264, 269–71
penitence, 145
performer, 19, 68, 70, 230–54, 287
perplexity, 63, 74

philosophy, 6–7, 17, 87, 95, 102, 188, 190, 207–8, 210
piety, 39, 47
pity, 40, 174, 189, 262
poetry, 69, 71, 98, 237, 269–72, 288
power dynamics, 8, 12, 63, 87, 140, 148, 187, 209, 212, 214, 236, 274–75, 277
prefiguration, 65, 114, 272, 289
prejudice, 46, 54, 63, 74, 88–89, 120–21, 163, 174, 199, 213, 240, 242, 268, 273
premediation, 4, 8, 10, 14, 18, 24n20, 51, 63–64, 67, 69–70, 74, 89, 94, 96, 102, 161, 168–69, 171, 173, 175–77, 199–200, 236, 259–60, 264, 267–70, 273–74, 278n2, 289
prison, 20, 43, 184–203, 215, 217, 222, 288
prisoner, 19–20, 133, 184–203, 287–88
prostration, 43-44, 46, 56n41, 136–41
Protestant, 22, 39–41, 47–48, 140
psychoanalysis, 93, 102, 208–9
psychology, 3, 6–7, 38, 97, 102, 173, 176, 194, 212–13, 247
Pussy Riot trial, 184–85

queer, 285, 294n12
Qing dynasty, 43–44, 136, 139

race, 23n2, 26n51, 94, 160, 162, 167, 177, 178n10, 238, 263, 268, 271, 283, 292
racism, 1–2, 15–16, 39, 47, 96, 120, 161, 163–64, 168–69, 179n40, 201n11, 259, 264–65, 273, 277, 286, 291
rage, 85, 101, 189, 208, 220, 248, 251, 262
reconversion, 188, 191
re-education, 172
re-enactment, 61, 79, 288–90
refiguration, 11, 114, 269, 274, 289
rehabilitation, 172, 185
rehearsal, 230, 243, 245–46, 250
reliability, 111, 123, 170–71
religion, 15–16, 37–57, 65, 140, 144, 146, 161–65, 167–68, 176, 178n10, 179n40, 186, 188, 191, 200, 201n30, 208, 215, 217, 258–59, 271–72, 283, 286, 290–91

remediation, 9–10, 71, 215, 219–20, 268, 277, 289
remorse, 145, 147, 208
reparation, 142–43, 152n60
resentment, 111, 139, 141, 144
respect, 42, 45, 76, 115, 133, 138, 141, 148, 164–65, 169, 174, 221, 238, 243, 245, 250, 268, 278n22
responsibility, 116, 119, 185, 210
reverence, 37–57, 136, 138, 140–41, 148, 210, 221
romantic, 71, 74, 77, 94, 160, 187–90, 220–21, 237, 246, 259, 269, 275, 277
Rorschach test, 97
rubescence, 175, 189

sadness, 49, 170, 221, 274
salvation, 50, 52, 188, 273
satisfaction, 17, 138, 142–44
serf, 191–92
sexuality, 70, 94, 195, 209, 232, 236, 238, 244, 269, 285, 292
sexual relation, 230–32, 236–38, 259–65, 269–71, 273
shame, 17, 133–34, 143–45, 147, 149, 171, 189
shaming, 134, 148
shock/shocking, 17, 61–62, 73–74, 94, 221, 273, 282, 291
Siemens (company), 112, 114–16, 119
Sikh, 48, 164, 168, 266, 274–75
similarity, 10–12, 63, 160, 167, 171–72, 176, 220, 244
slave/slavery, 20, 43, 48, 51, 53, 139–41
smile, 37, 100, 174, 194, 265, 268, 282
smoking, 20, 22, 166, 176–77
social capital, 38, 111
social location, 63
social media, 3, 184, 258, 290
social sciences, 6, 38. *See also* sociology
social status, 69, 167, 171, 189, 195
sociology, 39, 54, 102, 212–13, 290
soldier, 20, 160–63, 166, 168–73, 175–77, 191, 265, 290
solidarity, 17, 185, 195–99, 287, 292–93
solipsism, 173

sorrow, 68, 133, 144–45, 152n54, 152n60, 193, 208, 216, 219
sovereignty, 63, 71, 137–39, 141, 149, 150n33, 265, 291
space, 6–8, 10, 13–14, 20, 69–71, 162, 169, 186, 212, 233, 251, 270, 272–73, 277, 285–88, 294n14
'Stewart Emotional Response' test, 97
subjectification/subjectivation, 7, 86, 93, 96, 105n38, 186
subjectivity, 2, 7, 12, 19, 73, 291
submission, 20, 61, 71, 140–41, 148–49, 261, 275
subservience, 135, 140–41, 169, 177
suffering, 61, 94, 133, 192, 197, 208, 210, 215–16, 219, 221, 223
sympathy, 12, 15, 72–73, 123, 145, 164–65, 167, 173, 191, 216, 220, 272, 292

testimonial/testimony, 37, 187, 209–10, 215, 219
theology, 6, 271–72
tourism, 3, 20, 61–82, 162, 273, 286, 290
trader, 5, 14, 20, 62, 90, 92, 232, 260
translation, 3–4, 9, 11–13, 19, 41, 47, 55n23, 69, 71–72, 76, 102–3, 114, 124, 141, 146, 169, 213–14, 235, 243–44, 270, 276, 287–89, 294n20
transmission, 3, 9, 12–13, 176, 214, 225n41, 282, 288
traveller, 5, 14, 19, 22, 61–82, 88–89, 232, 240, 242, 248, 274, 284–86, 288
travelogue, 66, 68–69, 72, 87

Treaty of Tientsin, 138
Treaty of Versailles, 120
Treaty of Warsaw, 133–34
trust, 8, 17, 43, 110–27, 161, 164, 166, 173–74, 178n25, 243, 245, 250, 287

unfamiliarity, 8, 10, 14–15, 61, 102, 167, 232
United Nations Charter, 148
universalism, 3–4, 6–8, 10, 12, 16, 19, 22, 26n54, 86, 96, 100–1, 103, 164, 169, 179n40, 250, 283–85, 292–93
untouchables. *See under* Dalit
U.S. Congress, 124
U.S. Environmental Protection Agency (EPA), 110

violence, 8, 18, 39, 48, 51, 61, 76, 163, 171, 189, 192, 194–98, 214, 244
virtue and vice, 6, 69
Volkswagen (VW), 110, 124
vulnerability, 244

war, 73, 111, 138, 142; Cold, 176; First World, 120, 161, 167–69, 173, 267; Franco-Prussian, 142; Napoleonic, 216–17; Second Opium, 139; Second World, 77, 96, 133, 160–61, 174–75, 209, 242; Spanish-American, 161
weeping, 45–46, 218–19
wonder, 63, 68–73, 237, 241, 274, 286

zionism, 170–71
zoophilia, 195

Index of Names and Places

Abdullah of Saudi Arabia, 148
Abdullah, Morag. *See under* Murray, Morag
Abdullah, Syed, 267–68
Abramova, Zinaida, 194–95
Abu-Lughod, Lila, 97, 100–2
Akimych, Akim, 191
Alekhina, Mariia, 185
Alexander, J.E., 68
Alfonso XIII of Spain, 265
Aligarh, 72–73, 269
al-Tantawi, Sheikh Muhammad 'Ayyad, 67–68
Althusser, Louis, 207–10, 220–23
Amazonian, 37, 95
Ammar, Hamed, 87, 96–99
Amritsar, 274
Andrews, Charles Freer, 271–73
Anand, Valerie, 276–77
Arabian Peninsula, 67
Arendt, Carl, 145
Armenia, 22
Armfelt, Gustaf Mauritz, 62, 64–66
Asad, Talal, 87
Augsburg, 65
Aunay, 219
Auschwitz, 133
Australia, 89

Austria, 22, 175, 187
Awasthi, Suresh, 246

Baghdad, 67
Bahadur Shah II, 166
Barba, Eugenio, 242
Bareilly, 163
Basel, 145
Bate, Jonathan, 248
Begum Samru/Sumroo, 20–22, 236
Beijing, 40–43, 46, 289–90. *See also* Peking
Benares, 235
Benedict, Ruth, 93
Bengal, 234, 238
Berlin, 114, 116, 145–46, 148
Beseler, Hans Hartwig von, 169–70
Bharucha, Rustom, 239
Bhopal, 269
Blechynden, Richard, 260–63
Boas, Franz, 93
Branagh, Kenneth, 250
Brandt, Willy, 133, 149
Brazil, 37, 95–96
Brenner, Anita, 77
Briggs, Jean L., 99–100, 102, 284
Brno, Špilberg fortress, 187, 201n27
Brook, Peter, 242

Index of Names and Places

Bülow, Bernhard von, 147
Burgess, Ernest, 213
Burns, Robert, 269
Butcher, Charles Henry, 53-54
Buxoo, 261–63

Calcutta, 236, 259–63
Canada, 99
Canossa, 146
Cancún, 77
Carpenter, Mary, 73
Cashmere, 165
Churchill, Matilda, 49
China, 40-47, 56n41, 37–57, 121, 134–40, 142–44, 146–47, 152n54, 152n60, 153n89
Clark, Robert, 47
Codell, Julie F., 73
Collins, Randall, 214
Confucius, 42, 44
Cook, James, 19, 88
Count Daun, 65
Cyrankiewicz, Józef, 133

D'Abernon, Viscount, 120
Dalrymple, William, 261
Dasi, Binodini, 232, 237–39
Delgado, Anita, 265–68
Delhi, 166, 246, 271
Denby, Charles, 143
de Tournon, Charles-Thomas Maillard, 44
Devi, Rukmini, 240
Diamant, Gertrude, 74
Dick, Sheldon, 77
Dos Passos, John, 173
Dostoyevsky, Fyodor, 190–93, 287

Edinburgh, 267
Edwards, William, 163–67
Egypt, 67–68, 87, 97–98
Ehrensvärd, Carl August, 65–66
Eisenhower, Dwight D., 172
El Alberto, 78
Elbourne, Elizabeth, 40, 47
Elgin, Lord (James Bruce, 8th Lord of Elgin), 138

England, 2, 22, 26n51, 70–73, 114, 116, 120, 168, 243, 245, 258, 270, 272, 276, 285. *See also* Great Britain
Essen, 120
Etkind, Alexander, 192
Eulenburg, August Graf zu, 146
Everett, Daniel, 37–38

Fazl-e Haqq, 167
Feist, Siegmund, 169
Forbes, James, 233, 236–37, 240–41, 246
Forster, E.M., 269–72
Forster, Georg, 88–89
Foucault, Michel, 186, 196, 209–10, 216, 222
Fourier, Charles, 191
France, 22, 64, 138–39, 143, 150n29, 172–73, 209, 216, 220, 243
Franke, Otto, 147–48
Frazer, James, 90
Frederick II, 140, 145
French Algeria, 209
Fuchs, Elinor, 248

George III, 135–36
Germany, 20, 22, 110, 121–22, 124, 134, 142, 144, 146, 149, 152n60, 161, 167–68, 171–76, 290
Ghosh, Girish C., 238
Ginzburg, Eugenia, 193–95
Giovanella, 198
Goethe, Johan Wolfgang von, 64, 72
Gordon, Anne, 114
Gordon, Lewis D.B., 114–15
Gorissen, Stefan, 113
Goudie, William, 51
Gramsci, Antonio, 194
Granville, Earl, 140
Grass, Günter, 133–34, 148
(Great) Britain, 136, 138–39, 143, 161, 232–33, 235. *See also* England
Greene, Graham, 74
Griswold, Hervey, 50, 52, 54
Grotowski, Jerzy, 242
Guam, 161
Guangxu Emperor, 144–47
Gustavus III, 64–65

www.ingramcontent.com/pod-product-compliance
Lightning Source LLC
Chambersburg PA
CBHW050207130526
44590CB00043B/3050